WE THE PEOPLE

THE COMMISSION ON THE BICENTENNIAL
OF THE UNITED STATES CONSTITUTION, 1985-1992

Final Report

Library of Congress Cataloging-in-Publication Data

We the people : the Commission on the Bicentennial of the United
    States Constitution, 1985-1992 : final report.
        p.   cm.
        1. United States Constitution Bicentennial, 1987-1991.   2. United
    States — Constitutional history.   3. Commission on the Bicentennial
    of the United States Constitution.   I. Commission on the
    Bicentennial of the United States Constitution.
    KF4541.W4   1992
    342.73'029 — dc20   92-27417
    [347.30339]   CIP

Unless otherwise credited, all photographs are from the Archives of the
Commission on the Bicentennial of the United States Constitution, National
Archives, Washington D.C., Record Group RG 220.

CONTENTS

The Bicentennial Commission
came into being by Act of Congress,
and President Ronald Reagan
appointed me Chairman on June 25, 1985.

In **1987** the Commission led the nation in celebrating the 200th anniversary of the drafting of the United States Constitution with the Celebration of Citizenship, highlighted by nationally televised ceremonies from the West Front of the Capitol.

Foreword   V

There President Reagan led all Americans in the Pledge of Allegiance, a reaffirmation of our constitutional heritage and the ideals of human values that heritage represents.

I read the Preamble to the Constitution, Speaker of the House Foley, Senate Majority Leader Mitchell, and Chief Justice Rehnquist followed. Officials estimated that about 140,000 people attended the event.

Asymbolic linkage of past, present, and future was reflected on that day in the range of generations of Americans present. The nation's leaders on the main platform were surrounded by thousands of schoolchildren as representatives of future American leaders, who will see the 250th anniversary of the Constitution in 2037. They will, no doubt, then be recounting to their grandchildren memories of that warm late-summer day back in '87, when they witnessed the opening of the celebration of our Constitution's 200th birthday. We pointedly gave these children a prominent place on the platform to symbolize our emphasis on the education of America's youth contemplated by the Commission's programs, to give Americans "a history and civics lesson."

Such linkages with future commemorations are significant in the collective memory of a nation. But will the lives of those children—who will be grandparents 50 years hence— and the nation itself benefit because this celebration took place? Will Americans have learned from our "history and civics lesson" of 1985 to 1992?

There are indications that the efforts of the Commission have had, and will continue to have, a significant and long-lasting impact on the American public. At a congressional budget hearing in 1991, Representative Joseph D. Early of Massachusetts commented that there had been more public discussion, more awareness and display of the Constitution and the Bill of Rights since the creation of the Commission in 1985 than at any other time in his life. He noted that it is impossible to "measure what that does" for the country. Representative Neal Smith of Iowa echoed Early's sentiments, stating that "this Bicentennial Commission has done more than anything in my lifetime to help point out to people" the importance of understanding the Constitution.

Surveys in 1985 suggested that the Commission's "history and civics lesson" was clearly needed. A study conducted by the William Randolph Hearst Foundation, for example, revealed that both students and adults had an alarming lack of understanding of the history and structure of our system of government. When a pollster asked the source of the statement "from each according to his abilities and to each according to his needs," the answer almost universally given was "The Constitution." That seductive sentence came from a constitution of sorts; it was written by Karl Marx in *Das Kapital*. When some of the members of the Commission compared what we remembered from our school days with the survey results, we sensed that valuable lessons had been lost or forgotten in the past 35 or 40 years. One explanation seemed to be that with the advent of "social studies," other subjects such as history and geography had been given less and less emphasis.

We on the Commission decided that our mission was to leave a legacy of substance with special focus on the youth. Before the Commission began to function, we explored the possibility of undertaking a comprehensive study of all three branches of the government but soon abandoned the idea, concluding that, however desirable the study might be, to conduct it properly would likely absorb a disproportionate amount of the Commission's time and resources. We therefore decided that the chief focus of the Commission's programs should be educational, with particular emphasis on primary and secondary schools.

Accordingly, from the outset we dedicated the Bicentennial not so much to public celebrations with "parades and fireworks," useful as they are to gain public attention, but to long-term programs designed to improve Americans' understanding and appreciation of our heritage and to make them the "informed electorate" the Founding Fathers thought imperative to the preservation of democracy. Not that public celebrations played no part in the commemoration. For example, parades and fireworks were a dramatic part of the magnificent opening celebration in Philadelphia on September 17, 1987, sponsored by the Philadelphia Committee on the Bicentennial, with President Reagan reviewing the events. The main emphasis, however, was on education. To this end the Commission committed the major part of its resources to teaching materials, teacher training, and the development and dissemination of new publications on the Constitution.

More specifically, during the past six years our Bicentennial Educational Grant Program awarded over $12 million for teachers' summer seminars, in-service training, and curriculum development. We sponsored or cosponsored countless academic competitions at the primary and secondary school levels, ranging from essay contests to an oratory contest for the hearing-impaired. In addition, with the invaluable assistance of Betty Debnam, editor of *The Mini Page*, a children's tabloid supplement that appears weekly in 500 newspapers nationwide, the Commission was able to reach literally millions of elementary schoolchildren and tell them the story of their constitutional heritage in terms they could readily understand.

For three years the Commission conducted an innovative National Historical/ Pictorial Map Contest at three levels: one as a class project for fourth through sixth grades; a second as a class or group project for seventh and eighth grades; and a third for high school students in grades 9 through 12, who would compete individually. Working with the National Geographic Society, we supplied blank outline maps to thousands of schools each year. The National Geographic Society also provided a timeline chart that adroitly illustrated events from Columbus in 1492 to President Reagan's 1981 appointment of Sandra Day O'Connor as the first woman Justice of the Supreme Court. The contest required the students to study the evolution of the original 13 colonies and bring that history to life by illustrating the maps with what they considered to be the significant historical events between 1607 and 1803. According to teachers, the contest not only stimulated a renewed interest in history and geography and taught them to translate ideas into pictures, but also provided students with a valuable experience in "teamwork." The winners at each level were brought to Washington, D.C., and one year First Lady Barbara Bush presented the winners' prizes in a ceremony on the White House lawn with teachers and parents present.

Essay contests and other activities in foreign countries fulfilled the Commission's statutory obligation with respect to international programs. Many such contests were organized in Europe, Africa, Asia, and South America focusing on our concepts of ordered liberty. The impact of such projects is difficult to measure, but officials in those countries saw the results as significant.

The Commission also funded programs and educational materials to promote better understanding of our Constitution among adult Americans. These included the College-Community Forums program designed to engage teachers and citizens in public discussions on the Constitution, and the comprehensive exhibit of artifacts and illustrative materials relating to the Constitution we created in 1986 at Disney World in Orlando, Florida, in cooperation with the Disney organization; this exhibit was seen by millions of visitors from 1986 to 1991.

Over the years, we disseminated books, films, pamphlets, brochures, and well over 55 million copies of the immensely popular Pocket Constitution were published — many millions printed by the private sector — throughout this country and around the world. In addition, with the active support of the Department of Defense extension programs, more than 3 million copies of the Pocket Constitution were distributed to military personnel with a special Foreword from the President as Commander in Chief. A special Spanish edition was distributed at the 1992 World's Fair in Seville along with the English version. Special editions were also produced for millions of Boy Scouts and Girl Scouts. One unique feature included in our Pocket Constitution was a five-page descriptive word index.

The Commission's media campaign reached a broad segment of the nation's population through print, TV, and radio public service announcements. Comprehensive interviews on the Presidency with former Presidents Nixon, Ford, Carter, and Reagan were recorded and made available to public television and colleges and universities here and abroad. Not since Abraham Lincoln was elected to succeed James Buchanan in 1861 have we had four living former Presidents, and we concluded their experience in the Presidency should be preserved in some form. An outline prepared for the interviews enabled the interviewer and the former Presidents to focus on the office and function of the Presidency. Historians, political scientists, and leaders with extensive Washington experience were enlisted to plan the scope of the interviews. The interviewer, Hugh Sidey, a widely known journalist who had interviewed every President since Eisenhower, conducted the interviews. The series of one-hour programs produced by the Commission were aired by

Public Broadcasting Service stations nationwide and will be a permanent historical legacy.

In 1989, a reenactment of George Washington's inaugural journey and inauguration in New York took place. State and local Bicentennial Commissions actively participated in the event, and it received widespread media attention both here and abroad. The project focused on Washington's eight-day journey from Mount Vernon to New York, where on April 30, 1989, we reenacted his inaugural precisely 200 years to the hour after Washington took the oath. This was a colorful event with participants including the Presidential Guard of Honor in Colonial uniforms. President Bush was the principal speaker; the Mayor of New York, Senators Daniel Patrick Moynihan and Alphonse M. D'Amato, Representative Lindy Boggs, and I also spoke briefly.

The Commission also left a significant permanent legacy for the benefit of future generations of Americans with the publication of the "historical trilogy," three volumes by Jeffrey St. John: *Constitutional Journal,* on the daily work of the Constitutional Convention of 1787; *Child of Fortune,* on the state ratification conventions; and *Forge of Union, Anvil of Liberty,* on the establishment of the first National Government following ratification. The St. John trilogy was placed in every college and secondary school library in the country.

The Commission produced a book based on its popular 1991 calendar covering the history of the Bill of Rights that was also given to libraries around the country as part of "The Bill of Rights and Beyond" project. In 1992 the Commission published a book on the 106 Justices of the Supreme Court of the United States, with a brief history of the Court and important historical data on the Justices, that the Commission also placed in libraries nationwide. The Commission issued educational brochures on the Congress and financed the *Encyclopedia of Congress* and the *Documentary History of the First Federal Congress.*

In December 1991, the Commission approved funding of $250,000 for one of its last projects: the United States Information Agency's (USIA) Bill of Rights exhibit in the United States Pavilion at the Universal Exposition in Seville, Spain. Opening on April 20, 1992, Seville Expo '92 commemorated the quincentenary of Columbus's discovery of the New World. It promised to be the largest world's fair in history.

The Bill of Rights Exhibit celebrated the worldwide advance of constitutionalism and human rights, with special emphasis on the historical impact of the American Bill of Rights. It included an introductory video presentation, illustrations, quotations, and artifacts showing both the historical origins of the Bill of Rights and the quest for rights in the modern world. The exhibit's centerpiece was one of the original copies of the Bill of Rights, lent by the State of Connecticut.

One of two large geodesic domes, each centered in a pool of water, contained the Bill of Rights exhibit. The other dome housed an exhibit sponsored by the General Motors Corporation and included a courtyard with shops and space for special events and other activities. The front face of the pavilion was a "wall" of water. The large sails in the courtyard symbolized the anniversary theme of Columbus's voyage. The sails were decorated and configured so as to suggest an American flag.

This international exhibition of America's legacy of freedom provided a fitting close to the Bicentennial Era. The era began as a commemoration of the ideals and accomplishments of the eighteenth century and ended with a dramatic reaffirmation of those ideals in the collapse of twentieth-century totalitarianism, when long-subjugated peoples reached for the blessings Americans and others had enjoyed for 200 years. The principles embodied in the nation's founding documents — as those who shaped them realized — belonged not only to America but to all humanity. Millions of people would be reminded of this during their visit to the Bill of Rights exhibit at Seville, whose title and theme came from an ancient Latin aphorism, once the motto of American Founder James Otis: "Where Liberty Dwells, There Is My Country."

As this initial review of the activities of the Bicentennial Commission demonstrates, the investment of time, energy, and money in the Bicentennial commemoration was significant. We hope our focus on education will yield many dividends in the decades to come. Much will depend on the initiatives of the Bicentennial years being sustained by other programs in both the public and private sectors. Special thanks for these initiatives are due the countless individuals, private corporations, foundations, and groups in the public and private sectors who contributed to the commemoration. Without the dedicated efforts of teachers, civic leaders, civilian and military officials, business people, and private citizens from coast to coast, the mission could not have been accomplished. The teachers deserve special mention for their contributions. Whether we will have Madison's "informed electorate" in the future depends largely on them.

Fortunately, the Bicentennial has occurred at a time when there has been both a revival of the spirit of volunteerism in American life and a renewal in American education that promises to restore history, geography, and civics to their rightful places in our schools and colleges. Much has been accomplished, but much remains to be done and we are confident that the resources and desire are there to do it.

With the dramatic changes that have recently taken place in the world, including the "Gorbachev-Yeltsin Revolution," people of other countries long under arbitrary rule are taking a greater interest than ever in the American constitutional tradition and its legacy of ordered liberty. These global changes reaffirm the importance of that legacy and our need to understand it. As we move into an exciting if uncertain future, it is essential that we remember our past and how it has shaped us as a nation and a people.

Looking ahead to the task that will face the Commission established to observe the Constitution's 250th anniversary in 2037, several thoughts regarding logistics seem in order. The present Commission's initial efforts were hampered to some extent because it was not established until the very eve of the Bicentennial. The next Commission should be organized with a small staff not later than 2033 to undertake planning efforts well in advance of the anniversary dates. This would permit the organization to be staffed on a gradual and orderly fashion. It is also important to recognize that no Commission of this nature can be completely successful if assistance is not sought from existing groups and organizations that can help the Commission communicate its message to the people. We placed great emphasis on making contact and establishing good working relationships with such groups as the National Educational Advisory Committee, state Bicentennial Commissions, schools, campuses, and defense communities, the media, and advisory committees of the Judicial Conference of the United States and the National Center for State Courts.

As to appropriations, it is best to secure "no year" grants to give the Commission additional flexibility to respond to unanticipated opportunities for funding valuable projects. Congress should grant the Commission a mail frank. Without a frank a disproportionate share of our appropriated funds was consumed by postage costs. For example, annual postage costs for the National Historical/Pictorial Map Contest alone would have amounted to approximately $247,000. Although the United Parcel Service generously agreed to make two annual deliveries of this mailing for the Commission, postage costs on this project and others diverted substantial resources away from other programs.

Finally, the private sector's interest in, and ability to assist with, the commemorative effort should never be underestimated. We received invaluable assistance from many private corporations and organizations that financed the distribution of a wide variety of valuable educational materials, including the Pocket Constitution, at no cost to the Commission. Among the most generous were the American Express Company, the Food Marketing Institute, Gannett/*USA Today,* General Electric, IBM, International Paper, Kodak, McDonald's, Merrill Lynch, Xerox, Nabisco, *Parade* magazine, Polaroid, Walt Disney, and the Ad Council. In the aggregate, projects designed by the Commission and carried out by these and other private sector entities involved tens of millions of dollars of private money.

We hope this report of the work of the Commission will, among other things, serve as a guide to the Commission for the celebration in 2037. Many changes in travel and communication are bound to occur in the next half-century, but the objectives of the educational projects described in the following pages will remain essentially the same. In reading the explanations contained herein and enjoying the beautiful pictorial record of the Bicentennial events, one can only wonder what the celebration in 2037 will bring.

Chairman, Commission on the Bicentennial
of the United States Constitution
Chief Justice of the United States, 1969–1986

A CELEBRATION OF CITIZENSHIP and WE THE PEOPLE 200

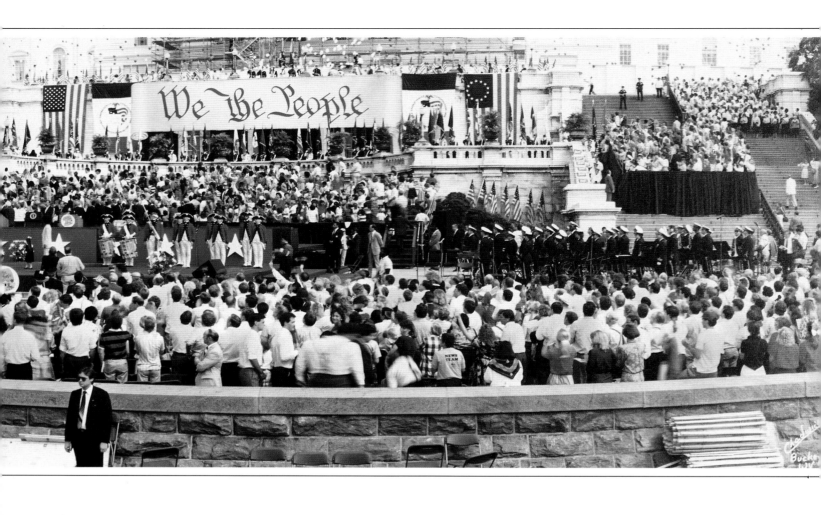

17. THE COMMEMORATION SHIFTS TO PHILADELPHIA.

Norfolk, Virginia

BUT CELEBRATIONS ARE NOT CONFINED TO WASHINGTON AND PHILADELPHIA.

Throughout the month of September, cities and towns in America and across the seas hold their own commemorative events.

*In **Niceville**, **Florida**, students listen attentively as Al Swihart, a local councilman and Bicentennial coordinator, conducts a "teach-in" on the Constitution. Swihart visited several schools throughout Okaloosa County to give students the opportunity to discuss their Constitutional heritage and the customs of the eighteenth century.*

*The **Twin Cities** in **Minnesota** are the site of a Constitutional Conference to honor the Bicentennial. One hundred high school students from around the state are transported 100 years into the future to a space colony about to declare its independence. As leaders of this colony, facing conditions and issues similar to those experienced by the Founding Fathers in 1787, the students work together to draft a constitution.*

*In **Piedmont**, **California**, a determined four-year-old participates in a "sign-on to the Constitution," part of a national program initiated by the National Conference of Christians and Jews in conjunction with local organizations.*

*At **Norfolk**, **Virginia**, more than 1,500 sailors in their dress whites form a "200" aboard the USS Dwight D. Eisenhower, and join President Ronald Reagan in reciting the Pledge of Allegiance.*

*In **London**, **England**, September 17 marks the launching of a campaign to restore the only known surviving house once occupied by Benjamin Franklin. U.S. Ambassador Charles Price presents British Prime Minister Margaret Thatcher with a bust of Franklin sculpted by Chief Justice Burger. In making the presentation, Ambassador Price refers to the Constitution as "a work of political genius," recalling Franklin's outstanding contributions to science, technology, and the arts, and his efforts as a participant in the drafting of the Constitution.*

President Reagan leads the nation in the Pledge of Allegiance.

© Art Stein

London, England

F. Thorp, Lt./U.S. Navy Photo

Kelly Hope

Piedmont, California

The Twin Cities in Minnesota

Niceville, Florida

We the People

of the United States, in Order to form a more perfect Union, establish Justice, insure domestic Tranquility, provide for the common defence, promote the general Welfare, and secure the Blessings of Liberty to ourselves and our Posterity, do ordain and establish this Constitution for the United States of America.

Article. 1.

Section. 1. All legislative Powers herein granted shall be vested in a Congress of the United States, which shall consist of a Senate and House of Representatives.

Section. 2. The House of Representatives shall be composed of Members chosen every second Year by the People of the several States, and the Electors in each State shall have the Qualifications requisite for Electors of the most numerous Branch of the State Legislature.

No Person shall be a Representative who shall not have attained to the Age of twenty five Years, and been seven Years a Citizen of the United States, and who shall not, when elected, be an Inhabitant of that State in which he shall be chosen.

Representatives and direct Taxes shall be apportioned among the several States which may be included within this Union, according to their respective Numbers, which shall be determined by adding to the whole Number of free Persons, including those bound to Service for a Term of Years, and excluding Indians not taxed, three fifths of all other Persons. The actual Enumeration shall be made within three Years after the first Meeting of the Congress of the United States, and within every subsequent Term of ten Years, in such Manner as they shall by Law direct. The Number of Representatives shall not exceed one for every thirty Thousand, but each State shall have at Least one Representative; and until such enumeration shall be made, the State of New Hampshire shall be entitled to chuse three, Massachusetts eight, Rhode Island and Providence Plantations one, Connecticut five, New York six, New Jersey four, Pennsylvania eight, Delaware one, Maryland six, Virginia ten, North Carolina five, South Carolina five, and Georgia three.

When vacancies happen in the Representation from any State, the Executive Authority thereof shall issue Writs of Election to fill such Vacancies.

The House of Representatives shall chuse their Speaker and other Officers; and shall have the sole Power of Impeachment.

Section. 3. The Senate of the United States shall be composed of two Senators from each State, chosen by the Legislature thereof, for six Years; and each Senator shall have one Vote.

Immediately after they shall be assembled in Consequence of the first Election, they shall be divided as equally as may be into three Classes. The Seats of the Senators of the first Class shall be vacated at the Expiration of the second Year, of the second Class at the Expiration of the fourth Year, and of the third Class at the Expiration of the sixth Year, so that one third may be chosen every second Year; and if Vacancies happen by Resignation, or otherwise, during the Recess of the Legislature of any State, the Executive thereof may make temporary Appointments until the next Meeting of the Legislature, which shall then fill such Vacancies.

No Person shall be a Senator who shall not have attained to the Age of thirty Years, and been nine Years a Citizen of the United States, and who shall not, when elected, be an Inhabitant of that State for which he shall be chosen.

The Vice President of the United States shall be President of the Senate, but shall have no Vote, unless they be equally divided.

The Senate shall chuse their other Officers, and also a President pro tempore, in the Absence of the Vice President, or when he shall exercise the Office of President of the United States.

The Senate shall have the sole Power to try all Impeachments. When sitting for that Purpose, they shall be on Oath or Affirmation. When the President of the United States is tried, the Chief Justice shall preside: And no Person shall be convicted without the Concurrence of two thirds of the Members present.

Judgment in Cases of Impeachment shall not extend further than to removal from Office, and disqualification to hold and enjoy any Office of honor, Trust or Profit under the United States: but the Party convicted shall nevertheless be liable and subject to Indictment, Trial, Judgment and Punishment, according to Law.

Section. 4. The Times, Places and Manner of holding Elections for Senators and Representatives, shall be prescribed in each State by the Legislature thereof; but the Congress may at any time by Law make or alter such Regulations, except as to the Places of chusing Senators.

The Congress shall assemble at least once in every Year, and such Meeting shall be on the first Monday in December, unless they shall by Law appoint a different Day.

Section. 5. Each House shall be the Judge of the Elections, Returns and Qualifications of its own Members, and a Majority of each shall constitute a Quorum to do Business; but a smaller Number may adjourn from day to day, and may be authorized to compel the Attendance of absent Members, in such Manner, and under such Penalties as each House may provide.

Each House may determine the Rules of its Proceedings, punish its Members for disorderly Behaviour, and, with the Concurrence of two thirds, expel a Member.

Each House shall keep a Journal of its Proceedings, and from time to time publish the same, excepting such Parts as may in their Judgment require Secrecy; and the Yeas and Nays of the Members of either House on any question shall, at the Desire of one fifth of those Present, be entered on the Journal.

Neither House, during the Session of Congress, shall, without the Consent of the other, adjourn for more than three days, nor to any other Place than that in which the two Houses shall be sitting.

Section. 6. The Senators and Representatives shall receive a Compensation for their Services, to be ascertained by Law, and paid out of the Treasury of the United States. They shall in all Cases, except Treason, Felony and Breach of the Peace, be privileged from Arrest during their Attendance at the Session of their respective Houses, and in going to and returning from the same; and for any Speech or Debate in either House, they shall not be questioned in any other Place.

No Senator or Representative shall, during the Time for which he was elected, be appointed to any civil Office under the Authority of the United States, which shall have been created, or the Emoluments whereof shall have been encreased during such time; and no Person holding any Office under the United States, shall be a Member of either House during his Continuance in Office.

CHAPTER I

1985

The
Creation
of
the
Commission

Organization of the Commemoration

The foregoing commemorative events in Washington, Philadelphia, London, and elsewhere did not simply happen by chance, and they did not stand alone. They were part of a carefully coordinated series of celebrations and educational programs marking the Bicentennial of the U.S. Constitution. Beginning in 1986, these activities led up to the anniversary of the Constitution's drafting in 1987 and extended through the commemoration of the "Bill of Rights and Beyond" in 1991.

The commemoration was spearheaded by the Commission on the Bicentennial of the United States Constitution, formed in 1985 on the basis of a 1983 congressional mandate. Joining in and contributing enormous amounts of time, hard work, and money were many U.S. Government departments and agencies, Congress, and the Judiciary; Bicentennial Commissions in all 50 states, the District of Columbia, and the U.S. territories; over 2,600 local communities; thousands of private companies and nonprofit organizations; schools, colleges, and universities; broadcasting groups; newspaper, magazine, and book publishers; and foreign governments and organizations throughout the world.

The national Commission, of course, was not responsible for all of the activities described in this report. In some cases, the Commission was a prime mover; in other cases, it may have been a principal source of funds or other support; in others, it merely stimulated activities and had little or no role at all, except as a cheerleader from the sidelines. In the cases of A CELEBRATION OF CITIZENSHIP and the reenactment of George Washington's first inaugural, the Commission provided the leadership. By contrast, in Philadelphia, although national leaders and members of the Commission played important roles, it was a local group, WE THE PEOPLE 200, that galvanized the leaders of some of the city's most important organizations into contributing to the Bicentennial commemoration. In thousands of additional events and activities, leaders and members of the state, local, and international groups involved provided the spark.

Purpose of This Report

This report offers a history of the Constitution's Bicentennial itself — not simply the activities of the Bicentennial Commission. It is the record of the great variety of activities across the landscape of America, undertaken individually and collectively by American citizens and by admirers of America's system of government around the globe. It describes the special commemorative events that took place during each year of the celebration. It also tells the story of the major programs and cooperative projects that continued during a significant portion of the life of the Commission. Finally, it presents examples of independent events, programs, projects, and other activities staged by diverse bodies within the context of the Bicentennial commemoration.

The report has two principal benefits: it is both a record of some of the things that happened and a form of accounting for the Commission's performance of its mission. In both respects, it will have value for posterity as a guide to those who may be responsible in the future for similar commemorations. Consequently, this report focuses not only on what happened but also on what it took to make these things happen: the application of people, resources, organization, time, effort, and planning—by the Commission and all those institutions and groups around the country and throughout the world that cooperated so splendidly in the commemorative enterprise. Thus, it is a compressed and selective account of an extraordinarily complex undertaking — carried on over seven years.

Courtesy, CIGNA Museum and Art Collection

Origins of the Commemoration
CALLS FOR A COMMEMORATION

Given previous commemorations of the Constitution, including the Golden Jubilee in 1837, the 75th anniversary in 1862, and especially the Centennial and Sesquicentennial celebrations, many individuals and groups naturally looked forward to 1987 and the Bicentennial. Different proposals were considered in an effort to find an appropriate way to commemorate the 200th anniversary of the Constitution. For example, proposals introduced in Congress in the mid-1970s called for a "bicentennial era," linking the celebration of the Declaration of Independence and the American Revolution with that of the Constitution. These proposals also recommended the establishment of a Federal entity that would use the occasion as a means of addressing the nation's current problems.

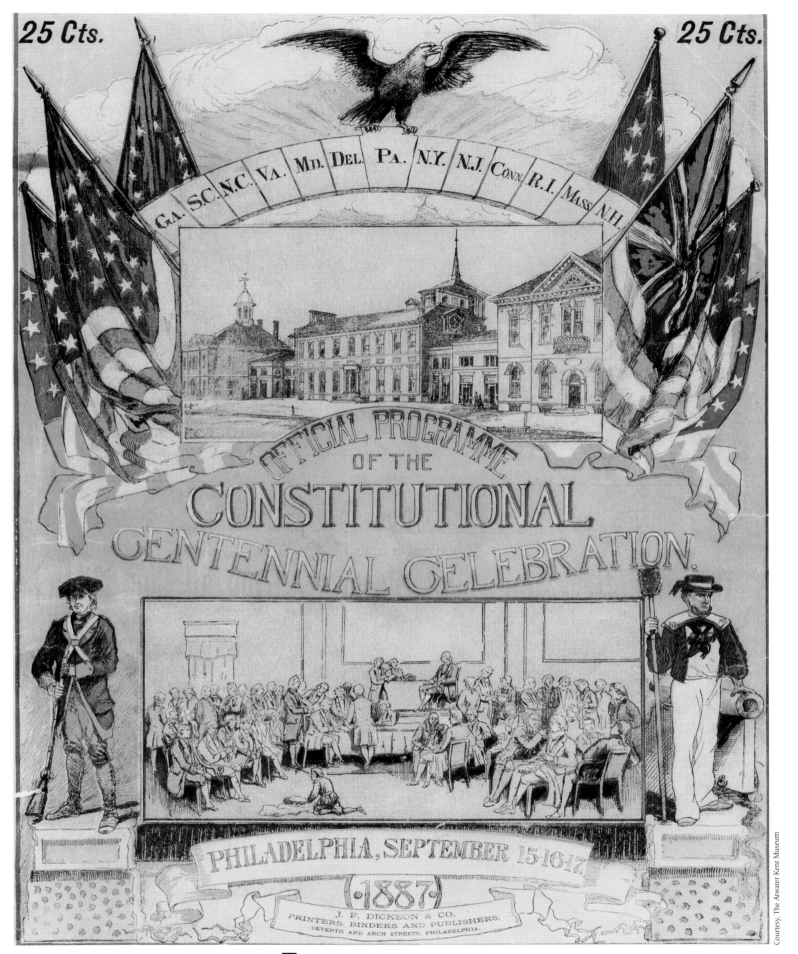

This silver tray, one of 13 made for the Governors of the original states, commemorates the 75th anniversary of the Signing of the Constitution (left). The official program of the 1887 Centennial celebration (above).

These broad reformative proposals did not make their way through the legislative process into law. In the end, those that focused more specifically on the framing and ratification of the Constitution and its history made more progress. Proponents called for a commemoration that would reeducate the American people about the principles underlying their form of government and way of life—one that would prompt Americans to rededicate themselves to those principles. Many believed such a commemoration was important as the United States looked toward its third century, continuing to govern itself under the world's oldest written constitution.

In the late 1970s and early 1980s, various individuals and groups with professional and personal interests in the Constitution called for such a celebration. In a speech on September 21, 1978, at the National Archives, for example, Chief Justice Burger proposed a three-year observance of the 200th anniversary of the Constitution, suggesting that "if we— collectively—use the 'lead time' now available to us, we can develop a program worthy of the importance of the occasion." In August 1979, the American Bar Association (ABA) joined the call for a Bicentennial celebration, urging that "public understanding about the Constitution, Bill of Rights, and the law generally . . . [be] . . . recognized as a national educational priority of the coming decade. . . ."

Philadelphia's Centennial parade featured many floats, including a one-room schoolhouse with the slogan "Education is the Basis of National Freedom" (top) and a float whose arch bore the ratification dates of the 13 original states.

The official poster of the 1937 Sesquicentennial celebration, by Howard Chandler Christy, shows Liberty triumphant above the signing Fathers.

Howard Chandler Christy also created the 1937 commemorative plaque, both sides of which are shown below.

National Archives (2)

BUILDING THE FOUNDATION

By the early 1980s, with the Bicentennial approaching, various organizations had begun to develop programs designed to educate young people and adults about the Constitution, the nation's form of government, and its way of life. One of the most important was Project '87, cosponsored by the American Historical Association and the American Political Science Association. The project—to run for nine years, until September 17, 1987, the 200th anniversary of the signing of the Constitution—had a distinguished advisory board, with Chief Justice Burger as Honorary Chairman and comprising members of the Federal Judiciary, the Senate and House Judiciary Committees, lawyers, educators, and representatives of the media. The threefold mission of Project '87 was to encourage research and sponsor conferences about the Constitution; improve the quality of teaching about history and government; and promote nationwide reflection on the Constitution, encouraging the widest possible participation in grassroots discussions of the constitutional system.

The ABA had also undertaken important initiatives. Its Special Committee on Youth Education for Citizenship, for example, initiated a special Bicentennial project to revitalize instruction about the Constitution and the Bill of Rights. The ABA's Committee on Public Understanding About the Law, with a planning grant from the National Endowment for the Humanities, conducted a model education program on the influence of the First Amendment in daily decision making.

The Bicentennial Council of the Thirteen Original States Fund, Inc., initiated the Great American Achievements Program. Annual conferences brought scholars, educators, political and public figures, and other interested individuals together to examine the relevance of a particular underlying theme of the Constitution and the Bill of Rights — from their historical origins to the present. The organization then prepared study materials for use by individuals and groups. By 1981, more than half of the 13 original states had some of the study kits in use.

CONGRESS BECOMES THE FOCUS

By 1981, Congress had become seriously interested in the 200th anniversary of the signing of the Constitution, by then only six years away. On September 17, 1981 (Citizenship Day), Senator Orrin Hatch of Utah, Chairman of the Subcommittee on the Constitution of the Senate Judiciary Committee, conducted hearings primarily to receive testimony about three Senate bills, each of which called for a national effort to commemorate the Bicentennial and for the establishment of a commission to lead the effort. Representatives from many of the private groups whose programs have been described also testified. Without exception, they supported the commemorative effort and the establishment of such an organization. They differed, however, in their conceptions of what functions the commission would perform.

Other groups contributed prepared statements. While the Senate hearings generated much enthusiasm for a national commemoration led by a government commission, none of the bills considered became law.

Not to be deterred, Senator Hatch held an extraordinary, even historic, hearing on this subject early in the first session of the 98th Congress. On March 1, 1983, his subcommittee considered Senate Bill 118, "a bill to provide for the establishment of a commission on the Bicentennial of the Constitution." Joining Senator Hatch in sponsoring this legislation were Senators Max Baucus of Montana, Dennis DeConcini of Arizona, Edward M. Kennedy of Massachusetts, Paul D. Laxalt of Arizona, Patrick J. Leahy of Vermont, Charles McC. Mathias of Maryland, and Strom Thurmond of South Carolina. Representatives of all three branches of government as well as distinguished representatives from the private sector either testified in favor of the bill or provided supporting statements. After Senator Hatch introduced the bill, former President Gerald Ford testified at length,* as did Chief Judge Howard T. Markey, United States Court of Appeals for the Federal Circuit and Chairman of the Bicentennial Preparatory Commission of the Judicial Conference of the United States. Representatives of the ABA, Project '87, and the Federal Bar Association all appeared to testify in support of the bill.

BILL BECOMES LAW

After approving various amendments, the Subcommittee on the Constitution unanimously endorsed S. 118, and on April 12, 1983, the Judiciary Committee of the Senate approved it as amended by voice vote. On April 28, 1983, the Judiciary Committee issued a report on S. 118 that effectively summarized the most cogent arguments advanced at the Hatch subcommittee hearings and strongly recommended passage of the bill with amendments.

The bill passed the Senate on July 18 and the House on August 4, 1983, with amendments. The amendments, which had been requested by the White House, increased the membership of the Commission from 16 to 23 as well as the number of commissioners the President could appoint; they also empowered the President to appoint the Chairman of the Commission. On September 14, the House returned the bill to the Senate, which concurred with the House amendments. Finally, on September 29, 1983, with President Reagan's signature, S. 118 became Public Law 98-101, ". . . an Act to establish a Commission to promote and coordinate activities to commemorate the bicentennial of the Constitution."

HIATUS

The legislation, however, was not put into effect immediately. In fact, the Commissioners were not appointed until the summer of 1985 — 21 months later.

*This marked the first time a former President had testified before Congress since former President Truman did so in 1959.

During this hiatus, however, activity related to the Bicentennial continued. The many private program initiatives already described, along with others, sustained the Bicentennial's momentum. The American Enterprise Institute, for example, sponsored a conference on constitution writing in September 1983 at the Supreme Court in Washington, D.C., with constitutional experts from around the world taking part. In the fall of 1984, a special pre-Bicentennial issue of *National Forum*, the journal of Phi Kappa Phi, featured articles from academic authorities, lawyers, and prominent public officials, including President Ronald Reagan, Speaker of the House Thomas P. "Tip" O'Neill, Jr., and Chief Justice Burger.

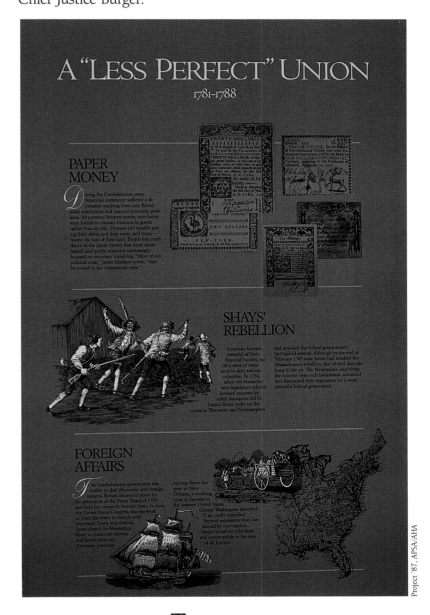

The Less Perfect Union, *from a series of 12 posters on the Bicentennial developed by Project '87.*

The Early Organization of the Commission

On June 25, 1985, President Reagan officially appointed Chief Justice Warren Burger as Chairman of the Commission on the Bicentennial of the United States Constitution and announced the names of the other individuals who were to serve as Commissioners. The Commission's authorizing legislation called for the designation of a portion of the Commission's membership by each of four individuals: the President, the President Pro Tempore of the Senate, the Chief Justice of the United States, and the Speaker of the House.

The law stated generally what was to be taken into account in the appointment of Commissioners:

Each of the individuals making recommendations to the President regarding appointments shall seek to achieve a balanced membership representing, to the maximum extent practicable, the nation as a whole. The Commission members shall be chosen from among individuals who have demonstrated scholarship, a strong sense of public service, expertise in the learned professions, and abilities likely to contribute to the fulfillment of the duties of the Commission.

President Reagan and Chief Justice Burger discuss the Bicentennial, White House, January 20, 1985.

In a White House ceremony on the morning of July 30, Vice President George Bush administered the oath to the members of the Commission. The original members were:

WARREN E. BURGER

FREDERICK K. BIEBEL

LINDY BOGGS

HERBERT BROWNELL

LYNNE V. CHENEY

PHILIP M. CRANE

WILLIAM J. GREEN

EDWARD VICTOR HILL

CORNELIA G. KENNEDY

EDWARD M. KENNEDY

HARRY M. LIGHTSEY, JR.

WILLIAM LUCAS

EDWARD P. MORGAN

BETTY SOUTHARD MURPHY

THOMAS J. O'CONNOR

PHYLLIS SCHLAFLY

BERNARD H. SIEGAN

TED STEVENS

OBERT C. TANNER

STROM THURMOND

RONALD H. WALKER

CHARLES E. WIGGINS

CHARLES ALAN WRIGHT

Senator DENNIS DeCONCINI was appointed to the Commission upon the death of Edward Morgan in 1986. Senator MARK O. HATFIELD was appointed after the resignation of Senator Stevens in 1989. Judge DAMON J. KEITH was appointed in 1990 after the resignation of William Lucas.

A Look at the People Involved

The Commissioners appointed reflected a diversity of perspectives, interests, and talents, whose mix would serve them well in their collective efforts. In addition to his administrative experience, Chief Justice Burger brought several abilities and attributes to his role as Chairman. He was steeped in the Constitution and its history and could talk authoritatively about it. A firm believer in the importance of the Constitution's Bicentennial and its potential value to the country, he proved to be an effective representative of the commemoration throughout the years of its existence. Jane Nevins wrote of him in the *The New York Times*, September 22, 1985:

. . .the Chief Justice downplays his own efforts to advance the tribute to the experiment, but disclaimers and the cautious language he uses cannot conceal the intensity of his feelings for the Constitution. Its creation and the founding days are so vivid to him that he effortlessly sees them as scenes on television. . . . A good national soaking in history to promote appreciation of the Constitution's genius is what Justice Burger is after. . . . "Basically," he says, "Americans for 200 years have been looking forward. The American mind should be looking back and ahead at the same time."

WARREN E. BURGER, *Chairman*
(Virginia)

As Chief Justice of the United States from June 1969 until September 1986, Warren Burger was also Chairman of the Judicial Conference of the United States — in effect, administrative head of the nation's Federal court system — and Chairman of the Federal Judicial Center, the research and education arm of the judicial branch. This followed a distinguished private and public career in the law. In 1933, he had become a full partner in the firm of Boyesen, Otis, and Faricy. In 1953, President Eisenhower appointed him Assistant Attorney General of the United States, Chief of the Civil Division. In 1956, he was appointed by President Eisenhower a Judge of the United States Court of Appeals for the District of Columbia Circuit, which position he held until his appointment to the Supreme Court.

FREDERICK K. BIEBEL
(Connecticut)

A businessman by background, Mr. Biebel had also made a distinguished career in public service before joining the Commission. Long active in the Republican Party, he served as State Chairman of the party and as Deputy National Chairman. He was a member of the Connecticut Historical Commission and the American Revolution Bicentennial Commission of Connecticut. Mr. Biebel continued to serve as the Chairman of the Bicentennial Council of the Thirteen Original States and Chairman of the U.S. Constitution Commission. Subsequently, he became the executive director of the *H.M.S. Rose* Foundation.

LINDY BOGGS
(Louisiana)

The first woman to be elected to Congress from Louisiana, Mrs. Boggs served over 17 years in the House of Representatives before retiring at the end of the 1988-1990 term. She was a member of the House Appropriations Committee and the Select Committee on Children, Youth, and Families, whose Task Force on Crisis Intervention she chaired. In 1976, she became the first woman to chair a national convention of a major political party when she presided over the Democratic National Convention in New York. A former schoolteacher, Mrs. Boggs was a regent of the Smithsonian Institution, a member of the National Historical Records and Publications Commission, and Chairman of the Commission on the Bicentenary of the House of Representatives.

HERBERT BROWNELL
(New York)

Mr. Brownell, an attorney specializing in corporate and private international law, brought decades of experience in public service to his work on the Commission. He served as Attorney General of the United States from 1953 until 1958 and, in 1972, as Special Ambassador to Mexico for the Presidential Study on the Colorado River Dispute. Long active in Republican Party politics, he was Chairman of that party's national committee. Mr. Brownell had been a principal architect of the 1957 Civil Rights Act and of the 25th Amendment. He became a Trustee of the White Burkett Miller Center of Public Affairs at the University of Virginia.

LYNNE V. CHENEY
(Wyoming)

At the time of her appointment to the Commission, Dr. Cheney was senior editor of *The Washingtonian* magazine. In 1986 she became Chairman of the National Endowment for the Humanities. She had served on the faculty of several colleges and universities, including George Washington University, and had published two novels and many articles focusing on women's history. She also coauthored a book profiling eight leaders in the House of Representatives from Henry Clay to Sam Rayburn.

DENNIS DeCONCINI
(Arizona)

Senator DeConcini was appointed to the Commission on June 23, 1986, to fill the vacancy created by the death of Edward P. Morgan. He had served since 1976 in the Senate, where he was a member of the Rules and Administration, Veterans Affairs, and Indian Affairs Committees. He was the ranking Democrat on the Subcommittee on the Constitution during drafting of the Bicentennial Commission's authorizing legislation. Before entering the Senate, Senator DeConcini practiced law in Arizona and was the Pima County Attorney.

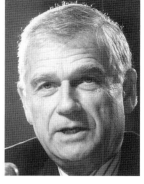

MARK O. HATFIELD
(Oregon)

Senator Hatfield was appointed to the Commission on September 6, 1989, to fill the vacancy created by the resignation of Senator Stevens. He had served Oregon in the Senate since 1966 and was Chairman of the Senate Appropriations Committee from 1980 to 1986. Before entering Congress, he served for many years in state government, including the governorship of Oregon. At one time an associate professor of political science, Senator Hatfield had written several books concerning various public affairs issues.

PHILIP M. CRANE
(Illinois)

At the time of his appointment, Representative Crane had served 16 years in the House of Representatives, where he was a member of the Ways and Means Committee as well as the Trade and Social Security Subcommittees. Before entering politics, he served as an administrator of a private school and taught history at the University of Indiana and Bradley University. Representative Crane was the author of three books as well as many articles on American history, government, and public issues.

WILLIAM J. GREEN
(Pennsylvania)

An attorney in private practice at the time of his appointment, Mr. Green had served seven terms as a Member of the House of Representatives for a district in Philadelphia and subsequently as Mayor of that city for four years. While in Congress, he was a member of the Ways and Means Committee and Chairman of that committee's International Trade Subcommittee.

EDWARD VICTOR HILL
(California)

Reverend Hill was the pastor of Mount Zion Missionary Baptist Church, Los Angeles, and vice president of the National Baptist Convention, USA, Inc. He also had leadership positions in a variety of religious and charitable organizations, including the World Christian Training Center, STEP (formerly Foundation for the Poor), and the United Benevolent Society.

DAMON J. KEITH
(Michigan)

Judge Keith was appointed to the Bicentennial Commission on June 18, 1990, to fill the vacancy created by the resignation of William Lucas. At the time of his appointment, he was Judge of the United States Court of Appeals for the Sixth Circuit. Previously, he had served as Federal District Judge and Chief Judge. Judge Keith's other services included chairmanship of the Michigan Civil Rights Commission and the national chairmanship of the Judicial Conference Committee on the Bicentennial of the Constitution.

CORNELIA G. KENNEDY
(Michigan)

At the time of her appointment, Judge Kennedy sat on the United States Court of Appeals for the Sixth Circuit, to which she had been appointed in 1979. Previously, she had served as Federal District Judge and Chief Judge for the Eastern District of Michigan and as Judge of the Third Judicial Circuit of Michigan. She had been Chairman of the National Conference of Federal Trial Judges and served on the Board of the Federal Judicial Center.

EDWARD M. KENNEDY
(Massachusetts)

At the time of his appointment, Senator Kennedy was in his fifth term in the Senate, where he served as Chairman of the Judiciary Committee and was a member of its Constitutional Rights Subcommittee. He was also Chairman of the Labor and Human Resources Committee and a member of the Armed Services and Joint Economic Committees. The author of four books, he served as a trustee or in other capacities for many projects and organizations in the fields of medicine, the arts, general philanthropy, and education.

HARRY M. LIGHTSEY, JR.
(South Carolina)

Dr. Lightsey was Dean of the University of South Carolina Law Center. Subsequently, in 1985, he became president of the College of Charleston in Charleston, South Carolina. Having both taught and practiced law for many years, he served as Assistant Attorney General for South Carolina and as Chairman of the South Carolina Human Affairs Commission. In 1985, he chaired the University of South Carolina's President's Commission to Study Undergraduate Education.

WILLIAM LUCAS
(Michigan)

Mr. Lucas was the Chief Executive Officer of Wayne County, Michigan, the fourth largest county in the United States. Prior to that service, he had been a police officer, social worker, and teacher in New York City. He also worked for the Justice Department as a civil rights investigator and attorney and as an FBI agent. He was the Sheriff of Wayne County for 14 years before becoming the county's Chief Executive. Mr. Lucas resigned from the Commission on November 9, 1989.

EDWARD P. MORGAN
(Maryland)

At the time of his appointment, Mr. Morgan had practiced law in Washington, D.C., for 37 years. He had been an FBI agent, rising to the position of Chief Inspector. For three decades he served in many special government appointments, including Chief Counsel of a Senate Foreign Relations subcommittee, Chief of the Enforcement Division of the Office of Price Stabilization, and, in 1980 and 1985, a member of the Presidential Commission on Executive, Legislative, and Judicial Salaries. Mr. Morgan died on March 3, 1986.

BETTY SOUTHARD MURPHY
(Washington, D.C.)

An attorney in private practice, Mrs. Murphy had also been Chairman of the National Labor Relations Board and Administrator of the Wage and Hour Division of the Department of Labor. A member of the American Bar Association's Commission on Public Understanding About the Law, she chaired several law association committees, including one on international law, and had testified before Congress on behalf of legislation establishing the Bicentennial Commission.

PHYLLIS SCHLAFLY
(Illinois)

Listed in the *World Almanac* as one of the 25 most influential women in the United States, Mrs. Schlafly was the president of Eagle Forum and the author of 12 books, as well as a monthly newsletter begun in 1967. Her activities also included a syndicated newspaper column and a daily radio commentary heard on 175 stations. An attorney and a member of the Administrative Conference of the United States, she served on President Reagan's 1980 Defense Policy Advisory Board.

TED STEVENS
(Alaska)

At the time of his appointment, Senator Stevens was the senior member of Alaska's Congressional delegation. He had served in the Senate since 1968. He had been both Assistant Majority and Assistant Minority Leader of the Senate and a member of the Appropriations, Commerce, Government Affairs, and Rules Committees. Before entering Congress, Senator Stevens served in the Alaska House of Representatives and held several positions in the Department of the Interior, including that of Solicitor. He resigned from the Commission on February 8, 1989.

THOMAS H. O'CONNOR
(Massachusetts)

Professor of American History at Boston College, Dr. O'Connor had written extensively about the Civil War era and the history of his native Boston. He was a member of the Massachusetts Civil War Centennial Commission, a historical consultant for the Boston 200 Program, and project director for Forum 350, which commemorated the 350th anniversary of Boston.

BERNARD H. SIEGAN
(California)

Distinguished Professor of Law and Director of Law and Economics Studies at the University of San Diego School of Law, Mr. Siegan had written and spoken extensively on various constitutional issues and was a specialist on the subject of economic liberties under the Constitution. He was a member of the President's Commission on Housing (1981-1982) and Chairman of its Regulations Committee. Professor Siegan was also a consultant to the Federal Trade Commission.

OBERT C. TANNER
(Utah)

Mr. Tanner was the founder and chairman of the O.C. Tanner Company, a jewelry business headquartered in Salt Lake City, Utah. He had also been a professor of philosophy at the University of Utah. Mr. Tanner served as Chairman of the Utah American Revolution Bicentennial Commission and in that capacity was responsible for several hundred community projects in his home state. He served on the Executive Committee for the White House Conference on Children and Youth and as an American delegate to the World Federation of the United Nations Association. In 1988 he received the National Medal of Arts from President Reagan.

STROM THURMOND
(South Carolina)

At the time of his appointment, Senator Thurmond had served 31 years in the U.S. Senate, where he had been Chairman of the Judiciary Committee, a member of the Armed Services Committee, and President Pro Tempore. Before entering the Senate, he had pursued many careers, including athletic coach, teacher, superintendent of schools, and attorney in private practice. He served his home state as a city and county attorney, State Senator, Circuit Judge, and from 1947 to 1951, as Governor. In 1948, Senator Thurmond was a candidate for President on the States Rights Democratic Party ticket.

RONALD H. WALKER
(Washington, D.C.)

Mr. Walker was a senior partner and managing director in the Washington, D.C., firm of Korn/Ferry International. He had held several positions in both government and the corporate world. His public career included service as Assistant to the Secretary of the Interior, Staff Assistant to the President of the United States, and Special Assistant to the President during the Nixon administration. From 1973 until 1975, Mr. Walker was the Director of the National Park Service.

CHARLES E. WIGGINS
(California)

Judge Wiggins sat on the United States Court of Appeals for the Ninth Circuit. Early in his career, he had practiced law in El Monte, California, where he also served as Chairman of the El Monte Planning Commission, a member of the City Council, and two years as Mayor. In 1966, he was elected to the U.S. House of Representatives, in which he served six terms and was a member of the Judiciary Committee. Judge Wiggins was also a member of the Advisory Committee on Federal Rules of Procedure of the Judicial Conference of the United States.

CHARLES ALAN WRIGHT
(Texas)

The William Bates Professor of Law at the University of Texas, Charles Alan Wright had taught at many universities in this country and abroad. An authority on the jurisdiction and procedures of the Federal courts, he had published more than 50 books on that and related subjects. He also had written extensively for both professional and lay audiences in various areas of constitutional law. Professor Wright had argued 11 cases before the U.S. Supreme Court and had served as a legal counsel to President Nixon.

COMMISSION STAFFING

On July 16, 1985, after the President's announcement of the Commission's membership and before its first meeting, the Commission's Chairman appointed a search committee to recommend a candidate for Staff Director. After an extensive review and upon the unanimous recommendation of the search committee, the Commission appointed Dr. Mark W. Cannon as Staff Director. Dr. Cannon served until September 1988 and was succeeded by Dr. Ronald L. Trowbridge. Dr. Trowbridge served as Staff Director until December 1989 and was succeeded by Dr. Herbert M. Atherton, who continued in that position until the expiration of the Commission in June 1992.

By the end of 1985, the Commission staff consisted of 25 people: four on the permanent payroll, who were paid out of funds appropriated to the Commission; eight detailed from other Federal agencies; and 13 volunteers.

STAFF DIRECTORS

MARK W. CANNON (1985-1988)

Before his appointment as Staff Director in August 1985, Dr. Cannon was Administrative Assistant to the Chief Justice of the United States. He had served in a variety of positions with the Institute of Public Administration, Brigham Young University, and the offices of Senator Wallace F. Bennett and Representative Henry Aldous Dixon of Utah.

RONALD L. TROWBRIDGE (1989)

Dr. Trowbridge joined the Commission in April 1986 as Director of Federal and International Programs. Before his appointment, he was Associate Director of the Bureau of Educational and Cultural Affairs, United States Information Agency. He became Acting Staff Director in September 1988 and Staff Director in January 1989.

HERBERT M. ATHERTON (1990-1992)

Dr. Atherton joined the Commission in August 1987 as Director of Educational Programs. Before his appointment, he was Dean of the College and Associate Professor of History at Connecticut College. He became Deputy Staff Director in January 1989, Acting Staff Director in January 1990, and Staff Director in March 1990.

Challenges Facing the Commission

From the outset, the Commission faced some formidable challenges, perhaps the greatest of which was the pressure of time. The Commission had been established three to five years later than was desirable for thorough planning. Because of legislative delay, it did not come into being until July 30, 1985, and so missed by several months the first important Bicentennial date: the Mount Vernon Conference (*see Chapter II*). The first major dates for commemoration were just over the horizon; the 200th anniversary of the Annapolis Convention was scarely more than a year away.

There was also a shortage of money and staff. Resources made available in the enabling legislation proved insufficient to the task ahead, with little expectation of significant increases. (Congress appropriated $331,000 for fiscal year 1985.) Moreover, the corporate community was still in the latter stages of raising over $200 million for the Statue of Liberty Centennial programs. The success of the Bicentennial therefore would depend on the spirit of volunteerism. The Commission could carry out only a few major projects itself; it would act primarily as a catalyst — a facilitator and coordinator of the activities of others. It was to make every effort to enlist the participation of other elements of government — Federal, state, and local — and to mobilize individuals and groups, public and private.

In addition, there was widespread ignorance in the country about, and apparent lack of interest in, the Bicentennial of the Constitution. The history of previous commemorations did not offer much encouragement or guidance. The Centennial and Sesquicentennial anniversaries of the Constitution, while realizing significant accomplishments, had not been popular successes. To many, the Constitution seemed a complex, abstract, and difficult subject for public celebration. Recent patriotic and historical commemorations in the United States seemed to favor festivity over substance. Some kind of balance had to be struck if the coming Bicentennial was to appeal to Americans of all backgrounds. All in all, the Commission had a formidable undertaking on its hands, particularly with so little time to get organized and operating before the next commemorative dates arrived.

EARLY MEETINGS OF THE COMMISSION

The Commission accomplished the basic work of organization in its first three meetings during the last half of 1985. Commissioners concentrated on an overview of the purposes of the commemoration: how the Commission would approach its task and organize its work. During the first meeting, the Commission's Chairman coined a phrase that would become the mission statement of the commemoration when he suggested that the Bicentennial provided a great opportunity for "a history and civics lesson for all of us."

The Commissioners also addressed the obstacles facing them. They passed a resolution requesting Congress to amend the legislation so as to provide the Commission with funding and staffing sufficient for its task and to extend its life through 1991 to accommodate the commemoration of the Bill of Rights. They adopted regulations concerning the acceptance of money, gifts-in-kind, and services from private sources. They discussed ways of energizing public and private bodies at every level of society through contact letters and a promotional brochure outlining the Commission's themes and objectives for 1986 through 1989. They established policies governing sponsorship, recognition, and other support of projects carried out by other organizations.

Ten advisory committees, formed to handle the details of the work, would strengthen the Commission's ability to deal with the complex and time-consuming issues ahead. These committees were:

EXECUTIVE COMMITTEE
chaired by Warren E. Burger

COMMITTEE ON FINANCE
chaired by Herbert Brownell,
with the Congressional members as Advisors

ADVISORY COMMITTEE ON PERSONNEL
AND ADMINISTRATION
cochaired by William Lucas and Ronald H. Walker

ADVISORY COMMITTEE ON EDUCATIONAL PROJECTS
cochaired by Philip M. Crane and Charles Alan Wright

ADVISORY COMMITTEE ON PRIVATE ASSOCIATIONS
AND ORGANIZATIONS
cochaired by Edward Victor Hill and Obert C. Tanner

ADVISORY COMMITTEE ON MEDIA
cochaired by Lynne V. Cheney and Edward M. Kennedy

ADVISORY COMMITTEE ON PROJECT ENDORSEMENT
AND SUPPORT
chaired by Cornelia G. Kennedy

ADVISORY COMMITTEE ON FEDERAL LIAISON
cochaired by Frederick K. Biebel and Lindy Boggs

ADVISORY COMMITTEE ON STATE AND LOCAL LIAISON
cochaired by William J. Green and Phyllis Schlafly

ADVISORY COMMITTEE ON INTERNATIONAL LIAISON
chaired by Betty Southard Murphy

THE BICENTENNIAL LOGO AND COMMISSION SEAL

An important accomplishment of the early Commission meetings was the selection of an official Bicentennial logo and an official Commission seal. In August 1985, the Commission authorized the Advertising Council to sponsor an open competition for the design of the logo. The Advisory Committee on Project Endorsements and Support considered 42 proposed designs for a logo before recommending three finalists to the whole Commission.

The Commissioners chose the design submitted by the Department of the Army's Institute of Heraldry. Its artist, Sarah LeClerc, featured a scroll with the inscription "We the People," an American flag, and a gold eagle capping the flag's staff. The official Commission seal featured the traditional heraldic representation of the American eagle and the scroll representation of the Constitution also used in the logo. The seal was intended for use on certificates of achievement awarded by the Commission and for special presentations. Public Law 99-549 granted permission for the Commission to market its logo for educational and commemorative purposes. In its November 1985 meeting, the Commission approved not only the design of the logo and seal but also the guidelines under which the Commission could grant official recognition to worthy projects and permit use of the logo. The guidelines were published in the *Federal Register* in 1986.

THE FIRST ANNUAL REPORT

During this early period, the Commission produced and distributed the first annual report, as required by law. On Citizenship Day, September 17, 1985, the Commission's Chairman presented copies of the report to President Reagan, to Senate and House officers, and to the Judicial Conference of the United States. House Speaker O'Neill and Senate President Pro Tempore Thurmond received the report on behalf of Congress. A limited number of additional copies were printed and distributed to key constituents.

In a sense, this report initiated the Commission's public education campaign. The report described the Commission's preliminary plans for commemorating the Bicentennial and proposed changes in Public Law 98-101. It also contained a calendar of key historical dates from 1785 to 1791, which provided themes for state and local commemorations and proposed a Bicentennial commemorative focus for each year:

• 1986 and early 1987 should concentrate on events leading up to the Constitutional Convention.
• The balance of 1987 should emphasize the writing of the Constitution, culminating on September 17, 1987,

the 200th anniversary of the signing of the document.
• 1988 should stress the ratification of the Constitution, completed June 21, 1788, when New Hampshire approved.
• 1989 should feature the establishment of the three branches of government and the inauguration of George Washington. Also during 1789, the first Congress proposed the amendments to the Constitution that became the Bill of Rights upon their ratification in 1791.

The report did not consider commemorative events beyond 1789 because at the time it was issued, the Commission was scheduled to terminate at the end of 1989.

THE FIRST PUBLIC HEARING

The Commission held its first public hearing at the Supreme Court on the same day it submitted the first annual report — September 17, 1985. The hearing, to learn about the plans of other governmental bodies as well as those of private organizations, provided a means by which these groups could suggest activities and provide general advice to the Commission. Representatives from 19 public and private agencies described their plans and projects, made suggestions as to Commission functions and activities, contributed offers of support for Commission fund-raising and the logo competition, and suggested projects for which funding support was needed.

GETTING FUNDS AND STAFF SUPPORT NECESSARY TO DO THE JOB

Public Law 98-101 had failed to provide the Commission with sufficient funds and staff support. The law reflected the belief that money and staff would be forthcoming from the private sector. Yet this notion was completely opposite, in spirit at least, to an important prescription in the report accompanying S. 118, the basis for Public Law 98-101. That report reflected accumulated wisdom about the practical interrelationship between the Federal Government and the private sector:

A Federal presence in the commemoration effort is also necessary to attract funding from private corporations and foundations. In the absence of a demonstration of interest by the Federal Government, private sources of funding may not be easily persuaded of the importance of supporting this commemoration, as they so generously backed the bicentennial of the Declaration of Independence.

The Commission thus faced the urgent task of obtaining a removal of restrictions on funding and staffing. The Commissioners who were Members of

Congress played an important role in accomplishing this, as did the leadership of both Houses. Initially introduced into Congress October 11, 1985, H.R. 3559 became Public Law 99-549 on October 27, 1986. This law extended the life of the Commission until the end of 1991, raised the ceilings on corporate and private donations, and eliminated limitations on staffing. It provided that all of the Commission's funding from Congress and private sources, as well as royalty payments, were to remain available for expenditure without time limitations to the Commission throughout its life.

OPEN OR CLOSED MEETINGS OF THE COMMISSION?

During the first few months of its existence, the Commission had to deal with one other important matter that was unrelated to its broad program of activities. During 1985, all Commission meetings had been closed to the press and public, except for the open hearing held on September 17. On October 10, Public Citizen, a nonprofit public affairs group established by Ralph Nader, brought suit against the Commission in Federal District Court in Washington, D.C. In its complaint, Public Citizen asked the court to order the Commission to give advance public notice about all future meetings and to open them to the public. The Commission's position favoring closed meetings was based on a belief that the free exploration and exchange of ideas necessary to effective planning and implementation would be inhibited if all meetings were open to the general public.

The Judge hearing the case, Louis D. Oberdorfer of the United States District Court of the District of Columbia, found for the Commission. He set forth his views in an order and memorandum opinion dated November 19, 1985, which stated that the Commission was not an advisory committee but primarily an operational agency, and it had functioned that way in practice. As such, it could conduct its business in public or in private, as it deemed appropriate. The Commission decided to hold open public hearings from time to time (as was the case with the first one in September 1985) to gather information and ideas and to encourage participation in the Bicentennial.

CONCLUSION

Despite delays in the legislation creating it and the need for additional legislation to widen its mandate and resources, the Commission had by the end of 1985 accomplished most of its organizational planning and preparation. It was ready to undertake the major commemorative events and longer-term programs that came to life in the years following.

CHAPTER II

1986

The
Commemoration
Begins

At the first Commission meeting on July 29-30, 1985, the Chairman emphasized that the Bicentennial provided a great opportunity for a "history and civics lesson for all of us." This suggested that the Bicentennial commemoration ought to be primarily educational in nature; obviously, students in classrooms and their teachers would be a key audience for the work of the Commission. The Commission's primary mission in 1986 was to create interest in and excitement about the Bicentennial commemoration and the opportunities it provided for citizens of all ages to participate in the "history and civics lesson," but with special focus on youth.

The Commission went about the task of trying to create interest and excitement in many different ways, working with a wide variety of individuals and groups. These included the organization of special events, the creation of ongoing programs and projects, and finally, the stimulation of other activities by the states and communities, schools and colleges and other educational organizations, Federal Government agencies, private organizations, the media, and institutions abroad. It would be impossible to treat each activity in detail in this report — so much went on. In this and in each subsequent chapter dealing with the years of the Bicentennial, the report selects a few of the major commemorative and special events for individual treatment. It provides a comprehensive summary of the ongoing Commission programs and a representative selection of other Bicentennial activities. This last category included projects that the Commission conducted jointly with others, as well as events, projects, programs, and activities carried out by organizations and groups entirely independent of the Commission. The year saw much planning and preparation for the Constitution's 200th birthday on the part of countless organizations and individuals around the country.

White House Photo

Strengthening the Commission

A number of administrative developments strengthened the Commission during 1986. On June 17, 1986, Chief Justice Warren E. Burger announced his intention to retire from the Supreme Court. In his letter to President Reagan, he explained his reasons:

I know we share the view that the story of our great constitutional system must be recalled to the American people — and indeed told to people everywhere who seek freedom. To tell the story as it should be told is an enormous and challenging task. I fear, however, it is now too late to enlist a new full-time Chairman. Accordingly, I have resolved to request that I be relieved as Chief Justice of the United States effective July 10, 1986, or as soon thereafter as my successor is qualified.

The announcement stimulated extensive coverage in the print and broadcast media. Nationwide and even worldwide press attention now focused on the Bicentennial commemoration and on Chief Justice Burger's role as Chairman. A significant example of this positive media attention was the hour-long interview Bill Moyers, then of CBS News, conducted with the Chief Justice on his retirement. While its main focus was on his 17-year service as the nation's chief judicial magistrate, the interview contained numerous references to the Bicentennial commemoration.

Even before assuming the Chairmanship of the Commission on a full-time basis, Chief Justice Burger had been very active in telling the story of the Bicentennial — and of the need for individuals and groups to get behind it — to important audiences all over the country. He met with the National Conference of Mayors in January of 1986 and with the National Governors Association a month later. On April 11, he spoke to the annual meeting of the American Society of Newspaper Editors (ASNE) in Washington, D.C., and on April 16 addressed the National Association of Broadcasters (NAB) convention in Dallas, Texas. On August 5, he spoke to the Business-Government Relations Council, a group of more than 100 Washington-based representatives of major American companies. In New York City, on November 25 and December 8, respectively, he addressed the International Radio and Television Society and the Economic Club of New York. In the months following, he made a special effort to speak to teachers' organizations, on which the success of the Bicentennial in reaching its educational objectives was to depend. On all these occasions, he called on individuals and groups to initiate or get involved in Bicentennial events and activities.

By the end of 1986, the Commission had greatly augmented its working space and staff, and the Congress had voted substantial additional budgetary resources. During the year, the Commission staff grew from 25 to 115 people: 86 paid from appropriated funds and 29 detailed from other Federal agencies. A few of the executive staff were still located at 736 Jackson Place (734 had been turned over to another agency), which continued to be the Commission's official headquarters. Only the Chairman and his immediate assistants remained housed at the Supreme Court. By late December 1986, most of the staff was consolidated into space on the eighth floor of Riggs National Corporation

BENJAMIN FRANKLIN
BY
WARREN E. BURGER

at 808 17th Street, N.W., donated rent-free for one year as a Bicentennial contribution by Riggs Bank.

The basic form of organization had been well established by this time, with a director in charge of each operating division. By early 1987, there were six principal program divisions: State and Local Affairs, Federal and International Programs, Educational Programs, Communications, Private Programs, and Marketing. In addition, there were three areas of staff support, including a division of Administration, a division of Commission Plans and Project Recognition, and an Office of the Legal Counsel.

With the enlarged staff, augmented space, new equipment, and the beginnings of a very active program, the Commission needed additional financial resources. Congress had appropriated $12.2 million in funds for the Commission for fiscal year 1986. The Commission also received $48,000 in donated funds during fiscal year 1986. All of these funds would remain available to the Commission for expenditure throughout its life.

The Franklin bust created by Chief Justice Burger (top); 736 Jackson Place, Washington, D.C. (right).

Another organizational step taken in 1986 was intended to strengthen the ability of the Commission to cope with the greatly increased responsibilities coming in 1987. This was the incorporation in March 1986 of the Foundation for the Commemoration of the United States Constitution. Originally intended to be the principal fund-raising organization for the Bicentennial, the Foundation was a nongovernmental, nonprofit corporation which was to serve as a fundamental link between the Commission and the private sector. Dwayne O. Andreas, chairman and chief executive officer of the Archer Daniels Midland Company, accepted the chairmanship of the Foundation. The other members of the Foundation's board of directors were Justin Stanley (president), Mrs. William P. Rogers (secretary-treasurer), Griffin Bell, Robert L. Clare, Jr., Kenneth Rush, and Bernard G. Segal. It was contemplated that the Commission itself would not engage in any direct involvement in fund-raising in the private sector.

In May 1986 Chief Justice Burger donated to the Foundation an original sculpture of Benjamin Franklin (executed by him at the age of 15). The Foundation, in turn, contracted with the Franklin Mint, whereby the Mint paid $50,000 to the Foundation for the right to make bronze replicas of the original sculpture and sell them as a commemorative item. The proceeds also went directly to the Foundation. Each replica, set on a hardwood base with a brass nameplate, carried an inscription of Chief Justice Burger's signature and was accompanied by a certificate of authenticity. Under the contract with Franklin Mint, each member of the Commission received a Franklin bust and sterling silver copies were made for President Reagan and his successor.

Major Events

ANNAPOLIS CONVENTION

The first major commemorative event of the Constitution's Bicentennial took place in Annapolis, Maryland, on September 11-14, 1986. This commemoration of the Annapolis Convention of 1786 witnessed the close cooperation between the national Commission, the Maryland State Archives' Office for the Bicentennial, the Maryland Humanities Council, and the U.S. Department of Defense. While the Maryland Office organized and staged most of the commemorative activities, the national Commission held its September meetings in Annapolis as part of the proceedings. The Commission's Chairman and other Commissioners participated actively in the commemorative events. The Commission also funded publication by the Maryland Office of a historical newspaper about the Annapolis Convention, 100,000 copies of which were distributed in Maryland and elsewhere. The Maryland Humanities Council

In a reenactment of the 1786 carriage ride, the Delaware delegation arrives in Annapolis.

conducted a major scholarly conference during the commemoration, and the Department of Defense arranged the stirring finale at Fort Meade.

Historical Background: The Annapolis Convention played a significant role in the history of the Constitution. Out of its deliberations came the call for the Confederation Congress to convene a convention in Philadelphia, which began in May 1787. The events that led to Annapolis and then Philadelphia actually began at George Washington's Mount Vernon home in March 1785. Delegates from Maryland and Virginia had met there to resolve jurisdictional and navigational problems involving the Potomac River and the Chesapeake Bay. From this meeting came the idea of inviting all the states to attend a commercial convention in Annapolis in September 1786.

Nine states named 40 delegates to Annapolis, but only 12 from five states — Virginia, Pennsylvania, New York, New Jersey, and Delaware — attended. Ironically, since the Maryland Senate feared an adverse reaction on the part of the Confederation Congress, Maryland sent no delegates and would not allow the meeting to be held in Maryland's new State House. At first, the delegates meeting at Annapolis, including Alexander Hamilton, James Madison, Edmund Randolph, and John Dickinson, were discouraged with the lack of representation. They made use, however, of the opportunity that permitted the discussion of "other important matters," such as the weaknesses of the central government under the Articles of Confederation. They drafted a resolution calling for a meeting in Philadelphia in May 1787 to discuss these problems and "to devise such further provisions as shall appear to them necessary to render

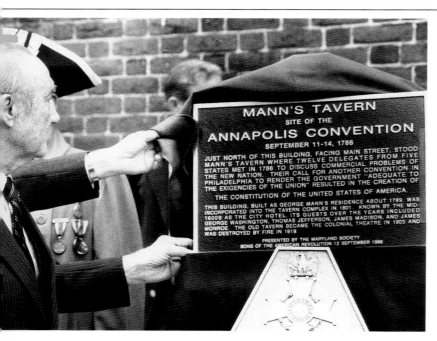

J. Connors/Maryland State Archives (5)

Maryland State Archives

*S*en. *Thurmond unveils historic site marker (top); Chairman Burger at Annapolis High School (above).*

*E*vening festivities at the Annapolis City Dock include actors portraying Jefferson and Franklin (top) and a gigantic translucent painting.*

the constitution of the Federal Government adequate to the exigencies of the Union." Copies of the resolution were sent to their own states, to the governors of the other states, and to the Continental Congress. Later that winter, state legislatures began appointing delegates, a development that finally convinced the Confederation Congress to call the Philadelphia Convention — "for the sole and express purpose of revising the Articles of Confederation."

Highlights of the Commemoration: The commemoration opened Thursday, September 11, 1986, with the dedication of the new Maryland State Archives building and the unveiling of an exhibit describing the Annapolis Convention. Governor Harry Hughes was the featured speaker. The next morning, Governor Hughes and the Commission's Chairman cut the ribbon inaugurating

Maryland's new Constitutional Resources area in the Silver Room of the State House. They then greeted a costumed delegation from Delaware, who had arrived by carriage at the front door of the State House following their reenactment of the 1786 trip made by the Delaware delegates to the Annapolis Convention.

Representing the Commission, Senator Strom Thurmond then stepped into the horse-drawn carriage which had transported the group from Delaware and proceeded to Conduit Street, historic site of George Mann's Tavern where the 12 delegates to the Annapolis Convention had met. Senator Thurmond unveiled a commemorative plaque donated by the Sons of the American Revolution to be mounted on the outside wall of the present Masonic Lodge, adjacent to where the tavern once stood. Meanwhile, at Annapolis High School, the Commission's Chairman responded to

Three views of the 18th-century fair on the campus of St. John's College in Annapolis, Maryland.

questions about the Constitution asked by high school students from all over Anne Arundel County. He sought to excite the young people, to encourage them to learn more about the remarkable document and its origins. "It is not a perfect document, but it is the most nearly perfect document that's ever come from the hand and mind of man," Chief Justice Burger declared, paraphrasing British Prime Minister William Gladstone.

On the afternoon of Friday, September 12, the national Commission held public hearings in Annapolis. Heading the list of participants was Governor Harry Hughes, who detailed Maryland's plans for the Bicentennial celebration, as did 15 other representatives of important groups, public and private. The hearings provided an opportunity for invaluable exchanges of information among the participants. That evening, Secretary of the Navy John Lehman hosted a reception

and dinner for the Commissioners at the Naval Academy, where participants enjoyed a play, "A More Perfect Union," written by Annapolis historian William K. Paynter. Elsewhere in the city that evening, the Ballet Theater of Annapolis staged both a special evening of ballet and a Colonial Ball.

The following day, Saturday the 13th, the Maryland Humanities Council, in cooperation with the Maryland Office for the Bicentennial and the Maryland State Archives, sponsored a scholarly conference, "The Annapolis Connection." The national Commission devoted Saturday to an all-day business meeting. In the evening, eighteenth-century music and dancing were featured in a program at the Annapolis City Dock, where actors impersonating Benjamin Franklin and James Madison talked about their lives and times. Highlight of the evening was the lighting of a gigantic translucent

Maryland State Archives (3)

During the Annapolis commemoration, Colonial encampments are established at Fort Meade, Maryland, where "Colonists" sew their clothes (above) and dip candles (right).

painting, a replica of an illumination created in Annapolis to celebrate the Constitution two centuries earlier.

The four-day commemoration concluded on Sunday, September 14, with an eighteenth-century fair on the St. John's College campus and a military review at Fort George G. Meade, near Annapolis in Maryland. A year in the planning, the fair was an authentic reproduction of life 200 years before. Activities included period games and pastimes and displays of eighteenth-century craftsmanship. Eighteen thousand people enjoyed a variety of military activities, displays, and ceremonies at Fort Meade. Before the official ceremonies, visitors witnessed battle reenactments and recreated Colonial encampments where "Colonists" could be seen cooking over camp fires, sewing their own clothing, and dipping candles. Elsewhere, visitors could view a Constitutional exhibit, military equipment displays from each of the services, and a Colonial March-Around with representatives from the 13 original colonies.

Following a concert by the United States Army Field Band, the Commission's Chairman, Secretary of the Army John Marsh, and several Commissioners planted five white oak trees (Maryland's official tree) as a "Constitution Grove." Soil from the five states that sent representatives to the Annapolis Convention was spread around the base of each of the trees. As the tree-planting ceremony drew to a close, a horseman arriving from Annapolis presented Chief Justice Burger with a copy of the "Call to Philadelphia," which 200 years earlier invited representatives to the Philadelphia Constitutional Convention. The day's events concluded with a military review.

"Colonial" soldiers encamped at Fort Meade (above).

The New Hampshire regiment joins the "March-Around" at Fort Meade (left); Commissioners Tanner and Wiggins help plant white oak trees (above).

*C*ongressional leaders host a
news conference in Statuary Hall (top);
Lady Bird Johnson inaugurates
PLANT A LIVING LEGACY.

CITIZENSHIP DAY, SEPTEMBER 17, 1986, WASHINGTON, D.C.

Citizenship Day and Constitution Week were fixtures on the nation's calendar long before the Constitution's Bicentennial. In 1952, Congress authorized an annual Presidential proclamation designating September 17 as Citizenship Day in commemoration of the signing of the Constitution. At the suggestion of the Daughters of the American Revolution (DAR), Congress in 1955 authorized the President to designate annually the week of September 17-23 as Constitution Week. In the years since, the President had issued a single proclamation each year designating both Citizenship Day and Constitution Week. The tradition continued through the years of the Bicentennial, providing a focus for each year's activities. Perpetuating this annual observance became one of the Commission's primary objectives.

Citizenship Day, September 17, 1986, was the occasion for several special events related to the Bicentennial. A joint press conference in Statuary Hall of the U.S. Capitol brought together Speaker of the House Thomas P. O'Neill, Jr., Senate President Pro Tempore Strom Thurmond, Republican National Committee Chairman Frank J. Fahrenkopf, Jr., and Democratic National Committee Chairman Paul G. Kirk, Jr., to announce their support for the celebration of the Bicentennial of the Constitution. At the end of the press conference, the two political party chairmen issued a joint statement calling on candidates of both parties for public office "to place a strong emphasis on the history and the enduring truth of our Constitution." Later that day, the 199th anniversary of the signing of the

Constitution was observed with a reception and dinner for the Commissioners, Supreme Court Justices, the Cabinet, Members of Congress, and other dignitaries at the historic Willard Inter-Continental Hotel, newly restored to its turn-of-the-century splendor and celebrating its grand reopening.

Citizenship Day 1986 also marked the inauguration of one of the Commission's continuing programs: PLANT A LIVING LEGACY. Lady Bird Johnson, former First Lady, returned to the nation's capital on that day to assist Chief Justice Burger and the Commission in unveiling the project at Constitution Gardens, near the Vietnam Veterans Memorial. The Commission's Chairman and Mrs. Johnson — well known for her work in beautifying America during and after her years in the White House — were joined at the public ceremony by Secretary of the Army John Marsh; R. Max Peterson, Chief of the Forest Service; William Penn Mott, Jr., Director of the National Park Service; and several Commission members. The Commission sponsored the event along with several Federal agencies and two dozen service and horticultural organizations. A Boy Scout and Girl Scout joined Chief Justice Burger and Mrs. Johnson in planting a "Constitution tree."

The goal of this program was to encourage communities to develop "living legacies" to the Constitution in the form of a park, garden, or other landscape creation, using trees, flowers, or other plants. As originally envisioned by the Commission, each local project developed in the year that followed would be dedicated on or about September 17, 1987, the Bicentennial of the signing of the Constitution.

During the year a network of 37 Federal agencies, corporations, and private associations joined with the

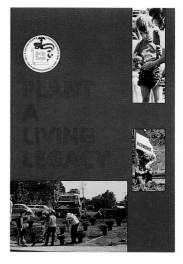

The LIVING LEGACY project encouraged local communities to develop parks, gardens, and landscapes honoring the Constitution.

George T. Henry

Lillian B. Dyhrberg

R. Edward Brown, Jr.

Some examples of PLANT A LIVING LEGACY at work: faculty and students dedicate a tree at Coe College (middle); a Bicentennial Garden blooms in Westbrook, Connecticut (above); a "Colonial" in Gloucester, Virginia, plants a tree (right).

Commission in promoting the program. By the end of 1987, over 5,000 LIVING LEGACY projects across the nation were completed. Tree plantings proved to be one of the most popular commemorative activities of the Bicentennial, bringing together the traditional symbolism of the Liberty Tree with current interest in improving the environment. A single organization, the National Society of State Garden Clubs, was responsible for the planting of over 5 million trees as part of LIVING LEGACY projects in every state. The Department of Defense coordinated similar projects on American military installations around the world. The PLANT A LIVING LEGACY program would continue to be a favored commemorative activity throughout the years of the Bicentennial, doing its part for the beautification of the American landscape.

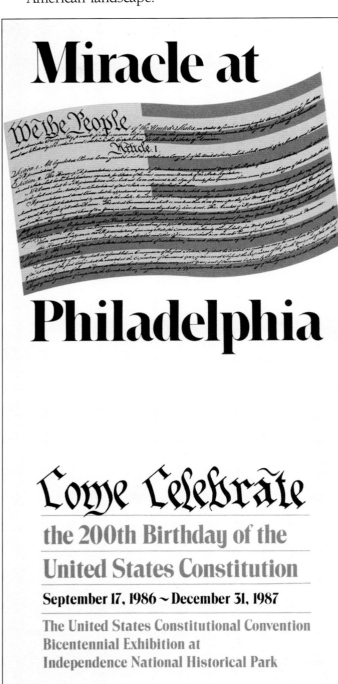

A *flyer for "Miracle at Philadelphia" (above); Chief Justice Burger introduces Nicholas Daniloff (right).*

Citizenship Day 1986 also saw the opening of the "Miracle at Philadelphia" exhibit at the Second Bank of the United States, Independence National Historical Park in Philadelphia. One of the premier Bicentennial exhibits, it displayed a collection of historical documents, including Benjamin Franklin's copy of the Constitution and James Madison's notes on the Constitutional Convention. Audiovisual programs, publications, and school materials were also part of the exhibit. "Miracle at Philadelphia" would draw 400,000 visitors during its two years at Independence Park.

DISNEY WORLD

Three weeks later on October 3, 1986, more than 5,000 journalists from 50 states gathered in Orlando, Florida, as guests of Disney World on the occasion of the 15th anniversary of that entertainment center and to celebrate the commencement of the Bicentennial. The Commission, along with key representatives of 45 state Bicentennial Commissions (also guests of Disney World), played a significant role in the proceedings. At the time, the event's sponsors claimed that this was the largest gathering in history of media people at a single event.

At the Orlando Convention and Visitors Center, Frank Wells, president of Disney World, began the proceedings with an eloquent tribute to the Constitution and some observations about the opportunities presented by the 200th anniversary commemoration. Chief Justice Burger then described briefly the events leading up to the signing of the Constitution and the difficulties attendant upon its ratification. Coining yet another phrase that was to become current in various forms

throughout the Bicentennial years, the Chief Justice noted that "the Declaration of Independence was the promise, the Revolution brought us our independence, and the Constitution was what we did with our independence." He then introduced a "special guest" with these words:

. . . by his conduct and by the extraordinary way this whole matter was handled by the President of the United States, there has been a dramatization of what our Constitution means, and it could not have come at a better time. I have the honor now to present to you, Mr. Nicholas Daniloff.

Marchers in the "We The People" parade promenade through the World Showcase at Disney World in Orlando, Florida. Disney World made the Bicentennial a theme of its many programs.

"Mr. Daniloff," the Commission Chairman added, "has seen and felt the difference." His appearance electrified everyone, including the thousands of media representatives in the hall. Daniloff had just been released from a jail in the Soviet Union. His arrest and interrogation had become a *cause célèbre* in U.S.-Soviet relations. This was Daniloff's first public appearance following his release. What he had to say in his brief appearance had a profound impact on his audience:

. . . I have been thinking as I traveled here what would be appropriate to tell you, and I had some trouble pulling my thoughts together before I came out on the stage. I met with the Chief Justice, and he gave me a copy of the Constitution. And very helpfully he wrote on it for me, "You have seen and felt the difference." I can tell you that as I languished in prison in Moscow, when I had spare time — you may not believe this — I really did think about the long hot summer of 1787, and I tried to rack my brains to remember what the debates were about and how the Constitution came to be written and how the Bill of Rights was later appended to the Constitution. . . .

He then went on to describe in a straightforward factual manner the circumstances of his arrest and the investigation that ensued. He concluded his remarks by saying:

. . . as I lay on my cot in the Lefortovo prison, I often thought about the Bill of Rights and about the protections that we have in the Constitution for the individual. The Bill of Rights, of course, is that part of our fundamental laws which bolsters the position of the individual against the awesome powers of a great state. In the Bill of Rights the First Amendment is one which is very dear to me, because it is the First Amendment which guarantees that there should be no laws abridging the freedom of the press. As you all know, in my case, the great interest and the enormous support of the press, of yourselves, was the thing which rocketed my case up to the top of the political and diplomatic agenda, and for that I am very, very grateful.

The celebrations formally concluded Saturday evening, October 5, with a huge "We The People"

The Commission's Chairman sits at a replica of James Madison's desk on display at EPCOT Center's Constitution exhibit.

Disney World parade. Members of the national Commission were in the reviewing stands as the parade wound its way through the World Showcase at the EPCOT Center. The parade featured floats and people dressed in Colonial garb and as Disney characters. The festivities included a choral group of 175 singers who performed "This is My Country," the National Anthem, and other patriotic songs. A Bicentennial flag was presented to Disney chairman and chief executive officer Michael Eisner.

Earlier that day, Chief Justice Burger, on behalf of the Commission, presented to Disney World several historical artifacts and replicas for display at the American Adventure Showcase at the EPCOT Center, where they were to remain for three and one-half years. While seated at the desk used by James Madison for drafting papers related to the Constitutional Convention, the Commission's Chairman explained the elements of the display to his audience. The display featured a replica of the "Rising Sun" chair used by George Washington when he presided over the Constitutional Convention, a replica of the original Constitution, and a large mural of the Howard Chandler Christy painting of the signing of the Constitution, the original of which hangs in the U.S. Capitol.

The Christy mural, commissioned by Congress as part of the Constitution's Sesquicentennial, was to become a familiar image in the Bicentennial as well — reproduced in publications and public displays around the country. Christy completed the painting in a makeshift studio at the U.S. Navy Yard in Washington, D.C. The canvas, measuring 20' x 30', was unveiled on May 29, 1940. The artist had painstakingly endeavored to reproduce the scene as it took place in Philadelphia at the moment of the Constitution's signing. He began by obtaining portraits of 37 of the 39 signers. The painting shows Richard D. Spaight of North Carolina as he completes his signature for his state, while the Secretary

of the Convention, Major William Johnson, indicates with four raised fingers the number of delegates waiting to sign for the next state, South Carolina. George Washington, as well as Franklin, Hamilton, and other delegates, is easily identified. The national Commission arranged for the creation of ten copies of the mural, designed as traveling exhibits. During the next five years these exhibits would log hundreds of thousands of miles as popular displays in conventions and meetings throughout the United States.

Since most states had formed Bicentennial Commissions of their own by October 1986, the national Commission used the occasion of the Disney World celebration to hold a national planning meeting with key representatives of the state Commissions. Forty-six states and the District of Columbia participated. The conference gave the Chairman, Commissioners, and staff of the national Commission a chance to get to know their counterparts at the state level better and to share perspectives with them on the coming Bicentennial commemoration.

The media coverage the Commission and the Bicentennial received from the October Disney World commemorations was extensive. According to Disney World figures, over 5,000 representatives from television, radio, and print media attended. The media coverage generated a total of 43 days of air time and 165 live television reports, as well as thousands of column inches in the print media. Disney World also made the Bicentennial a theme of its programs for a year by featuring Constitutional exhibits and musical theater presentations. Since Disney World was the world's number one tourist attraction, with more than 230 million visitors annually and as many as 138,000 visitors on a single day, it provided an ideal venue for launching the celebration.

Commission Programs and Publications

The Commission realized, of course, that if the "history and civics lesson" was to be taught, a major center for that teaching would be the schools of America, from the elementary grades to college. The schools would be a particularly important target in part because of the alarming degree of ignorance about the Constitution shown by surveys of the National Assessment of Educational Progress (NAEP), a congressionally mandated project to conduct national assessments of the educational attainments of young Americans. Carried out by the Educational Testing Service of Princeton, New Jersey, these studies had been the subject of much discussion in hearings on the legislation that led to the Commission's creation.

Their conclusions were confirmed by subsequent studies. A 1986 survey of 17-year-olds, funded by the National Endowment for the Humanities (NEH), showed that 68 percent of those interviewed could not place the Civil War in the correct half-century; 39 percent could not do the same for the drafting of the Constitution. The *Hearst Report* on public knowledge about the Constitution, issued in 1987, would confirm this alarming degree of ignorance. Nearly half of those surveyed (46 percent) could not identify the purpose of the original Constitution, and over half (59 percent) did not know what the Bill of Rights was. These and similar studies and surveys conducted about the same time all suggested the Constitution was poorly taught in the nation's schools.

Public Law 98-101, which authorized the establishment of the Commission, stated that:

In planning and implementing appropriate activities to commemorate the bicentennial, the Commission shall give due consideration to [among ten other criteria] . . . the need to encourage appropriate educational curricula designed to educate students at all levels of learning on the drafting, ratification, and history of the Constitution and the specific provisions of that document. . . .

In 1986, the Commission initiated a number of programs that continued through the Bicentennial commemoration. Two of the most important of these major educational programs — the Center for Civic Education's NATIONAL BICENTENNIAL COMPETITION ON THE CONSTITUTION AND BILL OF RIGHTS and the BICENTENNIAL EDUCATIONAL GRANT PROGRAM (BEGP) — had been signed into law (Public Law 99-194) by President Reagan at the end of 1985. The enabling legislation had authorized $25 million for these programs, but the Congress had made both of them subject to annual appropriations. On October 18, 1986, Congress appropriated and earmarked $2.7 million for the NATIONAL BICENTENNIAL COMPETITION and $1 million for the BEGP. Throughout the Bicentennial years, these were to be the centerpieces in the Commission's fundamental commitment to education.

CENTER FOR CIVIC EDUCATION'S NATIONAL BICENTENNIAL COMPETITION

The congressional conference report on the Commission's appropriation cites the Center for Civic Education (CCE) as the organization administering the NATIONAL BICENTENNIAL COMPETITION, with a directed grant from the Commission. CCE was a California-based nonprofit organization affiliated with the California State Bar. It conducted a variety of civic education programs for elementary and secondary school students and teachers nationwide. The Center's Executive Director, Charles N. Quigley, first appeared before the Commission at its second meeting on August 22-23, 1985. There he reported that his organization had spent the previous ten months developing a national high school program on the Constitution, to be held each school year between 1987 and 1991. The program's specially designed curricula were projected to reach over 2 million students and 60,000 teachers during the years of the Bicentennial. A competitive element, involving high school classes testing their knowledge of the Constitution at the congressional district, state, and national levels, would be the centerpiece.

At its April 1986 meeting, the Commission gave official recognition to the field-testing phase of the curriculum. During the remainder of the year, CCE tested the pedagogical and competitive elements of the program in 11th and 12th grade classes of 16 states. Both the curriculum-development and field-testing phases of the NATIONAL BICENTENNIAL COMPETITION had been covered by grants from the Departments of Education and Justice. These funds bridged the gap until Congress appropriated funds to carry out the first full year of the program. At its November 1986 meeting, the Commission approved a $2.7 million grant to CCE for the full program. This appropriation covered only a portion of the program's costs. The Center would raise approximately ten times that amount from state and local education sources and from the private sector.

By the time the field-testing was completed in the spring of 1987, a national network staff of state and congressional district coordinators necessary to administer the program had been recruited and prepared in national and regional training conferences. The network included head coordinators in all 50 states, the District of Columbia, Puerto Rico, and the territories of Guam, American Samoa, and the Virgin Islands, with over 400 coordinators at the congressional district level.

Approximately 500,000 students participated in the NATIONAL BICENTENNIAL COMPETITION during its first full year (1987-1988). The demand for the program's textbook, *We the People . . . ,* was so great that a second printing was required. In all, 215,000 copies were distributed to 6,000 teachers, 4,000 of whom had received in-service training in the program.

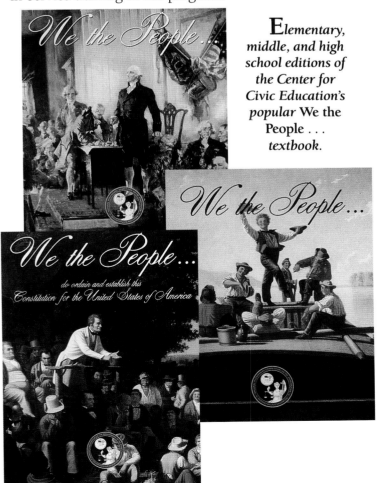

Elementary, middle, and high school editions of the Center for Civic Education's popular We the People . . . *textbook.*

The innovative six-week curriculum provided an in-depth examination of the philosophical and historical background of the Constitution and actively engaged students in the use of their analytical and communications skills. The six-part curriculum included: (1) the philosophical ideas of the Framers; (2) the English and Colonial historical background; (3) the issues of the Constitutional Convention; (4) the establishment of the new government; (5) guarantees of fundamental rights; and (6) the responsibilities of citizenship.

Classes using the *We the People . . .* text were free to participate, or not participate, in the competitive part of the program. While many classes chose the noncompetitive alternative, over one-third decided to compete in a series of mock congressional hearings at the district, state, and national levels. Students qualified their class

Center for Civic Education (3)

NATIONAL BICENTENNIAL COMPETITION *finalists compete at the Senate (top) and at Fort McNair (center); teachers discuss the program (above).*

for the competition after studying the six-week curriculum and then achieving a class average of over 70 percent on a multiple-choice test on the history and principles of the Constitution. For a simulated hearing, classes were divided into six groups, each of which would provide "expert" testimony on one of the six units in the curriculum. All students in a competing class were required to participate, and during the hearings they were evaluated by panels of judges comprising academics, jurists, public officials, and others knowledgeable about the Constitution.

The NATIONAL BICENTENNIAL COMPETITION garnered widespread support in the Congress. By the end of 1987, 75 Senators and 350 Representatives had agreed to assist the program by serving on advisory committees, participating in the teacher training, and providing administrative and other assistance through their state and district offices. The program's Advisory Committee included representatives of the three branches of the Federal Government, scholars, and leaders of public- and private-sector organizations.

THE BICENTENNIAL EDUCATIONAL GRANT PROGRAM

Of the $3.7 million earmarked for major ongoing educational programs in the Commission's fiscal year 1987 appropriation, $1 million was specifically designated for the BICENTENNIAL EDUCATIONAL GRANT PROGRAM.* This program was designed specifically to "teach the teachers." The enabling legislation signed by the President at the end of 1985 had authorized the Commission to make grants for teacher training programs and for the development of instructional materials and activities on the Constitution and the Bill of Rights for use by elementary or secondary school students. These grants were restricted to programs aimed at students at these precollege levels, where the need and potential investment for the future were greatest.

Unlike the NATIONAL BICENTENNIAL COMPETITION, which was developed and administered from the outset by CCE, the BEGP was administered from the beginning by the Commission. The Office of Justice Programs of the Department of Justice, through an interagency agreement, assisted with the budget reviews, accounting, and auditing of the grant awards. External reviewers and Commission staff undertook the initial screening of applications. Final decisions on grantees were made by the Commission's Advisory Committee on Educational Projects.

The Commission publicly announced the BEGP and its regulations and procedures in the *Federal Register* on December 30, 1986. Deadline for receipt of applications for the first round of competition was February 15, 1987. The program gave priority to proposals that focused on strengthening the ability of elementary and secondary teachers to successfully teach the basic principles and the history of the Constitution, the Bill of Rights, and subsequent Amendments. These ends could

be achieved through the development of instructional materials — audio projects and videotapes as well as printed curricular materials — or through conferences, institutes, or in-service training of teachers during the school year. Important ideas and texts about the Constitution and Bill of Rights were to be emphasized, and projects receiving Commission funds were to demonstrate how they benefited students.

The Commission was authorized to accept applications from, and award grants to, local educational agencies, private elementary and secondary schools, private organizations, individuals, and state and local public agencies in the United States. Colleges and universities could apply as long as they fell within one of the appropriate categories of eligibility and the proposed project was designed for use in elementary and secondary schools. As specified in the Commission's congressional mandate, the program gave paramount thematic importance to the origins, history, and enduring principles of the Constitution and Bill of Rights, rather than to the controversies and issues of the moment. The program also encouraged applications that addressed the contributions of the nation's diverse ethnic and racial groups to American society, as well as projects meeting special learning needs.

During the life of the Commission, over 250 projects were funded under the Bicentennial Educational Grant Program.

---

*For a more complete description of this program, see *Bicentennial Grant Program: A Report (1985-1991)*, Washington, D.C., 1991.

SCHOLASTIC AND WNEV-TV

The enlistment of the educational community in the Bicentennial was aided during the year by two special programs. On June 13, 1986, Chief Justice Burger welcomed to the West Conference Room of the Supreme Court 13 students from elementary, junior, and senior high schools. They had been selected from all over the country to interview the Commission's Chairman by teacher advisory panels serving Scholastic's three magazines for students, *Scholastic News, Junior Scholastic,* and *Scholastic Update.* For two hours, they asked questions ranging from the responsibilities of a Chief Justice and the workings of the Supreme Court to the effect of historic court decisions and the overall influence of the

Constitution in America. Where he could not comment directly on a matter before, or likely to come before, the Court, he responded to the student's question with a relevant historical example.

The interview, taped by WNEV-TV for broadcast July 17 and later in September, was the opener in the station's series of five one-hour specials on the Constitution. It also provided the basis for articles in all three Scholastic magazines. On September 8, *Scholastic Update,* with a readership of over a million in grades 8 through 12, came out with an issue entirely devoted to the Constitution. Its three-page cover story featured the Chairman's interview with the students and a box

Thirteen students selected from around the country interview Chairman Burger as part of a Scholastic/WNEV-TV promotion.

advertising the NATIONAL BICENTENNIAL WRITING COMPETITION, which the Commission would be co-sponsoring with *USA Today,* Gannett, and the American Bar Association in the coming year *(see Chapter III).* This issue, with a wraparound teaching guide and poster for classroom use, went to 150,000 social studies teachers and department heads across the country. *Scholastic Update* editors informed the Commission that this was "the most useful package on the Constitution ever to hit high school classrooms."

On September 12, *Scholastic News,* which aimed at an estimated readership of 1.9 million pupils in the third through sixth grades, featured in each of its separate

editions an article on the Bicentennial of the Constitution and on the two young reporters from elementary schools upon whose questions the articles were based. The teachers' edition of this issue contained a letter from the chairman of Scholastic, Inc., Richard Robinson, which described their projected yearlong citizenship program called "Project: Kids Care." The interview with Chief Justice Burger served as an introduction to that project. Finally, *Junior Scholastic,* reaching 3 million junior high school students, published a special November 17 issue containing lengthy excerpts from the interview. Promotional copies were sent to every teacher and department chairperson at the grade levels served.

THE NCSS CONFERENCE
FOR SOCIAL STUDIES TEACHERS

The Bicentennial held center stage on November 15, 1986, at the five-day National Council for the Social Studies (NCSS) annual meeting convened in New York City. Chief Justice Burger was the keynote speaker at an all-day workshop on the Constitution that the Commission had helped to fund. He then participated with three of his fellow Commissioners — Lindy Boggs, Lynne Cheney, and William Lucas — in a panel discussion about the Constitution. Bill Moyers opened and closed the session and moderated the 90-minute discussion. An audience of 5,000 elementary and secondary social studies teachers, teacher trainers, administrators, and other interested professionals had the opportunity to put questions to the panel during the last half hour.

The televised session also was broadcast live via the Learning Channel, a cable network, and the Public Broadcasting System (PBS) to 10,000 other NCSS members who were holding workshops on the Constitution at 100 locations in 34 states and the District of Columbia. In addition to promoting teacher viewing, NCSS mounted a major promotion of general audience viewing by developing a family viewing guide and working with a variety of national organizations to promote the program. These included the National Congress of Parent and Teacher organizations, the League of Women Voters, and the Veterans of Foreign Wars. As a supplement to the live broadcast, the Learning Channel and WETA-TV, Washington, D.C., one of the four principal producing stations in the PBS system, developed and made available for sale a one-hour video based on the program. The Learning Channel also aired it later, during school hours, to allow for classroom viewing.

THE "POCKET" CONSTITUTION

To make sure that the "history and civics lesson" reached as many people as possible, the Commission in 1986 began to develop an extensive publications pro-gram designed to reach a variety of audiences of diverse educational backgrounds. The single most important of these publications was a pocket-sized version of the Constitution, eventually to appear in 18 editions (17 in English and one in Spanish) and over 50 million copies. At its June 1986 meeting, the Commission approved the expenditure of $50,000 for wide distribution of this small Constitution. In response to requests up to that time, the Commission had distributed commercially prepared parchment copies of the document.

In the design and production of the official version, the Commission used original spelling and punctuation. As a proof text, the so-called "literal print" was provided and certified by the National Archives and Records Administration and reviewed by the Congressional Research Service of the Library of Congress (minor variations occur in the several copies of the original Constitution, making it difficult to decide on an "official" version). The pocket size selected (3½" x 6½") is historic, corresponding to a small Constitution included in the 1820 edition of Thomas Jefferson's *Manual of Parliamentary Practice*.

The Commission published the first edition of the POCKET CONSTITUTION in October 1986. The cover was tan (i.e., "parchment") in color with brown lettering. The booklet carried a foreword by the Chairman, the full text of the Constitution, the implementation resolution, all of the Amendments, and a page of "Dates to Remember" — but as yet, no index. An early pilot printing of 10,000 copies became part of the total run of 400,000 for 1986. The size and format remained essentially constant after that first printing, although many improvements and additions were made during the life of this extraordinary document during the next six years. At its November 1986 meeting, the Commission approved the expenditure of $250,000 for the printing and distribution of an additional 2.5 million copies of the POCKET CONSTITUTION.

In addition to its own direct distribution, the Commission encouraged private organizations and corporations to distribute copies to employees and customers, and to make them available to the general public. A number of Federal agencies printed their own supplies of the pocket-sized edition and made copies available to their employees. During the following year special editions of the POCKET CONSTITUTION appeared, underwritten by some of the nation's corporations, including Citicorp/Citibank, World Book, and Phillips Petroleum. In addition, Frito-Lay, Dow Chemical, General Dynamics, McGraw-Hill, and Sheraton Hotel-Towers were among others that printed and distributed large numbers of the Commission's editions.

In 1987 the POCKET CONSTITUTION's cover changed from the original parchment brown to white with red and black lettering. More important was the introduction that year of the document's distinctive subject index, enhancing its value as a convenient reference. The POCKET CONSTITUTION became the most familiar and widely used artifact of the Bicentennial — making the Constitution easily accessible to both Americans and other peoples around the world.

Several other editions of the Constitution were published in honor of the Bicentennial. The West Publishing Company of St. Paul, Minnesota, printed hundreds of thousands of a pocket-sized edition for use by lawyers, private groups, and the general public. The DAR also distributed easy-to-use versions of the Constitution, as did a number of state bar associations. The Library of Congress ordered a limited supply of 500 specially bound and printed Constitutions at $500 apiece, and a more popularly priced paperback edition. The following year, two other special editions of the Constitution appeared. Bantam Books' *Bicentennial Keepsake Edition,* with an introduction by President Reagan as well as essays by Chief Justice Burger and others, was one of the few commercial publications to be officially recognized and licensed by the Commission. Copies were distributed to college libraries. Under an NEH grant, the National Braille Press distributed 10,000 copies of a Braille edition of the Constitution. To ensure that every public library received a copy, the Commission purchased an additional 20,000 copies.

COMMEMORATIVE CALENDAR

An important basic educational tool that the Commission was to use throughout its life was an annual commemorative calendar featuring themes and historical material related to the Constitution. In 1986, the Commission printed and distributed the first edition of these calendars, which had been in development since late 1985. The printing of the 15,000 copies was underwritten by a donation from the National Association of Home Builders in Washington, D.C. The 1986 calendar included color photographs, one for each

1992 Harlee Little

Pocket Constitution editions printed 1986-1992.

Commission's Resource Information Center Display at 1717 H Street, N.W., in Washington, D.C.

month, depicting important sites throughout the nation related to the Constitution, and historical facts associated with the Constitution for each day of the year.

INFORMATION CENTER AND SPEAKERS BUREAU

In October 1986, the Commission's Resource Information Center began operating in the ground-floor space at 1717 H Street, N.W., in Washington, D.C. Visitors to the Center were able to view a video presentation about the Constitution, obtain brochures, pamphlets, fact sheets, and other promotional materials, and consult a small library of key reference books and periodicals. The Center also had a computer terminal programmed with information to answer queries on Bicentennial programs and projects in accordance with the Commission's legislative mandate to develop a Bicentennial clearinghouse. The clearinghouse, established to collect and disseminate information on events occurring throughout the nation, consisted of a computer database management system. To obtain accurate and complete information, the Commission developed a special form that was sent to event organizers and sponsors so that information they submitted could be incorporated into the database system. A staff of about 20, mostly volunteers, handled this important operation.

The Commission's Speakers Bureau also functioned as a part of the Resource Center. It provided, in collaboration with the Judicial Speakers Committee chaired by former United States Court of Appeals Judge Arlin M. Adams, a database of speakers and speeches available for events at both the national and local levels. It encouraged the creation of state and local speakers bureaus, coordinated regional speaking requests, and assisted speakers through the dissemination of the Commission's resource materials.

Other Activities

To assure the success of its important work, during 1986 the Commission reached out to organizations and groups throughout the country — educational organizations, Federal agencies, states and communities, private organizations, religious groups, the media, and groups involved in international activities. In a few cases, the Commission joined with a group to cosponsor an event or share in the financing. In other cases, it gave official recognition to projects or activities initiated, developed, funded, and carried out by another group. This provided extra encouragement and stimulation and allowed the sponsoring organization to use the Bicentennial Commission's official logo. In many instances, however, many organizations and groups sponsored projects without any involvement by the national Commission. A sampling of all these activities is included here.

EDUCATIONAL ORGANIZATIONS

In addition to the educational programs already mentioned, many more were put in place. One of the most important educational initiatives prior to the start-up of the Commission's own programs was Project '87, a joint undertaking of the American Historical Association and the American Political Science Association already referred to in Chapter I. This collaborative effort developed a set of classroom materials on the American Founding as well as a 12-part poster series entitled "The Blessings of Liberty." The posters depicted basic events, leaders, and ideas that contributed to the framing of the Constitution and were designed to stimulate commemorative activities in schools, libraries, and other community organizations.

Of projects officially recognized by the Commission in 1986, one of the most interesting was the MENTOR program in law-related education that had been under way since 1983 and which adopted Bicentennial themes during the school years 1986-1987 and 1987-1988. A cooperative project of the New York Alliance for Public Schools, the Federal Bar Council, and the New York City Board of of Education, MENTOR had by 1986 matched 27 New York City law firms with an equal number of public junior and senior high schools and had spread to ten other states. Through a program that combined speakers, visits, and discussions, the law firms worked closely with classes of 20 to 30 students to introduce them to the legal profession, to related

MENTOR *program participants in New York City (above); a speaker addresses the Dewitt Wallace Conference on "The Constitution, Freedom of Expression, and the Liberal Arts" at Macalester College (right).*

vocations, and to the New York State and Federal court systems. One of MENTOR's projects for the academic year 1986-1987 involved such activities as a moot court discussion of constitutional issues, simulations of the Constitution ratification debates, trips to a local courthouse to hear arguments, and meetings of classes in judge's chambers.

At the university and professional school level, many other programs began in 1986. An educational program carried out during the academic year 1986-1987 by James Madison University of Harrisonburg, Virginia, involved development of educational materials and programs for elementary, secondary, and college students in Virginia and nationwide. The University of California, Berkeley, sponsored a three-week summer institute for high school teachers on the subject "Constitutionalism: Two Centuries of Freedom Under Law."

During the same academic year, Macalester College of St. Paul, Minnesota, conducted the Dewitt Wallace Conference, sponsored by the Readers' Digest Foundation, on "The Constitution, Freedom of Expression, and the Liberal Arts." This yearlong program began with a conference in the early fall of 1986 at which seven distinguished speakers discussed the themes of the conference. The speakers returned to the campus for short periods during the year to meet with students, teach classes, counsel with faculty, and make contact with community groups. The University of South Carolina School of Law at Columbia conducted a Bicentennial symposium, September 19-20, 1986, on "The Federal Courts — The Next 100 Years," which featured distinguished speakers, commentators, and extensive panel discussions before an audience of lawyers, judges, academics, and students. In many ways, the Macalester and South Carolina programs foreshadowed the Commission's COLLEGE-COMMUNITY FORUMS program that appeared two years later (*see Chapter IV*).

FEDERAL GOVERNMENT DEPARTMENTS AND AGENCIES

In the autumn of 1985, the Commission had initiated a major stimulus to Federal departments and agencies. Letters to Cabinet members and agency heads encouraged their involvement in the Bicentennial commemoration, and representatives of departments and agencies met for the first time in mid-December of that year. President Reagan invited the Chairman to a Cabinet meeting to stimulate the interest of Cabinet members. By the third interagency meeting, April 23, 1986, Bicentennial projects from 41 agencies had been submitted to the Commission.

During 1986, the Commission conferred official recognition on many of these projects. For example, a major two-year exhibition called "An American Experiment: Creating the Constitution" opened in October 1986 at the National Archives. The exhibit featured original drafts of the Constitution, Declaration of Independence, and Bill of Rights, as well as other public

The *Department of Defense used this logo for all its Bicentennial activities.*

and private documents detailing the Founding Era. The Archives made facsimiles of the exhibit's documents available to schools, libraries, historical associations, and other organizations for a small fee.

The Department of the Army began its Bicentennial program for 1986 with a series of 23 six-page, three-color pamphlets on the "Soldier-Statesmen" who had signed the Constitution. The Army estimated that, with reprints included, these pamphlets would reach over 11 million readers. Under the leadership of Army Secretary John Marsh and later Secretary Patrick Stone, the Department would become the most active of government agencies in the Bicentennial. Its many publications, programs, organizational networks, and logistical support capabilities proved invaluable to the Commission in the years ahead. The Army also began development of a videotape series on the Framers of the Constitution, to be used both in educational programs and before general audiences. It also sponsored several Pentagon exhibits, including a "Hall of Military Signers" dedicated on September 17, 1986, in honor of the men who served their country in the military and helped to frame the Constitution. Secretary Marsh assigned retired Lt. Gen. Robert Arter to take primary administrative responsibility for the Department's Bicentennial programs.

The principal focus of NEH's Bicentennial initiative was the encouragement of "renewed scholarly interest in, and public reflection about, the principles and foundations of Constitutional government." Through grants under this initiative, NEH supported research projects and other Bicentennial activities, including a number of major media programs. NEH also announced plans for matching fund grants to public libraries for the creation of "Bicentennial Bookshelves," containing reference works and other books about the Constitution. Between 1982 and 1992, NEH awarded $27 million in grants for projects of various kinds related to the Constitution, including summer institutes, workshops, and lecture series.

The National Park Service, whose facilities at Independence Park in Philadelphia would become a principal geographic focus of commemorative activities in the coming year, had a variety of Bicentennial projects under way. In addition to the "Miracle of Philadelphia" exhibit described above, Independence Park's programs

Medals, struck annually between 1987 and 1991 by the U.S. Capitol Historical Society, illustrate the theme of each Bicentennial year.

Harlee Little (5)

included a computerized exhibit on the Constitution entitled "A Promise of Permanency," sponsored by Philadelphia Bell. The Park Service staff there took the lead in organizing a "Rocks Across America" project, which envisioned the construction of a new commemorative fountain for the facility made up of geologically representative specimens from each of the 50 states. In addition, the several hundred Park Service sites elsewhere in the nation initiated commemorative activities of their own. Together with the CIGNA Corporation, the Park Service also sponsored a one-act musical, entitled "Four Little Pages" (a reference to the four pages of the original Constitution). Written and produced by Franklin S. Roberts Associates, the musical told the story of the events leading up to the signing of the Constitution. During 1986 the musical toured National Park Service sites throughout the original 13 states, and a national tour was conducted in 1987.

The national Commission worked out a program early in 1986 with the U.S. Capitol Historical Society

that called for a joint sales and profit-sharing arrangement in connection with five medals to be struck annually, 1987-1991. Each medal — sculpted in deep bas-relief—illustrated the theme of one of the Bicentennial years. This program produced substantial revenue for use in Commission activities and represented a generous contribution by the Society to the Bicentennial commemoration, since normally all proceeds from the Capitol Society activities went towards the maintenance and beautification of the Capitol building. Society activities, which included symposia, publications, films, and a continuing commemorative medals program, all focused on U.S. history, especially that of the Capitol, Congress, and the framework of the American government. The Society, a nonprofit organization chartered by the Congress, sponsored several conferences and publications related to the Bicentennial.

STATES AND COMMUNITIES

The Commission also encouraged the development of state Bicentennial Commissions and Designated Bicentennial Communities during 1986. As a result, by the end of the year the number of state Commissions had grown from 19 to 43, and 350 Designated Bicentennial Communities were in operation.

States made significant strides in their commemorative planning during the course of this year. For example, the Committee to Commemorate the U.S. Constitution in Illinois, with assistance from a number of state and private groups, coordinated a Bicentennial program that eventually was to reach citizens throughout the state and in the surrounding regions. The Committee sponsored newsletters, event handbooks, television programs, regional training conferences, symposia, historical newspapers, exhibits, and teaching programs for high school students and teachers.

To assist states and communities in their planning for 1987, the Commission at its November 1986 meeting authorized the implementation of the Bicentennial Regional Program, which was to include up to eight Bicentennial Regional Conferences by 1987. The national Commission had already made available to state Commissions a Bicentennial flag with the official logo, and model bills, executive orders, proclamations, and resolutions that could be adapted to the individual needs of each state.

PRIVATE, NONPROFIT, AND RELIGIOUS GROUPS

Similarly, the Commission was actively engaged in drawing into the Bicentennial commemoration private, nonprofit, and religious groups. It conducted two meetings on March 17 and 20, 1986, at the National Archives in Washington, D.C. Representatives of more than 150 associations with a total membership of 64 million attended. The Commission's Chairman and Commissioners Phil Crane, Edward Hill, and Obert Tanner were the principal speakers. Trade and educational association representatives participated at the first meeting, while the second involved religious, civic,

"F_our Little Pages," a one-act musical about the drafting of the Constitution, was performed at National Park Service sites throughout the 13 original states and at Mount Rushmore, and went on a six-month national tour._

The leadership of the Northern and Southern Jurisdictions of the Scottish Rite meet with the Commission to announce their Bicentennial program.

social service, and labor associations. The consensus of these meetings confirmed that involvement of associations in the commemoration was vital in reaching all elements in American society.

By the fall of 1986, more than 375 private organizations, representing a cross-section of American society, had Bicentennial programs already planned, many of which received official recognition from the Commission. One of the many organizations was the DAR, the original sponsor of Constitution Week. The DAR would carry out over 50 separate commemorative projects at every level of its nationwide organization. It sponsored an annual essay contest, which focused each year on a Bicentennial theme and which was cosponsored by the Commission during the last three years of commemoration.

In November 1986, the Southern and Northern Jurisdictions of the Scottish Rite of Freemasonry, the Masons, signed a joint proclamation announcing a bipartisan undertaking to commemorate the Bicentennial. Titled "Keystones of Liberty," the Masonic program of commemoration included leadership in the creation of local Bicentennial Commissions, a national high school essay contest, and a series of articles in the two jurisdictions' publications, *The New Age* and *The Northern Light*. Chief Justice Burger met with the Sovereign Commanders of the two groups, the first time such a meeting between commanders had occurred since the Civil War.

PRIVATE CORPORATIONS

Participation of private corporations in the Bicentennial quickened during the year. For example, the General Motors Corporation underwrote important TV programs beginning in July with the CBS News Special "The Burger Years," the Bill Moyers interview with Chief Justice Burger described earlier. In September, GM supported a sequel to the CBS miniseries about George Washington, "George Washington: The Forging of a Nation." In connection with the latter, GM distributed educational materials to 8,000 schools. It also announced several future TV projects, including a mini-

series, "The Miracle at Philadelphia," which dramatized Catherine Drinker Bowen's classic story of the Constitutional Convention, and a multipart PBS series on the Constitution hosted by Bill Moyers.

Also in 1986, Merrill Lynch & Co., Inc., announced its cosponsorship of the largest corporate contribution to the Bicentennial up to that point — a multifaceted program to be carried out in cooperation with WQED-TV San Francisco and the American Bar Association. It consisted of a four-part public television series to be aired in the fall of 1987 and the underwriting of state ratification commemorations throughout the country between 1987 and 1988. The program, titled "We the People," included ABA plans for special educational newspaper supplements, public forums on Constitutional issues, and seminars and symposia for the public as well as for scholars.

MEDIA

Media interest in telling the story of the Bicentennial commemoration developed as excitement about the Bicentennial grew. One of the earliest to become involved was Betty Debnam, author of *The Mini Page,* a four-page tabloid newspaper insert for younger readers that ran in 450 newspapers across the country. At the request of the national Commission, Debnam began a series on the Constitution starting in March 1986 with an issue on the Annapolis Convention, and continuing until September 1987 with the anniversary of the Constitution's drafting. Throughout the Bicentennial period, she produced several projects and articles on the Constitution, including *The Mini Page* series on the Bill of Rights in 1991. For millions of young Americans, she became a teacher *par excellence* of the Bicentennial. In praising her efforts, Chief Justice Burger observed that no one person contributed as much to the education of youth about the Constitution as did Betty Debnam.

During 1986, TV and radio networks began to introduce Constitutional inserts. For example, CBS started its "We The People" program in late October. Its Bicentennial profiles ran weeknights in prime time and featured distinguished American leaders who offered insights into the history and meaning of the Constitution. The series included profiles of the Framers and vignettes on the history of the Constitutional amend-

Betty Debnam, *editor of* **The Mini Page,** *presents her plans for covering the Constitution.*

ments. ABC's "Bicentennial Constitutional Minutes," aimed at children, were televised on Saturday mornings, with inserts featuring Bugs Bunny and friends, who discussed the Constitution and Bill of Rights. Their message was: "The Constitution works for everyone — even kids." The NBC Radio Network launched a daily program called "Constitutional Minutes" in which TV personality Willard Scott explained the events of 1787 leading up to the signing of the Constitution.

The Associated Press released an educational filmstrip on the Constitution, a four-part audiovisual series designed for classroom use, to give students a historical overview of the Constitution and the formation of America's system of government. Entitled "The Constitution at 200 Years," the series was distributed to schools along with a teacher's manual. Newspaper editors across the nation were also beginning to take note of the Bicentennial. An editorial appearing in *The Wichita* (Kansas) *Eagle and Beacon* noted:

The observance of the Constitution's bicentennial is a time to reaffirm the country's commitment to the principles of individual freedom and democratic government. Modern Americans should approach the bicentennial with gratitude for the wisdom of the Founding Fathers and with determination that their work will endure for countless future generations.

By 1986, the publishing industry was commemorating the Bicentennial. Both scholarly works and books for the general public began to issue from the presses, in anticipation of the anniversary of the Constitution's drafting. The four-volume *Encyclopedia of the American Constitution,* edited by Leonard Levy, appeared during the year. This monumental work, eight years in the making, with over 2,000 articles by 262 contributing authors, made available to a general audience references for almost every conceivable constitutional topic.

The year also saw the appearance of a new history of the Constitutional Convention and the reappearance of another. Christopher and James Lincoln Collier's *Decision in Philadelphia: the Constitution Convention of 1787* brought current biographical and historical research to bear in a topical account of the deliberations of Independence Hall in the summer of 1787. In November 1986, at the urging of the Commission's Chairman, Catherine Drinker Bowen's *Miracle at Philadelphia* became the first book ever reissued as a main selection by the Book-of-the-Month Club. Atlantic-Little Brown, the original publisher, reissued the classic on September 17, 1986, the 199th anniversary of the signing of the Constitution. The Chairman wrote a review of the book for the November issue of the Book-of-the-Month Club's magazine and a foreword to the new Atlantic-Little Brown edition.

INTERNATIONAL

From the outset, it was clear that the Bicentennial would be more than a national experience; it would have an international message as well. The historical

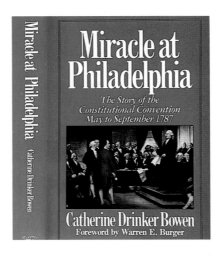

Book-of-the-Month Club edition of *Catherine Drinker Bowen's* Miracle at Philadelphia.

origins of the Constitution—in classical thought, British constitutionalism, and the European Enlightenment — invited transnational comparisons. So also did the extraordinary impact of the American experience in the rest of the world. Little could anyone imagine in 1986, of course, how events around the world during the years of the Bicentennial would throw a spotlight on the ideals of the U.S. Constitution and Bill of Rights.

The Commission provided leadership during the year in organizing the commemoration of the Bicentennial overseas. To this end, 52 representatives of corporations, Federal agencies, private organizations, and educational institutions gathered at the Supreme Court on February 24 at a meeting chaired by Commissioner Betty Murphy, who also chaired the Commission's Advisory Committee on International Liaison. Chief Justice Burger opened the session, which was devoted to the airing of ideas for international activities. At its April 13-14 meeting, the Commission approved the establishment of regional planning committees for Latin America, Europe, Africa, and Asia, each of which would recommend proposals to the Commission.

Among the major initiatives in international activities, the United States Information Agency's Voice of America announced plans for broadcast of a series of Bicentennial radio programs. These would include a 20-minute semidocumentary, a series of five-minute presentations in 40 languages on various Constitutional topics, and a series of biographical profiles of the Constitution's Framers.

CONCLUSION

The year 1986 had been one of constructive preparation. It saw Congress extend the Commission's mandate to 1991 and substantially increase the Commission's resources. The ceremonies at Annapolis and elsewhere created successful models for future commemorative events and historical reenactments. The gathering at Disney World brought increased media attention and public interest in the Bicentennial. Key educational and outreach programs had been established, as had useful networks in this country and abroad. The Bicentennial was now ready for 1987 and the anniversary of the Constitution's drafting.

CHAPTER III

1987

Drafting

and

Signing

of

the

Constitution

The Commission's organization and national network were essentially in place. Promotion of the Bicentennial through both the media and a variety of cooperating organizations was already well under way. Along with organizations and groups throughout the country and the world, the Commission was now ready to coordinate the challenging series of activities that would commemorate the great events of 1787—the writing and signing of the Constitution at that seminal meeting in Philadelphia attended by 55 remarkable men.

Major Events

ROADS TO LIBERTY TOUR

ROADS TO LIBERTY, a traveling exhibition of the great, fundamental documents of liberty — from the Magna Carta of 1215 to the Bill of Rights of 1791 — led off the major commemorative activities of 1987. President Reagan dedicated the exhibit at an opening ceremony on

the White House lawn on March 11. During his brief remarks, the President said: "The documents gathered here are the springs from which the great river of human freedom rises." The centerpiece of the exhibit was the Lincoln Cathedral copy of the Magna Carta, one of the four existing copies of the document signed by King John at Runnymede in 1215, which confirmed the liberties of free men, articulated the principle of the rule of law, and placed limits upon the power of the king.

The Roads to Liberty exhibit also featured other landmark documents of self-government, including a facsimile of the Mayflower Compact, an original copy of the Fundamental Orders of Connecticut (the first constitution in America), a printed broadside edition of the Declaration of Independence, an original copy of the Articles of Confederation, the draft of the Constitution used by Pierce Butler of South Carolina, and Maryland's copy of the Bill of Rights.

After a one-day public display at the Ellipse in Washington, the specially designed and outfitted semi-trailer truck carried the exhibit to Chicago where it

began its six-month tour. The display visited the Northwest Territory states (Illinois, Wisconsin, Minnesota, Michigan, Ohio, and Indiana) and several other states in the Midwest, Southwest, and South before returning to Washington for five more days of public viewing. The exhibit then embarked on a journey through the original 13 states, concluding its tour in Philadelphia during the September commemoration of the Constitution's signing.

The U.S. Constitution Council of the Original Thirteen States, the American Express Company (which also provided funding for the exhibition and the tour), and the national Commission cosponsored the Roads to Liberty exhibit, which was designed by the Commission with the assistance of the Smithsonian Institution. Frederick Biebel, a member of the Commission and also the tour chairman for the Constitution Council, was the principal organizer of the project. Magna Carta in America, a nonprofit educational organization based in Portland, Oregon, arranged for the loan of a copy of the Magna Carta. This organization had exhibited the same

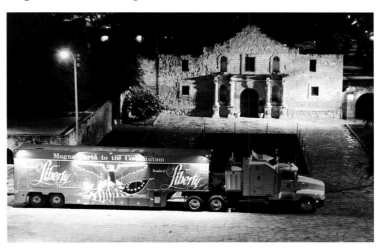

P resident Reagan opens the 25-state Roads to Liberty tour (top left); on the road (left); in Texas at the Alamo (top); visitors studying the precious documents aboard (above).

copy of the Great Charter and other key historical documents in several U.S. locations during the latter half of 1986 and early part of 1987, in a project given official recognition by the national Commission.

The contract with Lincolnshire Cathedral required a 24-hour armed guard for the document. The tour had a staff of 15 and five vehicles. The exhibit vehicle contained a generator that provided the electrical power required to expand its sides to accommodate visitors. The Smithsonian provided weapons and uniforms of the Revolutionary War era, which added vivid color to the truck's interior.

ROADS TO LIBERTY was well received around the country, drawing several hundred thousand visitors in nearly 100 cities and towns in 25 states. Waits of up to three hours to view the exhibit became common, eventually requiring the creation of an advance ticket distribution system. Special receptions held in each state capital visited by the exhibit included the Governors, the state Bicentennial Commission members, state legislators and officials, Mayors, and business and community leaders. Most of the details of local ceremonies as well as media promotion and police escorts were arranged by advance teams from American Express. Media interest was extensive, and specially trained docents traveling with the exhibit provided media interviews and interpreted the historic documents for the thousands of visitors.

NATIONAL BICENTENNIAL
WRITING COMPETITION

A number of national essay and oratorical contests were already under way. These academic competitions would be a key element in the Commission's educational

*C*ompetition billboard (top);
President Reagan congratulates the winners (above).

programs. One of the most important was the NATIONAL BICENTENNIAL WRITING COMPETITION for high school students, which took place during the 1986-1987 academic year and which the Commission cosponsored in association with *USA Today* and Gannett Co., Inc., as well as the American Bar Association (ABA).

In essays of no more than 1,500 words, competitors addressed the topic "The Constitution: How Does the Separation of Powers Help Make It Work?" Invitations went out to every school district in the country. The Office of State Court Administrators was responsible for conducting the contests at the state level. Winners from each state, the District of Columbia, and the combined territories and overseas schools received $1,000 and, together with their teachers, an all-expense-paid round-trip to Washington, D.C., to meet with President Reagan, Chief Justice Warren Burger, members of the national Commission, and leaders of the Congress. Second- and third-place winners of the state-level competitions were given $500 and $250, respectively, and the national winner of the competition received a grand prize of $10,000. The prizes were provided by Gannett, which also promoted the competition through its publications and the use of billboards. Gannett also produced a special supplement of *USA Today* for use by schools. The supplement, "USA Freedom: Bicentennial of the Constitution," included background information about the three branches of government and about court cases of special interest to young people. It featured a series of articles in the style of *USA Today* about life in 1787.

More than 13,000 students participated. In the end, the judges could not decide between two entrants for the national prize and so awarded it to both of them: Sara Elizabeth Johnson of Portsmouth High School, Portsmouth, Ohio; and Mahbub Alam Majumdar of Hanford High School, Richland, Washington, whose family had recently emigrated from Bangladesh. In a ceremony at the White House, President Reagan greeted all of the state winners and presented each of the national winners with their $10,000 grand prizes. Speaker of the House Jim Wright and Senate President Pro Tempore Strom Thurmond, together with other Members of Congress, honored the 52 students at a reception and Chief Justice Burger hosted a luncheon for them at the Supreme Court. Afterward, the two national winners appeared on "Good Morning America" and the "Today" show.

WILLIAMSBURG REENACTMENT
OF THE CONSTITUTIONAL CONVENTION

Earlier that week, the state winners of the NATIONAL BICENTENNIAL WRITING COMPETITION had participated in an all-expense-paid reenactment of the Constitutional Convention in Williamsburg, Virginia. This mock convention, which took place on September 4-8, was the result of a combined effort by the Colonial Williamsburg Foundation, the Institute of Bill of Rights Law (part of the College of William and Mary's Marshall-Wythe School of Law), and the national

Commission. The reenactment took place at the restored Capitol building in Williamsburg, home of Virginia's House of Burgesses in the eighteenth century. The Commission's Chairman delivered the keynote address for the event on September 4 at the Marshall-Wythe Law School. Commissioner Lynne V. Cheney, the new Chairman of the National Endowment for the Humanities (NEH), spoke at the closing banquet on September 7.

The students prepared for the meeting by completing a reading list before arriving in Williamsburg and attending a day of seminars on constitutional history and development at the Marshall-Wythe School. They engaged in their mock convention as if they were delegates meeting in 1787 and governed by the Articles of Confederation. They met in formal floor debates and developed resolutions for constitutional reform. They were greeted with appropriate pageantry by the President of the Convention, George Washington, who was portrayed in period costume by Rob Nagle, a high school actor and native of Williamsburg. Nagle presided over the debates. Though similar to the Constitution drafted in Philadelphia in 1787, the document produced at Williamsburg 200 years later offered some new departures. For example, it provided for the election of President and Vice President by direct popular vote, four-year terms for members of the House of Representatives, and a guarantee of free education.

NORTHWEST ORDINANCE COMMEMORATION

While most commemorative events in 1987 focused on the Constitutional Convention, the year included another very important anniversary of an achievement of the old Confederation Congress, which the Constitution would eventually replace. July 13, 1987, was the Bicentennial of the Northwest Ordinance, sometimes called the third most important document in American history. Little known to most Americans, this document created a system of government for the Old Northwest Territory, 6.5 million acres north and northwest of the Ohio River. The Ordinance provided for the eventual division of the Northwest Territory into three to five states. Over the next 71 years, five states and part of a sixth — Ohio, Illinois, Michigan, Indiana, Wisconsin, and part of Minnesota — would be carved out of the territory and admitted to the Union.

Equally important, the Ordinance anticipated the Bill of Rights by guaranteeing the people of these new states freedom of worship, trial by jury, and security of contract. It stated that "schools and the means of education shall be forever encouraged" in the territory. It banned slavery and opened the way for the systematic, orderly migration of American homesteaders westward. Passed in the twilight of government under the Articles of Confederation, in its timing the Northwest Ordinance was fortunately coincidental with the Philadelphia Convention. Some of the delegates to that Convention expressed great concern over the admittance of new states, and historically, few countries had granted newly gained territories equal political or social status. But others, including James Madison, Roger Sherman, and James Wilson, saw the importance of bringing future states into the Union as equals, and so the Convention followed the lead of the Continental Congress. Article IV of the Constitution allows new states to enter the Union, guarantees their right to a

*S*tudents reenact the Constitutional Convention at the Capitol in Colonial Williamsburg.

republican form of government, and ensures that their citizens are granted the same rights and privileges as citizens of other states. In all its implications, the Northwest Ordinance was to have a profound effect on the course of American history in the decades leading up to the Civil War.

President Reagan recognized the great importance of this document in a June 1987 proclamation calling upon American citizens to observe the 200th anniversary of the Ordinance with appropriate commemorative programs, ceremonies, and activities. The proclamation was authorized and requested by both chambers of the U.S. Congress in a joint resolution noting that the Ordinance provided "an early example of the commitment of the people of the United States to democratic principles, religious freedom and individual rights."

A yearlong Bicentennial commemoration of the Northwest Ordinance commenced July 13, 1987, through the cooperative effort of the Big Ten Universities Alumni Associations, the state Bicentennial Commissions in the Old Northwest Territory, a number of midwestern libraries and historical societies, and the national Commission. The commemoration featured several major programs. The Big Ten Universities Alumni Associations launched a series of conferences and symposia entitled "The Northwest Ordinance — Liberty and Justice for All," with regionally and nationally known scholars participating. The series was made possible through grants from the NEH and the Commission as well as contributions from the participating Big Ten universities.

The highlight of the commemoration was "Liberty's Legacy — Our Celebration of the Northwest Ordinance and the Constitution," a multimillion-dollar

traveling exhibit (also preserved in book form), which displayed 120 original documents, maps, and other historical artifacts, including a rare first printing of the Articles of Confederation, Thomas Jefferson's copy of the first printing of the Bill of Rights, and Washington's letter accepting the Presidency of the United States. The exhibit, which remained two months in each of the six states, was funded with grants from NEH, the Lilly Endowment Inc., the George and Francis Ball Foundation, the John W. Anderson Foundation, and the Commission.

The weekend of the 200th anniversary of the signing of the Northwest Ordinance (July 13) was celebrated by churches, schools, government agencies, and organizations throughout the states of the Old Northwest Territory. Vincennes, Indiana, onetime capital of the Territory, provided a focal point for this celebration. There the representatives of the Territory states gathered for three days of commemorative activities, which included a crafts fair and a parade with the theme "Northwest Ordinance Freedoms." Highlight of the celebration was a ceremony at the George Rogers Clark Memorial, where Governor Robert Orr and Senator Dan Quayle of Indiana spoke and a proclamation by President Reagan was read.

A CELEBRATION OF CITIZENSHIP

For the Commission, the 1987 commemoration highlight took place in Washington, D.C., on September 16, with A CELEBRATION OF CITIZENSHIP, vignettes from which appear in the Prologue of this report. Along with the ceremonies in Philadelphia the following day, it provided a focal point and a climax for all of the activities in this festive year.

What Happened: September 16, 1987, was a warm, sunny day in Washington. Police estimated that 100,000 to 120,000 people gathered before the West Front of the Capitol. They blanketed the lawn in front and extended beyond the reflecting pool to the Mall. Schoolchildren representing school districts in the metropolitan area filled the bleachers behind the stage where the ceremonies would take place. The Diplomatic Corps was there, as were representatives of all the branches and agencies of the government. The West Front, bedecked with flags, both American and Bicentennial, carried a huge banner stretched from one side to the other. On the banner were the first three words of the Constitution: "We the People." Before the formal ceremonies, the crowd enjoyed a nonstop program of entertainment despite the heat and humidity. Choruses, bands, and vocalists offered patriotic songs. Actors portrayed scenes from historical dramas, highlighting some of the events leading up to the signing of the Constitution.

Distinguished representatives of the three branches of government then entered and were introduced and seated. The formal program began at 1:15 p.m. with an introduction by the television master of

Poster for the Northwest Ordinance commemoration (above); view of A CELEBRATION OF CITIZENSHIP on the West Front of the U.S. Capitol (opposite page).

© Art Stein (4)

A Celebration of Citizenship: *some of the more*
than 100,000 jubilant participants on the Capitol lawn
(top); fife and drums (far left); the National Anthem (left);
Floretta MacKenzie, Superintendent of D.C. Public
Schools (above), tells the crowd: "Get involved. Volunteer."

ceremonies, ABC news anchor Ted Koppel. Mr. Koppel noted that "this wasn't meant to be a birthday party, but a reaffirmation. It is an invitation to get involved." The leadership of the three branches of the government — President Reagan, Speaker of the House Wright, Senate Majority Leader Robert Byrd, and Chief Justice of the United States William Rehnquist — paid tribute to the Constitution in brief remarks. Each emphasized different aspects of the document — its origins, characteristics, and meaning in the lives of Americans today. Bridging the generations were two young Americans: 14-year-old Stephanie Petit of Bethel, Pennsylvania, who spoke of what the Constitution meant to her generation and for the future; and Damien Atkins, a 17-year-old Washington, D.C., high school student, who introduced President Reagan.

Calling the Constitution a "blueprint for freedom," the President concluded his remarks by quoting from the speech his predecessor, Grover Cleveland, gave on the occasion of the Constitution's Centennial in 1887:

When we look down upon a hundred years and see the origin of our Constitution; when we contemplate all its trials and triumphs, when we realize how completely the principles upon which it is based have met every national need and national peril, how devoutly should we say with Franklin: "God governs in the affairs of men."

Two emotional high points punctuated the ceremonies. Chief Justice Burger recited the simple but eloquent words of the Constitution's Preamble. Later, at the conclusion of his remarks, President Reagan led a group of young Americans standing with him, as well as all those present or watching and listening elsewhere, in the Pledge of Allegiance. Floretta MacKenzie, Superintendent of the Washington, D.C., public schools, closed the formal program by noting that good citizenship meant not only reading and understanding the Constitution, it also enjoined all Americans to do what they could to make the country a better place in which to live. "Get involved," she said. "Volunteer. The people who wrote the Constitution did, and look at what they accomplished!"

The CELEBRATION OF CITIZENSHIP climaxed with a stirring musical note when the choirs, singers, actors, dignitaries, and the entire assembled crowd rose and joined enthusiastically in the singing of "God Bless America" as 50,000 red, white, and blue balloons lifted into the sky above the Capitol. The spectacle, however, was not confined to Washington, D.C. Via television cameras and radio microphones these events were broadcast from the West Front of the Capitol throughout the country and around the world. With the ceremonies at the U.S. Capitol as the focus, over 60 million students, teachers, and administrators in the nation's public and private schools were estimated to have participated in an all-day "teach-in" on the Constitution.

How the Event Happened: The concept of this event originated in a project proposed to the Commission by the American Newspaper Publishers Association (ANPA), later joined by 12 major educational associations.* The project, which the Commission agreed to support at its November 1986 meeting, called for a daylong educational program in elementary, middle, and senior high schools across the country. It would also provide the culmination to a year of educational activities about the Constitution. Every school was to receive promotional materials that provided historical background and suggested learning activities for this all-day teach-in. The activities emphasized the rights and responsibilities of citizenship and the importance of constitutionalism in the American political tradition and in people's daily lives. The promotional materials also suggested other educational activities for use during the school year and encouraged the participation of members of the local community.

The ANPA proposal also linked the national teach-in on the Constitution to the idea of a media event — a live radio and television broadcast in which Chief Justice Burger would recite and discuss the Preamble of the Constitution and President Reagan would lead students in a recitation of the Pledge of Allegiance. The idea of a simultaneous, nationwide Pledge of Allegiance had been considered and approved by the Commission earlier in the year.

Once the project was approved, there remained the formidable tasks of coordinating the national teach-in, finding an appropriate site for the special event, making television and radio broadcast arrangements, and seeing after a host of other logistical, scheduling, and security details. At a news conference February 19, 1987, at the National Press Club in Washington, D.C., the Commission's Chairman and Jerry Friedheim, executive vice president of the ANPA Foundation, together with representatives of the 12 participating educational associations, outlined the plans for A CELEBRATION OF CITIZENSHIP (as the project was to be called). They announced that in April the foundation would send every elementary, intermediate, and high school a packet of educational materials developed in consultation with all the participating organizations.

By early summer the project had evolved and expanded in scope. The students and educators in the nation's 103,000 public and private schools had been invited to participate in the national teach-in. But as it developed, A CELEBRATION OF CITIZENSHIP would provide Americans of all ages, at home or at work, with an opportunity to join in the commemoration, which now had the corporate support of Nabisco Brands, Inc., and the Xerox Corporation. In addition, the National Association of Broadcasters (NAB) joined in, coordinating electronic media coverage and promoting A CELEBRATION OF CITIZENSHIP on its video satellite network. ABC, which had agreed to televise the main event, began development of a three-hour television special, "The Blessings of Liberty," to be broadcast during the evening

*These organizations were the American Association of School Administrators, American Federation of Teachers, American Library Association, Council for American Private Education, National Association of Elementary School Principals, National Association of Secondary School Principals, National Association of State Boards of Education, National Congress of Parents and Teachers (National PTA), National Council for the Social Studies, National Education Association, National School Boards Association, and the National School Public Relations Association.

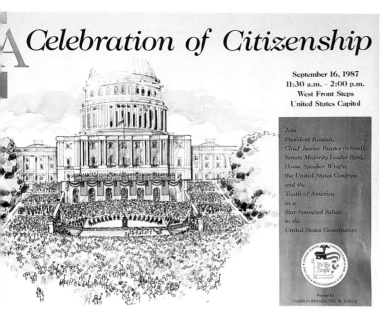

A Celebration of Citizenship

September 16, 1987
11:30 a.m. - 2:00 p.m.
West Front Steps
United States Capitol

*Join
President Reagan,
Chief Justice Burger (retired),
Senate Majority Leader Byrd,
House Speaker Wright,
the United States Congress
and the
Youth of America
in a
Star-Spangled Salute
to the
United States Constitution*

Funded by
NABISCO BRANDS, INC. & XEROX

address to join him in the celebration on September 16. Professional sports organizations ran scoreboard messages and other promotions focusing on the event.

In addition to the promotional activities of the various educational associations and the media, Nabisco distributed to local food stores 100 million "We the People" stickers. The International Paper Company produced 53 million milk cartons with Constitutional messages included on the packaging. Polaroid Corporation not only developed educational materials on the Constitution and distributed them to grade schools, but also, as an added incentive, provided a free camera and film to each school to use in its teach-in activities and to make a permanent record of the event.

Final arrangements, including transportation of schoolchildren and dignitaries to the West Front of the Capitol, were worked out primarily by the Commission, assisted by a corps of volunteers. Officials arranged

*Celebration promotion poster (top)
and news conference (above).*

of September 16. Arrangements were worked out for coverage abroad by the Armed Forces Network, the Voice of America, Radio Free Europe, Radio Liberty, and the U.S. Information Agency's (USIA) global television network, WorldNet.

By August, all of the key elements of A CELEBRATION OF CITIZENSHIP had fallen into place. The leadership of the three branches of government had agreed to participate. The essential legislation allowing the event to take place on the West Front of the Capitol had been passed by Congress, and the design and construction of facilities on that location were proceeding. Promotion of the event intensified with a press conference held at the National Archives on August 20. Chief Justice Burger also appeared on the Cable News Network (CNN) and on ABC's "Good Morning America." On September 12, President Reagan invited listeners to his weekly radio

for leave time for government workers to participate. In all its aspects, A CELEBRATION OF CITIZENSHIP was not only one of the most successful, but also one of the largest and most complex enterprises of the Bicentennial. Its combination of celebration and education provided a model for future commemorative events.

PHILADELPHIA 1987

The commemoration of the Constitution's signing culminated on September 17, 1987, the day following A CELEBRATION OF CITIZENSHIP, with ceremonies and a parade in Philadelphia. In a very real sense, Philadelphia's commemorations had begun exactly one year earlier with the opening of the "Miracle At Philadelphia" exhibit described in the previous chapter. Philadelphia's year of celebration was orchestrated by the WE THE PEOPLE 200 committee, chaired by William G. Rouse III, and was funded with the generous assistance of corporate sponsorship, as well as by a grant of $600,000 from the national Commission. That historic city witnessed many commemorative events and activities during the course of the year attended by hundreds of thousands of visitors as well as residents, but three major events deserve special mention here.

Opening of the Constitutional Convention: A four-day "All Roads Lead To Philadelphia" festival of events on May 22-25, 1987, marked the 200th Anniversary of the opening of the Philadelphia Constitutional Convention. The formal ceremonies, held May 25 at Independence Hall in Independence National Historical Park, featured Vice President Bush, Chief Justice Burger, Pennsylvania Governor Robert T. Casey, and Philadelphia Mayor W. Wilson Goode. Against the backdrop of a huge American flag configured with red, white, and blue balloons, each speaker discussed the Constitution and its blessings from a personal perspective. Remarks by Park Superintendent Hobart G. Cawood, Mr. Rouse, and actor James Earl Jones rounded out the program. Following the speakers, a 100-voice choir honored the Constitution with the premiere performance of WE THE PEOPLE 200's official song as thousands of balloons lifted into the sky.

Great Compromise: Lindy Boggs, a member of the national Commission and Chairman of the Bicentenary of the U.S. Congress, presided on July 16 over a

National Independence Park

Columns of balloons form an American flag at the opening of "All Roads Lead to Philadelphia."

Some of the many parade floats in Philadelphia (above, left, right); President Reagan addresses the crowd (opposite page).

ceremonial special session of Congress at Independence Hall in Philadelphia. There, 181 Representatives and 25 Senators, including the majority and minority leadership of both houses, gathered to honor the 200th anniversary of the Constitutional Convention's "Great Compromise," which provided states an equal standing in the Senate and proportional representation in the House. Legislative representation in the proposed new government was one of the Constitutional Convention's most difficult issues, and its successful resolution was one of the Convention's greatest accomplishments.

September 17, 1987: This date marked the 200th anniversary of the signing of the Constitution: the focal point of the year and, in a sense, of the entire Bicentennial. Unlike the preceding day in Washington, D.C., September 17 in Philadelphia dawned gray and wet. The festivities began with a WE THE PEOPLE 200 parade. Lasting three hours and involving over 30,000 participants, it was one of the largest parades in the city's history. The first part reenacted the "Grand Federal Procession," held in Philadelphia on July 4, 1788, to celebrate the ratification of the Constitution. The second part illustrated themes from the Constitution's Preamble, and the third part of the parade celebrated the people of America and the rich tapestry of their ethnic heritage. The morning's steady rain failed to dampen the enthusiasm of participants and bystanders as the floats and bands snaked their way from Penn's Landing through the narrow streets of the old city to Independence Hall, and then on to City Hall and the Museum of Art.

About noon (and before the third part of the parade), President Reagan emerged from Independence Hall to deliver a 15-minute address in which he described the Constitution as a "covenant" with the Almighty. The President underscored the difficult circumstances in which the Constitution had been born and suggested that the true American Revolution began in 1787. It was only then, he said, "that the noble sentiments and brave rhetoric of 1776 took on substance, that the hopes and dreams of the revolutionaries could become a living, enduring reality."

By mid-afternoon the sun came out, a propitious introduction to the day's concluding ceremony: a commemoration of the actual signing of the Constitution at the same hour that event had taken place 200 years before. Together with Hobart Cawood, the director of Independence Park, and Jacqueline Wexler, the executive director of the National Conference of Christians and Jews (NCCJ), Chief Justice Burger presided against the impressive backdrop of Independence Hall. The Chairman accepted on behalf of the national Commission the signatures of 6 million schoolchildren, who had been invited to "sign-on to the Constitution" in a national program of the same name sponsored by the NCCJ.

At precisely 4:00 p.m. — the historic moment of the Constitution's signing — Chief Justice Burger was scheduled to ring a replica of the Liberty Bell, provided for the event by the Liberty Bell Foundation. Instead of doing it as planned, he invited a group of schoolchildren to join him, saying, "It will be up to you to keep this bell ringing." The ringing of the bell was accompanied by the release of 20,000 red, white, and blue balloons. It was also the signal for bells, chimes, carillons, and whistles throughout the city, across the country, and indeed around the world to join in a great tintinnabulation lasting 200 seconds. This climactic event had been organized in the preceding months through the Commission's BELLS ACROSS AMERICA program (*see page 67*).

Courtesy of Liberty Bell Foundation Headquarters, Fort Washington, Penn.

Churches, synagogues, colleges, even cemeteries and prisons joined in. At military installations around the world, including Berlin, the bells were rung. So were the carillons at the U.S. Capitol and the Washington Cathedral. In London, the bells of St. Paul's Cathedral and Westminster Abbey honored the day. Steamboats joined in with their whistles; so did ships at sea. Staff at the Kyoto Air Force Base in Japan made T-shirts to commemorate the event. In a town of 1,300 at the northernmost point of Alaska, people gathered in the snow with hand bells and balloons.

The festivities continued with a TV gala at Philadelphia's Civic Center. A day dizzy with celebration ended where it began — at Penn's Landing, where spectators witnessed a spectacular illumination of the Benjamin Franklin Bridge, followed by fireworks. In all, the great shows of celebration in 1987 caught the public's eye, generated widespread interest in America's legacy of constitutional government, and thereby laid the basis for the Bicentennial's lower-profile but equally important ongoing programs.

Clarksville, Tenn./Ruth Porter

USS Sierra/U.S. Navy Photo

Rowe, Maine/E. Libbey

O*n September 17, 1987, Americans everywhere joined in* BELLS ACROSS AMERICA, *a joyful ringing tribute to the signing of the Constitution (this page and opposite page).*

Jacqueline Wexler of the NCCJ, sponsor of the SIGN-ON TO THE CONSTITUTION project, joins Chairman Burger and Hoby Cawood, Superintendent of National Independence Park, for the Philadelphia gala (left), concluded by fireworks at Penn's Landing (top).

Drafting and Signing   65

Commission Programs and Publications

Many Commission programs that had been established in 1986 peaked in 1987 as the nation geared up to celebrate the 200th anniversary of the signing of the Constitution. Other programs and publications introduced in 1987 would have a continuing importance during the remaining years of the Bicentennial.

BICENTENNIAL EDUCATIONAL GRANT PROGRAM

The BICENTENNIAL EDUCATIONAL GRANT PROGRAM, one of the Commission's most important commitments to American education, completed its first round in the spring of 1987 with the award of 29 grants totaling almost $1 million to programs in 19 states. Despite the short amount of time allowed for the program's start-up, it received 222 applications requesting almost $10 million in funding. Among the projects funded were the following:

The California State Department of Education sponsored a two-week institute for 45 primary and secondary teachers. Every participant developed a lesson plan with the assistance of master teachers and the resource staff provided by the department.

The Social Sciences Education Consortium, Inc., of Boulder, Colorado, sponsored a one-week institute for 25 elementary- and middle-school teachers on the history, literature, and art of the Founding era.

James Schick of Kansas developed a computer simulation of the Constitutional Convention and the ratification process.

The Mississippi Committee for the Humanities sponsored a teacher training conference, the program materials from which would be made available to every high school in the state. One hundred teachers, four scholars, and several consultants participated.

The American Studies Center in Washington, D.C., created a 44-minute film on the Constitution for secondary school students.

The Connecticut Humanities Council sponsored a four-week training course on the Constitution for 20 teachers. The project required each participant subsequently to provide in-service training for at least 10 teachers in his or her respective home school districts.

The History Teaching Alliance, a project of the American Historical Association, sponsored a series of yearlong seminars on the Constitution for elementary and secondary school teachers. The seminars were spread among 12 states and involved in each case the collaborative effort of four or five university professors working with 15 to 20 teachers taking the seminar.

A *teacher seminar held by the History Teaching Alliance.*

In August 1987, the Commission announced its second round of grant competition in anticipation of continued congressional support in fiscal year 1988. In December 1987, after providing $1 million for the program in the Commission's fiscal year 1988 budget, Congress increased funding for the program by $2.5 million ($1.25 million in supplemental appropriations and $1.25 million from the Commission's general appropriations through a reprogramming authority). The $3.5 million combined total would become the approximate level of annual funding for the program.

BICENTENNIAL CAMPUS PROGRAM

Most of the Commission's efforts in education would focus on younger students at the elementary and secondary school levels. Its programs, however, did not overlook older Americans of college age and beyond. To stimulate college and university participation in the Bicentennial commemorations, the Commission at its January 1987 meeting approved the BICENTENNIAL CAMPUS PROGRAM. Modeled after its DESIGNATED BICEN-

George Washington and friends entertain and educate in "The Next Amendment" — a tribute to the Constitution performed by students at Southwest Texas State University.

TENNIAL COMMUNITY (DBC) counterpart, through which cities, counties, and towns were officially recognized, the program required participating educational institutions to establish a Bicentennial Committee, broadly representative of the campus community. Each Bicentennial Campus would then develop plans for a commemorative program, to extend through 1991, designed to educate members of the community about the Constitution and the Bill of Rights.

The more than 1,200 two-year colleges and nearly 2,000 four-year colleges and universities in the country were eligible to participate. Universities with more than one campus could submit multiple applications, one for each campus with a separate administrative unit. In September 1986, the Commission sent a letter to college presidents, encouraging their institutions to participate in the commemoration. By the January 1987 meeting, the responses indicated a high level of involvement, and the BICENTENNIAL CAMPUS program would enable the Commission to reward the accomplishments of active institutions while encouraging others to develop plans.

BELLS ACROSS AMERICA

Though strictly speaking not a continuing program, the BELLS ACROSS AMERICA project had a major role in the September 1987 celebrations, and its story tells a great deal about how the commemorative activities of that year evolved and were eventually implemented. Moreover, it created a program activity and a network that would be used again during the years of the Bicentennial.

The idea of a nationwide (indeed, worldwide) bell-ringing to celebrate the anniversary moment of the Constitution's signing had been considered by the national Commission as early as 1986, but was tabled until the spring of 1987, when a detailed plan was developed for mobilizing the resources of churches, synagogues, educational institutions, carillon and bell-ringing societies, bell manufacturers, and other organizations in the effort. A promotional flier was produced and first distributed at the end of May.

Then in June, meetings were held with Jacqueline Wexler of the National Conference of Christians and Jews to discuss the Conference's "sign-on" program. The Conference had developed a five-year educational plan for commemorating the Bicentennial, which included a special curriculum for elementary and secondary school students and a SIGN-ON TO THE CONSTITUTION project, in which students read and inscribed their names to copies of the Constitution. From the meeting came the idea of merging that program with the bell-ringing ceremony; this was in effect the Commission's first substantial involvement in the activities in Philadelphia.

BELLS ACROSS AMERICA now had a major event on which to focus. Special packets were mailed to approximately 600 religious organizations. Fliers were sent to universities, colleges, private associations, and corporations. The resources of state Commissions and DBCs were mobilized. The Department of Defense (DOD) asked all military installations around the world to participate, and the National Park Service enlisted the participation of all of its facilities with carillons. Members of Congress contacted Mayors in their respective constituencies. Officials at the United States Embassy in London secured the participation of St. Paul's Cathedral and Westminster Abbey.

The Department of the Army's Institute of Heraldry developed a logo for the program, and Don Ameche recorded a public service announcement for radio. The country's four bell manufacturers sent special mailings to their customers. The United States Telephone Association and several phone companies included promotional inserts with their regular mailings to customers. As already mentioned, even the nation's penal institutions and cemeteries joined in. Additional staff were assigned the task of coordinating this massive effort, with special attention given to a synchronized ringing of bells in Philadelphia and Washington, D.C.

It is difficult to estimate the number of institutions and individuals participating in the event, but it was substantial. Afterward, approximately 4,000 certificates of recognition were issued to sponsoring organizations alone. The success of the effort, put together and carried out within a relatively short span of time, helped to provide one of the dramatic moments in this momentous year.

ADVERTISING CAMPAIGN

Among the most important of the media projects in terms of raising public consciousness about the Bicentennial was the campaign of public service announcements (PSAs) that the national Commission developed in collaboration with the Advertising Council and its participating agency, Scali, McCabe, Sloves, Inc. The campaign, on the theme "The Constitution: The Words We Live By," was launched on February 23, 1987, at a press briefing at the National Press Club.

Beginning in 1987 and continuing through the Bill of Rights commemoration in 1991, the Advertising Council created and disseminated PSAs to media outlets across the country (*see Chapter VI*). Over 900 television stations, all of the major networks, and approximately 400 cable TV outlets received 30-second and 20-second broadcast spots that addressed such subjects as freedom of religion, freedom of the press, and the right to vote. The most popular PSA featured several Presidents taking the oath of office. Radio kits with live announcer copy and recorded spots, in both English and Spanish, were distributed to more than 6,000 radio stations. Packets of print PSAs, containing ad slicks of various sizes, were sent to newspapers and magazines nationally for inclusion in their advertising space. During the first six months of its activity, this campaign generated $19 million worth of free advertising.

Each broadcast and print PSA contained the Commission's address, to which members of the public could write to obtain a "response kit" on the Constitution. This general purpose kit, printed on quality vellum, included a handsomely illustrated booklet that contained an introductory essay by Chief Justice Burger and a copy of the Constitution, a set of bookmarks —

COMMEMORATION OF THE BICENTENNIAL OF THE CONSTITUTION

CNCO 7330   "RECRUITS"   30 SECONDS

COMMANDER: May I have your attention? Raise your right hand and repeat after me. I do solemnly swear... RECRUITS: I do solemnly swear... COMMANDER: That I will support and defend... RECRUITS: That I will support and defend... COMMANDER: The Constitution of the United States... RECRUITS: The Constitution of the United States.
ANNCR: (VO) The Constitution...if it's important enough to fight for, don't you think it's important enough to know about? The Constitution: the words we live by.

CNCO 7430   "TALK TO GOD"   30 SECONDS

CATHOLIC PRIEST: Happy are they whose way is blameless, who walk in the law of the Lord. Happy... BARMITZVAH BOY: Baruch atah adonai elohainu... PROTESTANT MINISTER: Sure goodness... ANNCR (VO) In America because of the words of the Constitution... BAPTIST MINISTER: If you call on Jesus... (CONGREGATION SINGS) ANNCR: (VO) ...you can talk to God any way you want...Or not at all.
The Constitution: the words we live by.

CNCO 7320   "CENSORSHIP"   20 SECONDS

ANNCR (VO) Without the protection of the Constitution there would be something missing in your life.

The Constitution: the words we live by.

A Public Service Campaign of the Advertising Council

These two frames end all of the PSAs highlighted on this photoboard.

Volunteer Agency: Scali, McCabe, Sloves, Inc.

*T*elevision, radio, and print public-service announcements carry the message.

each reproducing a portrait, quotation, and signature of one of the Framers — a historical chronology and map, lists of the national Commissioners and state Commissions, and a selected bibliography. Nearly 135,000 copies of the kit were distributed during the year.

LOGO-LICENSED COMMEMORATIVES

Towards the end of 1986, with the legislative authority in hand and the regulations in place, the Commission began its logo licensing operation, in which an increasing number of commercial firms were licensed to use the logo for educational and commemorative products related to the Bicentennial. Along with the manufacturers, the Commission itself sold some products of special commemorative value. Eventually, it developed a series of promotional catalogs as part of an across-the-board effort begun in 1986 to create interest in and excitement about the Bicentennial.

In addition to souvenir merchandise such as pins, hats, and T-shirts, these commemorative products included heirloom-quality furniture, fine china and crystal, paintings and prints, records and tapes, sculpture, ornaments, and commemorative medals and stamps. Sales produced license fee income for the Commission, which helped to fund educational programs.

Although the program was not officially launched until late 1986, it quickly became a success. While the required legislation made its way through Congress and the Commission developed the necessary implementing regulations, manufacturers geared up to be ready to go as soon as the program became official. Once it did, the Commission was deluged with requests for logo licensing agreements. During the next year, 70 products would receive logo licenses. On December 29, 1986, the first license was issued to the Detra Flag Company to produce the Commission logo flag, the first of five flag manufacturers to be licensed.

Among the heirloom-quality items carrying the logo was a limited edition of 200 Constitution Bicentennial crystal prisms designed by Steuben. The prisms were topped by a stylized American eagle, with the Preamble, engraved in calligraphy, visible through the crystal. Stickley Furniture reproduced the original desk and chair used by the first Secretary of the U.S. Senate, the original of which is exhibited in the restored Senate chamber on the second floor of Congress Hall in Philadelphia. The Lenox Collection offered several products that became especially popular, among them a limited-edition Constitution Bowl, for which orders far exceeded production. Another china manufacturer, Edward Marshall Boehm, Inc., designed a porcelain bowl decorated with four gold eagles, which also proved very popular.

In 1987, the Commission also inaugurated a series of five 24-karat gold-plate ornaments, designed and manufactured by the licensee, Orion Marketing. Each of these ornaments captured one of the themes of the Bicentennial commemoration. The first edition, for example, was a representation of Independence Hall, symbolizing the drafting of the Constitution. Each ornament was boxed with a leaflet giving a brief history of the event represented.

Logo-licensed products include gold-plated ornaments (right); the Lenox Constitution bowl (below); and the Steuben crystal vase (below right).

WE THE PEOPLE NEWSLETTER

Shortly after it began in 1985, the Commission decided to publish a regular newsletter, *We the People*, to share with other groups and individuals information about commemorative activities and plans. The newsletter first appeared in November 1985 and quickly became the "town crier" of the Bicentennial. Issued free of charge, the newsletter increased its circulation to 2,000 by the time of its fourth issue in September 1986, and to more than 45,000 subscribers by 1987. Nine issues appeared during this year, including a special edition for the September celebrations.

In its 37 issues, *We the People* chronicled nearly every aspect of the Bicentennial. Its articles included not only descriptions of all the major national events and programs, but a wide selection of state and local activities as well, through information provided by the network of Bicentennial leaders and organizations. It included historical background about the Constitution and identified sources of materials for carrying out programs. Chief Justice Burger was a regular contributor in his "Chairman's Corner."

The newsletter eventually gained a circulation of 72,000, including many subscribers overseas. Its articles often became the source of program ideas for others. Many libraries, for example, displayed copies of the newsletter with their book exhibits on the Constitution, and some Bicentennial organizations took *We the People* as a model for their own newsletters.

OTHER PUBLICATIONS

The year's activities generated a great demand for publications of all sorts, for both the promotion of Bicentennial events and the satisfaction of public interest in the Constitution and its origins. The variety and quantity of the Commission's publications increased accordingly during the year.

In addition to the kit of educational materials already mentioned, a number of publications were developed for A CELEBRATION OF CITIZENSHIP. *World Book Encyclopedia*, in collaboration with the Commission, issued a special booklet that included a reprint of the *Encyclopedia's* article on the Constitution by Professor J. W. Peltason, an introduction by Chief Justice Burger, a promotional statement for A CELEBRATION OF CITIZENSHIP, and suggested learning activities and resources for teachers. The Commission distributed over 100,000 copies of the booklet and also issued two posters in large quantities promoting the event.

The Commission devoted several of its publications to media relations. During the year it issued a *Media Guide* in a layered flap format, which contained a summary of almost all the commemorative events taking place that year. It also published a *Media Relations Guide*, a booklet designed for sponsors of Bicentennial events, with suggestions about how best to work with the media.

With the editorial assistance of the Commission, BellSouth published *The Constitution; the Bicentennial; 1787-1987*. This publication in magazine-format included inspirational photographs and essays on the meaning of America's constitutional legacy. BellSouth

The We the People newsletter chronicled every aspect of the Bicentennial.

also assisted the Commission with the production of a Bicentennial poster.

Another Commission publication series increased its popularity during the year: the COMMEMORATIVE CALENDAR. The 1987 edition was illustrated with striking photographs of buildings, artifacts, and paintings associated with the Constitutional Convention. In the fashion of a diurnal, each day on the calendar contained an important historical fact associated with that date and with the development of the Constitution. A total of 250,000 copies of the COMMEMORATIVE CALENDAR were printed for distribution.

These publications, together with the other pamphlets, leaflets, brochures, posters, and Bicentennial documents, issued forth to meet the swelling demand. The Commission's Information Center handled over 287,000 inquiries from the public for information and publications, resulting in the dissemination of over 2.2 million items about the Bicentennial commemorations. Also busy handling requests, the Speakers Bureau helped to organize over 300 speaking engagements around the country.

ORGANIZATIONAL CHANGES AND RESOURCES

To undertake a project of the magnitude of A CELEBRATION OF CITIZENSHIP and the other commemorative events in 1987, the Commission reorganized and expanded its staff to 155, including 90 regular employees, 34 detailees, and 31 temporary volunteers. After the completion of these projects, the staff was reduced by the end of the year to 118, including 84 regular employees, 28 detailees, and six temporaries. For fiscal year 1987, Congress appropriated $13.2 million, to be supplemented by $253,000 in royalty income from logo licensing and medal sales, and by $201,000 from donated funds.

Other Activities

During 1987, the Commission continued its important work of reaching out to organizations and groups throughout the country and around the world and participating in many of their projects. In addition, other organizations created and put into effect programs and activities in which the Commission was not involved.

EDUCATIONAL ORGANIZATIONS

The Commission took a major step forward in 1987 in its ability to make contact with school administrators, teachers, and the educational press around the country when the National Educational Advisory Committee (NEAC) agreed to lend its support to the Bicentennial. NEAC included among its members representatives of almost all the major educational associations and publications. Elliot Richardson, one of the nation's most distinguished public servants, who had held several cabinet-level positions as well as the Ambassadorship to Great Britain during the Nixon and Ford administra-

tions, chaired the group. The Vice Chairman was Sidney Marland, a retired educator who had been the Superintendent of Schools in Pittsburgh, Pennsylvania, and New Canaan, Connecticut, as well as a member of the board of directors of Scholastic, Inc., and Assistant Secretary for Education at the Department of Health, Education, and Welfare. NEAC had played a major advisory role during the Statue of Liberty celebrations in 1986. Meeting periodically at the Supreme Court during

The National Educational Advisory Committee holds a meeting.

the years of the Bicentennial, the Committee served, in the words of its Vice Chairman, to "advise and advance" — advise the Commission on what it should do in education and advance Commission programs through the constituencies of its members.

Most of the organizations represented on NEAC sponsored their own Bicentennial activities during 1987, a few of which can be mentioned here. In addition to working with the Commission and Gannett/*USA Today* in the National High School Writing Competition, the ABA sponsored its National Mock Trial and Student Seminar Program, a week-long event in May for students from 34 states. The ABA also developed a resource kit to help local bar associations and other groups establish Bicentennial speakers bureaus. It cosponsored with the American Assembly four regional conferences on the Presidency and the Constitution, which began in 1987 and continued into 1988.

The National Association of Secondary School Principals worked with Scholastic, Inc., to develop materials for a high school citizenship education program, entitled "Make It a Class Act," in which graduating seniors were encouraged to register to vote before their graduation. The National Education Association, the American Federation of Teachers, and the National Council for the Social Studies each had their own projects to develop new curricula on the Constitution. The Anti-Defamation League produced teaching modules and a poster series on the Bill of Rights to promote the ethic of citizenship and combat prejudice among young Americans.

From pledges to pageants to a "living" map of the United States, schools nationwide celebrate the Constitution during Citizenship Day and Constitution Week.

Sylvania, Georgia

Norwood, Massachusetts

Jay, Maine

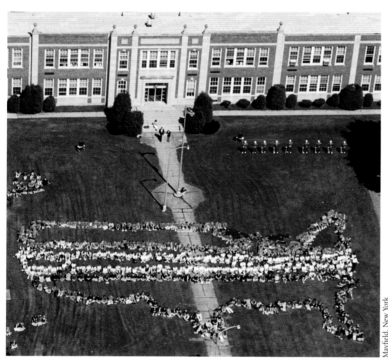

Mayfield, New York

The televised ceremonies on September 16 and 17 each provided a focus for school activities. The nation's schools, of course, had provided the principal audience of A Celebration of Citizenship, certainly one of the largest events of its kind ever. Across the nation, schools of every type — public, private, parochial — and every grade level, kindergarten through high school, devoted an entire day, and in some cases an entire week, to programs honoring the Constitution. Many schools took the occasion to initiate a series of activities lasting throughout the school year, whose range extended as far as local resources, opportunities, and inventiveness would allow. The activities included skits, mock trials and constitutional conventions, essay contests, research projects, film festivals, art displays, library exhibits, flag ceremonies, quilt makings, giant birthday cakes, special assemblies, playlets, and dramatic readings. The objective was to make this occasion something more than balloons and flag-waving, to engage the nation's youth in thoughtful consideration of the Constitution and the responsibilities of citizenship.

Nyack Public Schools in Nyack, New York, for example, devoted September 17 to a reenactment of the Constitutional Convention, to which the entire community, including local craftspeople, contributed. Participants gathered on the high school football field, where a life-size set of the interior of Independence Hall had been erected. With the assistance of a horse-drawn carriage, a musket salute from the Orangetown Militia, and period music provided by a school band and choruses, students, teachers, and administrators in period costumes re-created the drafting and signing of the Constitution. The day's festivities, however, marked only the beginning of a yearlong program of constitutional studies at every level of the city's school system.

In addition to the National Bicentennial Writing Competition, a great many other essay and oratorical contests took place all over the country during 1987, some of them national in scope, others regional or local in character. One such competition was the National Bicentennial Law School Essay Contest, which took place during the academic year 1986-1987. Cosponsored by West Publishing Company of St. Paul, Minnesota, and the national Commission, it invited students in every law school in the country to participate. The topic was "Does the allocation of power between the Federal and state governments and among the branches of the Federal Government contribute to the preservation of individual liberty and the functioning of our government?" The winner, Candace H. Beckett of Annapolis, Maryland, a student at the University of Maryland School of Law in Baltimore, received a newly published three-volume treatise on Constitutional law from West Publishing Company and a cash award of $10,000.

The Department of Education sponsored a Bicentennial essay contest for elementary school students. Commencing in January 1987, the contest focused on the theme "What the Constitution Means to Me and to Our Country." The *Weekly Reader* agreed to support this contest through its issues in 1987. The 150 representative

A skit on the Constitution was written and performed by students at the Norwood School in Potomac, Maryland

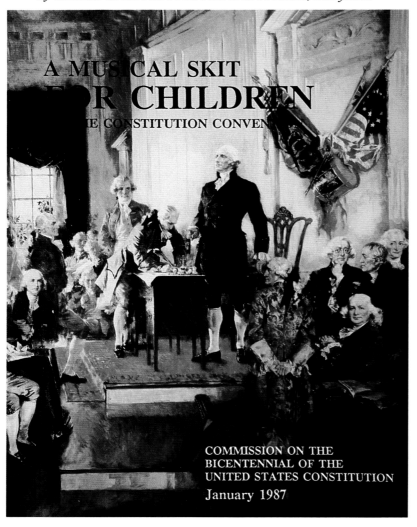

A MUSICAL SKIT FOR CHILDREN
THE CONSTITUTION CONVEN[TION]

COMMISSION ON THE
BICENTENNIAL OF THE
UNITED STATES CONSTITUTION
January 1987

student essayists came from all 50 states, the District of Columbia, and U.S. territories, as well as from Department of Defense, Department of Interior, and Department of State schools. The students attended special ceremonies in Washington, D.C., and visited with President Reagan at the White House.

The American Legion's 50th annual National High School Oratorical Contest, held in the spring of 1987, had received official Commission recognition as a Bicentennial project. Since its beginning, this annual competition sought to develop in students a deeper knowledge and appreciation of the Constitution. It encouraged contestants to think and speak clearly about the rights and responsibilities of American citizenship. They competed first at the local level and worked their way up via state, regional, and sectional contests to the national finals held in Kansas City, Missouri, on April 10. Maryagnes Barbieri of Milton, Massachusetts, a high school junior, won the national grand prize — a $16,000 scholarship. Substantial prizes also were awarded to the others competing in the national finals and to winners and participants at lower levels in the contest.

The Daughters of the American Revolution (DAR) annual Constitution Week essay contest took as its topic in the 1987 competition "The Checks and Balances of the U.S. Constitution." American history students in grades 11 and 12 were eligible to participate. The competition progressed through local, state, district, and national levels. Cash prizes were awarded to the national winners at the DAR's Continental Congress in April. The National Society of Hebrew Day Schools sponsored a contest based on the topic "Citizen Awareness: Constitutional Rights and Responsibilities," with students in the 525 affiliate schools participating.

In addition to these national competitions, a wide variety of similar contests throughout the country at the regional and local levels were sponsored by universities and colleges, companies, department stores, banks, newspapers, and private, nonprofit, and other groups. James Madison University, for example, cosponsored with the Virginia Canals and Navigations Society a writing competition on the topic "From Canal to Competition." Students attending colleges and universities in Maryland, Virginia, West Virginia, and the District of Columbia were eligible to participate.

Educational institutions and organizations set in motion a great many other programs during the year, of which only a sampling can be mentioned here. At their June 1986 meeting the Commissioners were entertained with "A Musical Skit for Children on the Constitutional Convention," written and performed by the Norwood School of Maryland. In the following year the Commission printed and distributed copies of the skit to all grade schools in the country. Students in West Chester County, Pennsylvania, wrote and recorded their own series of "Bicentennial Moments" — historical vignettes that were then broadcast regularly on two local radio stations and were also played each day on the public address system of local schools.

Role-playing was the main ingredient in various mock Constitutional Conventions held by schools and colleges throughout the country. For example, junior and senior high school students participated in a mock Convention sponsored by the Delaware Historical Society on March 27-29, 1987, at the Old Town Hall Museum in Wilmington. On May 2, Washington and Lee University in Lexington, Virginia, hosted a simulated national convention on its campus. Student delegates from area colleges, representing all 50 states, focused on current issues. Culminating a yearlong series of constitutional studies, the Clark County School District in Nevada sponsored in April a mock convention for local students. Among other topics, the convention delegates considered the idea of a balanced budget amendment.

Some individual colleges developed commemorative events that took advantage of their own historical legacies. Franklin and Marshall College, which began as Franklin College the same year the Constitution was signed, celebrated both Bicentennials in grand style. The college, located in Lancaster, Pennsylvania, scheduled a yearlong celebration, including scholarly, cultural, and festive activities. The commemoration began in January with a student-sponsored birthday party for Benjamin Franklin. Students performed an original opera by two faculty members, entitled *Benjamin: An Opera of Our Own Invention.* In June, students, faculty, alumni, and the local community joined in an all-day celebration of

Founders' Day, which included a parade, festival, and concert. With support from an NEH grant, the college also sponsored a series of "John Marshall Lectures" on the Constitution and the Supreme Court, in which noted scholars focused on contemporary constitutional issues. The college could claim another interesting historical legacy: one of its entering freshmen was Peter Bellamy, the great grandson of the author of the Pledge of Allegiance, Francis Bellamy.

Scholarly associations took up the Constitution as a theme at their annual meetings and conferences. For its 1987 symposia series, the U.S. Capitol Historical Society addressed the topic "To Form a More Perfect Union: The Critical Ideas of the Constitution." Several workshops at the annual meeting of the American Historical Association in December 1987 were devoted to constitutional subjects of one kind or another. The annual meeting of the East-Central/American Society for Eighteenth-Century Studies, at Ursinus College in Collegeville, Pennsylvania, examined topics on the theme "The American Constitution: Its Cultural Sources and Antecedents in Eighteenth-Century Europe and America."

FEDERAL GOVERNMENT DEPARTMENTS, AND AGENCIES

By midyear, departments and agencies representing almost the entire Federal work force had initiated Bicentennial programs. Some were intended primarily for employees, while others involved the general public. The potential impact of these Federal programs was impressive. The number of visitors to the facilities of the National Park Service each year, for example, was roughly equivalent to the entire population of the United States.

As principal custodians of the nation's documents and artifacts, the National Archives, the Smithsonian Institution, and the Library of Congress were expected to take a prominent role in the year's commemorations.

At 6:00 p.m. on September 13, the Archives began its 87-hour vigil for the Constitution. During the next three and one-half days, round the clock until 9:00 a.m. on September 17, some 21,000 visitors entered the Rotunda to view the Constitution, displayed in its entirety. A series of events, including concerts and dramatizations, were presented during the vigil, as well as two exhibits, "The American Experiment: Creating the Constitution" and "The American Experiment: Living with the Constitution." During the course of the year, the National Archives also sponsored a lecture series, symposia and debates, and a Constitution film festival.

The many facilities of the Smithsonian also played their part in reaching millions of Americans and foreign visitors with educational programs about the Bicentennial. In May it hosted, together with the ABA and the University of Virginia, an international conference on "Constitutional Roots, Rights, and Responsibilities," in which more than 70 scholars, jurists, and educators from around the world participated. The Smithsonian's Museum of American History staged an exhibit, "The Blessings of Liberty," that examined the development of the American political process under the Constitution.

Once the custodian of the Declaration of Independence and the Constitution, the Library of Congress commemorated the Bicentennial with an exhibit of its own, "The American Solution: The Origins of the U.S. Constitution," featuring some 200 original manuscripts and printed materials from the Founding era. The Library also published, in association with the Arion Press, its own limited edition of the Constitution, with a preface by Chief Justice Burger and an introduction by the Librarian of Congress, Daniel Boorstin.

The Library also cosponsored with the Commission the acquisition of the manuscripts of Jean de Crevecoeur, including his *Letters from an American Farmer*, which did as much as any writing to introduce the new nation to the rest of the world. The Commission and the Foundation for the Commemoration of the U.S.

At *Franklin and Marshall College, students, faculty, and alumni held scholarly, cultural, and festive activities on the Constitution during the year.*

The Bicentennial
of the Constitution of
the United States
of America

1787-1987   USA 22

We the people
of the United States,
in order to form
a more perfect Union...

Preamble, U.S. Constitution   USA 22

Establish justice,
insure domestic tranquility,
provide for the common defense,
promote the general welfare...

Preamble, U.S. Constitution   USA 22

And secure
the blessings of liberty
to ourselves
and our posterity...

Preamble, U.S. Constitution   USA 22

Do ordain
and establish this
Constitution for the
United States of America.

Preamble, U.S. Constitution   USA 22

*Special stamps
issued by the
U.S. Postal Service
throughout the
commemoration
included a block
of five stamps
with the Preamble,
and the
Constitution stamp.*

U.S. Constitution

We the People

1787-1987 22 USA

Constitution acquired this work, together with 23 other essays and letters, through a grant of $400,000 from the Morris and Gwendolyn Cafritz Foundation, and then presented the manuscripts to the Library of Congress for permanent keeping.

In May, Professor Forrest McDonald, a scholar of the Founding Era, delivered NEH's 1987 Jefferson Lecture in the Humanities in the Great Hall of the National Building Museum in Washington, D.C. Pro-fessor McDonald's presentation, "The Intellectual World of the Founding Fathers," offered a learned and eloquent defense of the brilliance of the Constitution's Framers, "the likes of which we shall not see again."

The many other initiatives of the NEH in support of the Bicentennial have been summarized in Chapter II. Many of its funded projects were undertaken by state Humanities Councils. The Kansas Committee for the Humanities, for example, sponsored a monthlong living history program called STAR ("Striving Toward America's Roots") that allowed citizens of various locations around the state to learn more about the fundamental principles of the Constitution through a series of mock debates, reading and discussion programs, seminars, and slide presentations. The Pennsylvania Humanities Council sponsored a series of reading and discussion groups on the U.S. Constitution in a program held at the Pennsylvania State University/Schuylkill Campus. The Maryland Humanities Council issued a poster, "The Annapolis Connection: Maryland and the U.S. Constitution," commemorating the Annapolis Convention. The Federation of State Humanities Councils, with an NEH grant, produced *Celebrating the Constitution: A Guide for Public Programs in the Humanities*, offering suggestions and a step-by-step guide for Bicentennial activities sponsored by local civic and educational groups.

The National Park Service, whose facilities at Independence Park in Philadelphia became the principal geographic focus for this Bicentennial year, used all of its facilities nationwide to promote the commemoration, through programs described earlier. The National Park Service's staff there also took the lead in organizing a "Rocks Across America" project, which envisioned the construction of a "Fountain of Freedom" for the facility, constructed of geologically representative specimens from each of the 50 states. With the assistance of both government and private foundation support, the National Park Foundation began the renovation of New York City's Federal Hall, and its transformation into an educational center (*see Chapter V*).

The U.S. Postal Service introduced a new series of stamps in honor of the Bicentennial. Subjects of the 1987 issues included the opening of the Constitutional Convention and the signing of the Constitution. The National Archives was the site of first-day-of-issue ceremonies in August for a booklet of 22-cent stamps, each featuring a portion of the Constitution's Preamble. The year also saw three stamps issued in honor of Delaware, Pennsylvania, and New Jersey, the first states to ratify the Constitution. Numismatists as well as philatelists benefited from this commemorative year. The U.S. Mint issued silver and gold commemorative coins in honor of the Bicentennial. The U.S. Constitution Coin Program was unveiled by Secretary of the Treasury James A. Baker in ceremonies at Philadelphia on July 1. A two-coin gold and silver proof set sold for $250. The Mint received initial orders for more than 2 million coins. During the commemoration, the public purchased more than $52 million worth of these coins from the U.S. Treasury.

Expressing America's success in providing for two centuries a military under constitutional and civilian control, DOD established itself as the most active of all the permanent Federal agencies in honoring the Bicentennial. Under the leadership of the Department of the Army, DOD initiated an impressive array of programs and publications during 1987. Focusing on the military's contributions to the Constitution, the Army continued its "Soldier-Statesmen" theme with videotapes and booklets on the men who signed the Constitution and who also fought in the Revolution. The Army also produced the first in a series of *Bicentennial Resource Guides*, offering a variety of suggested activities and background materials for Bicentennial observance.

Special events sponsored by DOD included a series of lectures on the Constitution, conducted by the Center for Military History at the National Defense University; a promotional record album produced by the U.S. Army Field Band, which featured a special composition, "We the People"; and a 200-mile relay run, sponsored by the U.S. Army Training and Doctrine Command (TRADOC), in which participants carried copies of the Constitution from the National Archives to Fort Monroe, Virginia.

Though the Department of the Army was the most active of the Services during the years of the Bicentennial, it was not the only one to get involved. Anticipating the salute of its sister ship, the *USS Eisenhower* on September 16 (see *Prologue*), in April the aircraft carrier *USS Ranger* assembled 1,350 sailors to configure "We the People" on its flight deck. In Boston harbor, the *USS Constitution*, celebrating its 190th birthday, provided the centerpiece for a series of activities during Constitution Week. On September 17 "Old Ironsides" served as the stage of a naturalization service, in which 100 immigrants became U.S. citizens. In addition to other commemorative activities, the Air Force arranged for "flybys" at Bicentennial events across the country.

To stimulate participation on the part of U.S. military installations around the world, the Commission joined with DOD to establish a Bicentennial Defense Communities Program. Similar to the Commission's DBC program for cities and towns, it provided for Commission recognition of defense communities whose

A *bald eagle against a flag backdrop was the visual theme used by the Department of Defense in many of its Bicentennial projects.*

United States Constitution Bicentennial

1787–1791 / 1987–1991

"*provide for the common defence - secure the Blessings of Liberty*"

On the USS Ranger, 1,350 sailors spell out three historic words.

PH3 Ron Wimmer/U.S. Navy Photo

Bicentennial applications had been approved by DOD.

As noted, some Federal agency programs were directed at government employees. A prime example was the Bicentennial program sponsored by the Office of Personnel Management. OPM dedicated a week in June to honoring the Constitution. The program included the opening of OPM's Bicentennial Civil Service exhibit, the showing of a film series on the Constitution, and a special ceremony at which OPM honored its employees for their role in America's constitutional system of government.

STATES AND COMMUNITIES

By May 1987, Nebraska, Texas, and Arkansas had formally established their own Bicentennial Commissions, thus making all 50 states (as well as the District of Columbia, Puerto Rico, and the Virgin Islands) official participants in the commemoration. By the time of the September celebrations, the Commission had also recognized over 1,800 DBCs throughout the country, with every state represented. The numbers did not necessarily correspond to population. Georgia led the way with 159 DBCs, one in each of that state's counties. New York State was second with 111, and North Carolina third with 88. Several states with relatively small populations, especially in the west, established an impressive number of DBCs. Utah, for example, had 47, Wyoming 22.

These state Commissions and DBCs took the initiative in sponsoring programs and events of their own. The New Hampshire Bicentennial Commission, the first to be created (1981), for example, began a joint program with the state's Humanities Council to research life in New Hampshire during the Founding Era. It selected eight communities as representative sites where historians, antiquarians, and other scholars studied all aspects of life as it was lived in those locations two centuries before. The research results were subsequently published in an illustrated book.

To help prepare these state Commissions and DBCs for the upcoming celebrations, the national Commission began its first series of regional meetings in February 1987, with a gathering of Midwest Bicentennial leaders in Chicago. In the next four months additional meetings were held in Charleston, South Carolina; Phoenix, Arizona; Princeton, New Jersey; Great Falls, Montana; and Boston, Massachusetts.

The first regional meeting in Chicago on February 6-7 illustrates the tenor and purpose of these events. State Commission Directors, Commissioners, and staff from six states in the Midwest attended the meeting and were joined by national Commissioners Phyllis Schlafly and William Lucas. The meeting was cosponsored by the national and the Illinois Commissions, with the latter serving as host. Officials from DBCs in Illinois, Michigan, Indiana, Wisconsin, Ohio, and Iowa also participated. This gathering provided a forum for the exchange of ideas among national, state, and local officials. It also allowed the national Commission representatives to brief attendees, as well as the media, on the Commission's plans. While in Chicago, Commissioners Schlafly and Lucas generated additional media attention as guests on a radio talk show and at a meeting with the *Chicago Sun-Times* editorial board. They also had an opportunity to meet with students in government classes at two area high schools.

Throughout the spring and early summer months, the Commission kept the state Commissions and DBCs informed and mobilized through a steady stream of communications. The investment in these networks paid off handsomely during the Bicentennial celebrations. Combining national programs and encouragement with local interest and opportunity, this galaxy of communities across the land demonstrated that there were almost limitless ways to commemorate the Bicentennial. A small sampling gives some idea of the diverse ways in which "hometown" America chose to celebrate.

Odessa, Delaware, for example, held a town festival in the traditional mold on September 12 in honor of the Bicentennial. Festivities included a reenactment of a Constitution ratification debate in period costume (with partisans orating from farm wagons), a bonfire, an ox roast, and a fife and drum parade. Bar Harbor, Maine, began September 17 with a sunrise service on the summit of Cadillac Mountain. Similar ceremonies elsewhere in Maine and along the eastern seaboard welcomed the dawn of this anniversary day. At the opposite end of the country, Buena Park, California, was the focus of the California Commission's activities on the 17th. Events there included the unveiling of a sand replica of Independence Hall at a local beach, naturalization ceremonies in the town's own Independence Hall (itself a replica of the original), a signing ceremony, and a Governor's Ball.

Fort Pierce, Florida, distributed 20,000 Bicentennial Bookmarks (designed by the winner of a special contest) throughout the local public school system and libraries; the town also planted a "Constitutional oak tree" at the city hall. Several longitudes and latitudes away, the University of Alaska's Bicentennial Committee chose a participant in the state's famous dogsled race, the Iditarod, to carry a copy of the Constitution on the thousand-mile route from Anchorage to Nome. Kokomo, Indiana, reenacted the signing of the Constitution at a natural earth stage created specifically for the event

Commissioners William Lucas and Phyllis Schlafly at a regional meeting in Chicago.

at Indiana State University at Kokomo. Various topics at the Constitutional Convention were debated. The Kokomo Symphony and Boys Choir performed a Bicentennial concert, which was followed by fireworks.

Helena, Montana, hosted a public ceremony on September 17 at the state capitol. The ceremony included a posting of the Colors, a gun salute by the National Guard, a flyover of F-16 fighter aircraft, and an address on the Constitution by a State Supreme Court Justice. Citizens throughout the state then participated in a 200-second bell-ringing. Scottsdale, Arizona, honored the 17th with a Bicentennial breakfast and two days later hosted an eighteenth-century festival on the

Scottsdale mall, featuring a student reenactment of the Constitutional Convention, a quilting exhibit and town criers, as well as arts, crafts, and music from the Founding Era.

Large cities as well as small towns got in on the act. New Orleans, Louisiana, chose Sunday, September 20, as its day of celebration. Activities included a morning mass at St. Louis Cathedral, a military parade and tree-planting in Jackson Square, a "Heritage Festival" with music in the French Market, student choirs and bands performing in the French Quarter, and an outdoor musical extravaganza with the New Orleans Symphony, accompanied by fireworks, cannonades, and the ringing of church bells. Chicago, Illinois, paid tribute to the Constitution on September 17 at a baseball game in old Comiskey Park. In a pregame program, Armed Forces bands performed in center field, and were followed by a parade representing Illinois's DBCs and Chicago's many ethnic groups. The national anthem was followed by a 21-gun salute and the release of 200 white doves and 10,000 balloons. The game itself was followed by a dramatic reading of the Preamble and a 10-minute fireworks display.

The Commission's network of DBCs included two Native American communities, which took the occasion the honor their own ethnic heritage. The Sac and Fox Tribe of Stroud, Oklahoma, celebrated the Bicentennial in conjunction with the Annual Sac and Fox Day. The Retro-Sparks Indian Colony in Nevada sponsored educational programs examining the impact of the Constitution's thought upon tribal self-determination and the elements of constitutional principles embodied in tribal relationships.

With the American "Main Street" of yesteryear having given way to the modern shopping mall, it was perhaps fitting that several of the year's commemorative programs took place in the latter. For example, the Great Northern Mall and Plaza of North Olmstead, Ohio (a DBC), offered a yearlong Bicentennial program, "The Great American Spirit," which included a junior and senior high school essay contest, a photo contest, and a musical salute.

PRIVATE, NONPROFIT, AND RELIGIOUS ORGANIZATIONS

A century and a half ago, Alexis de Tocqueville noted as one of the peculiar characteristics and strengths of America the capacity of its citizens to join together in private association, often in matters affecting the public weal. Perhaps there is no better testimony of the blessings of liberty under the Constitution than the thousands of private groups in American society, many of which contributed to the Bicentennial in 1987.

As already noted, the nation's major civic and service organizations took important leadership roles in the year's commemorative activities. Organizations such as the Masons, the DAR, the American Legion, and the Veterans of Foreign Wars sponsored academic contests and other educational programs. Many featured the Bicentennial in special editions of their magazines or

New Orleans, Louisiana/Charles Daehler

Helena, Montana/Tom Malee

Cadillac Mountain, Maine/Maria Higgins

Los Angeles County, California/NSA World Tribune Press

Community
*Bicentennial celebrations:
a Constitutional Convention
reenactment (top), a Heritage
Festival in New Orleans
(above), a flyover in Helena,
Montana (right), a sunrise
service on Cadillac Mountain,
Maine (far right, above),
and a community event in
San Diego, California
(right, below).*

Gilbert, Arizona

Salina, Kansas/Terry Evans

SALINE COUNTY HISTORICAL SOCIETY

A *Colonial bell-ringing in Saline County, Kansas (above).*

Camden — Wyoming, Delaware/Adriana Daniels

A *very popular Bicentennial program invited citizens of all ages to read and sign their names to a copy of the Constitution. Sign-on ceremonies took place in schools, malls, courts, and town halls nationwide (above).*

Drafting and Signing   81

The 600-foot-high Gateway Arch in St. Louis flew a gigantic flag to celebrate the Constitution (right). St. Louis dedicated its annual July 4th Veiled Prophet Fair to the Bicentennial, featuring a naturalization ceremony for 300 people at which Chief Justice Burger presided. American Legion posts placed Bicentennial Billboards all around the country (below).

newsletters. The Benevolent and Protective Order of Elks sponsored a portion of the ceremonies at Philadelphia on September 17. In addition to its oratorical contest, the American Legion placed "Bicentennial Billboards" all around the nation. Its Bicentennial program also included the publication of a one-act play on the Constitution, a Bicentennial coloring book for elementary school students, and distribution of copies of the Constitution. The Pennsylvania, New Jersey, and Delaware State Societies of the DAR commissioned artist Louis S. Glanzman to execute a painting of the Signing of the Constitution. The original was donated to Independence Park, and copies were made available

through the Eastern National Park & Monument Association.

The League of Women Voters, working with Project '87, sponsored two public forums on constitutional issues: "Mr. Madison's Constitution and the Twenty-first Century" and "The Constitution and the Courts: Text, Original Intent, and the Changing Social Order." The sponsors made available videotapes and discussion guides from these forums. The Council for the Advancement of Citizenship, in conjunction with the Center for Civic Education and the national Commission, sponsored a series of Bicentennial Leadership Workshops at several locations around the country. The series would continue throughout the years of the Bicentennial and thereby provide another important network for commemorative activities.

The Eagle Forum, whose president was Commissioner Phyllis Schlafly, put together a slide presentation on the Constitution. That same organization's Education and Legal Defense Fund produced a one-minute jingle, "Standing Proud for the Constitution," for use on radio as a public service announcement. The American Civil Liberties Union produced a radio series, "The Bill of Rights Radio Education Project," first broadcast in 1982. In 13 half-hour programs, the series examined current constitutional issues. The National Consumer Council took "Consumers Celebrate the Constitution" as its theme for Consumer Week 87. Held in April, this annual event took notice of the role that consumers play in the American system of free enterprise. With the help of Sears Roebuck, the Council arranged for posters and brochures with Bicentennial messages to appear in stores and other locations around the country. The American Association of Retired Persons produced a series of booklets and a videotape on constitutional issues for use by senior citizens. The program was based on the public television series, "The U.S. Constitution: That Delicate Balance."

Among the many ethnic organizations that took the occasion of the Bicentennial to celebrate their own respective contributions to the American experience was the Tuskegee Airmen, Inc., an organization of African-American pilots, renowned for their distinguished service during World War II. The organization saluted the Constitution at its annual meeting and encouraged the member chapters to undertake Bicentennial activities of their own.

Professional associations of all sorts also took a prominent role. The American Hotel & Motel Association produced a series of television, radio, and print ads, as well as a resource kit that it distributed to 10,000 of its members. The kit included a plan for hosting a "Colonial Open House" during "American Hospitality Weekend" (May 16-17), historical quotations and anecdotes to be included on menus and service cards, as well as camera-ready artwork and ad slicks. During the year the Association's members also distributed POCKET CONSTITUTIONS to guests.

Not only the great national libraries and archives, but thousands of state and local libraries, museums, historical societies, and other repositories of learning sponsored Bicentennial programs during the year. The New York Public Library's celebration of the Bicentennial, for example, included an exhibit, "Are We to Be a Nation? The Making of the Federal Constitution," and the American Library Association sponsored a national tour of an exhibit based upon the same theme. In May the Harry S. Truman Library in Independence, Missouri, hosted a "Constitutional Olympics," in which Missouri high school students tested their knowledge of the Constitution. The Missouri chapter of the DAR sponsored the event.

Together with the Virginia State Commission and the U.S. Army, the National Trust for Historic Preservation sponsored the formal opening of James Madison's home at Montpelier. The dedication ceremonies on March 15, the day before the 236th anniversary of Madison's birth, marked the beginning of several Bicentennial events at this historical location, available for the first time to the public after many years under private ownership.

Many state historical societies sponsored exhibits, lecture series, and other programs. The Pennsylvania Historical Society offered, with the city of Philadelphia as cosponsor, a summer History Camp program for students on the subject, "Constitutional Celebrations in Philadelphia." With the assistance of professional historians, the young participants enjoyed a program of discussions, field trips, and work with historical documents and artifacts. The Society also produced a three-part exhibit on the evolution of the Constitution. In another creative effort to reach younger Americans, the Friends of Independence National Historical Park produced a series of trading cards with likenesses and biographies of the Framers of the Constitution. Each of the 55 delegates at Philadelphia was represented in the set, designed in the style of baseball cards. The project was funded by NEH.

The "living museum" of Williamsburg, of course, was the location for a series of Bicentennial activities during the course of the year, including teacher workshops, special walking tours, and the mock Constitutional Convention described above. Another living museum, Old Sturbridge Village in Massachusetts, hosted a variety of projects and programs on the Bicentennial.

It is not surprising that the nation's religious institutions joined in the year's celebrations. For many, the Constitution's anniversary was cause for gratitude for the freedom of religion guaranteed by the First Amendment, as well as an inspiring example of the workings of Providence in the affairs of humanity. The participation of churches, synagogues, and other houses of worship was imperative to the success of several Bicentennial projects, including BELLS ACROSS AMERICA.

At a meeting in June, representatives of various denominations briefed the Commission on their plans for the year. Among the many events planned: the National City Christian Church of the Disciples of Christ sponsored its own nationwide "sign-on" to the Constitution. The nation's Jesuit colleges offered a series of symposia on freedom of religion. NSSA, the parent organization of American Buddhists, sponsored a "New Freedom Bell" project in which a replica of the Liberty Bell toured the nation and was presented to the city of Philadelphia. B'nai B'rith created a Bicentennial Constitutional Sabbath Project, focusing on the parallels between American constitutionalism and the Judaic heritage. The National Thanksgiving Foundation, with

CONSTITUTIONAL CONVENTION DELEGATE
Virginia

GEORGE WASHINGTON
1732-1799

A *set of "trading cards," featuring images of the Constitution's Framers, was produced by the Friends of the National Historical Park.*

the assistance of the Conference of Mayors and other organizations, sponsored a "National Year of Thanksgiving" for the blessings of the Constitution. The program was highlighted by Thanksgiving dinners on November 22, in which all Americans were urged to participate. Observed at hundreds of locations around the country, the dinner also served as a fund-raiser for needy charities.

Acknowledging the importance of volunteerism to the success of the American experiment in self-government, and to the work of the Bicentennial, the National Center declared April 26-May 2 "National Volunteer Week — Our Constitutional Heritage." The 400 Volunteer Centers around the country were urged to respond to the volunteer needs of state and local Bicentennial Commissions.

PRIVATE CORPORATIONS

Perhaps no event better symbolized corporate America's commitment to the Bicentennial than the New York Stock Exchange's suspension of its activities for several minutes on September 16, in order to join in the national Pledge of Allegiance. Some 2,000 traders on the floor of the Exchange watched the Washington, D.C., ceremonies on a big-screen television. Despite funding and in-kind support from the various levels of government, the Bicentennial would not have been possible without the generous assistance of American business. Events such as the ROADS TO LIBERTY TOUR, the NATIONAL BICENTENNIAL WRITING COMPETITION, A CELEBRATION OF CITIZENSHIP, and the events of WE THE PEOPLE 200 in Philadelphia were substantially underwritten by corporations like American Express, Gannett/*USA Today*, Xerox, Polaroid, Nabisco, Merrill Lynch, IBM, AT&T, and the Bell System.

A few additional examples will illustrate the variety and extent of projects developed by corporations during the Bicentennial year, many of them in cooperation with

© Neil Schneider, *New York Post*

The New York Stock Exchange suspends trading on September 16, 1987, to commemorate the Constitution (above); one of four McDonald's commemorative trayliners (right).

the Commission's Marketing Division. They proved effective in their own way in educating Americans of all ages about the Constitution.

General Mills included on 100 million of its cereal boxes historical vignettes about the Constitution and the Founders, and distributed them through food stores nationwide. McDonald's Corporation printed a series of four placemat trayliners including the Preamble, as well as educational pieces and pictures about the Constitution. Millions of sets were distributed to McDonald's franchises. The Eveready Battery Company published a collection of Constitutional documents and offered them during 1987 to the general public. As noted in Chapter II, several corporations printed and distributed copies of the Commission's POCKET CONSTITUTION or special editions of their own.

Apple Computers, Inc., and Scholastic Hardware collaborated on a computer/interactive video exhibit at the National Archives, entitled "Would You Have Signed the Constitution?" Ace Hardware sponsored an educational program on the Constitution for grade school teachers in each of its nearly 5,000 market areas throughout the nation. In cosponsorship with the Commission, West Publishing Company of St. Paul, Minnesota, commissioned an oil painting of the Constitutional Convention by the artist, Alton S. Tobey. Copies of the painting, "A More Perfect Union," were sent to every high school in the country. Not only large companies and corporations participated in the Bicentennial. For example, the Pasqua Coffee Bars, a California chain, distributed copies of the Commission's Pocket Constitution to its customers on September 17.

MEDIA

As activities and projects proliferated, the Bicentennial became increasingly interesting to the media, whose attention was drawn to both the commemorative activities and the subject of the Constitution itself. The commemoration provided many opportunities, not only in straight news coverage, but in feature pieces and editorials as well, to examine the story of the making of the Constitution, the lives of those who brought the document into being, and the relevance of the document to contemporary American life. Even if some of the coverage was critical of the Constitution and its celebration — focusing, for example, on the Constitution's failure to resolve the issue of slavery — it prompted attention and debate about its subject.

The Communications Advisory Committee, created in late 1986 and formally introduced at a public hearing of the Commission meeting on January 23, 1987, became an effective resource in this effort. Comprising executives from major media organizations in broadcast, cable, and print journalism, the Committee was organized to advise the Commission and help coordinate media efforts on behalf of the Bicentennial. The Committee was chaired by Edward O. Fritts, president of the National Association of Broadcasters (NAB). Jerry Friedheim, executive vice president and general manager of the American Newspaper Publishers Association, served as vice chairman.

General Mills includes historical vignettes on their cereal boxes.

Cheerios

THE CONSTITUTION
THE WORDS WE LIVE BY
☆☆☆☆☆☆☆☆☆☆☆

The Birth of a Nation.

In the year 1787, the United States was united in name only. Individual states had their own governments and were reluctant to give up any of the independence they had fought so hard for in the Revolutionary War.

The Constitution was the document that first spelled out exactly how our national government would be organized and operated. After four months of sometimes heated debate, it was signed by its authors or "Founding Fathers" on September 17, 1787, and approved later by the 13 original states.

The Constitution establishes the foundations of our federal government, the powers of Congress and the President, our court system and the relations between the states.

In 1789, James Madison introduced in Congress the Bill of Rights, which was added to protect the rights of individuals including: freedom of religion and speech, freedom of the press, the right to trial by jury, and more. In 1791, the Bill of Rights was ratified by the States and became part of the Constitution.

This educational program has been officially recognized by the Commission on the Bicentennial of the United States Constitution.

Series No. **6**

All of the networks, including CNN and C-SPAN, offered Bicentennial programs in 1987. NAB made monthly satellite feeds to TV stations throughout the country, informing them of Bicentennial events and encouraging stations to work with their state and local Bicentennial Commissions. NAB also distributed to radio broadcasters a series of 110 scripts on historical events in the Founding era and public service announcements on the Constitution. C-SPAN featured a weekly series, "Inside the Constitution."

Three programs underwritten by the General Motors Corporation represented a collaborative effort by the Public Broadcasting Service and commentator Bill Moyers. The first of these, "In Search of the Constitution," was a 10-part series produced by WNET-TV New York and WTVS-TV Detroit and was broadcast from April through September. The hour-long segments included interviews by Moyers of historians, educators, judges, and other constitutional experts. A second project, produced by the same two stations, was a single 90-minute show. Broadcast in September, "Moyers: In Search of the Constitution" focused on the impact of the Constitution today. A third television series on the Constitution, "Philadelphia Journal," ran from May through September. It consisted of nightly three-minute film reports from Philadelphia, with Moyers in effect "covering" the events of the 1787 Convention for each of

the days it was in session. ABC's coverage of A CELEBRATION OF CITIZENSHIP and its three-hour educational special on the evening of September 16 have already been noted.

The print media response to the Bicentennial was overwhelming. The Constitution became a frequent subject in almost every newspaper in the United States, from major national papers like *The New York Times and The Los Angeles Times* to small-town dailies and weeklies. Newspapers such as *The Chicago Tribune* dedicated their Sunday magazines to special issues on the Bicentennial. A special 12-page Bicentennial supplement produced by the Commission was reprinted in most of the 5,000 member papers of the National Newspaper Association, representing small dailies and weeklies reaching 30 million readers.

The media's extensive coverage of the Bicentennial in 1987 was recognized at a special awards ceremony in April 1988, at the National Press Club, where Commissioner Lynne Cheney presented the Benjamin Franklin Journalism Awards for outstanding newspaper and magazine writing on the Bicentennial and the Alexander Hamilton/Ohio State University Awards for outstanding radio and television coverage.

The Benjamin Franklin Awards, cosponsored by the national Commission and the National Press Foundation, recognized four examples of writing excel-

The cover of Time *magazine's special Bicentennial edition.*

lence on the subject of the Constitution's "import and impact on the nation and its people." These winners included a special supplement piece written by Jonathan Storm of *The Philadelphia Inquirer*, a series of articles by James C. Millstone of *The St. Louis Post-Dispatch*, a magazine article by Alice J. Hall of *National Geographic Magazine*, and an editorial piece by Jeffrey Hadden of *The Detroit News*. These winners were chosen from among 32 finalists.

The Alexander Hamilton/Ohio State Awards, cosponsored by the national Commission and the Ohio State University's Institute for Education by Radio-Television and administered by the University's public broadcasting stations, recognized eight examples of excellence in radio and television coverage "designed to instruct, inform, or enrich understanding about the Constitution of the United States." Recipients included "We the People," produced by television station KQED, San Francisco; "We Have Become a Nation," produced by radio station WMAL, Washington, D.C.; "Searching for Justice: Three American Stories," produced by WUSA-TV, Washington, D.C.; "The Living Constitution," produced by WBAL-TV, Baltimore; "The Constitution — the Virginia Connection," produced by WTKR-TV, Norfolk, Virginia; "A Matter of Honor," produced by Walter Teas, Illusion Inc., Baltimore; "The Benchbook," produced by WKSU-FM, Kent, Ohio; and "Main Street," produced by NBC Television, New York.

U.S. News & World Report, Time, People, American Heritage, Newsweek, and *TV Guide* were among the magazines that published substantial accounts of the Bicentennial. *Life* magazine prepared a special Bicentennial issue, which included the story of the creation of the Constitution, including portraits of the 55 delegates, a look at the various commemorative events and exhibits scheduled across the country in 1987, and photos of past celebrations related to American independence. Another Time-Life publication, *People* magazine, included in its end-of-the-year issue an article on the Framers of the Constitution and a two-page spread of Howard Chandler Christy's painting of the Signing. *Parade* magazine cosponsored a photo contest in association with Fuji Films, Inc., on the topic "A National Photo Contest for Everyone: We the People."

The anniversary year also prompted an avalanche of books and monographs, exceeding the numbers that had appeared the previous year in anticipation of the Bicentennial. Some of these publications were intended for scholars and other specialists on the Constitution; others reached a more general audience. William Peter's *A More Perfect Union: The Making of the U.S. Constitution,* published by Crown Publishers in March 1987, was featured as a Book-of-the-Month Club and History Book Club Alternate. It presented a dramatic account of the Philadelphia Convention and the thoughts and personalities of the delegates. Another Book-of-the-Month Club selection, *A Book of Days in American History,* offered historical facts for every day of the year. Barnes & Noble Books published *A Cartoon History of the United States* by the cartoonist Eric Lurio.

U.S. News & World Report's *special Constitutional issue.*

A series of 24 articles on the Constitution was written by the Commission's Chairman for syndication by the Associated Press. These articles appeared in hundreds of newspapers during the course of the year and were later adapted by Harcourt Brace into a textbook (*see Chapter VI*). Another series of articles published in 1987 was Jeffrey St. John's lively chronicle of the Constitutional Convention from the perspective of a journalist covering these events as they occurred. These articles were adapted later in the year into a book, *Constitutional Journal: A Correspondent's Report from the Convention of 1787,* copies of which the Commission would later distribute to schools and colleges (*see Chapter V*).

The published scholarship in 1987 also included a reissue of Max Farrand's *The Records of the Federal Convention of 1787,* incorporating a supplemental volume of new material edited by James H. Hutson of the Library of Congress. Garland Publishers, Inc., published a 20-volume series reproducing over 450 of the most important articles on the Constitution and related subjects. Titled *United States Constitutional and Legal History,* the series was edited by the historian, Kermit L. Hall. Richard Morris, one of the most distinguished historians of the Founding Era, published *The Forging of the Federal Union, 1781-1789.* His *The Framing of the Federal Constitution,* written originally for the National

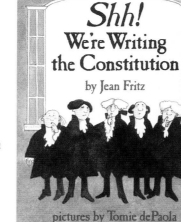

Jean Fritz's account of the Constitutional Convention, written for elementary students.

The need for younger readers to be exposed to interesting educational material about the Constitution was not overlooked. Jean Fritz, a member of the National Education Advisory Committee and noted author of children's books, published *Shh ... We're Writing a Constitution*, an account of the Constitutional Convention for elementary school students. Place in the Woods, a small independent publishing house in Minnesota, published *My Own Book*, by Roger Hammer. It included the text of the Constitution, together with a collection of short stories by child authors on how their respective cities, states, or schools got their names. Random House re-released several titles in its Landmark series of children's history books, including Dorothy Canfield Fisher's *Our Independence and the Constitution*.

One of the new books for children was *We the People: Bits, Bytes, and Highlights of the Constitution and Bill of Rights*, published by Storyviews. It was the story of two honeybees playing a computer game with the goal of discovering the "miracle" of the Constitution. Joan Anderson's *1787* was an historical novel for middle-

Park Service, was distributed to schools and colleges with the assistance of the Liberty Bell Foundation and the Commission.

In anticipation of 1988's ratification of the Constitution, Commissioner Thomas O'Connor, together with Alan Roger, published *This Momentous Affair: Massachusetts and the Ratification of the U.S. Constitution*. One of the Commission's staff, J. Jackson Barlow, was coeditor with Leonard Levy and Ken Masugi of a collection of essays entitled *The American Founding: Essays on the Formation of the Constitution*, which examined the philosophical roots of American constitutionalism. The year's titles also included Jethro Lieberman's *The Enduring Constitution*, Richard Vetterli's and Gary Bryner's *In Search of the Republic: Public Virtue and the Roots of American Government*, Walter Berns' *Taking the Constitution Seriously*, and Mortimer Adler's *We Hold These Truths*.

Sao Paulo, Brazil

Washington, D.C.

Manama, Bahrain

Vienna, Austria

Celebrating the Constitution worldwide: winners of the Latin American Essay Contest (top); Hong Kong officials with Commissioner Murphy in Washington (center); the U.S. Embassy in Bahrain (far left); Austrian composer R. Baumgartner rehearsing Missa Pacis *(left).*

graders about the writing of the Constitution as seen through the eyes of a teenage boy. Betty Debnam's series on the Constitution in *The Mini Page*, described in the previous chapter, continued to run in 1987 and reached millions of young Americans of elementary-school age.

INTERNATIONAL

As the preceding pages have shown, America's Bicentennial was not only a national event. A variety of programs, both in this country and abroad, had a significant impact overseas. Print, radio, and television coverage carried the major festivities around the world. USIA and its radio arm, the Voice of America, conducted programs focusing on the Bicentennial throughout the year. USIA published annotated and illustrated versions of the Constitution in English, Spanish, French, Arabic, Korean, Japanese, Dutch, Turkish, Indonesian, Finnish, and Nepalese for distribution abroad. It also developed a 50-panel poster exhibit and an exhibit of 125 books on the Constitution. Voice of America's series of semidocumentary broadcasts and talk shows on the Constitution continued through the year (*see Chapter II*).

Many Bicentennial programs directly involved overseas constituencies. American Embassies and Consulates, USIA stations, DOD's network of Bicentennial Defense Communities, other military bases, and Dependent Schools, as well as independent American schools abroad all participated in such programs as A Celebration of Citizenship and Bells Across America.

Many of the year's activities, in Philadelphia, Washington, D.C., and elsewhere were seen by thousands of foreign tourists. During the course of the year Chief Justice Burger and other Commissioners had many opportunities to meet with foreign dignitaries visiting this country. Commissioner Betty Southard Murphy, for example, met with a delegation of civil service representatives from Hong Kong to brief them on the Bicentennial in general and to examine in particular such topics as the overlapping roles of police authority in a Federal system and the status of the District of Columbia, subjects of special interest given the impending reversion of the Crown Colony to the People's Republic of China in 1997.

Visitors to this country were able to take advantage not only of exhibits and programs for the general public, but also some intended primarily for their benefit. "Constitutional Philadelphia," for example, offered a series of seminars on the Constitution designed specifically for a foreign audience. The International Visitors Center of Philadelphia sponsored the project with support from the J. Howard Pew Foundation and USIA.

The Foreign Policy Association focused on the Constitution in its 1987 "Great Decisions" program. Involving about 250,000 participants throughout the country, who met to discuss foreign policy issues and make recommendations on the basis of those discussions, this year's program focused on such topics as "The Constitution and Foreign Policy" and examined the Constitutional implications of a variety of current issues. One of the many conferences held abroad during the year was sponsored by the John Hopkins University-Bologna Center and the University of Rome. Meeting at the University of Bologna, the conference focused on the impact of the U.S. Constitution on European constitutions and the U.S. Constitution as an instrument for change, thereby reflecting the American pragmatic tradition.

The Bicentennial also stimulated interesting special projects. On July 1, as part of the year's celebrations in that city, Philadelphia hosted the world premiere of *Missa Pacis*, an orchestral-choral work by Austrian composer Roland Baumgartner. Undertaken with both government and private support, the composition was a gift to the people of America from the people of Austria and West Germany. In Great Britain, the American Franklin Friends Committee began a project to restore Benjamin Franklin's London residence. With support from the national Commission, the Committee sought to raise $2.5 million needed to restore the house and maintain it as a permanent museum about Franklin.

CONCLUSION

The Bicentennial commemoration of the drafting and signing of the Constitution offers a model for future commemorations of a similar kind. It combined a select number of special events (e.g., the ceremonies in Washington, D.C., and Philadelphia), providing a national focus for the Bicentennial, with a series of programs (e.g., A Celebration of Citizenship, Bells Across America, Plant A Living Legacy) designed to link those events to a vast number of local activities in the country and around the world. And it created networks that enabled the national Commission to work with the key organizations and agencies in an effective collaborative effort.

The Bicentennial year of 1987 affirmed not only the unity of America in its common ideals, but its diversity as well, in the myriad of ways Americans chose to affirm those ideals. Almost every corner of the land seemed to have been reached by this year of commemoration, in events that graced not only the most famous edifices of the nation but simpler venues as well: courthouses, churches, schoolhouses, and community centers. The celebration touched old and young, blue-collar and white-collar, and almost every ethnic group, each proud of its place in the tapestry of the American experience. The array of activities included reenactments, music and parades, martial pomp, proclamations and speeches, bell-ringings and bonfires, exhibits and tours, essay contests, dramatic productions, TV documentaries and extravaganzas, and a blizzard of publications — books, articles, editorials, feature stories, pamphlets, and posters. It was a bounty year for commemorative souvenirs and for actors — both professional and amateur—who could bring to life the images of Franklin, Madison, and other revered personages of the Founding era. Through a unity of purpose and the binding ties of modern communications the country became for a time a community — a national village — in which all could join, with solemnity and festivity, in thanksgiving for the blessings of liberty.

Dec 7, 1787 USA
Delaware 22

22 USA
Dec 12, 1787
Pennsylvania

Dec 18, 1787 USA
New Jersey 22

22 USA
January 2, 1788
Georgia

22 USA
January 9, 1788
Connecticut

22 USA
Feb 6, 1788
Massachusetts

April 28, 1788 USA
Maryland 22

25 USA
May 23, 1788
South Carolina

25 USA
June 21, 1788
New Hampshire

June 25, 1788 USA
Virginia 25

July 26, 1788 USA
New York 25

25 USA
November 21, 1789
North Carolina

25 USA
May 29, 1790 (Slater Mill, 1793)
Rhode Island

REDEUNT SATURNIA REGNA.

On the erection of the Eleventh PILLAR of the great Na-
tional DOME, we beg leave most sincerely to felicitate " OUR DEAR COUNTRY."

Rife it
will.

The FEDERAL EDIFICE.

1988

Ratification
by
the
States

*C*ommemorative
medal for 1988
(below left);
Project '87's
ratification poster
(left).

I‍n the aftermath of the commemoration of the drafting and signing of the Constitution, the Commission faced the task of sustaining the momentum of the five-year Bicentennial, only just begun. The Commission would build upon the success of its 1987 achievements during four more years of continuing activity. In so doing, it would ensure that the Bicentennial left an enduring legacy of appreciation for, and understanding of, the Constitution. To this end, the Commission joined with state and local Commissions, as well as other organizations and groups throughout the country, in extensive planning in the months following the September 1987 celebrations. This pause would be critical in charting the future course of the Bicentennial. Out of it emerged some of the commemoration's most important and successful initiatives.

Major Events

While this planning took place, the Bicentennial's focus in 1988 shifted from the national to the state level as the nation commemorated the ratification of the Constitution. Any assumption that the Bicentennial was "over" with the celebration of the Constitution's drafting and signing reflected a misreading of history. Acceptance of the Constitution was by no means assured when the delegates at Philadelphia concluded their work and presented the new frame of government to the Confederation Congress, which in turn referred the document to state ratification conventions. The ideas embraced in the draft sent to the Confederation Congress were so new to many, there were even suggestions that the delegates sent to Philadelphia be censured for exceeding their mandate simply to "revise" the Articles of Confederation. In the months that followed, more than 1,600 delegates at ratification conventions in most of the 13 states debated the merits of the proposed Constitution. But for a handful of votes in two or three critical states, the issue of the Constitution's acceptance might have gone another way — and with it the course of American history.

With the possible exception of the conflict leading to the Civil War, the struggle for the Constitution's ratification represents the only occasion in American history of a national debate over the seminal principles of government. Both sides believed passionately in their cause, and both had formidable champions. Those who supported the new Constitution — called the Federalists — included Washington, Madison, Hamilton, John Jay, and Edmund Randolph among their ranks. Those who opposed acceptance of the new plan of government were called Anti-Federalists, and they too had powerful advocates in such legendary figures as Patrick Henry, George Mason, Luther Martin, and Elbridge Gerry. This great debate produced some of the finest political writing of all time. It illuminated for future generations the key principles of American constitutionalism. Even though the Federalist cause prevailed in the end, the Anti-Federalists left their own enduring legacy in the subsequent passage of the Bill of Rights.

In its own way, then, the story of the Constitution's ratification was an episode in the Bicentennial as important as the document's creation. Its commemoration began with the anniversary of Delaware's ratification on December 7, 1987 — the first state to ratify — and continued through the anniversary of New Hampshire's acceptance of the Constitution on June 21, 1988. New Hampshire's ratification was the ninth, the number required to approve the Constitution and bring the new government into effect. But subsequent anniversaries were important, too, including those of Virginia's and New York's ratifications, without which the new union created by the Constitution would scarcely have been viable. Indeed, the Bicentennial of the Constitution's ratification provided the occasion for all 50 states to celebrate the anniversaries of their statehood. A selective description of these commemorative activities follows, with a focus on the first and last of the states needed to ratify the Constitution, as well as on three others whose actions were critical to ratification.

STATE RATIFICATION CELEBRATIONS

Delaware: On December 7, 1787, after meeting for four days at the Golden Fleece Tavern in Dover, all 30 delegates of Delaware's ratification convention signed their approval of the Constitution. Their concerns about a stronger national government had all been resolved during the Constitutional Convention. As citizens of the smallest, least-populated state in the nation, Delaware's delegates to the Convention wanted to make sure that their state would have equal representation in at least one branch of the legislature. The Great Compromise accomplished this by providing for all states an equal vote in the Senate and proportional representation in the House of Representatives. Delaware's delegates also wanted the assurance that Congress would no longer have to requisition money from the states. When the Convention gave Congress the power to raise money directly through taxation and the collection of duties, imposts, and excises, Delaware responded with a prompt and unanimous ratification of the Constitution.

Delaware Governor Michael N. Castle served as the state's official host and master of ceremonies during the commemorative events held in Dover on December 7,

Delaware Bicentennial Commission (3)

Governor Castle opens the Ratification celebrations in Dover, Delaware (far left); a commemorative plaque at the Golden Fleece Tavern (left); a high school band at the parade (below).

State House, Boston, Mass.

1987. Chief Justice Warren Burger, representing the Commission, joined the Governor in dedicating a plaque at the Golden Fleece Tavern, site of Delaware's ratification 200 years earlier. Members of the Delaware General Assembly, many in Colonial attire, convened in Legislative Hall. Invoking both the words of the original 1787 ratification document and those of a new resolution, they endorsed the Constitution. Visiting a fourth-grade class at East Dover Elementary School, the Chairman borrowed a phrase from one pupil's essay on the subject to explain the Constitution to the children: "It tells you when to stop and how far you can go."

A three-hour "First State Parade," which passed Legislative Hall, included bands, fife and drum units, an assortment of floats, and a "flyby" of an Air Force C-5A cargo plane. A public program featured remarks by several delegates as well as music by a Bicentennial Chorus. Public entertainment and educational films were available throughout the day, and "Celebrate the First State," Delaware's state history film, ran continuously at the Visitors' Center. Later, Delawareans and others viewed a laser light show projected onto a 40' x 60' screen, and 1,500 people gathered at Dover Air Force Base for a Ratification ball sponsored by Merrill Lynch & Co., Inc. The latter event raised $100,000 for the First State Constitutional Scholarship program to award four-year scholarships annually to outstanding Delaware high school students planning to study political science or government at a Delaware public college or university.

Massachusetts: Following approval by Delaware, Pennsylvania, New Jersey, Georgia, and Connecticut, Massachusetts became the sixth state to ratify the Constitution. Despite significant opposition in some states, especially in Pennsylvania where the demand for a bill of rights was first raised, the Constitution had so far been readily accepted with comfortable majorities. Massachusetts, which had been deeply divided by the recent Shays' Rebellion and where the Anti-Federalist camp was strong, presented the document's first serious test. If defeated in Massachusetts, the Constitution might be

New Hampshire Bicentennial Commission (2)

doomed in the still more critical state conventions to come. Three hundred fifty-five delegates convened at the Boston State House on January 9, 1788. Though initially outnumbered, the Federalists employed skillful political stratagems to secure the support of potential adversaries such as Governor John Hancock and Sam Adams. In the end, the Federalists' endorsement of a bill of rights proved decisive in securing a victory on February 6, when the convention voted 187 to 168 in favor of the Constitution. Boston "went wild with joy" in celebration as bells rang and cannons boomed throughout the city.

Two hundred years later, on Saturday morning, February 6, 1988, students from 240 high schools in Massachusetts and Maine (part of Massachusetts during the Founding Era) gathered in the chambers of the State House in Boston to recreate the original ratification convention. The reenactment was sponsored by the Massachusetts Council for the Social Studies and funded by a $50,000 grant from the national Commission. In preparation for the event, the participating students (designated "John Hancock Scholars") teamed with

Ratification celebration in Concord, New Hampshire;
painting of the Massachusetts Ratification convention at the State House in Boston (opposite page).

their teachers ("John Hancock Fellows") to do historical research. The young historical "reenactors," dressed in period costumes to resemble John Hancock, Sam Adams, and other Bay State leaders, debated controversial political issues and proposed amendments that would eventually be adopted as the Bill of Rights. One student from Belchertown, Massachusetts, Keith V. Kaplan, won special praise for the work he did in transcribing the original 1788 diary of an Anti-Federalist delegate, Justus Dwight. The diary, which had been recently unearthed by Kaplan's teacher, Robert Hansbury, added new insights into the political dynamics of the Massachusetts convention.

New Hampshire: On June 21, 1788, New Hampshire became the ninth state to ratify the Constitution when a convention of the delegates from the state's townships meeting in Concord voted 57-47 to approve the document unconditionally. Since Article VII of the proposed Constitution declared that a new national government would be established once nine (of the existing 13) states approved, New Hampshire had the honor of being the deciding state. That honor, however, did not come easily. At first, a majority of state voters and convention delegates disapproved of the Constitution, however, pro-ratification forces outmaneuvered their opponents with delaying tactics and by taking advantage of developments elsewhere.

The Federalists arranged the scheduling of the state convention late enough to guarantee that Massachusetts would have made its decision beforehand. They hoped that an affirmative vote there would weaken resistance to ratification in New Hampshire. New Hampshire's convention convened in Exeter on February 13, 1788, one week after the Bay State ratified the Constitution. Though outnumbered, the Federalist delegates arrived early and with their temporary majority seized the initiative. By a narrow margin they prevented the taking of an official vote and arranged for an adjournment of the convention until June. The intervening four months allowed time for a gradual shift in the balance of power, aided by an aggressive Federalist campaign in the press. When word arrived shortly before the convention's reconvening in Concord that South Carolina had become the eighth state to ratify, New Hampshire's delegates seized the opportunity at hand to cast the deciding vote. The convention's approval of the Constitution on June 21 provided (in the words of convention president John Langdon) "the Key Stone in the great Arch" of the new union.

New Hampshire celebrated its historic role exactly 200 years later — on June 21, 1987 — with a daylong celebration in Exeter. It began with an ecumenical service at St. Paul's Episcopal Church, followed by a parade and the burial of a time capsule. Chief Justice Burger delivered the keynote address at dedication ceremonies in Representatives Hall, which was followed by the first-day-of-issue ceremony of a stamp commemorating New Hampshire's ratification, one of a series by the U.S. Postal Service (see page 90). The 25-cent stamp featured New Hampshire's most prominent symbol: a granite relief of "the Old Man of the Mountain."

Special exhibits, entertainment, and craft demonstrations took place throughout the day, which also included a New England lobster bake and a dance on the State House lawn. Chief Justice Burger led a group of schoolchildren in Colonial costume in the ringing of a replica of the Liberty Bell provided by the Liberty Bell Foundation. The U.S. Military Academy Band from West Point entertained the crowd with "The Constitutional Overture," composed by Dr. Hubert Bird of Keene State College. A Governor's reception, cosponsored by Merrill Lynch and the state Bicentennial Commission, acknowledged individuals and businesses that had made contributions to a fund for a continuing-education program in the state. The program, "New Hampshire Legacy," established an endowment for teacher workshops and seminars on issues relevant to the Constitution, the Bill of Rights, and New Hampshire history.

Virginia: Though Virginia's ratification of the Constitution on June 25 (just a few days after New Hampshire's) was not part of the required mandate, it was vital to the fledgling nation. Centrally located on the eastern seaboard, Virginia was the largest and wealthiest state and also the most important in terms of national leadership. The proposed new union could not survive without it. Virginia's acceptance of the Constitution came only after a tense, dramatic debate lasting three weeks. Most of the key figures in the state assembled in Richmond for the ratification convention, but the stage clearly belonged to Patrick Henry, a man of legendary eloquence. A year earlier, he had declined to be a delegate to the Philadelphia Convention, saying he "smelled a rat." That "rat" — the Constitution the delegates in Philadelphia had produced — was now before the delegates in Richmond, and Henry was determined to kill it. He was joined in his opposition by George Mason. James Madison — of small voice and stature, but great in intellect and learning and the principal architect of the Constitution—responded to Henry's arguments. He was supported by Virginia Governor Edmund Randolph and John Marshall—and by George Washington, who, though not present at the Convention, lent his prestige to the cause of ratification. The outcome proved very close, with approval secured by a vote of 89 to 79.

On June 25, 1988, in Capitol Square in Richmond, music, living history, displays, and ceremonies marked a dual celebration of the Bicentennial of Virginia's ratification of the Constitution and the 175th anniversary of the state's Executive Mansion. The event's organizers erected a Bicentennial stage just north of the Capitol, where special activities all day culminated in a formal ceremony featuring an address by Secretary of the Army John Marsh. Governor Gerald L. Baliles and his wife cut a giant birthday cake in honor of the Executive Mansion, which was open to the public throughout the day. The First Virginia Regiment, encamped on the west side of the square, saluted the two anniversaries with a musket volley, and Hobart Cawood, Superintendent of the Independence National Historic Park in Philadelphia, rang a replica of the Liberty Bell, provided by the Liberty Bell Foundation.

On the Bicentennial stage — after a mid-morning program of freedom songs of the Revolution — actors performed a reenactment drawn from the debates between James Madison and Patrick Henry, "A Dominion Divided," twice during the day. In the early afternoon, the Festival Williamsburg Chorus, the U.S. Continental Army Band, and the U.S. Army Band entertained the crowd. Meanwhile at the Old Dominion stage erected on the south side of the Capitol Square near Bank Street, historical interpreters brought to life Dolley Madison, Thomas Jefferson, and other personages of the time. Throughout the day, stamp enthusiasts bought the first-day-of-issue Virginia Statehood Commemorative from a temporary U.S. Post Office set up on-site.

Official poster of Virginia's Ratification celebration.

Publication and convention scenes from New York's "Critical Choices" program, held in Poughkeepsie.

Critical Choices
New York and the Constitution

The New York State Commission on the Bicentennial of the United States Constitution

New York Bicentennial Commission (2)

"Critical Choices" Convention Delegates

July 25–26, 1988

Laura Kresch and Iris Nortman of White Plains.

Workshop C in progress.

Cindy Campbell of Syracuse at the Plenary Session.

Rodney Braxton delivers a stirring rendition of "America the Beautiful" at the Opening Ceremony. Stephen L. Schechter and Hon. Lucille Pattison look on.

Gov. Mario M. Cuomo addresses "Critical Choices" delegates at the Closing Ceremonies, July 26, 1988.

"Liberty Bell" Ceremonies, Main Street, Poughkeepsie.

New York: After Virginia's ratification, the battleground shifted to the other crucial state, New York, where Hamilton, Jay, and Madison had published a series of newspaper essays supporting ratification, later collected as *The Federalist Papers,* one of the greatest political commentaries ever produced. Despite such formidable support, the state's elections to the ratification convention elected 46 declared Anti-Federalist representatives, compared to 19 Federalists. The former were led by Governor George Clinton, then at the peak of his political power, and supported by their own corps of able polemicists. Although Anti-Federalist sentiments were predominant when the convention began on June 17 in Poughkeepsie, Hamilton and his 18 allies had several advantages in their favor. Many delegates feared that their state would suffer grave economic disadvantages if it were isolated outside a union that included Massachusetts and Virginia, and some feared that should New York vote against ratification, the southern part of the state, including New York City, might secede and join the union separately.

Once again, the Federalists' best tactic was delay: the balance in the convention might be tipped if New Hampshire and Virginia voted to ratify. To this end, the Federalists secured a resolution calling for the New York convention to debate the Constitution clause by clause. After a week of such tedious deliberation, on June 24 the delegates received news of New Hampshire's ratification, followed a week later by the same news from Virginia. The atmosphere changed, and on July 26, 1788, the delegates voted 30 to 27 to ratify without condition, but with amendments recommended that eventually provided a basis for the Bill of Rights.

New York's ratification commemoration in July 1988 differed substantially from most of those previously described in other states. The centerpiece was a public affairs program called "Critical Choices," sponsored by the New York State Bicentennial Commission, which culminated in a convention of delegates who gathered in Poughkeepsie on July 26 to discuss and debate issues of current importance. The commemoration updated instead of reenacted the events of 200 years before. Approximately 150 delegates considered proposals that had been adopted by more than 2,000 New Yorkers at regional town meetings held around the state on June 9. Young people as well as senior citizens, individuals representing various single-issue organizations, and others sharing the commitment to better government through constitutional reform attended these town meetings to discuss critical choices facing New York in 1988. Resolutions from these gatherings were taken up at the Poughkeepsie convention on July 25 in five workshops, focusing respectively on the right to privacy, freedom of expression, equal rights and economic opportunity, governance and home rule, and criminal justice. Eventually, the convention agreed on 29 resolutions and sent copies of its final report to the Governor and to the 1988 Republican and Democratic Presidential candidates, as well as to New York's state and Federal legislators.

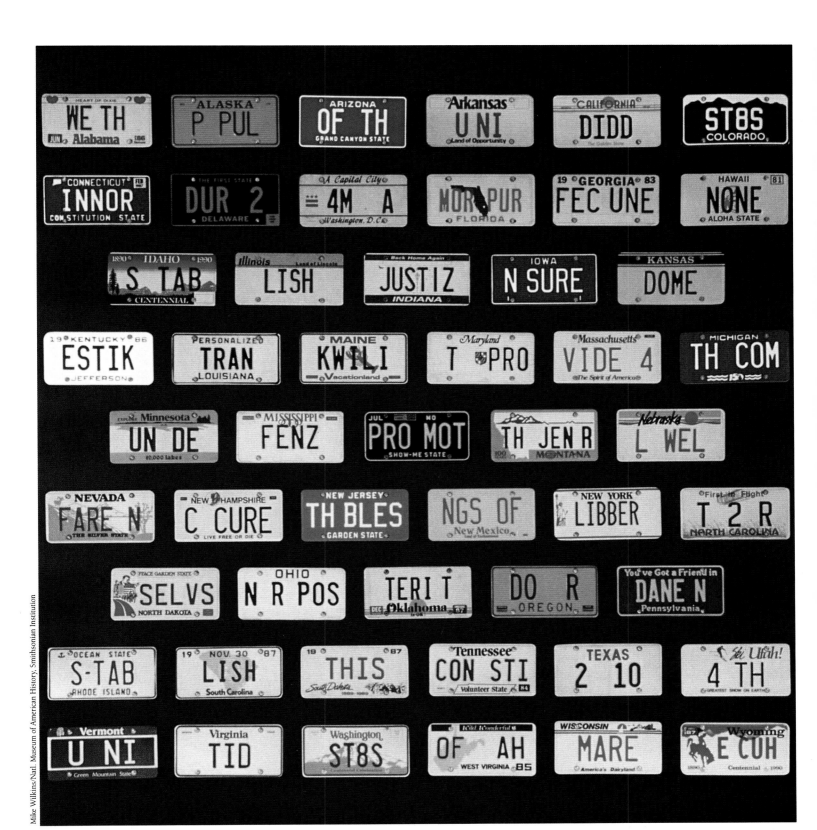

Mike Wilkins/Natl. Museum of American History, Smithsonian Institution

Other State Celebrations: Similar celebrations took place in the six other original states that ratified the Constitution in 1787 and 1788. (North Carolina did not ratify until 1789, Rhode Island, not until 1790). As mentioned, the anniversary of the Constitution's ratification also provided an opportunity for the rest of the 50 states to celebrate their own statehoods. One such event took place in Boise, Idaho, on July 19, where representatives of Idaho, Montana, North Dakota, South Dakota, and Washington gathered to celebrate the Constitution's ratification and to plan for their respective state centennials in 1990.

"We the People" poster by artist Mike Wilkins, spelling out the Preamble of the Constitution. The artist used 51 real auto license plates issued from all 50 states and the District of Columbia.

A *Bicentennial float in the Fourth of July parade.*

JULY 4TH PARADE

With fanfare and fireworks on the long Fourth of July weekend, Washington, D.C., saluted American independence and the 200th anniversary of the Constitution's ratification. A National Independence Day Parade highlighted the festivities. Cosponsored by the national Commission, this holiday parade took as its theme "A More Perfect Union." It commemorated the grand processions held throughout the new Republic on Independence Day, 1788, to celebrate the ratification of the Constitution. The procession — down Constitution Avenue between 7th and 17th Streets — featured high school bands from many states as well as military and mounted units. Floats sponsored by nonprofit associations and foreign countries added colorful pageantry to the line of march. An estimated 150,000 onlookers crowded the curbside. As a prelude to the parade, a flag-raising ceremony and a program of patriotic music, performed by a choir of young people from all over the nation, saluted the Constitution. With national Commission support, Channel 56 in Fairfax, Virginia, made its parade coverage available free of charge to all public television stations nationwide and promoted the event with talk-show interviews during the days prior to July 4th. Commentary for the television coverage of the parade included actor Ralph Archibald portraying Benjamin Franklin.

CONSTITUTION WEEK 1988

The Bicentennial of the Constitution's signing had provided a natural focus for the promotion of Constitution Week in 1987. In 1988 and subsequent years, the national Commission made a major effort to encourage and perpetuate the annual observance of Constitution Week and Citizenship Day. To this end, it developed a special logo for the observance and a series of publications, including a brochure, a poster, a Constitution Week public service announcement, and a 48-page booklet of ideas and suggestions for planning and implementing Constitution Week activities. The Commission mailed printed materials by the hundreds of thousands to state commissions, Designated Bicentennial Communities (DBCs), public libraries, civic organizations, and schools. Citizenship oaths in various forms provided the theme for the 1988 observance. New

citizens pledged the "Oath of Citizenship" and members of the military reaffirmed their oath to "support and defend," while rank and file Americans recited a newly drafted "Citizen Oath."

On Citizenship Day, September 17, 1988, in Washington, D.C., 174 new citizens gathered in the auditorium of the Department of Commerce on Constitution Avenue. From 62 countries, they now stood together to forswear previous allegiances and then to swear to "uphold and defend the Constitution of the United States" in the Oath of Citizenship administered by Chief Justice Burger.

In accompanying remarks, United States Attorney General Richard Thornburgh declared that "the Constitution and citizenship bind us together for the common good even as they free us to live, dream and plot our own destinies." Vice President George Bush observed that the presence and oath-taking of these new citizens "is the living expression of our political philosophy. It is the reason the nation endures. These new citizens and their talent, hard work, and hope will make a magnificent contribution to their new country, just as those who earlier came to our shores have done."

On September 19, hundreds of Federal employees gathered in Lafayette Park across from the White House to participate in a voluntary reaffirmation of citizenship hosted by the Veterans Administration, whose chief medical director, John A. Gronvall, served as master of ceremonies. The reaffirmation oath, prepared by the national Commission after consultation with constitutional scholars, judges, lawyers, and Members of Congress, stated: "I do solemnly swear that I will support and defend the Constitution of the United States against all enemies foreign and domestic, and that I will well and faithfully discharge my duties and responsibilities as a citizen of the United States."

To help promote the observation of Constitution Week, September 17-23, five members of the national Commission crisscrossed the continent. Commissioners Phil Crane and William Lucas visited Miami, Florida, where the two made appearances at Dade County public secondary schools and assisted in a military oath reaffirmation ceremony at the U.S. Coast Guard station at Opa Locka. After sitting on a discussion panel at the law school of Saint Thomas University, they presented a Constitution Week Plaque to Miami Mayor Xavier Suarez. Commissioner Frederick K. Biebel and Lt. Gen. Robert Arter of the Department of Defense's (DOD) Bicentennial Committee flew to San Antonio, Texas, there to visit Alamo Heights secondary schools and participate in a joint military induction-reaffirmation service at the Quadrangle at Fort Sam Houston, a city council function, and a naturalization ceremony. Commissioner Biebel and General Arter then flew to Portland, Oregon, where they joined Commissioners Betty Murphy and Bernard Siegan in school visits, a military oath reaffirmation on the USS *Okinawa,* a naturalization ceremony and a LIVING LEGACY tree planting in Portland's Washington Park.

DOD concluded Constitution Week with a ceremony at Mount Vernon. Members from each branch of

Bill Buckingham

Naturalization (top) and reaffirmation ceremonies in Washington (left); a Commissioner contingent in Miami.

the Armed Forces joined in expressing their devotion to "support and defend" the Constitution. Deputy Secretary of Defense William H. Taft IV reminded the crowd of the 23 soldier-statesmen who signed the Constitution, and emphasized the vital mission of the military in defending the country and the Constitution. After leading the assembled crowd in the Citizen Oath, Secretary Taft and Mrs. Robert Channing Seamans, regent of Mount Vernon Ladies' Association, dedicated a LIVING LEGACY oak tree — representing independence, strength, triumph, and virtue.

Commission Programs and Publications

Although the national Commission participated in various commemorations in 1988, its principal efforts during the year went into the development and implementation of ongoing programs intended to provide the "history and civics lesson" for all Americans. The Bicentennial, as it continued, was to be primarily an educational enterprise. As already mentioned *(see Chapter II),* recent national surveys had highlighted

Elliot Richardson speaks at the closing banquet of the National Meeting of Bicentennial Leaders.

widespread ignorance about the Constitution and the nation's history generally. The years preceding and including the Bicentennial, however, had seen the beginnings of a renewal in American education — an encouraging trend that gave impetus to the Commission during the last months of 1987 and the first few months of 1988 as it worked on this task in long-range strategic planning and creative "program engineering."

The Commission had an opportunity to share its plans at a National Meeting of Bicentennial Leaders in Washington, D.C., on February 6, 1988. Representatives of the Bicentennial Commissions of the 50 states, the District of Columbia, Puerto Rico, and the Virgin Islands joined with educators and community leaders at this meeting, which was hosted by the national Commission. Commission staff outlined plans for a variety of educational programs and special events, as well as publications, media products, and other activities. Private sector attendees described the new opportunities they saw for their continued help and participation. Afternoon workshops gave Commission staff, state leaders, and private sector representatives an opportunity to share and discuss respective plans and needs. Commissioner Lindy Boggs delivered a luncheon address in which she spoke about the importance of understanding history in the civic life of a nation. In an address following the closing banquet, Elliot Richardson, Chairman of the National Education Advisory Committee (NEAC), explored the constitutional and political implications of a government based upon powers derived from the people. All in all, this gathering was useful in providing both inspiration and coordination for the future work of the Bicentennial. The following description of the Commission's 1988 programs includes some of the most important projects that were initiated by the national Commission as part of this effort.

THE NATIONAL HISTORICAL/PICTORIAL MAP CONTEST

In a ceremony on March 1, 1988, at the Sumner School in the nation's capital, the Commission announced the winners of a map contest for students in the District of Columbia School System, kindergarten through the ninth grade. The Bicentennial Commission and the D.C. Public Schools had cosponsored this contest, which was won by students from the Anne Beers and Benning Elementary Schools, and from the Browne Junior High School. The Smithsonian Institution's Museum of American History subsequently displayed the winning maps. The Commission had originally developed the concept of a map-design competition as part of its effort to improve the teaching of history and geography in the nation's schools. To test the feasibility of this idea and refine its concept, the Commission enlisted the support of the D.C. Public Schools to undertake a pilot program early in 1988. The school system was able to design, implement, and complete the entire project all within the span of three months.

The enthusiasm of both teachers and students for the contest, together with the creative quality of the entries, persuaded the Commission to proceed with the development of a national program to take place during the next school year (1988-1989). The pilot test had shown that such a contest was an educationally useful and enjoyable activity for its participants. The principal purpose, of course, was to sharpen students' understanding of both history and geography. As the Commission's Chairman noted, "Geography and history are so closely related, they cannot be separated, and logically they should not be separated. If you do not understand both geography and history, you really cannot understand either one." The contest would eventually reveal other educational benefits. It engaged students not only in historical and geographic research, but in other skills as well, including artistic imagination and design. And it yielded one other benefit. Participation of groups of students in the contest required cooperation and teamwork as they organized themselves for the various tasks required to create their map. Such experience in its own way was a good preparation for citizenship.

The NATIONAL HISTORICAL/PICTORIAL MAP CONTEST, as it came to be called, was launched with the assistance of three organizations. The National Geographic Society provided expert advice in defining the contest's guidelines and in designing its centerpiece, a large black-and-white outline map of the eastern half of the United States, circa 1787. The time frame 1607-1803 was selected both for practical considerations of map size and to be consistent with the Bicentennial's focus on early American history. National Geographic also supplied the Commission with copies of its *America on Parade* timeline and its *Territorial Growth of the United States* poster. Copies of these materials, three copies of the outline map, a contest brochure, and a cover letter were distributed in the autumn of 1988 to every school in the country through the generosity of the United

The Commission Chairman explains the map contest to students.

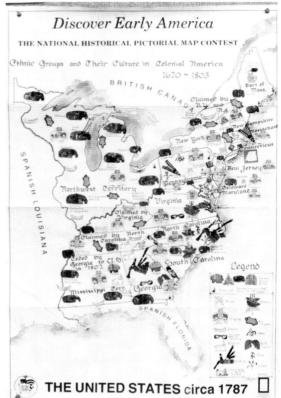

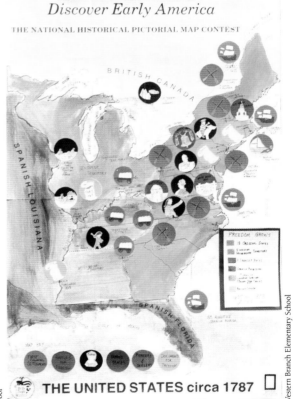

Winning maps of the three competitive levels from the first map contest: Western Branch Elementary, Chesapeake, Virginia (left); St. Andrews School, Tipton, Missouri (top); and Governor Mifflin High, Shillington, Pennsylvania (left).

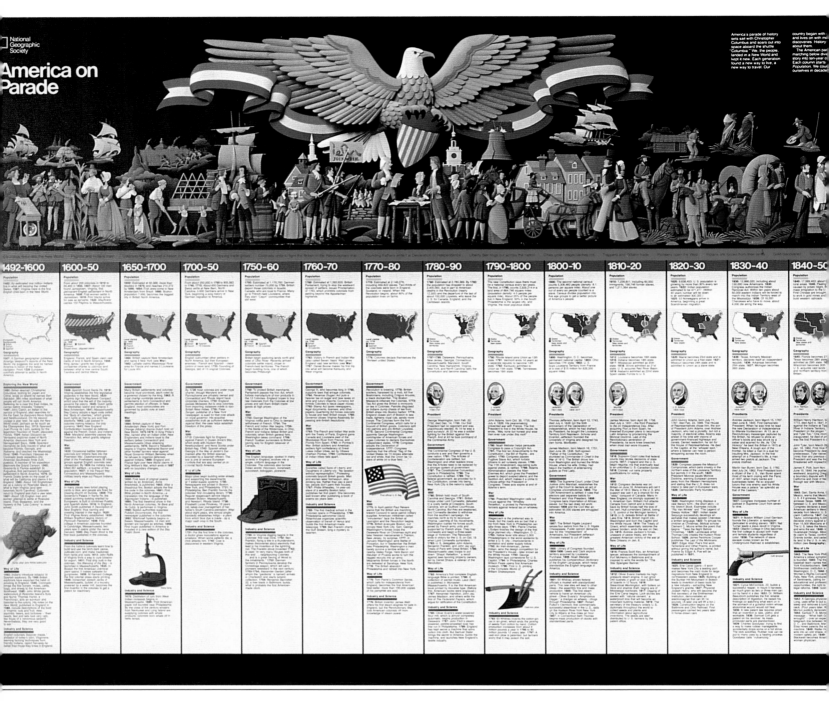

First-place winners meet Barbara Bush at the White House.

Parcel Service. An even more formidable problem was the administration of the contest, which was solved in the spring of 1988 through a special grant to the Center for Civic Education (CCE), whose network of state and congressional district coordinators could handle the complicated logistics of a national competition. The MAP CONTEST proved to be a suitable complement to the NATIONAL BICENTENNIAL COMPETITION, also administered by CCE.

The MAP CONTEST was organized into three competitive levels: elementary and middle school competitions, in which students participated as classes or groups; and a high school competition, in which either individual contestants or groups could submit entries. Each competition passed through three stages, beginning in congressional districts, then to state finals, and eventually to a national final. Overseas schools and those in the District of Columbia were also eligible. All

The National Geographic's *"America on Parade"* timeline.

entrants received a certificate of participation, and winning schools at the three stages of competition received special certificates as well as cash awards for the purchase of educational materials. National winners in the three levels of competition received $5,000 for first place, $3,000 for second, and $1,000 for third. The contest materials were designed to stimulate the interest and inventiveness of all participants. The guidelines and supplemental material included suggestions and background information, but students were confronted with a largely blank map that they were to fill with graphic imagery and words, depicting historically important people, places, and events. Creativity counted as much as historical accuracy. A teapot, for example, could represent the Boston Tea Party; a quill, the drafting of the Constitution. To help promote the contest nationwide, the Commission sent a letter in the spring of 1988 to every school superintendent.

Despite the short lead time for the implementation and promotion of the contest, over 4,000 schools registered, and an estimated 120,000 students participated. Over 240 entries in the three levels of competition provided a colorful decoration for the walls of the Duke Ellington School for the Performing Arts in Washington, D.C., where the judging of the national finals took place in May 1989. Contest entries ranged from a quilted version with hundreds of sewn-on patches to an elaborately colored map showing the eighteenth-century distribution of various religious and ethnic groups, including Native American tribes. First-place honors went to the Western Branch Elementary School in Chesapeake, Virginia, the St. Andrews School (a parochial middle school) in Tipton, Missouri, and the Governor Mifflin High School in Shillington, Pennsylvania. The winning high school entry had been designed by a senior, Suneeta Krish. The students who had created the winning entries and their teachers were honored at an awards luncheon at the Smithsonian's Air and Space Museum in Washington, D.C.

By every measure, the first year of this program proved successful. Teachers praised the contest as a stimulating learning activity that combined cooperative effort with a visual linking of geography and history. One of the many letters from teachers made the point:

We want to thank your Commission for developing such an entertaining way to learn history and geography. We are already winners because we have already gained by learning and working together. This exercise has helped teach us to work in groups of various sizes in a cooperative manner. We have added to our knowledge of how to do research. We have learned historical and geographical knowledge to aid us in our work. Thank you for giving us this means for learning.

The Washington Post paid tribute to the map contest in an editorial on June 18, 1989:

It was a classic example of what can happen when teachers are given materials outside the formal curriculum and allowed simply to run with the ball. . . . This graceful linking of visual skills, class teamwork, and the Bicentennial theme offers an easy to replicate approach to the otherwise large and slippery idea of "where" in context with "when" and "what." This is of course the larger goal of any geography coursework; it's all too easy, though, for curriculum-writing committees overwhelmed with "relevance" to get carried away and produce lesson plans that cover everything and nothing. The sharply defined Bicentennial theme ensures concreteness — and fun.

Because of the response, the Commission decided to sponsor the contest for a second year, with the CCE once again administering it. Scholastic, Inc. promoted the contest in its publications and *USA Today* eventually distributed a special mailing to 16,000 social studies supervisors. Over 7,000 schools registered for the competition. St. Andrews School in Tipton, Missouri, repeated as 1990 champion in the middle school competition, with the Kings Academy in West Palm Beach, Florida, and Long Beach High School in Long Beach, Mississippi, winning the elementary and high school competitions. (The high school entry was designed by Be Do, a senior.) The 1990 award ceremonies included a visit with Barbara Bush on the South Lawn of the White House. The First Lady commended the students on their winning creations and posed with them for pictures.

BICENTENNIAL SCHOOLS

The year 1988 saw the inauguration of the BICENTENNIAL SCHOOL RECOGNITION PROGRAM, another product of the Commission's "program engineering" the previous autumn. In many ways a companion to the DESIGNATED BICENTENNIAL COMMUNITY and BICENTENNIAL CAMPUS programs, it was in fact inspired by a similar project associated with the 1986 Centennial of the Statue of Liberty. Its intent was to encourage elementary and secondary schools to conduct Bicentennial activities engaging students, teachers, administrators, parents, and other members of the school community in planning and executing a variety of curricular and extracurricular events during the school year—from Constitution Week in September through Flag Day in June. Activities could include such things as special assemblies, intra-school competitions, field trips and other community programs, as well as a variety of classroom activities. To be recognized, a school had to develop a coherent plan of activities supervised by a committee whose membership was broadly representative of the school community.

Recognition by the Commission included a special certificate, the receipt of a set of educational materials, and a periodic Bicentennial Schools newsletter, which kept recognized schools abreast of Bicentennial activities, including exemplary activities of their fellow institutions. State Commissions played important roles in the recognition process by clearing and approving applications before forwarding them to the national Commission. To promote the program, application forms were included in the NATIONAL HISTORICAL/PICTORIAL MAP CONTEST packet, which was sent to every school. During its first year the program recognized over 270 schools. Though the number of schools did not increase in subsequent years as much as had been expected, the program established a useful network for future educational activities of the Bicentennial.

COLLEGE-COMMUNITY FORUMS

Under its congressional mandate the Commission from the beginning had focused its educational effort on elementary and secondary education. This reflected a generally shared belief that the improvement of teaching and learning in elementary and secondary schools represented the best investment in the future. The Commission was also conscious, however, of its obligation to reach all Americans, including adults of every age. The BICENTENNIAL CAMPUS PROGRAM, instituted in 1987, was the first major Commission initiative in higher education (*see Chapter III*). By the end of 1988, a total of 369 colleges and universities had joined the program, creating a valuable network for other initiatives in higher and continuing education. America's colleges and universities had already been active in other ways. With the support of Project '87, NEH, and other organizations, they sponsored lecture series, workshops, research projects, and other programs in constitutional studies. Moreover, the Commission's BICENTENNIAL EDUCATIONAL GRANT PROGRAM (BEGP) enlisted the resources of high education through its summer institutes, workshops, in-service training, and curricular materials.

Nevertheless, the Commission early on began considering the idea of college and university participation in the Bicentennial through sponsorship not of conventional academic conferences (which the schools were already doing), but of public forums that would include not only representatives of an institution itself, but the surrounding community as well. The idea for this program had perhaps been triggered by the Chairman's participation in such an event at Macalester College in 1986 (see Chapter II). In June 1987, Commission representatives met with a group of educators to discuss the project. Useful suggestions emerged from this meeting, but their development was shelved until after the September celebrations of that year. The Commission proceeded with the assistance of an ad hoc advisory committee of scholars and university administrators, and through consultation with the U.S. Department of Education, NEH, the Council on Higher Education, and several state humanities councils.

The project called for a nationwide series of public forums, involving not only colleges and universities, but other institutions as well, including public libraries, civic groups, and local educational organizations. The designation "College-Community" denoted the joint effort. The program's mission statement declared that the purpose of the forums was:

to increase public awareness of the Constitution, by linking important and perennial political issues to the principles and theory of the nation's Charter, and thereby underscore the importance of constitutional government that lies at the foundation of current attempts to resolve important issues of public policy.

Broadly conceived, these public discussions of constitutional issues followed the tradition of the American town meeting, though they could adopt any format or combination of formats — lecture, panel discussion, roundtable, etc. — so long as all in attendance were given an opportunity to participate and as the program afforded a fair and balanced presentation of the issues.

At its June 1988 meeting, the Commission approved up to $75,000 for a pilot test of the program, to be implemented in the next academic year. A program announcement was quickly prepared and distributed to the Commission's network of Bicentennial Campuses, which offered a useful vehicle for undertaking the pilot program. The Commission funded the initial series of forums by contract and subsequently by grants after its grant-making authority was expanded by Congress in 1989. A single event could receive maximum funding of $5,000. A program involving a series of forums or a consortia of schools could receive up to $15,000. Procedures for review and selection of applications mirrored in simpler form those of the BEGP, with initial reviews by Commission staff and outside experts and final approval by the Commission's Advisory Committee on Educational Projects. The Commission also developed procedures for evaluating the forums.

The pilot program awarded funding to 11 projects involving 24 institutions of higher learning, most of which were held during the 1988-1989 academic year and focused on the themes of Congress and the Presidency (though some took up other Bicentennial themes). For example, the University of Tennessee in Knoxville sponsored a forum in November 1988 that addressed the topic "Federalism: Original Intent and Current Reality." It brought together representatives of the city and county Bicentennial Commissions, the Knoxville Bar Associations, the county library system, and the East Tennessee Historical Society.

To promote the program, the Commission developed a handbook of suggestions for organizing a forum, as well as *The Legislative Branch and the Constitutional Order* and *The Executive Branch and the Constitutional Order,* the first two booklets of a planned series. Each booklet contained a brief explanation of the purpose of the program, an essay reviewing the history and key issues relating to its subject, and a selected bibliography. The Commission supplied the booklets and handbook for each of the events and distributed them elsewhere as part of the program's promotional effort. To showcase the project, the Commission's Chairman participated in a College-Community Forum at the University of South Carolina in October 1988. The event, which had received funding from the Commission and was broadcast on public television, addressed the topic "Congress into the 21st Century: Would the Framers Approve?" Other participants included Norman Ornstein of the American Enterprise Institute, Representative Butler C. Derrick, former Secretary of Labor William Brock, and United States Circuit Judge Jean G. Bissell. Veteran TV correspondent Edwin Newman served as moderator. Pleased with the initial response, the Commission in November 1988 approved up to $1 million to fund a full-fledged COLLEGE-COMMUNITY FORUMS PROGRAM in the upcoming 1989-1990 academic year.

COLLEGE-COMMUNITY FORUMS

The Legislative Branch
and the
Constitutional Order

One of the College-Community Forums program booklets produced to promote public discussions of constitutional issues (left); A forum held at the University of South Carolina in October 1988 (below).

THE CONSTITUTION

The words we live by

Let's talk about it!

Created by the Bicentennial Commission, the program
lets people begin again — to grasp
these important principles and apply them to contemporary issues, not just nationally,
but within their own communities. It is democracy in action.

Illustration by John Benson

ADULT EDUCATION

The Commission's ADULT EDUCATION PROGRAM,
yet another product of the planning and development
during late 1987, was also an interesting derivative of the
COLLEGE-COMMUNITY FORUMS project. Among the
individuals with whom the Commission consulted in
the development of the latter project was Dale Parnell,
president of the American Association of Junior and

Community Colleges and a member of NEAC. Dr.
Parnell suggested that the greatest contribution the
Commission could make to the world of adult and
continuing education would be to develop useful
reading and discussion materials on the Constitution.
He noted the absence of such materials in adult
education and offered the assistance of his organization
in their dissemination and use, should they become
available. Subsequently, the Washington Higher Educa-

tion Secretariat (a blue-ribbon group of representatives of all the major educational organizations in higher education) endorsed the suggestion. It had become clear that the Commission, for all its emphasis on reaching younger Americans, should not neglect the increasingly important world of adult and continuing education. The Commission considered the idea of a special set of educational materials at its December 1987 meeting and gave the go-ahead for developing a concept and plan, with final funding to be contingent on quality and feasibility.

During the winter and spring of 1988, the Commission worked on a plan, in consultation with constitutional scholars and educational experts in the field of adult education. Lacking the resources to develop such materials by itself, the Commission in October 1988 awarded a contract to Dual Associates, a consulting firm in Arlington, Virginia. The contract called for the production of four reading modules on the Constitution (covering the historical background, human rights under the Constitution, the fundamental principles of the Constitution, and the meaning of citizenship), together with supplementary materials and a dissemination plan.

A two-day planning meeting was held in December 1988. Participants included constitutional scholars, educational experts, and representatives of the American Association for Adult and Continuing Education, the American Bar Association (ABA), the Center for Applied Linguistics, the National Council on Aging, the Federal Bureau of Prisons, the U.S. Department of Education, and the DOD. At the meeting it was decided to expand the package to provide simplified versions of the modules for use by adults with reading difficulties in English.

The materials to be developed and tested during the following year included the four discussion units, a discussion leader's guide, a guide for tutors of new readers, and an introductory videotape. Adults of all ages and educational and cultural backgrounds were the intended users of these materials. The discussion leader's guide would offer discussion questions and activities tailored to the various audiences, including adult basic education classes, English-as-a-second-language programs, junior and community college courses, senior groups, civic organizations, and government employees. By the end of 1989, the contractor, working with the Commission and teams of outside experts, had produced polished drafts for three of the four discussion units and had completed the supplementary video. The remaining materials would be completed early in 1990. As part of their final refinement, pilot tests were scheduled for each primary audience. The first of these pilot tests was conducted in November 1989, with 22 low- and middle-income retirees, ages 65-85, one-third of whom were African-Americans. After a two and one-half hour reading and discussion session on those materials dealing with the Founding Era, the participants' responses to the materials included some insightful comments. When asked what the Constitution meant to them, one 83-year-old

woman said: "It means I don't have to sit on the back of the bus and I can go to any store I want." A 75-year-old man said: "Some people take the Constitution and pick out the raisins [i.e., the rights]. I tell them you have to think about responsibilities. They have to work at it."

Consistent with the program's original conception, the Commission devoted considerable thought and planning during the year to the task of disseminating the materials, training people in their eventual use, and encouraging adult educators to use them once they were available. A network of 32 national organizations — representing civic organizations, ethnic and racial groups, religious denominations, and the disabled — agreed to help, as did the Federal Government's Departments of Education and Defense, and Office of Personnel Management. A key supporting group was the American Association of Retired Persons (AARP), which also arranged for the use of other Commission materials in its education programs across the country.

OTHER COMMISSION PROGRAMS

The NATIONAL BICENTENNIAL COMPETITION ON THE CONSTITUTION AND BILL OF RIGHTS completed its first full year with national finals in late April 1988. The essentials of this program, administered by the Center for Civic Education in cosponsorship with the national Commission, have been described (*see Chapter II*).

Over 1,000 students and their teachers from 43 states gathered in Washington, D.C., for the finals, the preliminary rounds of which were held at Fort McNair. The top ten teams then vied for the national championship in facilities provided by the United States Court of Appeals for the Federal Circuit. The competition followed its usual format of a mock congressional hearing, in which panels of judges evaluated student performance in each of the six areas of study covered by the program's curriculum. The Gompers Secondary School in San Diego, California, won first place, with second and third place honors going to East Brunswick High School in East Brunswick, New Jersey, and Half Hallow Hills High School East in Dix Hills, New York, respectively. All of the participants in the national competition, including teachers and program coordinators, were honored for their efforts at an awards banquet the evening of April 27.

S*tudents from Gompers Secondary School earn first-place honors in the National Bicentennial Competition.*

Now fully funded, the Commission's BICENTEN-NIAL EDUCATION GRANT PROGRAM (BEGP) also expanded during fiscal year 1988, with the completion of two rounds of competition, in which the BEGP received 427 applications. The 74 grants awarded totaled $3.2 million. The funded projects — summer institutes, in-service workshops, the development of curricular materials — covered many topics. Some focused on the current year's subject of Ratification. Others looked to the following year's theme of the executive and legislative branches or pursued a variety of other constitutional subjects. Among the projects were the following:

Tennessee Technological University sponsored a two-week institute for 30 social studies teachers from the Upper Cumberland (Appalachia) region of Tennessee. The institute's sessions aimed at increasing the participants' understanding of the Constitution and providing tools to help them teach the content effectively in their rural school systems.

The Association for Retarded Citizens of the United States developed educational materials on the Constitution, including a workbook and audiotape, that were appropriate for students with mental retardation.

The Idaho Centennial Foundation developed and produced 50,000 facsimile kits and curricular materials, entitled "Documents West," that included reproductions of some of the key documents in the development and statehood of the territories in the Great Northwest.

Joe Dunbar of the Kokomo-Center Township Consolidated Corporation developed a "roving constitutional scholar" program, in which an educator in the role of Benjamin Franklin visited area schools to deliver talks on the executive and legislative branches. The program included a series of two-week seminars aimed at 8th, 11th, and 12th grade students.

Louisiana State University conducted a two-week institute for 30 secondary-school teachers on the ratification debates and *The Federalist Papers,* followed by a series of in-service workshops.

The Center for Educational Experimentation, Development, and Evaluation, University of Iowa developed curricular materials in computer format on the legislative and executive branches for use by secondary school students with limited English proficiency.

Salem State College in Massachusetts sponsored a four-week summer institute designed to provide 20 middle and secondary school teachers with new teaching strategies and curricular materials concerning their state's role in the struggle for ratification and in the election of the First Congress.

The Citizenship and Law-Related Education Center for the Sacramento Region of California sponsored a yearlong Constitution Mentor Teacher Institute for teachers in the 4th, 5th, 8th, 11th, and 12th grades. The program included a five-day summer institute and a series of in-service meetings during the school year, both concentrating on the philosophical foundations of the Constitution and the Bill of Rights.

The National Trust for Historic Preservation developed an educational program and exhibit at James Madison's home, Montpelier, in Virginia, designed to help both elementary and secondary students better understand the Constitution's evolution, framing, ratification, and interpretation.

The Center for Research and Development in Law-related Education (CRADLE) implemented its "Sharing Lessons in Citizenship Education" (SLICE) program, which involved the collection, evaluation, cataloging, and dissemination of lesson plans on the Constitution, produced by teachers across the country.

By 1988, the administrative and review apparatus necessary to operate the BEGP was in place. About a dozen Commission staff, together with panels of outside reviewers, staff from the Office of Justice Programs, and the Commission's Advisory Committee on Educational Projects were needed to administer the program. By 1988, the program's administration and record-keeping were fully computerized.

Now in its third year, the LIVING LEGACY program had produced over a thousand officially recognized projects for both new and restored parks across the country. The administration of the program was given to the various state Bicentennial Commissions, which encouraged projects at the local level, received applications for recognition, and supplied the certificates for approved projects. During 1988, a majority of LIVING LEGACY projects took place on the East Coast as the original 13 states commemorated their respective ratifications of the Constitution. Perhaps the most ambitious was an $8 million renovation of the ten-acre Capitol Square in Columbus, Ohio. Initiated with ground-breaking ceremonies during Constitution Week 1987, the plan included a central fountain and the restoration of historic diagonal walkways, whose junctions would be marked by restored monuments and plaques concerning the state's history.

In 1988, the Commission began a mail-order COMMEMORATIVE CATALOG program to increase the outreach of the logo licensing program, encourage existing licensees to continue their marketing, and attract new ones into the program. In addition, the catalog provided a way to respond to regular inquiries, by phone or mail, from DBCs and other constituencies about available products. The catalog began modestly as a simple listing of products, but soon evolved into a full-color booklet. Fifteen new firms joined the licensing program in 1988, many looking ahead to 1989 and the special opportunities presented by the 200th anniversary of the Presidency.

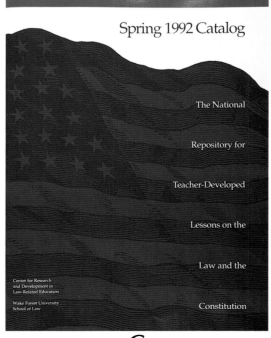

*C*RADLE *lesson catalog.*

"The Great American Patriot," one in a series painted by noted wildlife artist R. J. McDonald.

One of the Commission's licensed products was an original painting entitled "The Patriot." In May 1988, this portrait of an American bald eagle by artist R. J. McDonald was auctioned for $15,000 at the Southeast Wildlife Exposition in Charleston, South Carolina. Part of the proceeds of the sale went to the American Eagle Trust, dedicated to preserving the bald eagle and its habitat. Two signed limited-edition prints of the painting were featured at South Carolina's Ratification commemoration at Charleston in May. Commissioner Harry Lightsey, Jr., presented one of the autographed prints to the Mayor of Charleston and another to the chairman of the city's Bicentennial Commission.

PUBLICATIONS

During 1988 the Commission's range of publications began to grow along with the expansion of its programs. The POCKET CONSTITUTION continued to be the Bicentennial's most popular item. During the year, 1.9 million copies were printed and approximately 1.2 million were distributed by the Commission. The 1988 COMMEMORATIVE CALENDAR continued in the tradition of its predecessors, combining attractive illustrations with a chronology of historical facts about the Constitution. About 300,000 copies were distributed. It had become clear, however, that as the Bicentennial concluded its celebration of the Constitution's drafting and moved on to other themes, new publications would have to be developed. The advertising campaign response kit

continued to fill some needs, as did the Commission's information kit, which included a bibliography, a copy of the *Project Registry* of current projects in education, a listing of historical dates, and a poster copy of Howard Chandler Christy's painting of the Signing of the Constitution. Some new publications, such as the HISTORICAL/PICTORIAL MAP CONTEST material, the COLLEGE-COMMUNITY FORUM booklets and handbook, the new mail-order catalog, and the CCE's new texts, have already been discussed. Additional materials were needed, however, to address the new commemorative themes and to remind the public of the continuing Bicentennial.

In 1988, the Commission issued what was to become the first in a series of brochures providing historical information about a given year's commemorative theme and summarizing the principal programs and activities for that year. *"To Reap the Fruit of Our Labor" Ratification and Union: The Constitution Bicentennial Celebration Continues* was the first of these publications. The eight-panel brochure, mixing illustration and text, told the story of the Constitution's ratification and briefly described the year's plans for commemoration with suggestions as to how the public could get involved. Printed in the hundreds of thousands, this brochure (and its successors) became an effective promotional and educational resource of the Bicentennial. The Commission also issued *Celebrating the Bicentennial of the U.S. Constitution: A Resource Guide* for Bicentennial leaders across the country. The *Resource Guide* included historical background on the continuing Bicentennial, lists of commemorative ideas and suggestions, a bibliography, and other resources.

The Commission's Information Center continued to meet the public's need for a wide variety of published material and other data about the Constitution and the Bicentennial. To handle its increased responsibilities as a clearinghouse of information, the Commission added a new program area called Education Services that took over administration of the Speakers Bureau and its database of over 400 constitutional speakers, and continued with the regular publication of the *Project Registry* updates of current projects in education.

COMMISSION STAFF, ORGANIZATION, AND RESOURCES

In late 1987 and during 1988 the Commission reduced its staff from 155 (its highest level at the time of A CELEBRATION OF CITIZENSHIP) to 79, of whom 65 were regular employees and 14 were detailed from other government departments and agencies. Some areas, however, were expanded to meet additional program needs, most notably in the Education Division. Moreover, 12 exceptionally qualified college students joined the staff as summer interns to assist with the research and writing of Commission projects.

Leadership of the Commission's staff changed during the year with the resignation of Dr. Cannon to return to the private sector in September, to be succeeded by Dr. Trowbridge as Acting Staff Director (he became Staff Director in January 1989). With these changes, the Commission was reorganized into five program divisions: Education, Government Affairs, Marketing, Private Programs, and International (including Publications and Media Relations), with the Administration Division continuing as before.

Congress appropriated $21 million for the Commission in fiscal year 1988, earmarking a portion of that appropriation ($5 million) for directed grants to the WE THE PEOPLE 200 Committee, the National Trust for Historic Preservation (for the restoration of James Madison's home, Montpelier), and the establishment of constitutional law resource centers and professorships of constitutional law. The Commission received $16 million for its own programs, to which was added $8.7 million in carryover funds from the previous year. During the fiscal year, the Commission also received $441,000 in royalty income from logo licensing and the sale of ornaments, as well as $5,000 in donated funds from private sources.

Other Activities

As was expected, the level of Bicentennial activity slackened in the aftermath of the September 1987 celebrations, as the many organizations involved paused before moving on to new commemorative enterprises. Much of the work started in 1987 remained to be completed. The 1988 celebration of Ratification provided a special stimulus for the Bicentennial at the state

and local levels, especially in the original 13 states but elsewhere as well, as other states took the occasion to celebrate their statehood and history.

EDUCATIONAL ORGANIZATIONS

While the Commission moved ahead with its own programs in Constitutional education, other educational organizations did their part to sustain the momentum of the Bicentennial. NEAC's executive committee, for example, assisted the Commission during 1988 to develop the NATIONAL HISTORICAL/PICTORIAL MAP CONTEST and the BICENTENNIAL SCHOOLS RECOGNITION PROGRAM.

Another educational consortium doing its part was IMPACT II, a nationwide, nonprofit networking organization that recognized and rewarded innovative teachers within public school systems nationwide and provided them with grant support for the dissemination of new and creative in-school projects. Begun in the New York City public schools in 1979, IMPACT II had established a network of over 20 sites across the country by the start of the Bicentennial, with over 10,000 teachers participating. After 1987 it actively promoted the educational programs of the Commission and the Bicentennial generally. These programs included a grant awarded by the BEGP in 1988 to the New York Historical Society for the development of a mobile exhibit, "Government by Choice: Inventing the U.S. Constitution," based on the Society's 1987 exhibit on the Founding Era *(see Chapter III)*. Part of this project, called "The Bicentennial Connection," involved the development and dissemination of exemplary curricular materials on the Constitution through the IMPACT II network.

The year included a variety of interesting educational projects reaching students of all ages. During the spring of 1988, elementary school students in Texas had an opportunity to see a musical drama about the Constitution, written primarily for children and presented as part of the Southwest Texas State University's Children's Theater series. Professor of Theater Arts Charles Pascoe wrote the work, *The Next Amendment,* combining the stories of the Constitution and the Bill of Rights. Texas was also the site of an unusual high school mentor program on the Constitution, sponsored by the Free Enterprise Education Center of Houston. In this program, small groups of high school students, called "Constitution Corroborators," devoted hundreds of hours each to after-class study of the Constitution and then toured the state to present lectures, seminars, and slide presentations to various audiences on the meaning of the nation's charter.

In addition to the NATIONAL BICENTENNIAL COMPETITION, other national programs brought high school students together to consider topics related to the Bicentennial. One of these was the 13th annual Century III conference in March at Williamsburg, Virginia, where two outstanding high school leaders from each state gathered to discuss and debate issues of importance to America in her third century. The program, sponsored by the National Association of Secondary

*Century III
student leaders and
Chief Justice Burger
discuss freedom of
speech as guaranteed by
the Constitution.*

School Principals with funding support from the Shell Oil Company Foundation, provided college scholarships to the participants. Chief Justice Burger opened the conference and participated in a workshop on freedom of speech. Among interesting academic conferences held during the year was a February symposium in Atlanta, cosponsored by the Carter Center of Emory University, Georgia State University, and the Jimmy Carter Library. With former First Ladies Rosalynn Carter, Betty Ford, Lady Bird Johnson, and Pat Nixon participating, the symposium addressed the subject "Women and the Constitution: a Bicentennial Perspective" and examined women's roles in the Constitution's development and its subsequent impact upon them.

FEDERAL GOVERNMENT DEPARTMENTS AND AGENCIES

With Commission encouragement and support, the Federal Government's many entities continued to be among the most active participants in the Bicentennial. The commemoration remained a priority in DOD's special programs. By the middle of 1988, more than 140 military installations, including ships, National Guard and Reserve commands, and many overseas facilities, had been recognized as Bicentennial Defense Communities, and the national Commission had recognized nearly 60 military projects for "exceptional merit." General Arter continued to coordinate the military's Bicentennial activities and spoke about those activities at meetings around the country.

One Army project was the *Constitution Bicentennial Resource Guide*, 57,000 copies of which were distributed to schools coast-to-coast. With the assistance of the Commission, a special supplement to the guide on Ratification appeared during 1988, as did a brochure on the same subject. Military installations both within the United States and overseas continued to

make their ceremonial units, bands, and color guards available for Bicentennial events. In the spring of 1988, the Department adopted the Ratification theme for its annual military tattoo in tribute to the Constitution. The program, "Spirit of America," staged at the Capital Centre in Landover, Maryland, featured displays of military pageantry, history, and skill.

As already noted in connection with Constitution Week, the Armed Forces continued with their ceremonial and educational efforts to reinforce the importance of the military oaths pledging defense of the Constitution, taken at the time of enlistment and at graduation from basic training, and later renewed in oath reaffirmation ceremonies throughout a military career. The Army also developed programs to involve the civilian families of its personnel in these ceremonies. The commander in chief of Allied forces in the Persian Gulf War, Gen. H. Norman Schwarzkopf, described one of these oath reaffirmation ceremonies, which took place at Fort Lewis, Washington, on Law Day, May 1, 1987:

I was looking for a special way to bring home to the soldiers the fact that it was the Bicentennial of the Constitution and what a great thing the Constitution is. So I said, you know, "Why don't we renew our oath in front of each other?" And that's what we did. We gathered every single soldier at Fort Lewis and we filed them all out on the parade field in the wee hours of the morning . . . I gave a little talk. I raised my right hand and had every officer renew the oath to the Constitution in front of the troops. And then the troops did it for us. And we all sang "God Bless America." We lit the sky up with fireworks before the sun came up . . . the American soldiers cheered. Tears were streaming down their faces, and they were talking about it for weeks after — about how proud they felt to be an American. . . .*

*Dale Van Atta, "What Makes an American Soldier?" *Parade* magazine, July 7, 1991.

Spectacular finale of the "Spirit of America" military pageant presented in a Landover, Maryland, sports arena.

*C*ommunity support for the
Bicentennial continues with
PLANT A LIVING LEGACY
projects (above),
regional meetings (right), and
BELLS ACROSS AMERICA
tributes (below).

*W*inners of the Constitution essay contest
in 1937 (left) meet with winners of
the National Writing Competition at the
National Archives in 1987 (bottom).

Among other Federal programs in 1988, the Office of Legal Policy of the Department of Justice published a *Bibliography of Original Meaning of the United States Constitution,* edited by national Commissioner Bernard Siegan, with funding provided by the Department of Justice and research by Professor Siegan's students at the University of San Diego Law School. The National Archives, together with the national Commission and the Pennsylvania Commission, sponsored one of the most creative events to take place during the year. In May, surviving winners of a 1937 high school essay contest on the Constitution, sponsored by the Pennsylvania Sesquicentennial Commemoration Committee, came to Washington, D.C., to meet with the winners of the 1987 NATIONAL BICENTENNIAL WRITING COMPETITION, sponsored by the national Commission and Gannett/*USA Today (see Chapter III).* This intergenerational gathering allowed the older participants to consider what impact the Constitution had had on their lives during the half-century since the Sesquicentennial, and the younger participants to speculate on what the future had in store. The project was funded by the Prudential Foundation and USAir, Inc.

STATES AND COMMUNITIES

February's national meeting of Bicentennial leaders in Washington, D.C., did much to renew the commitment and enthusiasm of state Commissions. The workshops and other activities allowed for a useful sharing of ideas and collaborative planning for the future. So successful was this event that the Commission followed up with a series of 13 regional meetings held throughout the country in the spring, summer, and fall of 1988. There, national, state, and local Commissions shared their accomplishments and plans with local educators, private sector representatives, and public officials. The meeting in Boise, Idaho, in July coincided with the gathering of the states of the Great Northwest to plan their approaching Centennials *(see page 99).* A New England meeting in Portland, Maine, in October featured a college community forum on the subject "Congress: the Constitution and National Security." Such gatherings of Bicentennial leaders were a critical component in sustaining the momentum of the Bicentennial, one sign of which was the continuing expansion of the Commission's network of DBCs. By the end of 1988, the network encompassed over 2,500 DBCs, including cities, towns, and counties in every state.

Constitution Week, 1988, produced a proliferation of activity at the state and local levels. For example, residents of Immocolata Manor, a home for 28 developmentally disabled women in Liberty, Missouri, joined in the second year of BELLS ACROSS AMERICA with a bell-ringing tribute to the Constitution. The "Quill and Cube," a prize-winning sculpture, was unveiled on September 17 at Constitution Park, located on the site of the Golden Fleece Tavern in Dover where Delaware had ratified the Constitution. The Delaware Heritage Commission developed the park and the sculpture in honor of the Bicentennial. Dressed in Colonial garb, members of a local Scottish Rite Masonic lodge provided a color guard during a commemorative program at the Thomas R. Proctor Junior High School in Utica, New York. Representing all four Utica junior high schools, students attending the special assembly received the booklet *The Constitution and New York.* The program initiated a full year of Bicentennial activities for the state's schools, among the first institutions to be recognized by the national Commission's BICENTENNIAL SCHOOLS RECOGNITION program.

In addition to their participation in state Ratification ceremonies, regional meetings, and Constitution Week, the state Commissions pursued many projects of their own. Florida's Commission, for example, provided an $80,000 gift to the University of South Florida for a constitutional scholarship program. The California Bicentennial Foundation sponsored a "We the People" float in the 1988 Tournament of Roses Parade in Pasadena. The float, featuring the largest American flags ever constructed from flowers, had as its theme "The Constitution: 200 Years of Communicating Liberty," with depictions of the Constitution and Independence Hall connected by two giant flags to a representation of the future, symbolized by astronaut Edwin Aldrin standing amid a Martian landscape.

PRIVATE, NONPROFIT, AND RELIGIOUS GROUPS

The United States Capitol Historical Society continued with its collaborative enterprises on behalf of the Bicentennial. The Society's 1988 Bicentennial medal, inscribed with the legend "In Order to Form a More Perfect Union," featured profiles of Hamilton, Madison, and Jay (see page 92). The symposia series continued in March 1988 with a gathering of scholars to discuss "The Economy of Early America: The Revolutionary Period, 1763-1790." The Society also took the occasion of these annual symposia to honor outstanding high school students of history and their teachers.

In keeping with its original mandate, the national Commission made continuing efforts to engage Americans of all backgrounds, including the nation's many ethnic, minority, and special-interest groups, in the Bicentennial experience. In August 1988, the Commission met with representatives of various groups with special physical and learning needs to consider how best to involve these Americans in commemorative programs and activities. Before the meeting, extensive research identified key needs and opportunities. Thirty-three representatives of national organizations and agencies providing services to the disabled attended the daylong session. The meeting led directly to several initiatives, including the installation in the Commission offices of a telecommunications device to improve communication with the hearing-impaired, the distribution of Braille copies of the Constitution (see Chapter II) to libraries, the application of closed-captioning and voice-overs to television programs, films, and videos, and the distribution of specially prepared educational materials for those with reading difficulties.

The national Commission's efforts to address the problem of illiteracy have already been noted in the

*C*herry Blossom Princesses grace a Bicentennial float in Washington, D.C.

Disney donates Christy mural replicas in Statuary Hall ceremony.

discussion of the BEGP and adult education program. Another such effort was its support of Project Literacy U.S. (PLUS), a program launched by the Coalition for Literacy, Capital Cities/ABC Inc., and the Public Broadcasting System (PBS). A major public service campaign of ABC television, PLUS sought to capture the attention of the illiterate community through public service announcements (PSAs), inviting viewers to call an 800 number operated by the Contact Center of Lincoln, Nebraska, a nonprofit clearinghouse on literacy information. The Center matched individuals calling for help with resources available in their respective localities. At its June meeting, the Commission approved a grant of $350,000 to fund PLUS for one year and agreed to provide the Contact Center with a supply of POCKET CONSTITUTIONS, to be distributed to callers of the 800 number. ABC pointed out the natural connection between verbal and civic literacy ("The Constitution: The Words We Live By") in a television special about PLUS on the eve of July 4th, a program that included a PSA featuring Chief Justice Burger and fellow Commissioner Senator Kennedy at the National Archives.

There were other Bicentennial programs demonstrating the creative enterprise and collaborate efforts of America's private sector. At their Private Management Association convention in Chicago that year, the nation's chiropractors adopted a program, "Chiropractors for the Constitution," to donate sets of "The Right Connection" — an electronic teaching system — to libraries, schools, and adult education centers in the chiropractors' home communities. This computerlike game, which quizzed its users on a variety of topics, including the Constitution and American history, was developed by Madonna Educational Systems of Clearwater, Florida, a Commission logo licensee.

The Boy Scouts of America honored Chief Justice Burger, a former Scout, with their highest award, the Silver Buffalo, for distinguished public service. Presentation of the award was made at the National Bicentennial Competition awards banquet on April 27 in Washington, D.C. The Commission's Chairman, in turn, paid tribute to the Boy Scouts and presented them with the bugle he had used as a Scout in St. Paul, Minnesota. As one of several Masonic programs and publications on the Constitution, the Masonic Grand Lodge of the District of Columbia sponsored a Bicentennial float in the annual Cherry Blossom Parade in Washington, in

the spring of 1988. The float, featuring Cherry Blossom Princesses representing the original 13 states, had been granted official recognition by the Commission and took third-place honors in the float competition.

PRIVATE CORPORATIONS

The Walt Disney Company continued with its support of the Bicentennial in several different ways, including Disney World's EPCOT exhibits on the Constitution which ran throughout the year. Disney also arranged for coverage of the National Bicentennial Competition finals on the Disney Channel. On March 14, in a ceremony in the U.S. Capitol's Statuary Hall, Disney donated to the national Commission over 200 mural replicas of the Christy painting of the Signing of the Constitution *(see Chapter II)*. This gift made possible the distribution of the 6½' x 9' replicas to 50 state capitol buildings and 157 Federal courthouses around the country. The General Services Administration agreed to assist in the installation of the mural in all of the Federal buildings.

The Christy painting had been featured on the cover of many telephone yellow pages in 1987, thus reaching millions of Americans during the course of the year. The Bell Atlantic Corporation, the regional parent of six telephone operating companies and one of the sponsors of the 1987 campaign, initiated a new Bicentennial program in 1988 providing elementary schools with a six-foot poster entitled "We the People," including a timeline display of important dates in American history between 1787 and 1791. The company distributed 100,000 copies of the timeline free of charge to schools in Virginia, Delaware, Pennsylvania, Maryland, New Jersey, and the District of Columbia. Included in each mailing was a brochure with instructional ideas for teachers.

The American dairy industry continued with its efforts to reach schools with educational material about the Constitution. In 1987 the industry, with the sponsorship of the International Paper Company, had included on the panels of its milk cartons educational messages about the Constitution's drafting and signing *(see Chapter III)*, thereby enabling students throughout the country to learn some constitutional lore as they opened their milk cartons during the school lunch hour or recess. This program continued in 1988 under the same sponsorship. An estimated 30 million milk cartons carried one of 13 brief illustrated messages about the Constitution's ratification.

MEDIA

During 1988 there was outstanding media coverage of the Bicentennial, which was recognized by the Benjamin Franklin Awards. Awards went to Roger Pilon, for his article "On the Foundations of Economic Liberty" in *The Freeman,* a monthly publication of the Foundation for Economic Education; Lewis E. Moore, Jr., for a series of articles in *The Daily Herald* of Columbia, Tennessee, on the delegation of powers, the creation of the national government, and the ratification process; Jeffrey St. John, for a series of articles in the *Roanoke Times & World News* on the Virginia Ratification Convention; and Denis J. Hauptly and David A. Sellers, coeditors of *Supreme Court Spotlight,* for their monthly coverage of cases and activities of the Court. The Awards were presented to the winners at the second annual Benjamin Franklin Awards ceremony at the National Press Club, in April 1989.

With the encouragement of the Commission, CBS broadcast an eight-week series on American history created for younger Americans by cartoonist Charles Schulz. It was broadcast in two four-week phases: the first in the autumn of 1988; the second in early 1989. The series, "This is America, Charlie Brown," made its debut on October 21, 1988. Featuring the popular "Peanuts" characters, it dramatized and enlivened important events in American history. The second episode, broadcast on October 28, took up "The Birth of the Constitution," as the animated "Peanuts" gang traveled to 1787 Philadelphia, where Linus informed his friends that they had to clean up the meeting hall for the Constitutional Convention. Attentive witnesses to the painstaking deliberations of the Convention, Charlie Brown and Linus worried about delegates threatening to leave before the task was accomplished, while Lucy urged the election of a queen.

Journalist receives the Franklin Award.

The year produced nothing to compare with the deluge of books published in 1987 on the Constitution. There were, however, some titles worthy of note and in keeping with the year's focus on Ratification. One of these was *The Constitution and the States: The Role of the Original Thirteen in the Framing and Adoption of the Federal Constitution,* edited by Patrick T. Conley and John T. Kaminski. A collection of essays by outstanding scholars on the Founding Era, the book was sponsored by the U.S. Constitution Council of the Thirteen Original States and the Center for the Study of the American Constitution; both organizations played important roles in several Bicentennial programs. Chief Justice Burger noted in his foreword to the book: "To accurately interpret the Constitution — to fully understand its meaning — one must have some idea of what the document meant to those who participated in its ratification . . . the original meaning of the Constitution from the perspective of the states that ratified it deserves further study."

"THIS IS AMERICA, CHARLIE BROWN!"

"**T**his Is America, Charlie Brown" features the popular "Peanuts" characters in a TV history lesson for young viewers, broadcast by CBS (right and overleaf).

© 1958 United Feature Syndicate Inc.

Acknowledging the importance of *The Federalist Papers* in the story of the Constitution's ratification — and, indeed, to all future generations' understanding of the document — Public Research Syndicated (PRS) of Montclair, California, in 1983 launched "The New Federalist Papers" project. With funding from NEH as well as from private foundations, PRS enlisted more than 100 scholars, journalists, and public officials to provide contemporary constitutional commentary in the spirit of the original *Federalist* essays. Beginning in January 1984, some 250 articles were syndicated to nearly 2,000 newspapers across the country. In November 1988, a collection of 85 essays selected from the newspaper series was published by University Press of America, entitled *The New Federalist Papers* and coedited by J. Jackson Barlow, Dennis Mahoney, and John G. West, Jr. The essay authors took the occasion of the Bicentennial to reflect on the past, present, and future of the American experiment in limited government and considered the enduring themes of American politics — federalism, separation of powers, the three branches of government, foreign policy, civil rights, constitutional reform, and other issues.

INTERNATIONAL

Some of the impetus from the 1987 celebrations also carried over into the following year's international programs. American embassies and consulates, as well as the United States Information Agency (USIA) through its overseas posts and its broadcast arm, the Voice of America (VOA), sustained much of this momentum. The VOA, for example, took the occasion of Constitution Week, 1988, to do a series of programs and interviews on the Constitution.

In addition, several special projects involved international constituencies. The chairman of the Commission's Advisory Committee on International Liaison, Betty Murphy, organized a tribute to the Lahore High Court Bar Association, which was working to promote civil liberties and the rule of law in Pakistan. With the cooperation and support of the Library of Congress and the USIA, Judge Kenneth Starr of the United States Court of Appeals for the District of Columbia presented a set of *Corpus Juris Secundum* with accompanying law reports to the Bar Association in a ceremony at the Association's library in Lahore.

When the U.S. Olympics team departed for the Summer Games of the 1988 Olympics in Seoul, Korea, they took with them copies of the POCKET CONSTITUTION, "We the People" lapel pins for trading with fellow athletes of the Games, and a salutation from the Chairman of the national Commission:

As we celebrate the 200 years that the United States has lived by the Constitution, we must recognize the influence it has had around the world. With all eyes turned toward South Korea, you, too, will be setting a standard for many to look up to and follow for years to come.

In the Philippines in February 1988, Chief Justice Claudio Teehankee and his successor, Chief Justice Marcelo B. Fernan, hosted a Regional International Conference in Manila, sponsored by the Philippine Supreme Court, the Asia Foundation, the American Bar Association, the AFL-CIO, and others. Distinguished officials from other Asian countries, five from each country, participated as discussants on comparative constitutions within the region, including that of the Philippines, which was being redrafted at this time. Each delegation was comprised of a professor, legislator, judge, union leader, and a politician or journalist. Three thousand people attended the conference on its first day. Assessing the conference's impact, the head of the AFL-CIO delegation noted that labor leaders were present from nearly every Asian country and that the conference established, for the first time in Asia, the basis for a good working relationship between labor, management, and government.

In Washington in 1988, Chief Justice Burger joined with leaders from both sides of the Atlantic in toasting the permanent installation, in the Exhibition Hall of the Department of State, of a bust of the Baron de Montesquieu. This eighteenth-century French philosopher's observations about separation of powers and other constitutional principles had a profound influence upon the Framers of the U.S. Constitution. Others participating in the ceremony were Madame de Margerie, wife of the French Ambassador to the United States, and Senator Charles Mathias, who chaired the American Committee on the Bicentennial of the French Revolution. The Baron Charles de Montesquieu, chairman of the Bicentennial Community of the City of Bordeaux and a direct descendant of the philosopher, made the presentation.

Early on in the Bicentennial, jurists in Great Britain approached the Commission with the idea of bringing the story of the Constitution to that country with some kind of special program. In May 1988, with financial support from the John M. Olin Foundation, a group of American jurists and academics, including Professor Richard Morris of Columbia University, former Presidential counsel Lloyd Cutler, New York attorney Robert Clare, Commission members Thomas O'Connor and Herbert Brownell, and Chief Justice Burger, traveled to the British Isles to present a symposium on the principle of separation of powers.

The symposium began with three brief lectures on the historical background of the Constitution, summarized by Chief Justice Burger and Professors Morris and O'Connor. There followed a moot court based on the U.S. Supreme Court case of *Goldwater v. Carter*. It focused on the power of the President to cancel treaties without the consent of Congress and, conversely, on the right of Congress to demand confidential documents from the Executive. Herbert Brownell represented the Executive; Robert Clare, the Secretary of State; and Lloyd Cutler, the Senate. The three opening presenters, together with local representatives, sat as judges of the moot court. Afterward, there were questions from the floor and open discussion.

The symposium was first presented at Oxford to a packed house of faculty and students at All Souls College. The Middle Temple in London hosted the second presentation in its Great Hall before an audience that included members of all of England's Inns of Court. The tour then crossed over to Ireland for a repeat performance at University College, Dublin, witnessed by barristers, solicitors, and academics from both the Irish Republic and Northern Ireland.

Pakistan law group honored (below); symposium participants at the Middle Temple in London (bottom).

CONCLUSION

The commemorative activities of 1988 reminded Americans of the importance of the least appreciated chapter in the story of the Constitution: its ratification by the people. It was a year for honoring statehood and the Federal system. And it was a year that even without any specific national event to commemorate, sustained the momentum of the Bicentennial through the development of educational and other programs that would have a lasting impact.

CHAPTER V

1989

Establishment
of
the
New
Government

Having marked the 200th anniversaries of the Constitution's drafting and ratification, the Bicentennial moved on in 1989 to commemorate the Constitution's implementation in the establishment of a new government. During the year, the national Commission joined with states, local communities, other elements of the Federal Government, and private groups in producing major commemorative events honoring the creation of the legislative and executive branches. Meanwhile, the ongoing programs initiated in the previous year and earlier continued to carry forward the long-term educational work of the Commission, as did the many projects undertaken by organizations and groups throughout the United States and in other countries.

The year was not lacking in important anniversaries on which to focus: the creation of the First Congress; George Washington's first inaugural; the formation of the various government departments; and, in anticipation of future Bicentennial themes, the establishment of the judicial branch and the drafting of the Bill of Rights. The year 1789 was seminal in the life of the new Republic.

NEW YORK

Hudson River

Rye

Newark ○   ○ New York

Elizabethtown ○   Apr. 23-

Apr. 22 ○ Woodbridge

○ New Brunswick

○ Princeton

Trenton

Apr. 21

Delaware River

Harrisburg

Susquehanna River

PENNSYLVANIA

Philadelphia ○   Apr. 20

Chester ○

Apr. 19 ○ Wilmington

NEW JERSEY

York

○ Hagerstown

Havre de Grace ○

Apr. 18

Potomac River

Apr. 17

Baltimore

MARYLAND

Apr. 16

VIRGINIA

Georgetown ○

Annapolis

Alexandria ○

Mount Vernon ○

DELAWARE

Chesapeake

Bust of George Washington, by Houdon (top); map showing the original and reenactment route of George Washington's inaugural journey (above); George Washington's entry into Trenton, New Jersey, in an 18th-century drawing by Charles Willson Peale (opposite page).

Major Events

THE COMMEMORATION OF
GEORGE WASHINGTON'S FIRST INAUGURAL

The Constitution went into effect on June 21, 1788, when New Hampshire became the ninth state to ratify. On September 13, in one of its last acts, the Confederation Congress designated New York City as the temporary capital of the new government, issued instructions to the states for the choosing of Presidential electors and, in turn, their selection of a President and Vice President, and fixed the date for the meeting of the new Congress. On November 1, the old Congress concluded its business and adjourned, in effect leaving the country without a national government for five months.

On February 4, 1789, Presidential electors in ten of the 11 states (New York not having yet chosen its electors) cast their ballots and forwarded them to New York for counting by the new Congress, which itself had been elected the previous fall. The First Congress was scheduled to convene at Federal Hall in New York on March 4, 1789, but the absence of a quorum prevented both Houses from conducting any business until April. On April 6, the Senate counted the votes of the Presidential electors, which confirmed that George Washington had been chosen unanimously as President and that John Adams, with the second largest tally of votes, had been elected Vice President.* The President Pro Tempore of the Senate, John Langdon, dispatched messengers to inform the two men of their election. Charles Thomson, Secretary of the old Congress, was given the responsibility of traveling to Virginia to notify Washington.

On April 16, 1789, having borrowed $50 to cover his travel expenses (currency then being scarce), Washington departed his beloved Mount Vernon by coach, accompanied by Thomson and his former aide-de-camp, Col. David Humphreys. They traveled through Virginia, Maryland, Delaware, Pennsylvania, and New Jersey, much of the journey on the Old Post Road, and arrived in New York City April 23. Whatever Washington expected in making this trip, it became a triumphant progress, rivaling the glories of ancient Rome. All along the route, in town and hamlet, dignitaries, old army comrades, and citizens from all walks of life honored the nation's hero with a great outpouring of emotion. Military escorts attended his simple coach-and-four. At every stop Washington was the recipient of proclamations, addresses, banquets, toasts, fusillades, cannonades, and huzzas.

Approaching the bridge into Philadelphia, the President-elect was greeted by magnificent arches of evergreens and laurel, the work of artist Charles Willson Peale, whose daughter placed a hero's wreath of laurel on Washington's brow. Another arch awaited him at Trenton, where the ladies and girls of the town strewed his path with flowers. Perhaps the most touching displays of affection came from former comrades in arms, greeting their old Commander in Chief and remembering the harsh days of the Revolution.

This remarkable journey reached its climax in New York City, where Washington, ferried across the harbor in a ceremonial barge, was cheered by thousands of onlookers who crowded the shoreline and other vessels, some of which fired broadsides in salute. A week later, on April 30, the President-elect took the oath of office on the balcony of Federal Hall, to the acclaim of his fellow citizens assembled in windows, on rooftops, and in the street below. On cue, the flag of the new Republic unfurled above the Hall, a 13-gun salute sounded at the Battery, and the city's church bells began to peal. This momentous day closed with fireworks and illuminations.

Washington's journey to New York and his inauguration had a significance which surpassed the sentiment and ceremony of the moment. This extraordinary event—without precedent or sequel in American history — did much to cement popular support for the Constitution and the new government it had realized. In a sense, the people bestowed on the new Constitution the confidence they had in George Washington.

---

*Before the adoption of the Twelfth Amendment in 1804, which established the present election system, each elector in the Presidential election was allowed to cast two votes. The individual receiving the highest number of votes was elected President; the individual with the second highest tally was elected Vice President. In the absence of a majority or in case of a tie, the election went into the House of Representatives.

Reenactment of the Event: The reenactment of George Washington's journey to New York and his inauguration was one of the most complex projects undertaken during the Bicentennial. Although the reenactment did not involve as many people as did A CELEBRATION OF CITIZENSHIP, the sheer complexity of such a journey's organization and logistics surpassed anything else attempted. The entire event was a classic example of teamwork, involving several hundred individuals from dozens of Federal, state, and local authorities, and still more private organizations and groups. The journey was at least a year in the planning, which continued right up to the moment of departure from Mount Vernon on April 16, 1989.

For the historical reenactment, the individuals portraying Washington and his companions traveled the 250 miles from Mount Vernon to New York — most of that distance in a horse-drawn carriage — recreating many of the events of 1789 along the route. On April 30, the journey climaxed at Federal Hall with a reenactment of the First Inauguration in the presence of the nation's 41st President, George Bush.

The event began Sunday, April 16, on the east portico of Mount Vernon, aglow in a spring morning's sunshine, where the formal notification of Washington's election to the Presidency and his formal acceptance of the office were reenacted before a small audience of dignitaries and media representatives. The main ceremony began shortly thereafter on the west front of the mansion, where a large crowd was gathered. Postmaster

General Anthony Frank unveiled a new first-class commemorative postage stamp featuring a profile of Washington. White House Chief of Staff John Sununu and Mount Vernon Regent Eugenia Seamans spoke about the impact of Washington upon the nation's history. In his remarks, Chief Justice Burger observed that "this journey is a celebration of a journey that has lasted 200 years. Let us hope and pray that it will last many hundred more."

The ceremonies concluded with a staged reenactment of Washington's departure, produced by the Mount Vernon Ladies Association. All went smoothly until the noise of the crowd and camera flashes startled the horses. The coach-and-four pulled away and hit a stanchion, breaking the carriage's tongue in the process. Though it seemed at the time an inauspicious start, the breakdown would be the only significant mishap in an eventful two weeks of travel and ceremony. Fortunately, careful planning had provided for a backup carriage, in which the three "historicals" (as the three principal reenactors came to be called) proceeded to Alexandria, escorted into Old Town by a troop of mounted yeomanry. There the party dined at historic Gadsby's Tavern. Toasts and speeches were relived by Alexandria Mayor James Moran and local citizens dressed in period costume. After a brief visit with well-wishers gathered outside, Washington and his fellow travelers proceeded north on the Parkway named in honor of the First President, against the backdrop of the Washington Monument across the Potomac.

In 1789 Washington had crossed that river by ferry. The reenactment party entered the city named for him via the Key Bridge and made a brief visit to the Forrest-Marbury House in Georgetown, where they were honored with the reading of a poetic tribute to Washington, written 200 years before by Phyllis Wheatly. The first day of the journey concluded that evening at the eighteenth-century Montpelier Mansion, in Laurel, Maryland. A daylong fair, complete with period music, military units, and crafts demonstrations, preceded the Washington party's arrival. After reviewing his troops, Washington presented his hosts with samples of the gifts he would bestow throughout the journey: a commemorative inaugural journey flag and a boxwood cutting from Mount Vernon. Later, he delighted his guests by dancing the minuet.

Early on the morning of the second day (Monday, April 17), Willard Scott of NBC-TV's "Today Show" interviewed Washington in Riverside Park, Maryland, before the General and his party rode to Federal Hill, site of the Maryland ratification convention in 1788. Hundreds of schoolchildren were on hand to greet him, many dressed in homemade period costume. In an exercise he was to repeat countless times during the journey, the President-elect asked the children to join him in reciting the Preamble to the Constitution, which they did with youthful vigor. A chorus of rousing "huzzas" for the Constitution closed the program. After a parade through the Inner Harbor area led by the U.S. Army's famed Old Guard, Washington and his party were greeted by another group of exuberant school children at the Charles Carroll Mansion in Baltimore. Wrote one of the reenactors afterward:

There was the endless panorama of faces along the roadsides, from every environment and circumstance. . . . I recall with special poignancy the crowds of school children who flanked our carriage at so many stops, or who simply came out to stand along the road as we passed by; we could feel their electric excitement. I shall remember from that first Sunday, as we passed through Washington, D.C., the Hispanic ghetto kids running alongside our carriage yelling "El Presidente! El Presidente!" And then there were the prep school boys at Lawrenceville, waving to us in the dusk . . . the Quakers of Trenton; the proud townspeople of Havre de Grace; the newly naturalized citizens at Elizabeth; . . . military units in their eighteenth-century uniforms, obviously pleased to pass muster and inspection by their Commander-in-Chief. And I shall remember a country road bathed in the yellow glow of sunset, when two elderly ladies hurried up to our carriage and waved to us with tears in their eyes.*

That afternoon the 1st Maryland Regiment and the Sons of the American Revolution (SAR) Color Guard escorted Washington's party to an outdoor reception at the elegant Mount Clare Mansion in Carroll Park. The day concluded with an evening of music and dance at The Rectory, where Washington was saluted with the strains of "Hail, Thou Auspicious Day."

When Washington left Baltimore in 1789, a large group of citizens escorted his carriage for seven miles beyond the city. Two hundred years later, on the third day of the journey (Tuesday, April 18) the Washington reenactment party drew another cheering throng of youngsters as the carriage drove up to the Hampton National Historic Shrine in Towson, Maryland, the 1789 home of Charles Ridgely. Washington's hosts saluted him with the Revolutionary War hymn "Chester" and the Masonic March— in honor of Washington's Masonic affiliation. Standing on the front step of the mansion, the General — as he was to do countless times during the journey — called upon his favorite prop, a pair of spectacles, and began with a phrase Washington himself had once used: "Not only have I grown gray in the

© 1989 Peter Souza

D*eparting Mount Vernon (above and below, left); a friendly toast in Gadsby's tavern, Alexandria, Virginia (above).*

---

*Herbert M. Atherton, "On the Road with George Washington," *Public History News* (Spring 1991), p. 2.

Two hundred years after Washington's journey northward
to the first inaugural, the coach-and-four used in the reenactment negotiates 20th-century
traffic while passing the monument named for the first President.

service of my country, but nearly blind." He then spoke reverently of the Constitution and once again invoked the words of the Preamble. The young students presented their guests with cornbread, a proclamation, and a map showing the route of their remaining journey.

Another celebration by schoolchildren greeted the traveling party at the Paca and Old Post Elementary Schools as it proceeded along the Old Philadelphia Road, where the travelers made an impromptu stop at a center for retarded citizens. After a brief rest at the

Washington *dances a minuet at Montpelier (right) and mingles with a crowd of children in Colonial attire at Federal Hill, Baltimore, Maryland (below).*

Bill Fitzpatrick (5)

Crossing Key Bridge (left); greeting a very young lady (below); and entering Mount Clare Mansion (bottom).

The travelers journeyed through landscapes seemingly unchanged since the early years of the Republic (overleaf).

Bill Fitzpatrick

Soldiers, young and old alike, gather to greet the former Commander-in-Chief (left and below).

Department of Defense's (DOD) Aberdeen Proving Grounds, where the coach-and-four traveled along what may have been a remaining portion of the Old Post Road that Washington himself had used in 1789, the reenactment party proceeded to Havre de Grace for a formal ceremony in the town square. Then, after crossing the high bridge over the Susquehanna, they concluded their long day with a reception at the Rodgers Tavern in Perryville, Maryland.

Remarkably for April, almost all the journey was blessed with unremitting sunshine, so much of it that the passengers in the open carriage were eventually forced to use twentieth-century sunscreen. The fourth day (Wednesday, April 19), however, dawned cool and wet, forcing Washington and his companions into Navy capes. By the time the entourage reached Christiana, Delaware, the weather had cleared. There they visited the Cooch House, site of the only battle of the Revolutionary War fought in Delaware and the home of nine generations of the Cooch family. More memories awaited the General at the Hale-Byrnes House in Stanton, which had served as Washington's headquarters before the battle of Brandywine. To commemorate the event, the reenactment party participated in the planting of a white oak tree.

After a brief visit with students at the Newport, Delaware, Town Hall, Washington and his companions moved on to Wilmington, escorted into Caesar Rodney Park in the city's center by bands playing "Chester" and "Yankee Doodle." Before a large lunchtime crowd,

New Government   135

Colonial storefront display welcomes Washington (below); the President-elect addressing a crowd in Wilmington, Delaware (right).

Bill Fitzpatrick (2)

Governor Michael Castle and Chief Justice Andrew Christie of the state Supreme Court welcomed the General, who was presented with a Delaware Fighting Rooster. This was one of many unusual gifts Washington received during the journey. Others included a set of false teeth and a quilted pillow to ease his journey, as well as food, flowers, and an assortment of proclamations, certificates, plaques, maps, thank-you letters, and student artwork and essays.

In 1789 Washington had begun the fifth day of his journey with breakfast in Chester, Pennsylvania. At the reenactment 200 years later (Thursday, April 20), city and county officials entertained Washington's party at the Old Court House in that city. With as much fidelity to the original event as modern conditions would allow,

Washington crossed the Schuylkill River into Philadelphia and entered the city upon a magnificent white horse (this one a 13-year-old Lipizzaner named Revere), passing beneath a modest re-creation of the archway of flowers that had been erected on the Market Street Bridge. Escorted by the First City Cavalry Troop, Washington rode his white mount to City Hall, where he joined his two companions and Philadelphia Mayor Wilson Goode in the carriage for the ride to Independence Hall. There, 202 years before, Washington had presided over the Constitutional Convention. Before a large crowd gathered in the park opposite, Mayor Goode and other dignitaries paid tribute to Washington. "All I can offer you, my fellow countrymen," the President-elect said in response, "is fairness and integrity. No

A *few of the many items presented to Washington by schoolchildren, town officials, and citizens along the journey to New York.*

Harlee Little

matter how arduous the Presidency, these qualities will never desert me." Throughout the journey, Washington reminded well-wishers that the nation was about to embark on "untrodden ground" and he asked for their support in that venture. After a photo session in the room where the Constitution was drafted, Washington and his two companions strolled the grounds of Independence Park and visited with both children and reporters. One reporter asked the General what it was like to portray George Washington. Keeping in character — as he always did during the reenactment — the General replied: "Sir, I am George Washington." That evening his party dined at the City Tavern, as Washington himself had, two centuries before. He was saluted with toasts and musket fire in the tavern's courtyard.

On Friday, April 21, the reenactment party reached New Jersey, where they would travel entirely by coach and visit the sites of two of Washington's most significant victories in the War of Independence. The triumphant entry into Trenton in 1789 was reenacted, as the General, again mounted on Revere, crossed Assunpink Creek on Broad Street and passed beneath a Triumphal Arch, to the greetings of matrons and young girls, one of whom was a direct descendant of one of the ladies who saluted Washington two centuries before. In the midst of a large, exuberant crowd at the Capital Center, Governor Thomas Kean welcomed Washington. "This is an astonishing contrast to my former entry into Trenton," the General noted, in reference to his surprise attack on December 26, 1776. Asked by a reporter if he actually

Members of the Militia fire a salute in honor of the General's arrival (above); Washington strolls the grounds of Independence Park with children (right) and pauses to answer a few questions (opposite page).

Bill Fitzpatrick (3)

stood up in the boat as he crossed the Delaware, he replied, "Sir, only a fool stands up in a boat."

The day in Trenton was dedicated to several brief visits to historic houses of worship, where Washington laid wreaths on the graves of old comrades, and a stop at the Trenton Battle Monument. During a reception at the Core State Bank, on the site of the City Tavern where Washington dined in 1789, the General displayed a side of himself glimpsed by few. He was introduced to a little girl of Polish-American extraction, three or four years old, who handed him a copy of the Constitution to sign. In Polish she thanked Washington, who responded in Polish and then said with a wink: "Count Kosciuszko

Entering Trenton, New Jersey, under a triumphal arch (top); experiencing the arduousness of travel on 20th-century thoroughfares (above); rolling down Main Street USA (right).

*Everywhere,
there were crowds of
onlookers eager
for a glimpse of the first
President-to-be (far left),
who found time
to inspect a troop of
Boy Scouts along
the route (left).*

MAIN STREET

Bill Fitzpatrick (3)

[the Polish nobleman who fought in the War of Independence] taught me that." At the Old Barracks in Trenton, site of the battle in December 1776, Washington relived memories of that day and recalled comrades who did not live to share in the freedoms for which they fought. The reenactment party concluded this long day with a carriage ride in the dusk along Route 206 and an evening ceremony at the Phillips House in Lawren-ceville, where they spent the night. Dawn of the next day (Saturday, April 22) found the carriage and its

Washington's carriage enters the campus of Princeton University (left); he shakes hands with newly naturalized citizens (top); a welcoming crowd gathers in Woodbridge, New Jersey (above).

passengers on the road to Princeton, where Mayor Barbara Boggs Sigmund and other dignitaries gathered at Morven (once the Governor's Mansion) to welcome the President-elect. Washington and his party then proceeded to Princeton University for a meeting with faculty members at historic Nassau Hall and a recitation of the address delivered there in 1789.

After a brief stop for refreshments at the Bainbridge House in Nassau Street, Washington and his compan-ions rode on to Kingston and North Brunswick. At New Brunswick the reenactment party was joined by John Kean, portraying Governor William Livingston, who 200 years before had accompanied Washington, Thom-son, and Humphreys on the remainder of their trip to New York. At Buccleuch Mansion, they were greeted by an elementary school marching band and by a Mid-dlesex County Militia unit, which Washington reviewed. After a welcoming ceremony and lunch at the Mansion, Washington's party continued on to Highland Park and Edison. An unscheduled stop at a nursing home near Edison gave Washington a chance to speak to citizens who were born not long after the Centennial commemo-ration of the First Inaugural in 1889. The day culminated with a jubilant entry into Woodbridge, with swelling crowds and a crescendo of excitement as Washington, standing in his carriage and escorted by cavalry, proceeded down the city's main street to the Memorial Municipal Building and a ceremony highlighted by artillery fire and a musket *feu de joie*. That evening

Washington and his companions were honored at a private banquet at the Knights of Columbus Hall.

On the last day of the journey (Sunday, April 23), several hundred people welcomed the reenactment party at the Merchants and Drovers Tavern in Rahway, New Jersey. Washington entered to the sound of church bells, breakfasted with local dignitaries, and laid a wreath at the grave of Abraham Clark, a signer of the Declaration of Independence. Pausing for brief stops in Linden and Roselle, the carriage headed for Elizabeth, where the General participated in a naturalization ceremony for 200 new citizens at the Union County Courthouse. Washington and his companions handed out copies of the Commission's POCKET CONSTITUTION to their new fellow countrymen.

After a lunch at Boxwood Hall in Elizabeth, to commemorate Washington's official greeting by Members of Congress in 1789, the carriage traversed the old streets of the city, to the cheers of hundreds of well-wishers crowded on the sidewalks and in doorways and windows along the way. At about 2:00 p.m., it arrived at Municipal Pier, where a re-creation of the 47-foot ceremonial vessel of 1789 waited to take Washington and his party to New York City. Rowed by a crew of midshipmen from the U.S. Merchant Marine Academy (with the assistance of a Coast Guard vessel across New York harbor), the shallop passed through the Kill Van Kull and past Liberty Island, was saluted with a broadside from the frigate H.M.S. *Rose*, and arrived at the South Street Seaport in Manhattan within minutes of the landing time 200 years before. Mayor Edward Koch led dignitaries and a large crowd in welcoming the President-elect to New York City. In reply, Washington echoed the words from two centuries earlier: "My dear friends, I take on the burden and the challenge of the First Executive of the United States."

Washington and his party had reached their destination after traveling eight days through six states and participating in over 50 ceremonial activities. Although the journey ended on April 23, the reenactment was not over. Its climactic event, the inauguration, was still a week away. In 1789 Washington had spent the intervening time visiting friends, listening to petitioners, and assembling his administration. Preparations, parties, academic symposia, exhibits, a naval flotilla, an ecumenical religious service, and "Presidential Fireworks" filled the corresponding week in 1989.

On Sunday, April 30, the inaugural of the First President was reenacted at the newly renovated Federal Hall, in the presence of the nation's 41st President, 100 descendants of other U.S. Presidents, ambassadors from the five countries represented at Washington's inaugural in 1789, and numerous dignitaries. The Chairman of the New York City Bicentennial Commission, Joseph H. Flom, and the Mayor gave welcoming remarks followed by tributes to the Bicentennial of the U.S. Congress from Representative Lindy Boggs and from Senator Daniel Patrick Moynihan of New York. Chief Justice Burger, as Chairman of the national Commission, introduced the reenactment ceremony.

A *re-created ceremonial shallop carries Washington across New York harbor (above) to South Street Seaport (opposite page).*

William Sommerfield,
*portraying George Washington,
takes the oath of office at
historic Federal Hall in New York,
surrounded by descendants of
the original participants
of the event 200 years earlier.*

Wearing a replica of the brown suit of "American manufacture" that Washington himself had worn at the 1789 inaugural, the President-elect arrived at the Hall by carriage, escorted by the fifes and drums of the 3rd Infantry's Old Guard. Henry Livingston, a direct descendant of the Robert Livingston who administered the oath of office in 1789, presided. The oath was repeated with the same Masonic Bible used 200 years earlier and followed by the words "So help me God" that the First President had added impromptu in 1789 and that by tradition have accompanied the Presidential oath ever since. Washington then delivered an abbreviated version of the First Inaugural Address. "The preservation of the sacred flame of liberty, and the destiny of the republican model of government," he said, "are justly considered as deeply, perhaps as finally staked, on the experiment entrusted to the hands of the American people."

Following the reenactment ceremony, Senator Alfonse M. D'Amato of New York introduced President Bush, who observed that "everyone here today can still feel the pulse of history, the charge and power of that great moment in the genesis of the nation. The Constitution was, and remains," he said, "a majestic document. But it was a blueprint, an outline for democratic government, in need of a master builder to ensure its foundations were strong." Washington provided that service. President Bush urged his fellow citizens to follow Washington's example by heeding the summons of citizenship and public service.

The ceremony closed in traditional New York fashion with a deluge of multicolored confetti catching the sunlight above the gray canyons of Wall Street, followed by a ticker tape parade up Broadway. The day ended with a gala ball at the Waldorf Astoria.

*It was a journey of physical exhaustion and emotional highs, punctuated by enough sweet vignettes to crowd the memories of a lifetime . . . the pregnant pause that followed our aborted start at Mount Vernon; the driver of the Rolls-Royce who pulled alongside us on the George Washington Parkway to ask, "Grey Poupon anyone?"; the minuets and country dances at Maryland's Montpelier; the mists and first light near Federal Hill in Baltimore . . . the rounds of hearty huzzas and recitations of the Preamble of the Constitution; the Georgian elegance of Hampton and Mount Clare; our tricky crossing of the high bridge over the Susquehanna; the tumultuous entry into Woodbridge . . . the chop and winds of New York harbor, threatening the curls in Washington's hair; the shower of confetti at New York's Federal Hall. . . . What was perhaps most extraordinary about this venture — beyond the fact that we were able to pull it off at all — was its almost uniformly positive impact. . . . To judge from the reactions of many along the way, our little carriage, moving along the highways and byways, keeping its schedule against all obstacles, building its momentum of excitement, was in a very special way honoring the memory of Washington and the founding of our national government.**

In *New York's grandest style, a deluge of multicolored confetti concludes the reenactment of Washington's inauguration (overleaf).*

Bill Fitzpatrick

*Ibid., pp. 2, 15.

How It Happened: There was ample historical precedent for commemorating the First Inaugural. Indeed, precedent suggested that this was perhaps the one unavoidable event in the entire Bicentennial. In 1839, former President John Quincy Adams delivered an address organized by the New York Historical Society to mark the anniversary. Fifty years later, President Benjamin Harrison traveled from Washington, D.C., to Elizabeth, New Jersey, by train and from there, on April 29, participated in a Centennial reprise of the crossing to New York City. The following day, he marked the anniversary of the First Inaugural with brief remarks at a ceremony on the site of old Federal Hall, followed by a "Grand Military Procession." As a permanent monument to the anniversary, the Centennial Committee arranged for a memorial arch to be erected in New York City's Washington Square.

Both the journey and inaugural were part of the Sesquicentennial reenactment of 1939, when New York City artist and cartoonist Denys Wortman (chosen because of his resemblance to Washington and his interest in American history), made the 250-mile journey by carriage and bus, accompanied by actors playing the roles of Charles Thomson and David Humphreys. President Franklin Roosevelt initiated the

reenactment with a radio broadcast from the portico at Mount Vernon. Eight days later, Mayor Fiorello LaGuardia officially welcomed the traveling party to New York City. Instead of Federal Hall, the inaugural reenactment itself took place at Flushing Meadows, Long Island, as part of the opening ceremony of the 1939 New York World's Fair, which had been planned originally to mark the 150th anniversary of the 1789 inauguration. Governor Herbert Lehman unveiled a 65-foot statue of Washington on the fair's Constitution Mall, where the reenactment was staged. As the extensive coverage in *The New York Times* of the day makes clear, the project was a success, drawing media attention and large crowds much of the way. The record also suggests, however, the difficulties of such an enterprise, especially the logistical problems involved with the staging of so long a carriage journey. These difficulties soon became evident in the planning of the 1989 Bicentennial reenactment.

The long gestation period of this project began early in 1988 with informal meetings between representatives of the national Commission and various groups with a potential interest in the enterprise, including Commissions of the several states involved, the Mount Vernon Ladies Association, the Carriage Association of America, and others. The purpose of

New York City Commission On the Bicentennial of the US Constitution

In 1889 President Harrison crossed New York harbor as part of the Centennial reenactment of Washington's inaugural journey (opposite page); the 1939 World's Fair in New York (left) featured a statue of Washington.

Journey planners meet at Mount Vernon to discuss details of the reenactment (below).

these meetings was exploratory — to consider in a very preliminary way the feasibility of so large and complicated an undertaking. It became clear from the discussions that an immense amount of planning would be required. This planning got under way at a meeting of key participants on August 25, 1988, and continued in greater detail at a two-day meeting at Mount Vernon, September 28-29, 1988. By this time, representatives of the DOD, the District of Columbia, and New York City had become involved.

Despite the ample precedent for the reenactment, there was precious little information about how to undertake such a project. No manual existed explaining how one went about organizing and executing an event of such complexity in an age of superhighways and

Bill Fitzparrick

traffic congestion. The planners would have to start from scratch. The conference at Mount Vernon was therefore critically important in putting a project team together and defining the essential issues to be resolved. Three working-group sessions on logistics, press and public relations, and education and historiography produced reports that raised key questions and suggested possible directions in which further development might go. What should be the main purpose and program emphasis of the project — ceremony or education? Should the project attempt a complete mile-by-mile reenactment of the original journey, or compromise with current logistical realities? What should be the division of labor? Who should handle the overall planning and logistical coordination? Who should have primary responsibility for the historical events reenacted along the way? How and to what extent should the project be funded?

With the anniversary scarcely six and one-half months away, it was obvious that there would be real problems in carrying out the project at all. All of the participating constituencies looked to the national Commission as the organization that would have to take primary responsibility for overall planning and coordination if the deadline was to be met. It also became clear that certain states crucial to the reenactment would not be able to participate without an infusion of funds.

The Commission's Government Affairs Division was put in charge of the project, with primary responsi-

bility for the administration of all its aspects. Gradually, bit by bit, the questions raised at the Mount Vernon meeting began to be answered and the complex structure of the project took form. It was decided, for example, that the reenactment would be predominantly ceremonial but also have a number of educational features, including the extensive participation of school groups and the distribution of educational materials to schools in advance.

The national Commission awarded grants to states, communities, and various private organizations to permit them to move ahead with their plans. Where necessary, outside organizations were contracted to carry out specific aspects of the reenactment. Representatives of the national Commission began to work with state and local leaders in the tedious process of refining the details of an eight-day journey along the 250-mile route. This proved difficult for a number of reasons. First, not all particulars of Washington's original journey were known. Even with the best of historical research, there were gaps in the story of what happened 200 years before. After a potential route, combining historical fidelity with contemporary feasibility and opportunity, had been determined, each mile of the journey had to be surveyed and timed so that a precise schedule for both transportation and events along the way could be worked out.

As the 1939 reenactment had shown, adequate arrangements for transportation were crucial to the success of the enterprise. This task fell to Jack Seabrook and his colleagues at the Carriage Association of America, based in Salem, New Jersey. Seabrook recommended that several drivers and teams of horses participate, rotated and paced according to a carefully arranged schedule. After an extensive search, two antique carriages (a regular carriage and a backup) were selected for the journey. Owned by Henry E. I. du Pont of Delaware and John Allen, Jr., of New Jersey, they combined authenticity with reasonable comfort and safety. Mr. Seabrook had a special interest in the project that transcended his love of carriages and horses. As a senior at Princeton in 1939 he had witnessed the visit of the Sesquicentennial reenactment team. For sentimental reasons, he drove the 1989 carriage to the campus of his alma mater. The Pegasus Riding Academy at Philadelphia provided the Lipizzaner ridden by Washington in that city and in Trenton.

The Department of the Army volunteered to provide almost all the logistical support for the journey: transport vehicles, communications equipment, and personnel. Throughout, constant contact had to be maintained between those aboard the carriage, support vehicles, the Commission's advance staff, local personnel, and state and local security, who handled all the traffic problems.

As our odd little caravan snaked its way through city and countryside, over expressway and back road, along what is now called the "Northeast Corridor," it carried in its baggage a number of ironies and anachronisms. To create the illusion of an event that took place eight generations ago required the best efforts of a tireless support staff and a considerable amount of twentieth-century technology — walkie-talkies, an RV conveyance with microwave and TV, police cars and electric road signs, a helicopter, military equipment, even computer-generated scripts — all to keep a simple horse-and-four with its three foppish-looking passengers on the road and on schedule.*

All of the effort that went into the organizational and support side of the reenactment would have been for naught, however, if the "three foppish-looking passengers" were not up to their roles. They would provide the critical interaction with all those involved along the route: dignitaries, other reenactors, schoolchildren, and the general public. Herbert Atherton, then the Commission's Deputy Staff Director and Director of Education, was selected to portray Charles Thomson. David Dutcher, the Chief Historian at Independence Hall National Historic Park, took the part of David Humphreys. As scholars of eighteenth-century life and politics, both Atherton and Dutcher were well qualified to undertake the support roles. The critical selection, of course, was the man to play Washington. Many professional actors and other candidates were suggested and considered. Finally, Franklin Roberts of Franklin S. Roberts Associates in Philadelphia (*see Chapter II*), who had been contracted to script Washington's speeches

*Ibid., p. 2.

Mike Falco, *Statan Island Advance* (3)

The 20th century yields briefly to the 18th, as the cavalcade makes its way northward under escort.

*T*he three reenactors:
Herbert Atherton as Charles Thomson,
David Dutcher as David Humphreys,
and William Sommerfield as George Washington.

Bill Fitzpatrick

and provide costuming and makeup support for the three reenactors, suggested William Sommerfield.

Sommerfield was a professional actor associated with the Royal Pickwickians, a Philadelphia theatrical organization that specialized in historical reenactments. He had played Washington many times before on national, local, and foreign television and in hundreds of personal appearances. A well-read man, Sommerfield had spent almost a lifetime studying and researching Washington and his times. Dressed in period costume, he carried himself with a striking resemblance to the nation's first President. The simple dignity, seriousness of purpose, and historical fidelity with which the reenactment was carried out must be credited in large measure to Sommerfield's portrayal. He handled both the planned and the unexpected with grace, elegance, savvy, and wit. The Commission's Chairman perhaps put it best when he noted of the reenactment's success that "the top man set the tone."

In its execution and outcome, the reenactment of the First Inaugural provided an excellent example of teamwork. It was not unlike a relay, in which the coach and its three passengers, closely tracked by the staff of the national Commission and other support personnel, was passed from one jurisdiction to another according to a precise timetable. Each group of organizations along the route was equally vital to the reenactment. All involved could take credit for the success of the journey.

Impact of the Reenactment: Despite a lack of promotional resources and sufficient lead time, media coverage — both national and local — was extensive. Several factors explain this interest. The event itself was a natural feature item. Public interest in the anniversary may have been heightened by the coincidence of President Bush's inauguration three months before. Moreover, the event took place in one of the most

populated, media-intense areas of the country. Finally, the carriage's untoward accident at Mount Vernon had the compensation of generating additional media attention at the outset.

The reenactment received advance coverage through news items and feature stories in several newspapers, including *The Washington Times*, *The Baltimore Sun*, *The Philadelphia Inquirer*, *The Philadelphia Daily News*, and *The News Journal* of Wilmington. Other advance coverage was featured in *The Mini Page* (which appeared in the Sunday supplements of hundreds of newspapers across the country), Amtrak's bimonthy magazine *Express*, and *Capper's*, a biweekly farmer's magazine published in Topeka, Kansas.

The television and radio networks, as well as wire services, covered both the departure ceremony at Mount Vernon and the ceremonies in New York. The stop in Baltimore was featured on NBC's "Today" show, and the reenactment received intensive local news coverage as it made its way through the six states. Helping to publicize the event locally were radio traffic reports, which alerted drivers to the congestion generated by the carriage and its companion vehicles.

The *Staten Island Advance* reported on the entire reenactment with a special correspondent and photographer, who produced a vivid chronicle of what took place. Station WNVT-53, northern Virginia's public television station, also covered the entire journey with a series of three-minute pieces focusing on the historical significance of the reenactment. As many as 50 or 60 public television stations and 15 to 20 school divisions around the country taped segments of this coverage, which was also picked up by 20 commercial stations. WNVT granted all stations and schools unlimited rights to the use of this material.

The reenactment of George Washington's inaugural, along with 1987's A CELEBRATION OF CITIZENSHIP and the events of WE THE PEOPLE 200, ranks as one of the high-profile events of the Bicentennial. One way or another, it reached millions of people, poignantly reminding them of the legacy of Washington and the founding of the nation's government under the Constitution. Perhaps most important are the unforgettable images impressed on the memories of the thousands of people from Mount Vernon to New York, in town and countryside along the way, who participated in the reenactment or observed it:

Perhaps most eery was the way in which all this affected people, including those of us directly involved. . . . If one looked into the eyes of the many who reached out to touch Washington or who just stood clapping along the roadside — adults as well as children — one sometimes had the feeling that they believed, if only for a moment, they were in the presence of Washington, they were caught up in history . . . past and present, fantasy and reality magically merged. We brushed the edges of history in a very profound and personal way. And perhaps herein lies the most important message of this experience. . . .*

*Ibid., p. 12.

Mike Falco, *Staten Island Advance*

COMMEMORATION OF THE FIRST CONGRESS

George Washington's journey to the Presidency was not the only major subject of commemoration in 1989. Indeed, it was not the first. March 4 of that year marked the 200th anniversary of the convening of the First Congress and the establishment of the legislative branch. In a sense, the nation's government under the Constitution began here. Commemorated with special events, exhibits, publications, and a variety of other activities, this anniversary added to a crowded Bicentennial year.

As already mentioned, on September 13, 1788, the Confederation Congress set the calendar for the first Federal elections and directed the state legislatures to conduct them. The new Constitution mandated a decennial census to determine congressional representation, but for the interim before the completion of the first census, it specified a temporary apportionment of the House of Representatives. Pennsylvania was the first

Bill Fitzpatrick

T*ending the teams along the journey's route was a full-time job (top); Washington waving good-bye to the crowd (above).*

After taking the oath as the first chief executive of the infant nation, a bareheaded President Washington rides out into history.

House Speaker Langdon (top left) and Senate President Pro Tempore Muhlenberg (top right), leaders of the First Congress. To honor it, three commemorative coins were minted at the Capitol.

state to respond at the end of September, when its General Assembly selected two U.S. Senators. During October and November other states followed in the selection of Senators by their respective legislatures and with the popular election of Representatives in congressional districts.

The First Congress convened at Federal Hall in New York City on March 4, 1789, but in the absence of a quorum (only eight Senators and 13 Representatives were present) was not able to begin its business until the beginning of April—the House on April 1, the Senate on the 6th. The House selected Frederick Muhlenburg of Pennsylvania as its first Speaker, and the Senate chose John Langdon of New Hampshire as its President Pro Tempore. Since North Carolina and Rhode Island were not yet represented (neither had yet ratified the Constitution), the First Congress initially had 59 Representatives and 22 Senators. Eventually, it would include 20 men who had attended the Constitutional Convention in Philadelphia, eight who had signed the Declaration of Independence, two future Presidents, and one future Vice President.

The task before it was worthy of such an illustrious membership. Determining the election of George Washington and making arrangements for his inaugural was only the first in a series of fundamental accomplishments. The First Congress created the executive-branch offices and departments necessary to enable the new government to function. Its tax legislation established a Federal revenue system. It passed the Judiciary Act of 1789, thus creating the third branch of government. And it drafted, approved, and passed on to the states 12 proposed amendments to the Constitution, ten of which

A special joint meeting of Congress celebrates the Bicentennial of the first Congress.

became the Bill of Rights (*see Chapter VII*). Because of these and other measures of seminal importance, the First Congress has sometimes been called the "Second Constitutional Convention."

To plan and coordinate the commemoration, the 99th Congress in 1985 had established a Commission on the United States House of Representatives Bicentenary. This bipartisan entity was chaired by Representative Lindy Boggs, who was also a member of the national Commission. It consisted of six other Members of Congress and two former Members, appointed by the Speaker in consultation with the House Minority Leader. In overseeing the commemoration of the birth of Congress, the Bicentenary Commission worked closely with the Office for the Bicentennial of the House of Representatives, created by Congress in 1982 and headed by its professional historian, Dr. Raymond W. Smock. The Senate's activities for the commemoration were directed by a Senate Bicentennial Commission, created in 1986 and chaired by Senator Robert C. Byrd, with eight other members. This Commission worked closely with the Senate Historical Office, headed by Dr. Richard A. Baker. The office had begun planning for the Bicentennial in 1980 when the Senate established a Study Group on the Commemoration of the United States Senate Bicentenary. From their inception the two Commissions and their research support staffs developed a large number of projects, including publications, exhibits, video productions, symposia, and special commemorative ceremonies, only a few of which are described here.

Special Joint Meeting of Congress: On March 2, 1989, the two Houses met in a special joint session to celebrate the convening of the First Congress. C-SPAN televised the session, which was attended not only by Members of Congress, but other dignitaries, who were invited to sit on the floor of the House. The United States Army Band and the Old Guard Fife and Drum Corps provided musical accompaniment.

Speaker of the House Jim Wright presided in a ceremony that included a ceremonial presentation of the first journals of the House and Senate in 1789, as well as the Mace of the House and Gavel of the Senate. Speakers included Wright, the Chairmen of the congressional

Commissions, Representative Boggs and Senator Byrd, Senate Majority Leader George Mitchell, Senate Minority Leader Robert Dole, House Majority Leader Thomas Foley, and House Minority Leader Robert Michel. The Poet Laureate of the United States, Howard Nemerov, read a poem written specially for the occasion, which included the lines:

> *For here the million varying wills*
> *Get melted down, get hammered out*
> *Until the movie's reduced to stills*
> *That tell us what the law's about.*

Taking as his metaphorical theme Simon Willard's clock and Carlo Franzoni's statue of Clio (the Muse of history), which stand in Statuary Hall, historian David McCullough delivered the program's major address. He spoke of the historical "echoes and resonances" of the great men and women who had walked the halls of Congress, and of their great accomplishments. The special session also included the unveiling of designs for the House and Senate postage stamps and for the Congressional Bicentennial Coins, with Postmaster General Anthony Frank and Secretary of the Treasury Nicholas Brady participating.

Congressional Stamps and Coins: On April 4 the U.S. Postal Service, working with the Office of the House Bicentennial and the Postmaster of the House, conducted a first-day-of-issue ceremony for the House commemorative postage stamp, which featured the Franzoni statue of Clio. The House's Majority and Minority Leaders, together with Representative Boggs and Postmaster General Frank, participated in the ceremony in Statuary Hall, once the old House chamber. Two days later, on the anniversary of the Senate's first meeting with a quorum, first-day-of-issue ceremonies were held in the Old Senate Chamber for the Senate Bicentennial commemorative postage stamp. Senator Byrd and Postmaster General Frank delivered brief remarks.

At a ceremony held on the East Front of the Capitol on Flag Day, June 14, the two Houses celebrated the minting of three commemorative coins (five-dollar gold, silver dollar, and half-dollar), honoring the Congressional Bicentennial. For the first time in history, coins were struck outside a Mint facility. Four seven-ton presses were moved from the U.S. Mint facilities in Philadelphia for this purpose. In her remarks, Representative Boggs observed that "for the first time, Congress literally invoked its powers under Article I, Section 8 of the Constitution to coin money." Proceeds from the sale of the commemorative coins, projected at $22 million, were to be used for restoration work at the Capitol.

Exhibitions: In addition to many other Bicentennial projects, the Library of Congress and the National Portrait Gallery mounted major exhibitions to commemorate the anniversary of the First Congress. The Library of Congress's first exhibition, "The Tides of Party Politics: Two Centuries of Congressional Elections,

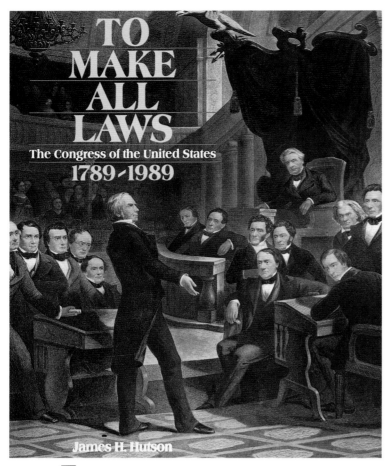

The Library of Congress's exhibit "To Make All Laws."

1789-1989," opened on February 8, 1989, in the foyer of the Library's Madison Building. It featured detailed maps showing every congressional district and the outcome of each congressional election in American history. The exhibit, which ran through August 1989, was based upon the research of Professor Kenneth Martis of the University of West Virginia. The Library's second exhibition, "To Make All Laws," opened to the public on September 29, 1989, in the Madison Building. Depicting events during Congress's two centuries in reproductions of portraits, cartoons, manuscripts, posters, and other items, the exhibit ran until February 18, 1990, after which it went on tour to 30 U.S. cities. The exhibit catalog, prepared by Dr. James Hutson of the Library staff, eventually formed the basis of a new senior high school and college textbook on Congress. The third of the Library's special exhibits, "'My Dear Wife': Letters from Members of Congress to Their Spouses, 1791-1944," opened in the Madison Building on September 13, 1990, and continued through the following January. These letters from the Library's Manuscript Division offered insights into the personal lives of Members as well as historical information about the history of Congress and its politics.

On March 1, 1989, the Chairmen of the two congressional Commissions, Senator Byrd and Representative Boggs, opened an exhibition at the National Portrait Gallery of the Smithsonian. The exhibition, "The First Federal Congress, 1789-1791," which went on public viewing the following day, featured rare pieces of art and artifacts, including portraits of the Members and

their wives. Complementing the exhibit were a catalog prepared by Margaret Christman of the Smithsonian staff and a lecture series on the First Congress. The National Portrait Gallery, the Smithsonian, and the 101st Congress cosponsored the exhibit, with the assistance of a grant of $109,000 from the national Commission.

"The Encyclopedia of Congress" Project: Among several research projects and publications occasioned by the Bicentennial of Congress was the "Encyclopedia of Congress" project, made possible by the D. R. Hardeman Bequest and developed into a project through a series of meetings of historians and political scientists, arranged by the two historical offices of the Congress. These discussions resulted in a plan for producing a comprehensive "Encyclopedia of Congress," which would bring together the best scholarship in various fields.

At its meeting in January 1989, the national Commission granted a request to fund this project in the amount of $789,000. The Lyndon Baines Johnson Library in Austin, Texas, administered the project, though most of the editorial work was done at the Library of Congress in Washington, D.C. Three authorities on Congress, Donald Bacon, Roger Davidson, and Morton Keller, served as editors of the encyclopedia, scheduled to be published by Simon and Schuster in 1993 or 1994 in four illustrated volumes, including almost 500 articles and 400 authors. Plans also included a one-volume condensed version without illustrations.

THE EXECUTIVE DEPARTMENTS CELEBRATE 200 YEARS

The formation of the new government in 1789 occasioned other commemorations in 1989, including the anniversaries of the formation of the judicial branch and the drafting of the Bill of Rights, which will be discussed in the next two chapters. Each of the original executive departments marked their respective Bicentennials. On July 27, 1789, Congress authorized a Department of Foreign Affairs, whose name was changed to the Department of State on September 15 of that same year. Thomas Jefferson was appointed the first Secretary of State. A Bicentennial exhibit in the lobby of the State Department commemorated the anniversary. Other exhibits were displayed at the Department's overseas posts. The Department's representatives also referenced the 200th anniversary in speeches and public announcements.

On August 7, 1789, the War Department became the second of the major executive agencies to be established. In its early days, the Department was headed by a Secretary of War (Henry Knox) and one clerk. The Department of the Navy was created four years later. Not until 1947 were the three armed services (including the Air Force) consolidated into a single Department of Defense, which on August 7, 1989, celebrated the anniversary of its ancestor with a ceremony at Fort Myer, Virginia. Cohosted by Secretary of Defense Richard Cheney and Army Secretary John Marsh, the ceremony included an Armed Forces Honor Guard and the dedication of a LIVING LEGACY planting, the "Commander-in-Chief's Oak." President Bush was the guest of honor.

On September 2, 1789, Congress created the Department of the Treasury, and nine days later Alexander Hamilton was named its first Secretary. The Department marked its anniversary with a colorful gala on September 11, 1989, including balloons and banners at the Old Treasury Building, attended by the President and heads of other Federal agencies and departments.* Part of the Judiciary Act that the First Congress passed on September 24, 1789, established the office of Attorney General, the nation's chief law officer. Two days later Edmund Randolph became its first occupant. While the Department of Justice did not come into being until 1870, the Department celebrated the Bicentennial of its origin with a commemorative program in Washington, D.C., September 22, 1989, in which President Bush, Attorney General Thornburgh, and past Attorneys General delivered remarks. The Department also published a book, *200th Anniversary of the Office of Attorney General, 1789-1989*, tracing the history of that office.

*P*resident Bush participates in an Armed Forces commemorative review.

*T*he original executive departments marked their own Bicentennials, the Treasury Department with a commemorative logo (below left), the Department of State with a special exhibit (below right). Former Attorneys General gathered (above) to honor the founding of the office of the Attorney General 200 years before.

*A fifth department was initiated in 1789. Congress authorized a national postal service under the Treasury Department on September 22, 1789, and created the office of Postmaster General to run it. Four days later, Samuel Osgood became the first Postmaster General. There were no Bicentennial ceremonies in 1989 for the U.S. Postal Service because it had already commemorated its Bicentennial in 1975, the 200th anniversary of Benjamin Franklin's creation of the country's first "national" postal service. In 1996 it would celebrate the 25th anniversary of the creation of the U.S. Postal Service (which replaced the U.S. Post Office Department in 1971).

CONSTITUTION WEEK 1989

In 1989 the national Commission continued its efforts to promote Constitution Week and Citizenship Day as annual observances. Updated publications were distributed to state and local Commissions, schools, organizations, and cities and towns throughout the country. These promotional materials included a new poster intended for schools. It featured the reproduction of a watercolor by a senior high school student from Florida, Catherine DiMare; the poster included suggested teaching activities for Constitution Week. The Commission also created a 30-second video public service announcement featuring the Preamble, for broadcast and closed-circuit use.

Nevada City, California, population 2,800, was small in numbers but committed and resourceful in honoring the fundamental principles of the Constitution. The town had celebrated Constitution Week and Citizenship Day every September since 1967 and was known for its parades, attracting about 10,000 spectators each year. The theme of the 1989 parade (the 23rd annual) was the 200th anniversary of Washington's inaugural. Its centerpiece was a display of "Marching Presidents" — impersonations of the 41 Chief Executives, portrayed by actors and ordinary townspeople in period costumes and guarded by trench-coated, radio-equipped "Secret Service agents." A town-wide celebration on September 8-10 featured band concerts, square dancing in the streets, battle reenactments, a tea-garden party, and an eighteenth-century ball.

Elsewhere in September 1989, a variety of activities honored the Constitution, some emphasizing the founding of the national government, others paying tribute to the Constitution in more general ways. Local businesses, banks, and libraries in Antlers, Oklahoma, for example, featured Constitutional exhibits, while the town's schools took up special learning activities on the Constitution, including spot announcements over the school intercoms, special bulletin boards, and a community ceremony. Activities in Union Beach, New Jersey, included an essay contest for students on "What the Constitution Means to Me," a naturalization ceremony for new citizens, and dedication of a "Constitution Avenue." In Spirit Lake, Iowa, the American Legion and the Veterans of Foreign Wars sponsored a Constitution Week ceremony that was broadcast on local television and radio stations.

Colleges and schools observed the week with festivities and educational activities. The University of Tennessee in Knoxville, for example, sponsored a daylong symposium on the Constitution and the Presidency, while Mississippi Delta Community College in Moorhead, Mississippi, hosted a "Constitution Quiz" for its students and a "Colonial Fare" dinner for its faculty. Schools everywhere were active participants in the commemoration, with special displays, contests, visiting speakers, and classroom studies (*see Bicentennial Schools, page 171*). In Shreveport, Louisiana, local DAR members dressed in period costumes performed a skit for first to fourth grades and provided historical

information about the Founders in an informal, conversational presentation.

BELLS ACROSS AMERICA once again rang out to promote Constitution Week. A new flier was developed and distributed as part of the Commission's packet of materials. It encouraged houses of worship and other organizations to mark the 202nd anniversary of the Constitution's signing with bell-ringing at 4:00 p.m. (EST) on September 17. Military installations at home and abroad and ships at sea joined in the observance with bells, oath reaffirmations, band concerts, park dedications, displays, and contests in adopted schools. In Jemez Springs, New Mexico, the American Legion Auxiliary added a potluck luncheon to the ringing. In Machias, Maine, Scouts led a bell-ringing ceremony at the local high school, joined by representatives of local churches. At Federal Hall in New York City, members of the Hugh O'Brian Youth Foundation held a similar ceremony, which also featured a discussion of the Constitution.

To reach large numbers of citizens in a new way, the Commission persuaded several supermarket chains to imprint a Constitution message on their shopping bags. Customers were encouraged to cut out the message and mail it to the Commission for a free POCKET CONSTITUTION. Nearly 3,000 supermarkets across the country — Safeway, Piggly Wiggly, Dillon, Giant, Winn-Dixie, Lucky Stores, and others — participated in this promotion and related activities, including ads,

A *watercolor poster was developed for Constitution Week (above); the Week celebration at Federal Hall (right).*

HUGH O'BRIAN
YOUTH FOUNDATION
SEMINAR
NEW YORK SOUTH
1989 LEADERSHIP

bag stuffers, and in-store promotions. At a U-Save store in Enterprise, Alabama, an "Uncle Sam" handed out free balloons and flyers for ordering POCKET CONSTITUTIONS.

The American Library Association alerted its members to the Constitution Week observance, and many libraries arranged special displays. The public library in Hutchinson, Kansas, for example, featured a historical flag display. The Silverton, Oregon, library organized a tree planting. Meanwhile, taking advantage of Citizenship Day falling on a Sunday this year, professional football and baseball teams across the country featured commemorative activities in their pregame and halftime ceremonies. Several stadiums showed the Commission's video on their giant scoreboard TV screens.

Commission Programs and Publications

During 1989 several new Commission programs completed their first year while older ones continued. The year also saw a continuing increase in the quantity and quality of Commission-sponsored publications.

THE DAR ESSAY CONTEST

In April 1988, the Commission entered into an agreement with the National Chapter of the Daughters of the American Revolution to cosponsor the latter's essay contest in the 1988-1989 school year. Since the 1986-1987 school year, the DAR had sponsored a "Constitution Week" essay contest for high school students who had completed or were taking a course in American history or government. The contest was administered through the DAR's network of chapters, with the entries evaluated at the local chapter, state, division, and national levels. Each year eight divisional winners and one national champion were selected and honored at the DAR's Continental Congress in Washington, D.C. In cosponsoring the 1988-1989 contest, the Commission assisted the DAR in the selection of an essay topic, promotion of the contest, and selection of judges. For the 1988-1989 contest, the two groups selected the topic "Under the Constitution, how do our responsibilities as 'We the People' influence the Presidency and Congress in the discharge of their duties?" Essays of 600 to 1,000 words in length were to be submitted to sponsoring chapters of the DAR no later than January 16, 1989.

The national winner, Michael Rather of Blackstone, Virginia, submitted an essay entitled "Our Responsibilities as 'We the People.'" As part of its New York City activities in celebration of Washington's inaugural, the Commission hosted the winning students and their teachers at a luncheon banquet at historic Fraunces Tavern in Manhattan, where an ongoing exhibit, "The Changing Image of George Washington," was on display, with engravings, etchings, and lithographs about the life of the First President. Earlier, on April 18, all of the division winners were honored by the DAR in ceremonies at Constitution Hall in Washington.

OTHER EDUCATION PROGRAMS

The NATIONAL BICENTENNIAL COMPETITION concluded its second year with national finals at the beginning of May. The preliminary rounds, in which over 1,000 students representing 44 states competed, were once again held at Fort McNair in Washington, D.C. The final round, involving the top ten teams, took place in hearing rooms of the U.S. Capitol. The national winners were announced at an awards banquet on the evening of May 3. First-place honors went to Lincoln Southeast High School in Nebraska, while second place was awarded to the Half Hallow Hills High School in New York. The previous year's champion, Gompers Secondary School from California, took third place. The following day President Bush met at the White House with students representing the three winning teams. This year's competition introduced for the first time special recognition awards for teams that had excelled in specific categories, e.g., each unit of the competition's textbook.

The program on which the competition was based continued to expand. During the 1988-1989 school year, over 1 million students were reached by the program's educational materials. Almost 2 million students had used the program's innovative textbooks, which now included adaptations of the high school text for use at the upper elementary and middle school levels. Approximately 9,000 classes participated in the competition. To encourage and recognize the many classes that used the materials but chose not to enter the competition (about 20,000 classes in 1988-1989), the Center during the year introduced a new program, WE THE PEOPLE . . . CONGRESS AND THE CONSTITUTION, which recognized schools using the materials with noncompetitive mock congressional hearings.

During 1989, the Commission's BICENTENNIAL EDUCATIONAL GRANT PROGRAM awarded 61 grants of $3.4 million to educational organizations of all kinds in 30 states and the District of Columbia. Many of the projects focused on the executive and legislative branches, the year's Bicentennial themes. Others looked forward to the next year's emphasis on the judicial branch. Among the grants awarded were the following:

President Bush with some of the winners of the National Bicentennial Competition.

The Connecticut Consortium for Law-Related Education sponsored a week-long teacher training and curriculum development seminar for 21 middle and high school students. The seminar was devoted to an intensive study of the First Congress.

Southwest Texas State University hosted a three-week institute for 30 middle and high school teachers. Its subject was Congress and the development of the executive branch. Participants subsequently trained other teachers through in-service programs.

The National Park Foundation in Washington, D.C., produced a 30-minute videotape, student books, and lesson plans called "Constitution Tools," all intended as support materials for the "Constitution Works" program, housed at the new Museum of American Constitutional Government at the Federal Hall National Memorial in New York City.

Asuza Pacific University hosted a two-week teacher training project, "Institute on the Principles of American Democracy," for 30 high school teachers from the Los Angeles area. This was a response to the requirements of California's new curriculum framework.

Forest Hills High School in Forest Hills, New York, developed, reproduced, and disseminated nationally four "Jigsaw Cooperative Learning Strategies" on the Bill of Rights. Each strategy included a hypothetical case, work sheets, and abstracts of relevant constitutional cases.

KIDSNET, Inc. in Washington, D.C., created a compendium of Constitution-related educational materials for grades K-12., which included a comprehensive listing of Constitutional materials in both print and electronic media. The compendium was distributed through PBS affiliates nationwide.

The Oklahoma State University College of Arts and Sciences created a computer bulletin board on *The Federalist Papers* offering original text, commentary, and lessons for classroom use. This curriculum resource served both teachers and students from 7th grade through college.

The National Council for the Social Studies developed, field-tested, and produced a poster series on the Judiciary. The posters, with appropriate educational activities included on back, were designed for use at all educational levels.

Vanderbilt University, in collaboration with the American Federation of Teachers, the Education Excellence Network, and other organizations, undertook the development of a computerized interactive video project on the Bill of Rights.

The Commission's other venture in adult education, the COLLEGE-COMMUNITY FORUMS PROGRAM, continued to expand in 1989. It received requests for applications from over 400 institutions in response to a December 1988 announcement. The program offered two rounds of competition in 1989 and supported 44 projects with over $301,000 in funding. The forums addressed a variety of issues. Conflict between the legislative and executive branches headed the list of topics considered at St. Vincent College in Pennsylvania, Pearl River Community College in Mississippi, College of the Redwoods in California, and Empire State College in New York. The War Powers Act was debated in a mock trial sponsored by Florida State University, in which the audience assumed the role of jury to determine the facts of the case. Lincoln Memorial University in Tennessee debated the future of the Electoral College in a forum that was broadcast on the campus radio station. During the 1989-1990 school year, American University in Washington, D.C., sponsored a forum on "Understanding Congress, the Presidency, the Courts, and the Constitution," which explored the functions of each branch of the government and the relations between them.

LOGO-LICENSED PRODUCTS

Since 1989 was the Bicentennial of both Congress and the Presidency, as well as the year a new President was inaugurated, it proved a boon for the Commission's logo-licensed products and other commemoratives. During 1989, the Commission licensed an additional 13 vendors and issued two full-color promotional catalogs. The first catalog, a special inaugural issue entitled *200 Years of the Presidency*, featured many new licensees and their products designed for the inauguration of President Bush. The products included an umbrella whose cover was imprinted with the names or initials of all former Presidents; a crystal vase with the Presidential seal carved between polished columnar cuts; and china plates by Lenox and Mottahedeh. Honoring George Washington were a replica of his favorite wine coaster with a 1989 Washington quarter set in the base, and a set of brass blazer buttons copied from the buttons on the coat Washington wore for his inauguration in 1789. An older licensee, the board game of Presidential electioneering, "Hail to the Chief" by Aristoplay, Inc.,

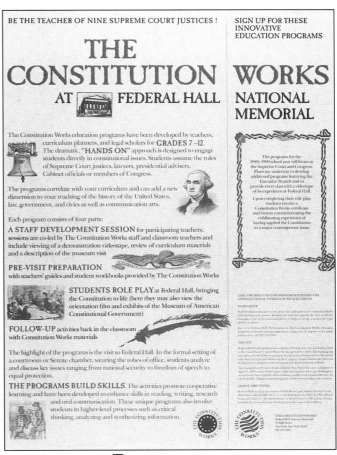

Promotional poster.

became especially popular during the year. At the time of President Bush's inauguration, the inaugural committee distributed many of the 200,000 copies of the inaugural catalog through Washington, D.C., hotels, tourist offices, and airlines. The Commission also sent copies to hotels along the route of the inaugural journey reenactment.

Promotional efforts during 1989 helped gross catalog sales increase to an average of more than $15,000 a month for the first four months, topping $133,000 for the year. Customers included the gift shops at the libraries of the four former Presidents, and representatives of Federal agencies and departments used Bicentennial commemoratives as official gifts during their travels. In November, the Commission began circulating a second commemoratives catalog.

Examples of the logo-licensing program: china plates by Lenox (above) and Mottahedah (right).

1989 AD CAMPAIGN

As part of its educational effort, the Commission issued a new series of radio and print advertisements in 1989. Like the previous series issued in 1987 (*see Chapter III*), these public service announcements were produced in collaboration with the advertising agency of Scali, McCabe, Sloves, Inc., and distributed by the Advertising Council, Inc. The 60-second radio spots were distrib-

uted to stations in both English and Spanish. One spot, "Tough Decisions," highlighted difficult decisions Presidents have made through the nation's history and the role the Constitution played in guiding those decisions. Another radio spot, "Oval Office," pointed out that such important decisions as declaring war are not made by the President but by Congress. Print advertisements followed the same themes.

THE ST. JOHN TRILOGY

Throughout the Bicentennial, the national Commission supported the publication and distribution of various books on the Constitution. Among the most important was a trilogy of books by former radio and television commentator Jeffrey St. John. The first of the series, *Constitutional Journal: A Correspondent's Report from the Convention of 1787*, had appeared in 1987, adapted from a series of articles in the *Christian Science Monitor* published earlier that year (*see Chapter III*). Based on James Madison's notes and the correspondence of other delegates at the Convention, the book provided a lively day-by-day narrative of the drafting of the Constitution from the perspective of a journalist covering the events as they happened.

With funding from the Commission, 28,000 copies of *Constitutional Journal* were printed and distributed in 1989 to high school, college, law school, and public libraries, as well as to other institutions in the United States and overseas. A sequel, *A Child of Fortune: A Correspondent's Report on the Ratification of the U.S. Constitution & the Battle for a Bill of Rights* appeared in 1990, and with Commission support a similar quantity was distributed to libraries. This was, in some respects, an even more important work than its predecessor, since it provided an exciting week-by-week account of the little-known story of the Constitution's ratification.

After two books about the Constitution's drafting and ratification, St. John completed his story with an account of the Constitution's implementation. In the spring of 1992, *Forge of Union, Anvil of Liberty: A Correspondent's Report on the First Federal Elections, the First Federal Congress, & the Bill of Rights* was published, and funding from the Commission made possible the placement of copies in libraries throughout the nation and abroad. In monthly installments, the book reported on the election of the First Congress, the election and inauguration of George Washington, the establishment of government departments and the judicial branch, and the drafting of the Bill of Rights.

This three-volume "eyewitness" chronicle of the creation and founding of the government of the United States would become a lasting resource for teachers, students, and the general public — helping to perpetuate the Bicentennial's "history and civics lesson" for all.

OTHER PUBLICATIONS

No doubt reflecting interest in the 200th anniversary of Washington's inaugural, the Information Center handled over 60,000 requests for information and

material in 1989. At the same time, the number of Commission program and special event publications increased significantly. As already mentioned, the promotion of Constitution Week required several new items. So did the Washington inaugural reenactment, for which the Commission developed a foldout brochure, *George Washington — Journey to the Presidency*, that included historical background, a summary of the journey to New York, and color illustrations. For schools the Commission created a blue-and-white brochure of the same title, which offered suggested learning activities appropriate for the commemoration. The Commission also issued the second in its series of general purpose brochures, providing historical background to the year's commemorative theme as well as a summary of projects and activities for the year. The eight-panel document, *The Grand Experiment Begins: Government under the Constitution, Congress and the Presidency 1789-1989*, featured the Houdon bust of Washington on its cover. Because of the significant increase in the number and range of its educational programs, the Commission created a leaflet describing these programs and made copies of the brochures available to teachers and educational administrators.

The year also began a series of popular and successful teaching tools that the Commission produced

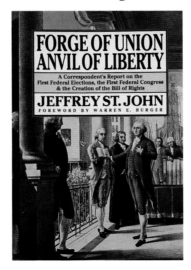

The three volumes of the Constitution trilogy by Jeffrey St. Johns, distributed to high school, college, law school, and public libraries across the nation.

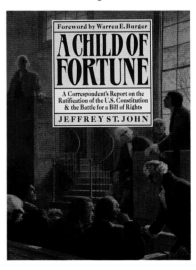

in collaboration with Scholastic, Inc. These materials included a poster entitled *United States Presidents 1789 to 1989* and a "Skills Handbook" on the Congress. The poster's front displayed, on a field of blue, enlarged reproductions of postage stamps containing portraits of all the U.S. Presidents from Washington to Lyndon Johnson, together with photographic portraits of the four living former Presidents and President Bush. On the back, in each of two versions, one for elementary school students, the other for secondary school, were eight panels of learning activities and information on the Presidency. The Skills Handbook also appeared in two editions, one for elementary schools, *Happy 200th Birthday: The U.S. Congress, 1789-1989*; the other for secondary school, *200 Years of the U.S. Congress, 1789-1989*. The handbooks contained fact and work sheets, historical timelines, map skills exercises, and other activities related to the history and functioning of Congress. Both editions were illustrated with sketches and political cartoons. These publications were initially distributed by Scholastic to its teacher subscribers as supplements to special editions of that organization's regular magazines. The Commission also distributed 120,000 copies to teachers upon request. The demand for the posters and Skills Handbooks ultimately required a second printing.

It was also a banner year for the POCKET CONSTITU-TION, which appeared in two special editions. Of these, one was a Special Limited Inaugural Edition, with a new foreword. Copies of the edition were distributed along with the commemoratives catalog to hotels, travel agencies, and other organizations at the time of President Bush's inauguration. The Commission also published a Special Military Edition of 3.7 million copies for use by the Armed Forces. At a Pentagon ceremony attended by the Secretaries of the three services and by ranking enlisted personnel, Chief Justice Burger presented the first copy of this edition to Defense Secretary Cheney. The edition featured a special foreword by President Bush as Commander in Chief, in which he said: "May studying this remarkable document renew not only your appreciation for the blessings of liberty and self-government but also your sense of pride in serving as one on whom our nation relies for protection." During 1989, the Commission distributed 1.2 million copies of the POCKET CONSTITUTION, its most popular and widely circulated publication.

The Commission's COMMEMORATIVE CALENDAR for 1989 was the fourth in the series, in which the calendar's format continued to evolve. In addition to the listing of key historical events for each day of the year, the calendar included biographical vignettes — complete with color portraits — of major U.S. Government officials appointed or elected during the course of the year as well as large color photographs that captured some of the excitement of 1987-1988 Bicentennial events. The Commission printed over 120,000 copies of the calendar for commercial and free distribution.

COMMISSION STAFF, ORGANIZATIONS, AND RESOURCES

Dr. Ronald L. Trowbridge became Staff Director in January 1989, and the basic organization of the Commission remained unchanged. By year's end, the Commission had a staff of sixty-four — 51 who were paid from appropriated funds, 12 detailees from government departments, and one part-time person on contract; there were also eight summer interns. In fiscal year 1989 the Commission received from Congress $6,936,000 in appropriations (added to funds carried over from the previous fiscal year). It also received $57,000 in donated funds and $176,000 in royalty income.

Other Activities

The anniversaries associated with the founding of the national government spawned a great variety of commemorative events, projects, and activities. Schools and colleges, Federal agencies, states and localities, and private organizations joined in celebrating the commemoration of Washington's inaugural, the convening of the First Congress, and the creation of the executive departments. A sampling of these celebrations is described below.

EDUCATIONAL ORGANIZATIONS

As already noted, schools were an important element in the year's principal event, the reenactment of

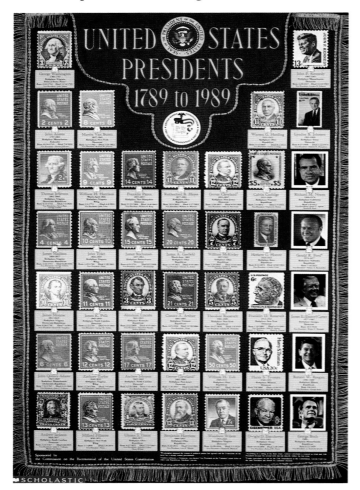

S*cholastic's Presidents Poster, featuring presidential portraits from Washington onward on postage stamps.*

George Washington's inaugural journey and inauguration. The national Commission and others involved in the project structured the reenactment so as to maximize its educational potential. Many, indeed most, of the major ceremonies of the journey involved schools. Thousands of schoolchildren either participated in these ceremonies or had an opportunity to see and cheer Washington from the roadside along the way. In the weeks before the reenactment, copies of the Commission's educational materials (as well as state Commission publications) were distributed to school districts on the route. In preparing for Washington's visits, teachers and students engaged in a wide range of learning activities, including research and writing projects, map exercises, contests, the construction of historical replicas, dramatic presentations, school assemblies, and musical exercises.

The anniversary generated other educational programs and publications as well. The Mount Vernon Ladies Association, for example, cosponsored with National History Day (see Chapter VII) a nationwide essay contest for students in grades 6 through 12 on "George Washington: The Unanimous Choice for First President." The Association also prepared a special lesson plan for students in Virginia. Its centerpiece was a series of "Scratch and Learn" cards, each of which included ten questions about George Washington. Students selected answers by rubbing off a latex film; those who answered all ten questions correctly found the word "W-A-S-H-I-N-G-T-O-N" underneath.

The results of many of these school activities greeted Washington as he proceeded on his way — student-prepared proclamations, letters, artwork, representative food of the period, personal gifts, and musical salutes. The educational opportunities of the reenactment were not restricted, however, to schools in those states directly involved. Teachers throughout the nation received materials on the reenactment prepared by the national Commission and other organizations, and could thereby focus their activities on the establishment of the executive and legislative branches.

By September 1989, a total of 278 elementary, middle, and high schools had joined the Commission's BICENTENNIAL SCHOOLS PROGRAM (see Chapter IV). Many of these schools shared common themes and activities. Some participated in the NATIONAL BICENTENNIAL COMPETITION and the NATIONAL HISTORICAL/PICTORIAL MAP CONTEST. At the suggestion of the Commission, many sought the assistance of their PTAs and local community organizations in framing copies of the National Geographic timeline, America on Parade, for display in their school lobbies or libraries (see Chapter IV). Other schools, granted recognition during the 1988-1989 school year, incorporated the November 1988 elections into classroom and extracurricular activities on the Constitution.

Diversity, enterprise, and creativity, however, were the most common characteristics among the dozens of elementary and secondary schools that joined this program. The Laurel Middle School in Laurel, Montana, established a History Club, whose projects included the creation of a "Freedom Hall" with patriotic artwork by

Scholastic's Skills Handbooks, with fact sheets, historical timelines, and map exercises.

Harlee Little

St. Helena Island, South Carolina

students, faculty, and local residents, and a museum of American history. Among the Bicentennial activities at the Marie Archer Teasley Middle School in Canton, Georgia, was the creation of a Constitutional research room in the school library and the naming of the room after William Few, a signer of the Constitution from that area. Students in the St. Helena Elementary School on St. Helena Island, South Carolina, created a large quilt on the Constitution. Every student in the first through sixth grade participated in the project. The quilt's 216 patches featured the 13 original states and South Carolina's signers of the Constitution.

Many Bicentennial Schools focused on the institution of the Presidency during the 1988-1989 school year. Heards Ferry Elementary School in Atlanta, Georgia, for example, staged a "Presidential Reception," with fifth-grade students portraying past Presidents and their First Ladies. Each student was expected to research the background on his or her respective historical character. Students of the W. B. Patterson Elementary School in the District of Columbia created a skit depicting a visit by George Washington to the District today.

In their plans, some schools developed not only special projects but comprehensive curricula of constitutional studies extending over several years. The Winston Park Junior High School in Palatine, Illinois, for example, put together a series of study units, field trips, in-service training for teachers, and special school lectures. Spanning the years 1987 to 1991, the school's activities included a Bicentennial Newspaper Project;

Atlanta, Georgia

Diversity, enterprise, and creativity were key features of the Bicentennial School program.

interdisciplinary study units on the Constitution; the electoral process; the 1990 census; the Bill of Rights; field trips to local historical societies; and guest speakers, including the "Circuit Court Jesters," whose mock trial production promoted student awareness of the judicial system.

Not all of the Bicentennial Schools were located in the United States. The network reached into the Department of Defense Dependent Schools (DODDS) and independent schools overseas. The DODDS' Schweinfurt American School in Schweinfurt, Germany, engaged its students in the production of a videotape series of portraits of the U.S. Presidents. The school also presented a framed copy of the Constitution to the Lord Mayor of Schweinfurt.

One of the many examples of the outstanding creativity and resourcefulness displayed by America's schools during the Bicentennial era took place during 1989 in Durham, North Carolina, where students from the Hillsdale High School in that city commemorated the Bicentennial by lobbying a bill through the state legislature. In their studies of the Constitution, the students discovered that North Carolina had never ratified the 24th Amendment, adopted in 1964, banning the poll tax and other discriminatory levies designed to prevent the poor from voting (North Carolina had abolished its own poll tax in 1928).

The students decided to correct the oversight. Under the direction of their teacher, the students launched a campaign to have a ratification bill passed retroactively. They lobbied individual legislators, appeared before legislative committees, and held press conferences. Their efforts led *The News and Observer* of Raleigh to observe: "The General Assembly can put the icing on this Constitutional birthday cake by voting long overdue approval of the legislation . . . to acknowledge the amendment and as a tribute to a group of high school students who learned well the lessons of American history and acted accordingly." The ratification bill passed the legislature. The students then hand-carried it to Washington, D.C., and presented it to the Archivist of the United States, Dr. Don W. Wilson. "You are to be congratulated on this imaginative project," Dr. Wilson told the students, "and on the perseverance you have shown in working toward its successful conclusion. You may be sure that this ratification will be preserved carefully at the National Archives."

During Constitution Week 1989, U.S. Supreme Court Justice Antonin Scalia participated in a live satellite broadcast interview to high schools. When asked which branch of government was most important in the protection of rights, Justice Scalia surprised some with his response that "the most important protection of the Constitution is not the Supreme Court or the Federal courts generally, but really the Legislature and President and the process by which they all have to agree that something is desirable and lawful before it happens." The program, sponsored by the Louisiana State University Law Center, the Center for America's Founding Documents at Boston University, and the Louisiana Commission on the Bicentennial, was made available to schools through facilities of the TI-IN Satellite Network, San Antonio, Texas.

The Commission's BICENTENNIAL CAMPUS PROGRAM continued to grow. By November 1989, a total of 389 colleges and universities around the country had joined in this campus network. Each institution had established a committee responsible for organizing its Bicentennial activities and was engaged in holding lecture series, conferences, symposia, and other programs on the Constitution. Columbia State Community College in Tennessee, for example, sponsored a lecture series on the legislative branch, "The People's Representatives: the Evolution of the U.S. Congress." A fellowship program was established at another Bicentennial Campus, the University of Missouri at Kansas

City. The program awarded two $1,000 "Bicentennial Graduate Student Fellowships" during the 1989-1990 academic year. To be eligible, a student had to be enrolled as a degree-seeking graduate student in the University's School of Law or in the Department of History.

With funding from the national Commission, the National Council for the Social Studies (NCSS) sponsored a teleconference in November 1989 on "Citizenship in the 21st Century." Approximately 10,000 teachers at the NCSS's annual meeting in St. Louis and at workshops around the country participated in the event, which addressed various issues related to the citizenship education of the nation's youth. The teleconference was aired live by The Learning Channel, with additional distribution through the Public Broadcasting System. In 1986, NCSS collaborated with the national Commission and other educational organizations in sponsoring a similar teleconference on the Constitution.

The National Teacher of the Year Award in 1989 went to Mary V. Bicouvaris, a government/international-relations teacher from Bethel High School in Hampton, Virginia, whose students had participated in the 1989 NATIONAL BICENTENNIAL COMPETITION. Mrs. Bicouvaris organized other Bicentennial activities, including a school-wide commemorative celebration and an idea/resource booklet, which was disseminated nationwide. At a White House ceremony in which President Bush presented her with the Award's coveted crystal apple, Mrs. Bicouvaris said: "As a naturalized citizen, I have an abiding love for my chosen country. It has been my goal to help young Americans understand and appreciate their country, its government, and its crucial role in international affairs."

FEDERAL GOVERNMENT DEPARTMENTS AND AGENCIES

Federal institutions were the principal focus of commemorative activities in 1989. Moreover, the coincidence of the inauguration of the nation's 41st President in this anniversary year of the executive branch afforded many program opportunities, some of which have already been described. Among other projects, the national Commission placed its Bicentennial float in the nationally televised inaugural parade up Pennsylvania Avenue on January 20, 1989. Added to the float's large scroll of the Constitution was George Washington, portrayed by the Commission's Staff Director, Ronald Trowbridge, wearing a replica of the brown suit used by Washington at his inaugural. Inside the suit was the label "Made in the USA," a double entendre referring both to the American manufacture of the attire and to the Constitution.

While much of the national Commission's interaction with Federal departments and agencies during the year concentrated on establishing liaisons with the new Administration, DOD continued to provide a strong element of continuity in support of the Bicentennial (including its participation in the reenactment of Washington's inaugural). In January, when much of the nation's attention was focused on the new Administra-

tion, DOD staged a tribute to the departing Commander in Chief, President Reagan, in a ceremony at Andrews Air Force Base outside Washington. There, President Reagan was saluted by units and ranking officers of the Armed Services, and presented with several awards, including an official Bicentennial flag. That same month, the national Commission honored the outgoing Secretary of the Army, John Marsh, for his outstanding leadership in the Bicentennial. At a dinner held in his honor, Secretary Marsh was presented with a replica of the Franklin bust. Later in the year, Patrick Stone became the new Army Secretary and continued his Department's role in leading the military's commemoration of the Bicentennial.

STATES AND COMMUNITIES

State and local government agencies had also performed a key role in the Washington journey reenactment. The six state commissions involved were central players in the planning and implementation of this extraordinary event. So too were the many city Commissions and Designated Bicentennial Communities (DBCs) along the way. For example, the New York City Commission chaired by Joseph Flom took the lead in orchestrating the inaugural reenactment and many other related activities in that city. Moreover, state and local police in the several states provided vital support in securing smooth passage of the project's entourage.

Although the year's principal commemorative event — the reenactment — focused on the Middle Atlantic states, the national Commission encouraged all states and U.S. jurisdictions to join in the commemoration. The nation's governors engaged their citizens in the commemoration by issuing proclamations and by holding special ceremonies. The Mount Vernon Ladies Association sent boxwood cuttings to the governors, with the suggestion that these cuttings be planted with

appropriate ceremony on their respective state capitol grounds. Alabama's governor, together with representatives of the SAR, planted boxwoods at the State House in Montgomery. The reenactment of Washington's inauguration provided a commemorative scenario for many other ceremonies across the country. Some communities sponsored exhibits, buried time capsules, and organized contests and other programs for local schools.

The anniversary of another important event in 1789 occasioned many commemorative activities in New York State and New England. Six months after assuming the Presidency, Washington visited the new country's most northern states. He wanted to reacquaint himself with an area he had known only in wartime and, undoubtedly, to generate some of that same goodwill and support for the new government his inaugural journey had realized in the middle states. Between mid-October and mid-November 1789, he visited New York, Connecticut, Massachusetts, and New Hampshire.

Two hundred years later, several communities in New York and New England commemorated this journey. The Wallingford (Connecticut) Historical Society, for example, re-created the visit to that community with special ceremonies and educational activities. Costumed as Washington, Neal Mackenzie, the Historical Society's chairman, visited local schools and recounted details of Washington's journey. An adult education class in Wallingford spent a year creating a quilt depicting the story of the Constitution. Featuring a scrolled representation of the Constitution, together with the seals of the 13 original states and representations of the three branches of government, the quilt was presented to the town of Wallingford for display in the county courthouse. In Rye, New York, the former president of the White Plains and Westchester Historical Societies, Stephen Holden, Jr., portrayed Washington during the reenactment of his visit there. The Rye Historical Society prepared an exhibit illustrating the town as it was 200 years before.

The year saw the Constitution honored in many other ways by states and communities throughout the country. The Nevada Bicentennial Commission, with the Nevada Humanities Commission, cosponsored a series of school appearances around the state by "Thomas Jefferson." An Oxford scholar, Clay Jenkinson, visited schools in seven cities, portraying Jefferson. In this role, he spoke to his young audiences about the philosophy and politics of the author of the Declaration

Governor plants boxwood cuttings from Mount Vernon during special ceremonies in Montgomery, Alabama.

Commemorative postage stamp marking North Carolina's Ratification of the Constitution.

of Independence and presented Jefferson's views on states' rights and the Bill of Rights.

For North Carolina, the major Bicentennial event of 1989 was the anniversary of that state's ratification of the Constitution on November 21, 1789. North Carolina had refused to ratify until the addition of a bill of rights was addressed by the First Congress. Once Congress had submitted a proposed bill of rights to the states on September 25, 1789, North Carolina ratified the Constitution less than two months later by a vote of 194 to 77, and thus became the 12th state to join the Union. To mark the event, the North Carolina Museum of History in Raleigh sponsored an exhibit, "Your Constitution: Private Rights and Public Freedoms," offering a historical overview of the state's role in ratification of the Constitution and a perspective of how that document affected North Carolinians in the contemporary world. The exhibit included videotape reenactments, artifacts, and other displays on various subjects in the state's history having to do with civil rights, censorship, and Prohibition. The exhibit featured an original draft of the Constitution, on loan from the Library of Congress, and Washington's letter of congratulations to North Carolina Governor Samuel Johnston.

Chowan College in Murfreesboro, North Carolina, a Bicentennial Campus, sponsored a series of activities including the dedication of a "Ratification Walk," the burying of school items in a time capsule, a "Ratification Buffet" offering the same bill of fare served to the delegates at the state's ratification convention in 1789, and a "Ratification Soliloquy," delivered by the college's chaplain.

The number of DBCs continued to expand, though at a much slower rate than two years before. By the end of the year, there were over 2,500 DBCs with some unusual additions to the network; early in the year, for example, the Commission recognized a penal institution, the Michigan Reformatory in Ionia, as a DBC. "We the People" provided the theme for the 1989 "Harvest of Harmony" parade in another DBC, Grand Island, Nebraska. An annual event, the parade this year featured over 200 units, including bands, floats, and antique vehicles. The Grand Island-Hall County Bicentennial Committee cosponsored a float to honor Nebraska's 19 DBCs. A new town library in West Allis, Wisconsin, opened a "Constitution Room," furnished with framed reproductions of the four pages of the Constitution, the Declaration of Independence, the Bill of Rights, and the Howard Chandler Christy painting. The $4.5 million library was completed in September 1989, with the dedication ceremonies covered by local television.

PRIVATE, NONPROFIT, AND RELIGIOUS GROUPS

Private organizations also had a hand in the inaugural reenactment. The Mount Vernon Ladies Association, the Carriage Association of America, the DAR and SAR, and the National Society of Colonial Dames of America contributed to the project, as well as dozens of state and local historical societies, museums and historic sites, veterans' organizations, ceremonial military units, civic groups, and churches. The initiatives of these organizations in honoring the anniversary of Washington's Presidency were not confined, however, to the reenactment itself. The Mount Vernon Ladies Association, in conjunction with the Founders Society of the American Studies Center, sponsored a three-day conference at Mount Vernon in September, "Commemorating the Bicentennial of George Washington's Inauguration as First President of the United States." Scholars, journalists, and others devoted the three days to an examination of the nation's First President, both the man and the myths, from several perspectives. Television correspondent David Brinkley delivered the conference's keynote address.

PRIVATE CORPORATIONS

Some of the nation's corporations participating in the Bicentennial tied their efforts to the year's commemorative theme: the establishment of the national government. Several dozen corporations, banks, and professional firms contributed financial support to

A*n actor in Kokomo, Indiana, portrayed Benjamin Franklin in a series of videotapes for grades 3 through 9.*

Learn about America and make yourself brighter.

Learn about America and make yourself brighter.

Learn about America and make yourself brighter.

Learn about America and make yourself brighter.

d the Gang

GE a NUT

Learn about America and make yourself brighter.

RATTA-TAT-TAT!

From G PEANU

From GE and the PEANUTS® Gang

From GE and the PEANUTS® Gang

Young readers of American history received these "Peanuts" bookmarks from General Electric.

Harlee Little

reenactment activities in New York City and elsewhere. The Brooklyn Union Gas Company, for example, sponsored radio advertisements promoting the reenactment. Radio City Music Hall Productions, Inc., produced the inaugural reenactment ceremony in New York. The Nabisco Corporation's Oreo Division donated 40,000 posters highlighting the history of the Presidency for educational use in conjunction with the reenactment project. The national Commission distributed the posters to schools and public libraries nationwide.

In support of 1989's designation as "The Year of the Young Reader," General Electric sponsored a national program to encourage reading and learning about American history and the Constitution. Through its "Read About America in the Best Light" program, GE encouraged youngsters to read two books on the nation's history. Participants received a free bookmark, each featuring a member of Charles Schulz's "Peanuts" gang portraying a historical character; they were also eligible to win a $500 U.S. Savings Bond. GE promoted this program through "Peanuts" posters displayed in retail stores and in "Reading is Fundamental" (RIF) Centers nationwide. During the life of the program, GE distributed nearly 600,000 bookmarks and more than 25,000 young readers fulfilled their reading assignments. GE also provided 80,000 RIF volunteers with copies of the Commission's POCKET CONSTITUTION to help those volunteers educate young readers about the Constitution's role in American history. The Midwest retail chain Carson Pirie Scott sponsored an "America Week" in its department stores. The company placed full-page ads promoting the program in major regional newspapers, sponsored an essay contest on the writing of a constitution for a future space colony, and staged a constitutional convention for the contest's winners in Illinois and Minnesota. POCKET CONSTITUTIONS and calendars were given to all participants.

MEDIA

In addition to media coverage of the Washington inaugural reenactment, other outstanding examples of both print and electronic journalism were produced during the year. Among some excellent television documentaries was "The Congress: The History and Promise of Representative Government," an award-winning 90-minute documentary film funded by Ameritech and produced by Ken Burns and public television station WETA, with research support from the offices of the two congressional historians. The film, premiered at the National Theater in Washington, D.C., on March 13, was subsequently broadcast over most PBS stations and distributed to schools. The video documentary, "An Empire of Reason," underwritten by the New York State Bar Association and the New York State Bicentennial Commission, re-created the fierce debate in New York State over the ratification of the Constitution. The arguments, characters, and key issues adhered to the historical facts, but the language, dress, and medium of debate were modern. Columnist William F. Buckley, Jr., hosted one segment showing a debate between the

Federalists and Anti-Federalists. This production won several awards, including an Emmy. With support from the New York Telephone Company, sponsors distributed 1,600 copies to New York schools. Cox Cable San Diego and C-SPAN together sponsored an essay contest during 1989 on the subject "How Does Television Promote Freedom of Speech in America?" More than 100 entries were received from 15 area schools. The winners and their families were awarded a five-day visit to Washington, D.C.

Among the books on the Constitution that appeared in 1989 were Charlene Bickford and Kenneth Bowling's *Birth of a Nation: The Federal Congress, 1789-1991* and editors Stephen L. Schechter and Richard B. Bernstein's *Well Begun: Chronicles of the Early National Period*. The former was produced by the First Federal Congress Project, and the authors were also the project's coeditors. A legacy of the Sesquicentennial Commission, this great enterprise had been engaged since 1966 in the research and writing of *The Documentary History of the First Federal Congress*, with support from the National Historical Publications and Records Commission and other sources. At its April 1989 meeting, the national Commission awarded a $120,000 grant to the project to expedite work on Volumes 10-14 in the *History*. Those volumes would comprise all the existing records of the debates of the House of Representatives in the First Congress, including major debates on the drafting of the Bill of Rights and the creation of the District of Columbia as the nation's capital.

In anticipation of the 200th anniversary of Washington's inaugural, two biographies of the nation's first President appeared the year before. One, Paul K. Longmore's *The Invention of George Washington*, focused on Washington as a young man and his early political career. The other, John E. Ferling's *The First of Men*, offered a psychological portrait of Washington.

The *National Geographic Magazine* covered the Bicentennial of Washington's inaugural with two articles, both focusing on a box of memorabilia from the 1889 Centennial. The second article, "A Bygone Century Comes to Light," which appeared in the September issue of the magazine, described the opening of the box, which had been sealed by its owner, Benjamin P. Field of Babylon, New York, a hundred years before. The article also included pictures and text on the Bicentennial reenactment.

INTERNATIONAL

The Bicentennial of the U.S. Constitution coincided with several other national commemorations. The years 1988-1989 marked the tercentenary of England's Glorious Revolution. In 1989 Australia celebrated the

A *box containing memorabilia from the 1889 Centennial was opened after 100 years.*

The Jefferson Memorial was the premiere site of 1989 Bastille Day ceremonies in the United States (top); former Senator Mathias presents a Franklin bust to French President Francois Mitterrand (below).

Bicentennial of its founding. That same year was the 200th anniversary of the French Revolution. Despite important differences between the American and French Revolutions, the common antecedents of the U.S. Bill of Rights and the French Declaration of the Rights of Man and the Citizen— the Declaration was created just 30 days before the proposed Bill of Rights was sent to the states for ratification — expressed the historical kinship between the two nations.

In a ceremony at the Jefferson Memorial on July 14, 1989 (Bastille Day), Chief Justice Burger and Army Secretary Marsh paid tribute to the country that had helped to bring about America's independence. "Without the aid of France," the former said, "we might not have gotten our Constitution as soon as we did." Former Senator Charles Mathias, Jr., Chairman of the American Committee on the Bicentennial of the French Revolution, spoke of the two great documents of human rights that were drafted in 1789. French Ambassador Emmanual de Margerie acknowledged the "wind from

Commemorative postage stamp.

America" — the spirit of liberty — that did so much to inspire the overthow of the ancien régime in France. Students from the Washington International School sang the national anthems of the two countries and recited the preambles to the U.S. Constitution and the French Declaration. Parallel portions of the latter and the U.S. Bill of Rights were read by former United States Solicitor General Erwin Griswold and Senators John Warner and Nancy Kassebaum. Postmaster General Frank displayed a new 45-cent stamp commemorating the French Revolution. The red, silver, and blue stamp, featuring personifications of Liberty, Equality, and Fraternity, was issued jointly by the U.S. Postal Service and the Postal Administration of France.

The anniversary of the French Revolution occasioned other celebrations during the year. A program at the University of California, Los Angeles, featured a *bal populaire* with song and spectacle. In Boston, the French Library sponsored a multimedia event including performances by the Boston Lyric Opera Company and street dancing. The Cercle Culturel de la Langue

Francaise in Buffalo, New York, organized a six-month series of programs, culminating with festivities on Bastille Day. New York City staged an outdoor French *fête* at Lincoln Center Park Plaza, followed by a Mozart Concert at Avery Fisher Hall. St. Louis and Detroit, both of which had once flown the flag of France, celebrated Bastille Day, the former with a concurrent celebration of the 108th anniversary of the French Society of St. Louis, the latter with a fund-raising dinner to benefit the Detroit Symphony Orchestra.

The Alliance Francaise, an organization that seeks to promote the study of the French language and French culture in the United States, sponsored an essay contest in the United States in 1989 to honor the French Revolution Bicentennial. Open to college and high school students enrolled in Alliance classes, the contest required essays written in French that focused on the question: "Do different perceptions exist . . . concerning the fundamental values . . . as reflected in the Bill of Rights and Declaration of the Rights of Man?" More than 600 students in 44 cities and 23 states participated. The national Commission awarded all contestants copies of the *Keepsake Constitution*, and the 30 winners (in the various categories of competition) received copies of Catherine Drinker Bowen's *Miracle at Philadelphia*, autographed by the Commission's Chairman.

There were international essay contests on the Bicentennial during 1989. Two students from the American School in Tokyo, Kohki Kubota and Kathleen Vaughan, won first and second place in an annual essay contest held by the American Chamber of Commerce in Japan, examining the influence of the U.S. Constitution on the Japanese political system. In their essays both pointed out that before World War II, the concept of "equal justice under law" and the democratic process were alien to Japan. Since 1977, the American Chamber of Commerce had sponsored an essay contest for 11th and 12th grade students in international schools in Japan. Northwest Airlines provided free round-trip transportation to Washington, D.C., for the winners, and the national Commission arranged a two-day program for the students, including visits with Senator Edward Kennedy and Mike Mansfield (former U.S. Ambassador to Japan), tours of the U.S. Supreme Court, the U.S. Capitol, and the National Archives, a luncheon hosted by Representative Boggs, and a dinner hosted by the Asia Foundation. National Commissioner Betty Murphy helped to coordinate the contest and suggested its Bicentennial theme.

During the year, the United States Information Agency, its overseas posts (USIS), and its radio arm, the Voice of America, continued to include Bicentennial themes in their programs. USIS-Paris supported the publication of *The Federalist Papers* in French. Chief Justice Burger appeared on USIA's Worldnet and other USIA broadcasts targeted at overseas audiences. The national Commission provided material on *The Federalist Papers* for use in Voice of America feature stories broadcast in various countries. USIA also distributed 20,000 copies of the Commission's POCKET CONSTITUTION around the world.

Among the other international initiatives undertaken during 1989 were the American-Canadian Association national high school essay contest and the Bicentennial Conference at the University of Calgary. The Association had been organized in 1986 through the efforts of Commander Robert Joergensen, an American citizen living in Canada, to foster understanding among the youth of both countries of the U.S. Constitution and "to sanctify our relationship by our devotion to material helpfulness." Its membership included educators and government officials throughout Canada.

Sen. *Kennedy greets the Tokyo essay contest winners.*

One of the most interesting and unusual reverberations of the Bicentennial during this year occurred halfway around the globe in the People's Republic of China. In 1988-1989, Patricia Dyson, who had been awarded a Fulbright scholarship to teach American constitutional and labor law at Jilin University in Changchun, Jilin Province, northeast China, requested that the national Commission provide her with Bicentennial materials. She took along a supply of the Center for Civic Education's *We the People* high school texts, which she used in teaching a college course on constitutional law. To help Chinese students understand the rights and responsibilities guaranteed by the Constitution, Ms. Dyson furnished them with copies of the Commission's POCKET CONSTITUTION. One of the most difficult concepts for her students to grasp, Dyson learned, was the right of Americans to criticize their government without fear of penalty. On a lecture visit to Beijing she saw some of the historic 1989 demonstrations in Tiananmen Square and gave her last two copies of the POCKET CONSTITUTION to students there.

CONCLUSION

The year 1989 had been an eventful one, crowded with commemorations in honor of the founding of the national government. They affirmed — as President Bush observed in his speech honoring the anniversary of George Washington's first inaugural—the extraordinary strength and continuity of American government through 200 years. The commemorations would continue into 1990, when the Bicentennial turned its attention to the third branch of government, the Judiciary.

JOHN MARSHALL

CHIEF JUSTICE OF THE UNITED STATES
FROM 1801 TO 1835

CHAPTER VI

1990

Two
Hundred
Years
of
the
Judiciary

Following the 1989 commemoration of the establishment of the executive and legislative branches under the Constitution, the Commission in 1990 continued with the celebration of the next major event of the nation's founding — the Bicentennial of the Judiciary. Although the judicial branch of government dates back to 1789 (with the Judiciary Act of September 24 in that year), the United States Supreme Court did not hold its first session until February 2, 1790. The commemorations of this event 200 years later included many impressive accomplishments in law-related education, an important educational area in which many organizations — particularly the judicial branch and the legal profession nationwide — had been involved for many years. To promote better teaching and understanding of America's judicial and legal systems, during 1990 the Commission sought to stimulate all existing law-related education programs in schools, colleges, and other educational organizations.

"To what quarter
will you look for protection
from an infringement
on the Constitution,
if you will not give
the power to the judiciary?"

John Marshall, 1788
*Responding to Patrick Henry
in the Virginia Debate on the
Ratification of the Constitution.*

© Lee T. Anderson

Major Events

THE BICENTENNIAL OF THE U.S. SUPREME COURT AND THE JUDICIARY

Background: The 13 original colonies each had a judicial system based on English common law. Colonial courts of general jurisdiction heard all kinds of cases, of which a significant proportion were admiralty cases. Judgments of courts in one colony were not always honored in other colonies. Following the Revolution, the Articles of Confederation attempted to correct this problem — its Article IX declared that Congress would be the court of last resort in cases that arose between states or involved international affairs — but the Continental Congress had no judicial system to implement or enforce its decisions. The sensitivity of the states to impositions on their sovereignty carried over into the 1787 Constitutional Convention in Philadelphia. While the delegates recognized the need for some national court system to ensure that the Constitution would work, there was some disagreement over its structure and powers. The delegates ultimately concluded that the resolution of the judicial-system problem should be left to the new Congress. Thus, Article III of the new Constitution broadly stated that the judicial power should be vested "in one supreme Court and in such inferior courts as the Congress may establish. . . ." But the Constitution said little about actually setting up and bringing to life this third branch of government; that task was left to the new Congress.

In the First Congress, opponents of a judiciary act in the Senate maintained that to implement the proposal would cost too much money. Others feared possible conflict in a dual system of Federal and state courts. However, under the leadership of Oliver Ellsworth, who later became the third Chief Justice, the Senate passed the bill, with just six nay votes cast out of 22. The House soon followed suit, although according to Senator Robert Morris of Pennsylvania, some critics of the judicial legislation there "snarled at it." This attitude reflected the latent hostility toward a strong central government. The Judiciary Act of 1789, signed into law September 24 by President Washington, created a dual Federal-state judiciary system for the new nation. It included a Supreme Court with six Justices; and one Federal District Court with a District Judge within each state, each state constituting a Federal District. It also provided three Federal circuits, each with a court of appeals consisting of two Supreme Court Justices and a District Judge. The Act gave Federal courts exclusive jurisdiction in certain important areas and concurrent jurisdiction with the state courts in other matters.

Scheduled to meet for the first time on February 1, 1790, in the nation's temporary capital of New York City, the United States Supreme Court, with only three Justices present, waited until the next day to convene in an upstairs room of the old Royal Exchange building at the intersection of Broad and Water Streets. Situated on the second floor over a farmer's market and across the

street from the Fulton Fish Market, the Justices had to cope with the bleating of animals and the cries of farmers hawking their produce. During the first session, the Court had no cases but admitted lawyers to the bar and appointed a court crier and a clerk. It heard no cases until after it moved with the rest of the Federal Government to Philadelphia in late 1790. And even thereafter, the Court would hear only a few cases in the first ten years. Because of this inauspicious beginning—the Court's current prominence was achieved only gradually over the years—there was no single dramatic event to celebrate the anniversary of, 200 years later. In 1989, by contrast, the Bicentennial of the first President's inauguration had provided an ideal focus for commemorating the founding of the executive branch.

What the Commission should focus on in 1990 therefore became something of a challenge. It turned for recommendations to a special ad hoc committee chaired by Judge Howard Markey, then Chief Judge of the United States Court of Appeals for the Federal Circuit. During the summer of 1989, this committee explored various options and made several recommendations, many of which were adopted. The Commission decided on participation in a special January 1990 ceremony planned for the Supreme Court. Meanwhile, state and Federal courts, local governments, schools, and other organizations across the country responded to the Commission's encouragement of commemorative activities. The Commission sent letters and copies of its brochure *To Establish Justice (see page 197)* to these constituencies in late 1989 and early 1990.

U.S. Supreme Court (3)

Royal Exchange in New York, site of the first Supreme Court (above); first Chief Justice John Jay (left); third Chief Justice Oliver Ellsworth (right); Court's 1990 commemorative medal.

Bicentennial of the Supreme Court: On January 16, 1990, the Supreme Court commemorated its 200th anniversary in a Special Session with a capacity audience including the Court staff along with invited dignitaries and guests. Chief Justice of the Supreme Court William H. Rehnquist characterized the idea of a constitutional court — an independent judiciary with authority to enforce the provisions of a written constitution — as "the most important single American contribution to the art of government." Then, referring to the three original Justices who met on February 1, 1790, the Chief Justice said:

[They] could not possibly have foreseen the future importance of the court upon which they accepted the call to serve. I am confident that even those who gathered here [in a similar commemoration] fifty years ago could not have foreseen the changes and developments in the law which would come in the next half-century, nor the influence that this institution would have outside its borders during that time. And surely the same is true of those of us who have gathered here today to commemorate the bicentennial of the Court's first sitting. We have no way of knowing with certainty where the quest for equal justice under law will lead our successors in the next half-century.

Reviewing the difficult early days of the Court, Chief Justice Warren Burger described to the audience the hardships of circuit riding, instituted by Congress in the belief that if the Justices of the Supreme Court were "kept busy riding circuit they would be less troublesome to the other branches of government." Several nominees to the Court in fact declined their appointments because of this arduous duty, the removal of which the first Chief Justice, John Jay, urged. The Chairman continued: "Congress finally did respond to the urgings of Chief Justice Jay and his successors by providing judges for the Courts of Appeal and eliminating the circuit riding burdens, but that was done, to borrow a phrase from the English equity law, 'with all deliberate speed.' It was done in 1891."

Chief Justice Burger explained that "the young Supreme Court did not enjoy the prestige that it has today. It was not really regarded as a coequal branch, and some questioned whether it could survive." Nevertheless, the appointment of John Marshall in 1801 as the fourth Chief Justice marked the beginning of "a great epoch in the history of this Court and of this country." Noting the rising demands for freedom prevalent throughout the world, Chief Justice Burger concluded with a reference to the newly emerging democracies:

Our history is their hope, and our hope for them must be that whatever systems they set up in place of the tyranny they have rejected will include a judiciary with authority and independence to enforce the basic guarantees of freedom, as this Court has done for these two hundred years.

Solicitor General Kenneth Starr, who represented the U.S. Government before the Supreme Court, noted that some — among them Alexander Hamilton — saw the judiciary as "the least dangerous branch," but that over time it has become a "truly coequal, coordinate branch with the Legislature and the Executive." Rex Lee, a former Solicitor General representing the Supreme Court Bar, said that members of the bar "of this court are proud of the institution whose two-hundredth birthday we celebrate, proud of what it has meant and what it has done for our country and its people. . . ." The proceedings of this ceremony were recorded in the *Journal, Supreme Court of the United States* and were later published in the *1990 Yearbook of the Supreme Court Historical Society*.

First-Day-of-Issue Ceremony: The Supreme Court was the site of another ceremony, held on February 2, 1990, to commemorate the actual anniversary of the Court's first meeting. At the event, held in the Lower Great Hall, a new U.S. Postal Service stamp was unveiled honoring the Bicentennial of the Judiciary, bearing a likeness of Chief Justice John Marshall. Joined by

Postmaster General Anthony Frank, Associate Justice William Brennan, and former Associate Justice Lewis Powell, Chief Justice Rehnquist honored the man featured on the 25-cent stamp:

There may be some who will feel that John Marshall has already had more than his share of stamps depicting him

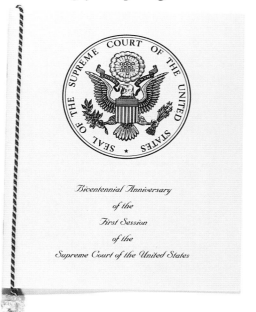

*P*rogram for the *Special Session (right); Judiciary stamp unveiling (far right). United States Supreme Court Building. (opposite page)*

Bicentennial Anniversary
of the
First Session
of the
Supreme Court of the United States

as compared with other distinguished members of this Court. But this issue is designed to represent the judicial branch of the United States Government, and surely there can be no doubt that if one person is to be selected to embody that branch, it must be the man who is referred to by all simply as "The Great Chief Justice."

The stamp, the fourth and last in the series marking the Bicentennial of the three branches of government (*see Chapter V*), was black and trimmed in red with an off-white likeness of Marshall.

Special Order of Congress, February 1990: The legislative branch also sponsored special events honoring the anniversary of the Court and the Judiciary, with several members of the national Commission taking part. On February 1, Speaker of the House Thomas Foley granted a special order for recognition of Congress's role in the founding of the Court and the Federal judicial system in the Judiciary Act of 1789. In her remarks at the ceremony, which she had helped plan, Representative Lindy Boggs said, "The Court was the last branch of government to go into operation, almost 11 months after the House convened, and was more a product of congressional deliberation than the decisions of the Federal Convention." Representative Boggs also placed in the *Congressional Record* a statement by the Commission's Chairman that described the gradual ascent of the Court to a level of coequality with the other two branches of government. Representative Phil Crane said, "Our Constitution, which was drafted as a contract ensuring the rights of all people in our Republic, would mean much less than it does today were it not for the judicial branch of the Federal Government."

The Senate reserved time on February 2 for its own special commemoration of the Judiciary. Senator Mark Hatfield said, "In the 200 years since that day when the Court first met, the political winds in this Nation have blown in a great many directions. But the Court has remained firmly founded on law, and has remained a beacon of liberty and justice." Senator Edward Kennedy remarked that "again and again, the Court has fulfilled its role of vindicating the constitutional rights of all Americans." Senator Kennedy also inserted in the record the text of a pamphlet prepared by the Committee on the Bicentennial of the Constitution of the Judicial Conference of the United States, *The Bicentennial of the Federal Judicial System.*

Judiciary Commemorations Nationwide: But perhaps the most far-reaching and impressive aspects of the Judiciary Bicentennial were the many commemorative events and educational activities that took place not in the nation's capital but in various states and communities across the country. At the annual meeting of the Conference of State Supreme Court Justices at Lake Tahoe, Nevada, in August 1989, Chief Justice Burger urged the state courts to join in the 1990 nationwide Judiciary commemoration and to conduct ceremonies on February 2 in honor of the first meeting of the Supreme Court. He noted that this anniversary honored

not only the Federal Judiciary, but America's independent dual judicial system, with the state courts continuing to transact most of the nation's legal business.

In 1990, the nation's courts responded to the Chairman's call by sponsoring commemorative ceremonies, and by initiating lectures, mock courts, seminars, swearing-in citizenship ceremonies, and various programs and activities in schools and colleges. The Chairman of the 1989 Conference, Chief Justice Harry L. Carrico of the Virginia Supreme Court, who had endorsed the Commission's recommendations and encouraged participation, set a proper example of the Federal-state partnership in 1990 by joining Federal Judge Harry Michael, Jr., of the Western District of Virginia in a special ceremony commemorating the Bicentennial of the Judiciary and the first session of the Supreme Court. A special commemoration later in Virginia Beach, Virginia, both honored America's dual court system and announced the construction of the city's new judicial center building.

To commemorate their own Bicentennial while honoring the Federal court system, the ten counties of eastern Pennsylvania, which constituted the first Federal District to be organized under the Judiciary Act of 1789, formed "Federal Courts 200." The first Federal Judge for the Eastern District of Pennsylvania had been commissioned just two days after the Act became law. Launched in November of 1988, the "Federal Courts 200" commemoration featured Supreme Court Associate Justice William J. Brennan, Jr. Awards named after Justice Brennan honored Philadelphia law firms, and individual attorneys, that had made a firm commitment to outstanding *pro bono* service. The yearlong education program concluded in September 1989 with a public convocation of Federal Judges at Independence Hall where winners from the various contests were honored.

The United States District Court in Kansas conducted a naturalization ceremony at the state capitol in Topeka, with Chief Judge Earl E. O'Connor administering the oath to 176 new Americans who came from 44 nations. The National Archives (Central Plains Region) sponsored the proceedings, which included the premier performance of a musical tribute commissioned by

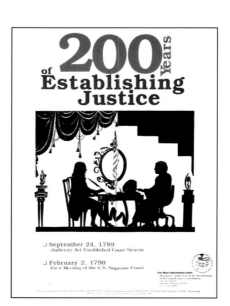

Michigan sponsored student art and writing contests on the Judiciary.

Kansas's state Commission. In honor of the first meeting of the United States Supreme Court, Federal Judges in Michigan explained the history of the Constitution and the Federal court systems to over 1,000 high school and college students assembled in their courtrooms. The program began simultaneously throughout the state at 10 a.m. on Friday, February 2, 1990. Believed to be one of the largest such programs in the country, it was sponsored by the Michigan Bicentennial Commission in cooperation with the Bicentennial Committee of the Judicial Conference of the United States, chaired by Judge Damon Keith, later to become a member of the national Commission.

In Utah, trial courts suspended operations at 10 a.m., February 2, for the reading of a resolution marking the first meeting of the United States Supreme Court. The resolution stated: "We commend the continuing work of the highest court in the land, and the dual system of state and Federal judicial institutions, which have effectively preserved the rights and freedoms of Americans for two centuries. . . ." Three District Court judges, a bankruptcy judge, and two U.S. magistrates presided over a special ceremony on February 2 in Jacksonville, Florida, in which 59 attorneys were admitted to the Federal bar. Chief Justice Ernest Clay Hornsby of the Alabama Supreme Court invited all appellate justices and judges and all district and circuit judges in the state to participate in commemoration of the 200th anniversary. He noted that "as big as the Federal judiciary has become, and as vast as its jurisdiction has expanded, still, the overwhelming majority of all civil and criminal cases in this country are heard in state and local courts."

Alaska Governor Steve Cowper issued an Executive Proclamation designating February 2, 1990, as Federal Judiciary Day and stating that "it is appropriate for Alaska to acknowledge the role of the U.S. Supreme Court in preserving and protecting the rights and freedoms of both the State of Alaska and its residents." The Museum of American Constitutional Government at Federal Hall in New York provided a challenging educational focus as part of its regular program, "The Constitution Works." Students, dressed in suits or judicial robes, took the parts of judges, lawyers, Members of Congress, Cabinet members, and lobbyists to debate issues ranging from freedom of the press to equal protection of the law. While learning how courts and the Congress work, the students also learned the history of the Federal Judiciary and the first meeting of the Supreme Court in 1790. Returning to their classrooms, the students reported on how they had arrived at their positions or decisions.

One of the recommendations of Judge Markey's advisory committee was to invite the nation's younger students to create, and send to the Court, birthday cards honoring the anniversary. Hundreds of elementary students from across the nation responded. Fifth-grade students from Coopertown Elementary School in Springfield, Tennessee, for example, wrote, "We the kids . . . wish you 200 Happy Years of Justice" and "We hope you stay another 200 years" (see page 197).

Students mailed birthday cards to the Court.

Exhibits: Special exhibits also marked the Judiciary's Bicentennial. Visitors to the Supreme Court building in 1990 viewed "The Supreme Court: 1790-1990," an exhibit that traced the 200-year history of the Court from its establishment by the Constitution. Cosponsored by the Court and the national Commission and running from January through September, the exhibit included the Supreme Court Bar, the former seats housing the Court, the Supreme Court building, landmark cases, and an explanation of the workings of the Court. Two hundred objects made up the display, including engravings, documents, photographs, busts, portraits, furniture, and memorabilia from several university libraries, the Library of Congress, the National Archives, and the Curator's Office of the Supreme

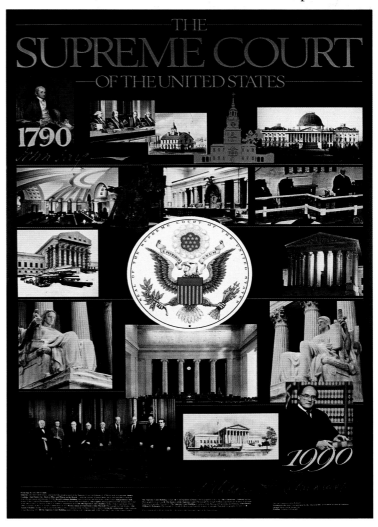

Poster for the Supreme Court's Bicentennial exhibition.

Court. Original documents included handwritten minutes of the first Court session and the notes of Abraham Lincoln on a case he argued as a lawyer before the Court.

Elsewhere, the United States District Court for the Southern District of New York placed a display at Fraunces Tavern, New York City, site of George Washington's 1783 farewell to his troops. The chronological exhibit, "'To establish justice . . .': The 200th Anniversary of the U.S. District Court in New York," remained open during 1989 and 1990, tracing the history of the Federal court system from 1789. It featured constitutional themes and legal decisions marking the history of the courts. A companion exhibit was on display at the Foley Square Courthouse in lower Manhattan.

CONSTITUTION WEEK 1990

Another opportunity for the commemoration and study of the Judiciary was provided by the annual observance of Constitution Week (September 17-23) and Citizenship Day (September 17). Continuing its efforts to institutionalize these commemorations as recurring annual events, the national Commission, at its March 3 meeting, approved the use of $100,000 for promotion of this observance, with special focus on the Judiciary. "In this 4th year of the Constitution's bicentennial, we commemorate the establishment of the Nation's judicial system," said President Bush in his 1990 annual proclamation on Citizenship Day and Constitution Week. He described the early history of the Constitution and outlined the structure of the Judiciary — with the "form and substance" provided by the Judiciary Act of 1789 — that Congress had built from the powers provided by Article III of the Constitution. Acknowledging that the Nation's independent Judiciary had upheld law and individual rights and "reaffirmed time and again the inestimable value of our Constitution," the President then said:

Asserting that no person shall be "deprived of life, liberty, or property, without due process of law" and guaranteeing every American "equal protection of the laws," the Constitution has remained a powerful governing tool and an effective instrument of justice to this day.

In May, the Commission disseminated to state and local Commissions 100,000 packets of Bicentennial materials, including an updated *Constitution Week, An American Legacy* booklet, a six-panel brochure of suggestions for "Honoring the Judiciary," a press release containing an article by the Chairman entitled "The Bicentennial of the Federal Judicial System," a Constitution Week poster, and public service announcements. The same packets also went to judges, city and county officials, and others. The packets prompted hundreds of requests from throughout the country for the Commission's Constitution Week materials and other educational publications *(see page 196).* Many of these requests came from judges. They disseminated the materials the Commission sent them to schools in their

The celebration on Constitution Hill.

Worchester Telegram & Gazette

areas and, in many cases, participated in educational activities at those schools. For example, Chief Justice John Mowbray of the Nevada Supreme Court distributed hundreds of Constitution Week posters and kits to every school district in the state. In New York, the State Supreme Court marked Constitution Week by hosting over 100 high school students at the Jamaica Court Building in Queens County and giving them demonstrations of how the judicial system works — from the courtroom and trial phase to the administrative system of record-keeping that enables the system to function. The program included a videotape on the legal system, observation of a trial in progress, a presentation on jury selection and the duties of jurors, and an information session on career opportunities in the courts.

In other activities, Constitution Hill, a commemorative shrine in Worcester, Massachusetts, was the 1990 site of Constitution Week ceremonies, as it is each year. The emotional highlight of the 1990 observance was the sight of 285 flag-bearing pupils from Heard Street School marching up the hill to take part in the program. At the State House in Boston, the Massachusetts Senate presented to Mr. and Mrs. Thomas A. Jolly of Worcester a Senate Resolution honoring their role in the dedication of Constitution Hill and in the organization of annual events commemorating Citizenship Day. Youngstown, Ohio, residents marked Constitution Week 1990 with a naturalization ceremony for 24 new citizens from Asia, Europe, and the Middle East on the steps of the Mahoning County Courthouse. New citizens from 50 nations participated in naturalization ceremonies at the Old Orange County Courthouse in Santa Ana, California, as part of the Orange County/Huntington Beach Bicentennial Commission Citizenship Day celebration. Events at the courthouse included a BELLS ACROSS AMERICA ceremony, a band concert, a Marine Corps color-guard salute, and a special U.S. Postal Service cancellation of the Chief Justice John Marshall commemorative stamp.

COMMEMORATING THE CREATION OF THE U.S. MARSHAL SERVICE

The Judiciary Act of 1789 provided still another opportunity for commemoration. Just two days after signing the Act, President George Washington nominated U.S. Marshals for each of the 13 original Judicial

Districts, and they were immediately confirmed by the Senate and began to enforce Federal laws and decisions of the Federal courts. To commemorate 200 years of this service, the national Commission and the U.S. Marshals Service Foundation cosponsored "America's Star," an educational traveling exhibit that began in Washington, D.C., in the spring of 1989 and ended two years later at Federal Hall in New York City. The exhibit, including

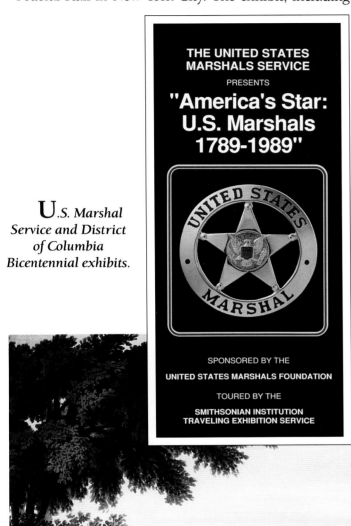

U.S. Marshal Service and District of Columbia Bicentennial exhibits.

more than 300 artifacts of famous "lawmen and desperados," traced U.S. Marshal involvement in major episodes of American history, from the Whiskey Rebellion in 1794 to the 1973 incident involving Native Americans at Wounded Knee, South Dakota. *Weekly Reader*, an educational newspaper for elementary schools throughout the country, helped to design an educational package, and each local museum made use of educational outreach programs for schools.

BICENTENNIAL OF THE DISTRICT OF COLUMBIA

Unlike any city before it, the national capital, Washington, in the District of Columbia, was the product of a written constitution, and 1990 marked the beginning of its Bicentennial. The Constitution called for the creation of a Federal District as the seat of government, and the Framers, to symbolize the experiment in self-government, wanted the capital to be free from the jurisdiction of any state. The selection of the site was a compromise. Secretary of State Thomas Jefferson, representing the views of the Southern states, agreed to support a Northern proposal by Alexander Hamilton, Secretary of the Treasury, that the Federal Government assume the states' revolutionary war debts only if the national capital was located in the South. The

Residence Act approving the site passed by a close vote in both the House and the Senate and allowed ten years to prepare the new Federal city. President George Washington signed the Act into law on July 16, 1790.

The District of Columbia Bicentennial Commission coordinated public and private initiatives for the District commemoration and worked with numerous outside organizations to develop commemorative programs. This Commission, a 39-member volunteer body appointed by the Mayor, members of the City Council, the Courts, and the D.C. Bar, had been established in 1987 by the City Council. Although the Residence Act anniversary fell in 1990, the D.C. Commission selected 1991, the 200th anniversary of the establishment of the

specific site and its boundaries, as the official beginning of a decade-long commemoration of the city's founding and building, to conclude in 2002, the anniversary of the first D.C. Charter. As a prelude to this commemoration, several new publications appeared in 1990. The Parks and History Association of the National Park Service produced *City of the Constitution: A Guide to Selected Sites*, a 64-page illustrated guide to 25 famous Constitution-related places in Washington, D.C. National Archives staff member Bruce Bustard compiled and wrote a 108-page book with more than 100 reproductions of documents, maps, photographs, and drawings showing the history of the city and its people. The book accompanied a special Archives exhibit entitled "Wash-

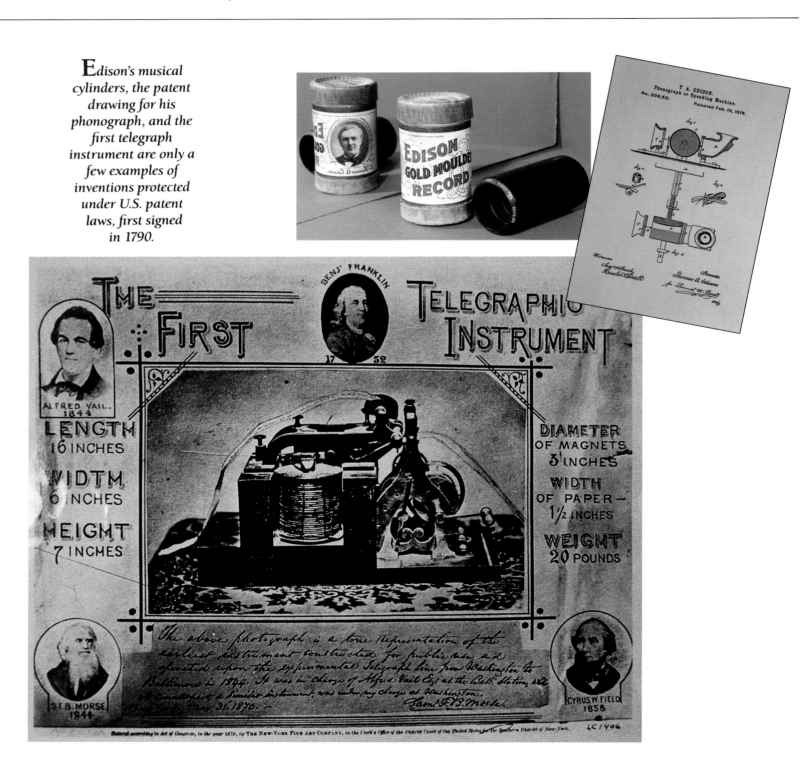

Edison's musical cylinders, the patent drawing for his phonograph, and the first telegraph instrument are only a few examples of inventions protected under U.S. patent laws, first signed in 1790.

ington: Behind the Monuments." The National Archives also produced and distributed two commemorative posters in connection with the exhibit: *City of Washington from beyond the Navy Yard*, depicting an 1834 engraving by W. J. Bennett from a painting by George Cook; and *Scene in March on Anacostia River, Washington, Capitol in Distance*, circa 1882, a tri-tone reproduction of a photograph by John K. Hillers.

THE BICENTENNIAL OF PATENT AND COPYRIGHT LAWS

On August 15, 1990, President Bush honored the patent and copyright laws of 1790 with a proclamation calling on all Americans "to foster recognition of . . . the bicentennial year of our nation's first patent and copyright laws." Enacted to supplement the Commerce Clause of the Constitution (Article I, Section 8), these two laws were of vital significance to the nation's prosperity. Before the Constitution went into effect, each state had its own rules governing the granting of patents and copyrights, but one state did not necessarily or automatically respect another's protections. The Constitution resolved this problem, giving Congress the power "to promote the Progress of Science and useful Arts, by securing for limited Times to Authors and Inventors the exclusive Right to their respective Writings and Discoveries." (Article I, Section 8). Once the Constitution

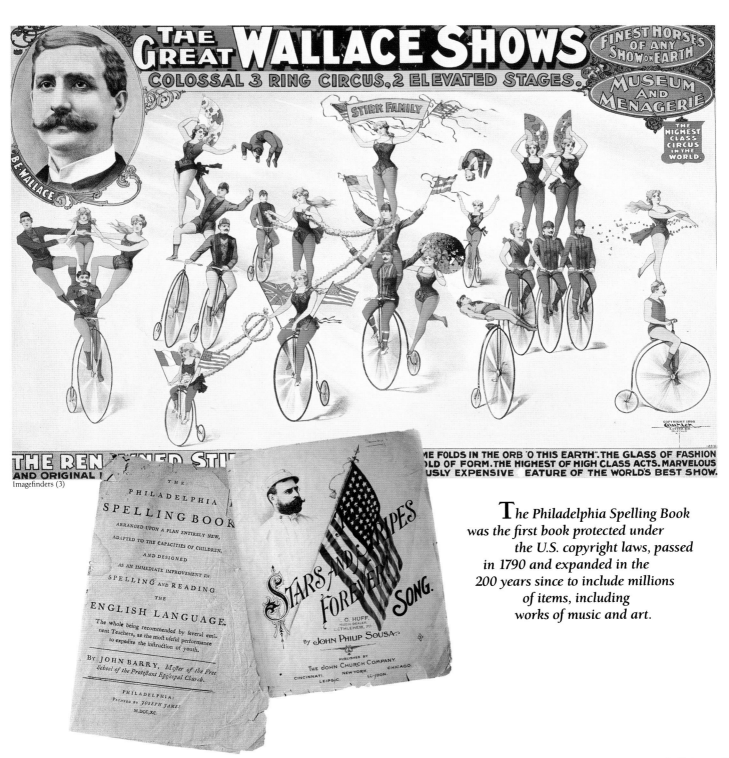

Imagefinders (3)

The Philadelphia Spelling Book was the first book protected under the U.S. copyright laws, passed in 1790 and expanded in the 200 years since to include millions of items, including works of music and art.

became widely read and known, the First Congress—by the time it met in 1789—was inundated with petitions for copyrights and patents. During its second session, the Congress passed an "Act to Promote the Progress of Useful Arts." President Washington signed it on April 10, 1790, and the United States patent system was born. On May 31, Washington also signed the Copyright Act, which, when subsequently refined, protected an author's original "writings" — literary, dramatic, musical, and artistic works as well as maps and charts — from copying by others without permission. Together with the Constitution's Commerce Clause, which created an unrestricted free trade area within the new republic, the patent and copyright laws laid the basis for America's growth and prosperity in the years to come.

Third Century award honorees (above); the winners of the Young Creators and Inventors Contest (right).

The national Commission granted official recognition on March 24, 1989, to the Foundation for a Creative America, a nonprofit organization set up to coordinate the 1990 commemoration of the patent and copyright laws. The Foundation planned for a series of events to recall the proliferation of inventions and intellectual creativity unleashed by the laws 200 years earlier, which catapulted the United States onto the world stage as an economic power — and which over two centuries produced some 28 million registered and protected inventions and creative works.

In early May in Washington, D.C., the Foundation highlighted its series of seminars, banquets, lectures, and exhibits with the presentation of the Third Century Award to 11 American geniuses in the creative arts and sciences. In addition, the Foundation, along with the American Lawyers Auxiliary, an American Bar Association (ABA) affiliate, sponsored a nationwide Young Creator's and Young Inventor's Contest to encourage creativity and inventiveness among young Americans. Of more than 5,000 entries received from all 50 states, the 36 winners each received a U.S. Savings Bond and a

four-day visit to the nation's capital. "America Creates," an exhibit developed by the Foundation to represent the history of American creativity and technology, opened May 10 at the Library of Congress, following a preview at the National Inventors Hall of Fame in Akron, Ohio. The exhibit displayed selected samples from the millions of registered creative works, and it included several oversize, interactive replicas that children could touch and manipulate. After closing in Washington, D.C., on June 15, the exhibit went on a nationwide three-year tour to Louisville, Kentucky; Kansas City, Missouri; Chicago, Illinois; Midland, Michigan; Los Angeles, California; Baltimore, Maryland; Portland, Oregon; and Jacksonville, Florida, with several more set for 1993.

COMMEMORATION OF THE CENSUS ACT

The year 1990 was also the Bicentennial of the Census Act, which was needed by the new government to meet the Constitution's representation requirements (*see Chapter V*). On March 1, 1790, therefore, Congress authorized the first census, which was completed three years later and reported a national population of 3,929,326. Plans to honor the 1790 Census Act on its 200th anniversary had begun on May 17, 1989, with a U.S. House of Representatives resolution stating that the national Commission and the Secretary of Commerce (who administers the Bureau of the Census) should "observe the bicentennial of the census of the United States with appropriate ceremonies and activities." The focus of the commemoration was the 21st Decennial Census itself, the most complex in history, which showed that the national population had grown more than 63-fold in 200 years, to 248,709,873 in 1990. Several Bicentennial publications were issued by the Census Bureau, including *200 Years of U.S. Census Taking: Population and Housing Questions, 1790-1990*. The Commission's 1990 commemorative calendar featured the founding of the census during the month of March.

Enumerating the 1890 Census, from Harper's Bazaar.

Commission Programs

To a great extent, the national Commission channeled its 1990 efforts through its ongoing programs.

The American Spirit

"...one supreme Court,..."

Although the year had no single major commemorative event, observance of the 200th anniversary of the Judiciary enabled the Commission to encourage projects in many areas of law-related education. The numerous educational programs focusing on the importance of an independent Judiciary and the rule of law provided excellent preparation for the Bicentennial's focus, during the concluding year, on the Bill of Rights.

BICENTENNIAL EDUCATIONAL GRANT PROGRAM

The BICENTENNIAL EDUCATIONAL GRANT PROGRAM (BEGP) provided an excellent example of the success of educational initiatives taken during the commemoration of the judicial branch. It should be noted that, next to the Bill of Rights, the Judiciary was the most popular specific subject among the 250 or so grants awarded by BEGP. This no doubt reflected not only a keen interest in

law-related education, but also the Judiciary's primary role in upholding the Constitution. In anticipation of the Judiciary commemoration, the Commission during the previous year had funded some grants focusing on that subject and funded several in 1990 as well. Among grants awarded in the previous year was one to the National Council for the Social Studies (NCSS) to produce two sets of posters, with curriculum materials, on the Judiciary. Another allowed Kennesaw State College in Georgia to collaborate with the National Archives, the Georgia Department of Education, and secondary schools in the Atlanta area to develop a supplemental teaching unit on the Federal courts.

The major emphases of BEGP continued to be teacher training and curriculum development. As with the previous two years of the program, 1990 had two rounds. In the first round, 31 out of 139 applications were funded, at an average amount of $56,817, for a total of nearly $1.8 million. Of 130 applications in the second round, 25 were awarded funds at an average amount of $63,846, for a total of $1.5 million. A few examples highlight the program's range of objectives:

Phi Alpha Delta Public Service Center in Maryland developed *A Resource Guide for Lawyers and Law Students: Teaching About the Bill of Rights in Elementary and Middle School Classrooms* and provided a lawyer and a law student training program to facilitate the guide's use nationally. The guide contained instructions on how lawyers and law students can work with young students and classroom teachers in law-related education.

The Council for Basic Education hosted a two-week summer institute on the Judiciary and on important Supreme Court decisions in modern history. The institute, for 30 secondary history teachers in the Washington, D.C., public school system, incorporated scholarly presentations and discussions using the Socratic method to encourage intellectual debate on important issues.

The Wayne County (Michigan) Intermediate School District developed guidelines for teaching the fundamentals of the Constitution and the U.S. Government in a multicultural education program, in kindergarten through grade 9. In seven one-day workshops, parents, educators, and cultural representatives participated in panels and development sessions.

Project PATCH of the Northport-East Northport Union Free School District, in conjunction with the New York State Bar Association, sustained ten regional teaching centers—training 1,000 teachers—and developed and distributed to all elementary schools in New York State a free *Bill of Rights Fun Book for Elementary Students*. It also produced a new supplementary text for ninth through 11th grades, *The United States Constitution and Its Amendments: A Global Legacy*.

The San Elizario Independent School District in Texas hosted in-service seminars for teachers that connected local history with the U.S. Constitution. The seminars were aimed at developing lesson plans for incorporation into the existing Texas social studies curricula. The elementary school approach focused on the three branches of government. The middle school approach focused on the two houses of Congress. The high school approach focused on the Bill of Rights and subsequent Amendments, and their impact on civil rights.

The Western Reserve Historical Society produced a 28-minute documentary film and teacher's guide on the possession, survey, and settlement of Connecticut's Western Reserve lands in Ohio. Focusing on the Constitution and the frontier of the Western Reserve, to which both Connecticut and Ohio had claims, the film was shown regionally on public television and other instructional channels, and videocassettes were made available for classroom use throughout New England and the upper Midwest.

PATHS/PRISM in Pennsylvania hosted a four-week summer institute for 25 teachers of first through eighth grades — from six major urban centers and one rural area nationwide — and produced materials and curricula, including computer software on the Bill of Rights and subsequent Amendments.

The South Carolina Bar Association produced four one-hour national civics television lessons on the Constitution, which relied on scholarly input and teaching techniques as well as development of video resources for the students. Two of the telecasts aimed at the high school level, while the others were for elementary and middle schools.

COLLEGE-COMMUNITY FORUMS

From its pilot run in 1988-1989, the COLLEGE-COMMUNITY FORUMS PROGRAM continued to grow, assisted by the Commission's expanded grant authority

T*aping a TV lesson in South Carolina.*

enabling it to grant awards at the college level. Community organizations as well as institutions of higher learning applied for funding. The Commission provided up to $5,000 for a single event and up to $15,000 for a series. Focusing each year on a commemorative theme, the program during 1990 emphasized the Bicentennial of the Judiciary. One highlight of the year was the third booklet in the forum series: *The Judicial Branch and the Constitutional Order*. From 46 applications received during the 1990 round of funding, the Commission awarded a total of $200,000 to 23 applicants from 15 states. Among the funded projects were the following:

Averett College officials in Danville, Virginia, joined with representatives from eight community groups in planning and hosting two public forums designed to encourage audience involvement; ten civic-group mini-forums; and two 30-minute radio broadcasts on "The Separation of Powers: Invitation to Conflict, But Safeguard of Our Liberties," which aired on WBTM Danville, reviewing the issues and discussing the points raised in the forums and mini-forums. At Rocky Mountain College in Billings, Montana, a forum on the history of the Constitution and the formation of Indian law attracted over 100 participants, more than half of whom were Native Americans. A series of panel discussions covered the rights of tribal and state governments to control taxation, zoning, and gambling on reservation land; criminal and civil jurisdiction and civil rights; and Federal trust responsibilities.

Drake University Law School in Des Moines, Iowa, sponsored a two-day forum in March on the Judiciary and freedom of the press. The symposium marked the 25th anniversary of the landmark decision *New York Times* v. *Sullivan*, with lectures by scholars Kermit Hall, Frederick Schauer, and Rodney Smolla. Focusing on the origins, operations, and impact of the Federal Judiciary, a series of forums sponsored by Albany State College in Albany, Georgia, was entitled "The Federal Judiciary: Non-elected Defender of Democracy." Conducted during the spring semester of 1990, the forums explored the tenure and removal of Judges, the Federal Judiciary's powers as related to those of the executive and the legislative branches, and judicial review.

LIBRARY PROGRAM

The national Commission, in cooperation with the American Library Association, introduced in January 1990 a two-year public service project, "With Liberty and Justice for All," honoring the Bicentennials of the Judiciary in 1990 and the Bill of Rights in 1991. The project invited the nation's 15,000 public libraries to become "active partners in educating the American public about the American judicial system, the Bill of Rights and other Amendments, and the United States Constitution." The Commission produced and distributed a brochure of the same title containing suggested program ideas for libraries, Bicentennial chronologies, lists of resources and resource organizations, and biographical information on John Marshall. A second brochure followed in September, this one on the Bill of Rights and subsequent Amendments.

Early in 1989, the Commission completed production and distribution of a four-cassette videotape series, "Equal Justice Under Law." These courtroom dramas, reenacted by professional actors, covered four historic court cases: *Marbury* v. *Madison*, *McCulloch* v. *Maryland*, *Gibbons* v. *Ogden*, and *United States* v. *Burr*. The first three represented landmark decisions of Chief Justice John Marshall that defined the role of the Supreme Court as an equal partner in the Federal Government. The fourth covered the trial of Aaron Burr, over which Chief Justice Marshall, sitting as a District Judge, presided, and which set a precedent for limiting executive privilege. Through the National Audio-Visual Center, the Commission produced 10,000 copies of the series, together with teaching guides, and distributed over 8,400 sets to film libraries, educational media centers, law schools, and selected institutions. The Commission made the remaining sets available to nonprofit organizations for a discounted price of $50 each. To promote use of the series, particularly in connection with the 1990 commemoration of the Judiciary, the Commission's eight-panel illustrated brochure described the series and suggested ideas on how to use it for educational purposes. WQED of Pittsburgh had produced a similar version of the series, which it had broadcast on public television two years before.

OTHER PROGRAMS

The finals of the third annual NATIONAL BICENTENNIAL COMPETITION ON THE CONSTITUTION AND BILL OF RIGHTS took place on May 7, 1990, in Senate hearing rooms on Capitol Hill in Washington, D.C. More than 1,000 students representing 43 states competed in the first two rounds, but as in previous years, only the top ten teams contended in the final round for the national title. The 29 students from Lincoln High School in Portland, Oregon, captured first-place honors. Coincidentally, Senator Mark Hatfield of Oregon, on behalf of the Commission, awarded the winning school an engraved walnut plaque of the Constitution and each student a gold medallion. Findlay High School of Findlay, Ohio, took second place, and East Brunswick High School of East Brunswick, New Jersey, placed third. Schools with the highest scores in each of the six units of the curriculum, and those with the highest overall scores from five geographical regions, were also recognized. In the 1989-1990 school year, 2.2 million

students (of whom nearly 800,000 were secondary students) participated in the total program, including some 14,000 classes in the six-week competitive course of instruction and 32,500 classes in the noncompetitive program.

The Center for Civic Education (CCE) added a new feature to the program in 1990. Partly to accommodate the growing number of classes participating in a noncompetitive way, and also to encourage greater participation by schools in noncompetitive use of its texts, it introduced WE THE PEOPLE . . . CONGRESS AND THE CONSTITUTION. Unlike the NATIONAL BICENTENNIAL COMPETITION, this new noncompetitive program permitted classes to prepare and present statements and answer questions on constitutional topics before a panel of representatives in their own community. Schools that registered for the noncompetitive program were designated "We the People" schools and received certificates for participation and priority consideration for free teaching materials. Each student completing the course, passing the final test, and participating in the community hearing received a Certificate of Recognition.

The 1990 national winner of the annual DAR CONSTITUTION WEEK ESSAY CONTEST, cosponsored by the Daughters of the American Revolution and the national Commission, was Mark Montgomery, a senior from Center High School in Kansas City, Missouri. In his essay on the assigned topic, "Why Are Independent Judges Important in the Preservation of our Constitutional System of Government?" he wrote that "independent judges ensure that all people receive equal justice under the law. Without this independence, Americans would have a federal judiciary controlled by the government." The winning prize was a $1,000 DAR scholarship and a copy of the bronze bust of Benjamin Franklin sculpted by the Commission's Chairman when he was a teenager. The nine regional winners and their

*S*en. *Hatfield and the National Bicentennial Competition winners (above).*

teachers, as guests of the Commission, enjoyed a VIP visit to the nation's capital, including a special Oval Office tour of the White House, visits with their Representatives, and other memorable activities.

During 1989-1990, the Commission granted OFFICIAL PROJECT RECOGNITION to 30 new Bicentennial projects, bringing to 336 the total number of projects granted recognition since 1986. Those recognized included the Freedom's Foundation Bill of Responsibilities, programs sponsored by the Foundation for a Creative America, the Department of the Army *Resource Guide*, and the Constitutional Issues Module prepared by the U.S. Office of Personnel Management.

To coordinate advertisement of the LOGO-LICENSING PROGRAM with the current Bicentennial theme, the Commission changed its commemorative catalog to an attractive 16-panel foldout gift brochure to be used for all response mail. Revised every four months, each edition of the catalog included a four-panel educational essay on the current theme. The two 1990 brochures — one on *The Bicentennial: An Ongoing Celebration* and the other on *200 Years of the Judiciary* — produced 2,500 orders totaling some $100,000 in royalties. The Commission

The *"George to George" (Washington to Bush) medal.*

granted three more logo licenses during 1990: a colorful poster depicting the Declaration of Independence, the Constitution, and the Bill of Rights surrounded in the margin by state flowers, birds, and ratification dates of these documents; a "George to George" medal (Washington to Bush); and a Bill of Rights plaque entitled "The Four Freedoms," with four sterling proof medals patterned after works of Norman Rockwell.

PORTRAITS OF THE JUSTICES

As a lasting memento of the Bicentennial of the Judiciary, the Commission produced a historical reference book, *The Supreme Court of the United States: Its Beginnings & Its Justices 1790-1991*, with biographical vignettes and portraits of all 106 Justices who have served on the Court. High-quality color reproductions of all the portraits were used. The book included a preface by the Commission's Chairman, a foreword by Chief Justice Rehnquist, a transcript of the Supreme Court Bicentennial Anniversary Ceremony, and appendices comprising a chart of Supreme Court members, a table of succession, and bibliographies covering the

Supreme Court and the Justices. Assisted by the Supreme Court Historical Society, the Curator's Office of the Supreme Court, and the National Geographic Society, the Commission published 30,000 copies of the book in the spring of 1992. The distribution list included colleges and law school libraries, court and government officials, public and court libraries, embassies, the United States Information Agency (USIA), and foreign high courts.

OTHER PUBLICATIONS

The 1990 edition of the COMMEMORATIVE CALENDAR appeared in January. It represented a significant departure in design and content from the approach used in earlier editions. Its expansive illustrations and text made the calendar a valuable educational resource. For the first time, the Commission mass-distributed its print run of 198,000 copies to courts, colleges, schools, and public libraries as well as interested individuals and groups. In a new format and a larger size, the calendar carried the Judiciary theme for eight of the monthly entries, while one month featured the first U.S. census and three months concentrated on the patent and copyright laws. The innovative calendar proved to be very popular with educators and others, and it provided a model for the 1991 edition covering the Bill of Rights.

A special limited edition of the POCKET CONSTITUTION in 1990 took advantage of the dramatic political changes then occurring in Eastern Europe. With the cooperation of the USIA, the Commission produced an Eastern European edition totaling 100,000 copies. This ninth edition included the Declaration of Independence and a new foreword by the Chairman. The POCKET CONSTITUTION went through three more editions during 1990. Special Boy Scout (tenth) and Girl Scout (11th) editions, with covers carrying their respective logos, totaled 7.1 million copies. Like the Eastern European

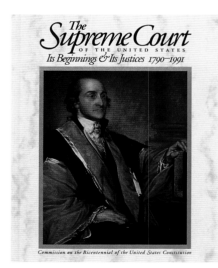

Portraits of all 106 Justices are featured in **The Supreme Court: Its Beginnings & Its Justices 1790-1991**

edition, the 12th edition carried the Declaration of Independence (thereafter a standard feature), and added the Bill of Rights transmittal notice. Besides these special editions, the Commission fulfilled requests for over 900,000 copies during the year. In April, copies of the POCKET CONSTITUTION, along with several documents relating to the Bicentennial of the Judiciary, traveled

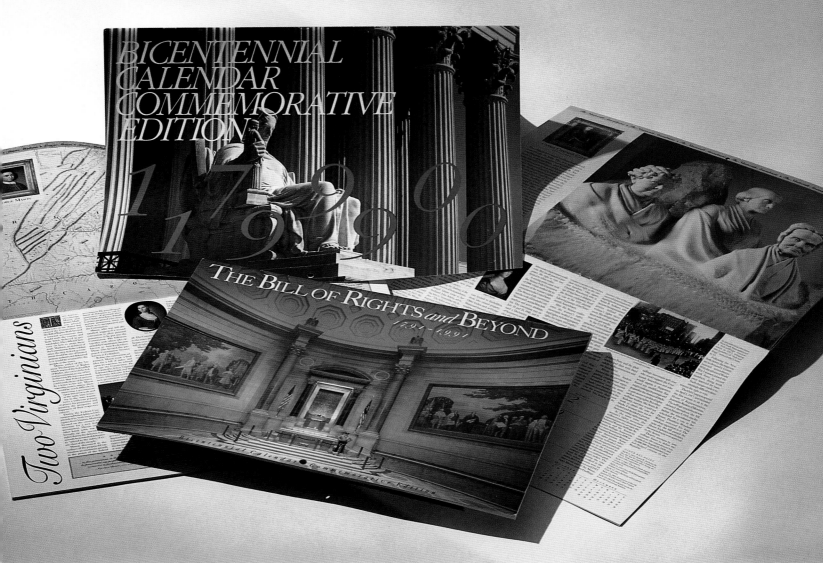

aboard the space shuttle *Discovery* on the historic flight when it placed the famous Hubble telescope in orbit. This marked the second time the Constitution had been launched on a trip into space, the first being the ill-fated flight of the space shuttle *Challenger*, January 28, 1986.

To Establish Justice, the third in the Commission series of general information brochures, with a distribution of over 400,000, reviewed the creation of the Federal Judiciary under Article III of the Constitution and the Judiciary Act of 1789. Like its predecessors, it also offered suggestions on how to observe this anniversary and listed Commission programs and resources available to the public. As sequels to the earlier Presidency poster and the Skills Handbooks on Congress, which the Commission had sponsored in collaboration with Scholastic, Inc., the Commission produced with Scholastic two Skills Handbooks on the Judiciary. The elementary level handbook was entitled *Happy 200th Birthday, The U.S. Supreme Court*, and the secondary level handbook, *200 Years of the U.S. Judiciary, 1790-1990*. The former encouraged younger students to create birthday cards for the Supreme Court (*see page 187*). Over 144,000 teachers nationwide received copies of these materials, which were included as supplements to that organization's regular publications. The Commission distributed an additional 50,000 copies. During 1990 the Commission's Information Services Division responded to 57,574 requests from the public. The

Commission's Speakers Bureau produced a new leaflet in 1990 and boosted its 400-speaker roster when the Federal Judicial Center, a collaborator since 1986, provided the names of an additional 100 speakers, including jurists, attorneys, and law scholars, to assist with the Judiciary commemoration.

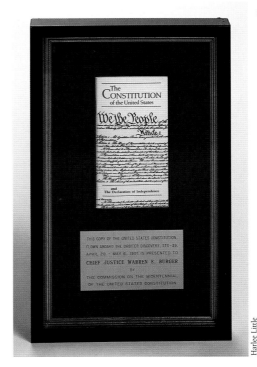

COMMEMORATIVE CALENDARS (*top*); this POCKET CONSTITUTION (*left*) traveled on the space shuttle.

COMMISSION ORGANIZATIONAL CHANGES

Among the organizational changes during 1990 was President Bush's June 18 appointment of Judge Damon Keith as a new Commissioner after the resignation of Commissioner William Lucas on November 9, 1989. At the March 3, 1990, Commission meeting, Dr. Herbert Atherton was named Staff Director; he had been Acting Staff Director since the departure January 6 of the previous Director, Dr. Ronald L. Trowbridge, to return to the academic world. By the end of 1990 the Commission staff, by attrition, had dropped in number to 57, including five part-time employees and ten detailed from other agencies. The Commission also began preparations for the eventual conclusion of its activities with a personnel phaseout plan that was approved near the end of the year. Once again in 1990, the Commission benefited from the work of ten summer interns who came from various colleges and universities throughout the United States. The six Commission divisions at the end of the year were Administration, Education, Government Affairs, Private Sector Programs, Communications and International Programs, and Archives.

Late in 1989, the Bicentennial Commission established, as a nonprofit corporation in the District of Columbia, the Trust for the Bicentennial of the United States Constitution, and subsequently transferred to the Trust the balance of its donated private funds from the Foundation for the Commemoration of the United States Constitution. The mission of the Trust also involved supplementing the activities of the Commission through special projects and, eventually, carrying on and concluding Bicentennial activities after the termination of the Commission. Elwood Davis was the first President of the Trust, with John Boice as Secretary. Burnett Anderson, Joseph Hennage, Howard Markey, Barnabus McHenry, Norman Murphy, and Ronald L. Trowbridge were Trustees.

Outside Activities

As already noted, the major activities honoring the Judiciary in 1990 are best illustrated by events undertaken by organizations and individuals at the local level throughout the country. A selective sampling of these activities appears below.

EDUCATIONAL ACTIVITIES

Programs and activities in law-related education became focal points in 1990. A number of organizations of national stature had for some years engaged in supplementing the programs of educational institutions with materials and projects about the Constitution. During this year these programs' impact increased.

The ABA continued as one of the most active organizations in law-related education throughout the entire Bicentennial period. The 1990 ABA theme for Law Day USA, "Generations of Justice," focused on the legal rights of children and the elderly. Commemorated annually on May 1, Law Day USA was established by

Presidential proclamation in 1958 as a "special day of celebration by the American people in appreciation of their liberties and to provide an occasion for rededication to the ideals of equality and justice under law." For 1990 Law Day USA, the ABA prepared and distributed a detailed planning guide to assist individuals and organizations, as well as promotional and educational materials ranging from buttons and balloons to brochures, booklets, speech texts, and mock trial scripts. Schools, libraries, churches, community organizations, and law enforcement agencies sponsored no-cost legal consultations, mock trials, court ceremonies, poster and essay contests, and television and radio call-in programs.

The National Institute for Citizen Education in the Law (NICEL), with support from the national Commission, conducted a series of activities in celebration of the Bicentennial of the Constitution. Looking forward to the Bill of Rights commemorative year, NICEL researched and wrote a six-lesson unit on famous civil rights cases from the 1940s and 1950s that reached the Supreme Court from the District of Columbia. These lessons, field-tested by lead teachers and demonstrated at workshops during the school year, then were showcased at a two-week summer institute, "Liberty Under Law," where participants heard from 30 presenters from several scholarly institutions. Washington public radio station WAMU-FM covered parts of the proceedings for later broadcast on National Public Radio's "Morning Edition."

The Iowa Chapter Federal Bar Association, with *Des Moines Register* editorial cartoonist Brian Duffey, produced an informative cartoon poster that became part of a junior and senior high school student kit, which included two national Commission brochures and a Constitutional Rights Foundation article on political cartoons and freedom of speech.

The BICENTENNIAL SCHOOL RECOGNITION PROGRAM grew during the year to 328 member institutions. To participate, schools formed committees of teachers, students, administrators, parents, and community representatives to plan and implement appropriate commemorative and educational activities during the school year from Constitution Week in September to Flag Day in June. Bicentennial Schools in Mesa, Arizona, for example, collectively participated in a series of Constitution Week activities coordinated by the city's and the school system's Bicentennial Committee. Events included an afternoon ceremony featuring a flyover of aircraft from Williams Air Force Base and a sounding of the city's sirens. The events concluded with an evening program in the city's amphitheater, where Commission certificates were awarded to the city's Bicentennial schools.

Students at Quail Valley Elementary, a Bicentennial School in Missouri City, Texas, learned about the operation of the justice system through a program in which they acted out solutions to legal questions. The school's "Blind Justice" bulletin board informed the students every six weeks of a new judicial issue, which then became the subject of background material and class discussion. Each class divided into three groups:

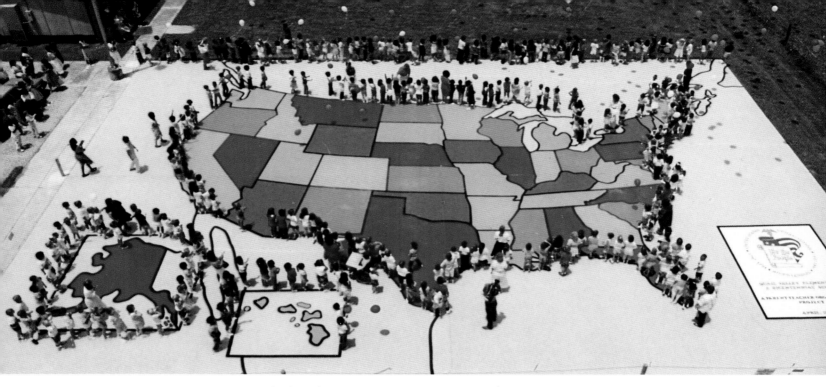

pro, con, and a seven-judge panel that heard the arguments. Each "judge" announced and explained his or her opinion to the class, which then analyzed the opinions and settled on a unified class "decision." Each class posted its "decision" on the "Blind Justice" bulletin board scales, and the issue was finally "weighed" by the entire school.

Weber Junior High School in Port Washington, New York, organized a Bicentennial Field Day, in which students competed in eighteenth-century sports. Weber students also presented "Bicentennial Minutes" each morning on the school public address system, featuring such announcements as the first meeting of the U.S. Supreme Court and President Washington's visit to Long Island in April 1790. Fifth graders from Porterdale Elementary School in Covington, Georgia, presented a Constitution quilt they had made to Montpelier, the Virginia home of James Madison. The red, white, and blue quilt—featuring pen sketches of the signers of the Constitution on the white muslin squares and a cross-stitched Preamble in the center—resulted from a hands-on learning activity to complement student lesson materials provided by the CCE. In preparing the quilt, the students researched the history of the signers and copied their likenesses.

By the end of 1990, the Commission's BICENTEN-NIAL CAMPUS PROGRAM had leveled off in enrollment with 380 two- and four-year institutions, about 12 percent of the total eligible in the country. Each campus had a committee responsible for organizing Bicentennial activities, including lectures, symposia, and conferences, and the appeal of the approaching 1991 Bill of Rights focus stimulated renewed planning. At Fitchburg State College in Massachusetts, for example, design students created visual presentations of the Bicentennial of the Constitution for a project that was eventually exhibited at the Fitchburg Art Museum and reviewed in the *Boston Globe*.

Clemson University in South Carolina, another Bicentennial Campus, recorded and distributed to other institutions, audiotapes of lectures delivered by Archibald Cox, Carl Rowan, Arthur Schlesinger, Jr., and Charles Mathias on "The Judiciary: Active or Restrained," "Civil Rights," and other themes. Morehead State University in Kentucky offered a seminar, "The Supreme Court and the Constitution: A Continuing Constitutional Convention."

*Q*uail Valley *elementary students worked on many Constitution and Judiciary projects (top, above, left).*

Quail Valley Elementary School (3)

The Revenue Cutter Eagle Captures Bon Pere *by* Wendell Minor

FEDERAL GOVERNMENT DEPARTMENTS AND AGENCIES

In addition to the extraordinary participation of the Federal courts during this Bicentennial year of the judicial branch, other Federal agencies contributed in a variety of ways. As noted earlier, the Department of Defense — without doubt the most vigorous Bicentennial partner and contributor of all Federal agencies — carried on activities through its network of Designated Bicentennial Defense Communities. The U.S. Army published Supplement III of its *Resource Guide* on the Judiciary, and the new 1990 poster in its poster series carried a Judiciary theme. In addition, however, other instances of Federal activity were worthy of note.

The United States Coast Guard commemorated its own Bicentennial in a yearlong series of over 300 events featuring a variety of aircraft and vessels, for example, the Coast Guard Sailing Vessel, the *Eagle*. Many of these events also included the Coast Guard Band and Ceremonial Honor Guard. A new Bicentennial art show displayed 24 original paintings depicting historic moments of the service. The commemoration reached its climax on August 4, 1990, in a celebration involving 500,000 people at Grand Haven, Michigan. That date marked the 200th anniversary of the congressional authorization for production of ten cutters and the effective creation of the Coast Guard. The initial events of this special year of commemoration recognized the October 1789 establishment of the Federal Lighthouse

The Introduction Of Reindeer Into Alaska by Shannon Stirnweis

The U.S. Coast Guard celebrated its Bicentennial with new publications (below) and artwork (far left and bottom). Historic lighthouses such as Point Vincent in California (left) were also the site of special observances.

Moments in History

program, originally a separate function, which was transferred to the Coast Guard in 1939.

To commemorate the 200th anniversary of the Judiciary, the National Archives, 11 Regional Archives, and participating Federal courthouses across the nation displayed a collection of posters illustrating landmark court cases drawn from two centuries of court history and representing each major region of the country. The exhibits included facsimiles of court records held by the Regional Archives. The national Commission and the Bicentennial Committee of the Judicial Conference of the United States assisted in funding the exhibits. The Archives also released a series of fifty 30-second public service announcements (PSAs), which began airing over participating radio stations on September 17, 1989, and

ran through February 28, 1990. The PSAs described the court system and significant cases and events. Then, with the ABA and the Association of Trial Lawyers of America as cosponsors, the Archives continued its public awareness effort through a mock trial program in six of the 11 regions.

The Bureau of Land Management in the Department of the Interior commemorated the Bicentennial in January 1990 in a special ceremony recognizing the completion of the prototype phase of its project, "Preserving America's Heritage." This project involved the microfilming and preservation of the records of the General Land Office, originally in the Treasury Department, and included patents and tract books dating back to the original public domain of 1789. Recognized by the

Rhode Island's ratification celebration (above); a parade of tall ships at Fall River, Massachusetts (right).

Rachel Barnet

national Commission in 1988, the completed project would provide public access to a comprehensive automated system of all Federal land records.

With the encouragement of the national Commission, the Office of Personnel Management (OPM) increased the emphasis on constitutional subjects in its executive training programs. Early in 1990, the Commission recognized one such program, "Constitutional Issues: Consideration in Management Decision Making," developed and conducted for Federal agencies by OPM. Directed at senior-level government executives and managers, the training module included sections on the Constitution and its implications for public management, constitutional values and principles, and constitutional considerations in managerial decision making.

STATES AND COMMUNITIES

States and communities across the nation participated enthusiastically in hundreds of activities and events on the theme of the Judiciary in 1990. As noted earlier, state courts took a lead role, especially in law-related education efforts. For example, the Colorado Supreme Court took the court into the community, with the seven Justices traveling to various judicial regions to hear oral arguments before local audiences, including high school students already briefed on the case. One popular session, at Otera Junior College in La Junta, involved 24 high schools in that region. The students had been prepared by speech/debate teachers who had attended in-service training for the session. Volunteer attorneys from local bar associations visited classrooms in advance to discuss significant case facts, legal precedents, and issues that could be raised during the arguments. Students from each of the participating high schools joined the Justices in a discussion of what they had observed during the hearings.

Even in this fourth year of the Bicentennial, communities continued to apply for official recognition as Designated Bicentennial Communities (DBCs). With the additions of Gypsum, Kansas; Worcester, Massachusetts; Novi, Michigan; Norwich, New York; Fairfield and Mahoning Counties, Ohio; Sumner County, 18th Judicial District, Tennessee; and Reston, Virginia, the total number of DBCs surpassed 2,500 by the end of 1990. The continuing vitality of this network testified to the deep commitment of people throughout the country to the objectives of the Bicentennial.

In Illinois, the village of Glenwood's vehicle sticker carried a Bicentennial message reminding the drivers of their constitutional heritage — a practice begun three years earlier. In a ceremony at the State House in Annapolis, Maryland, Governor William Donald Schaefer presented a proclamation to Jeffrey M. Samuels, Acting Commissioner of Patents and Trademarks, in recognition of the 200th anniversary of the first patent and copyright laws. Maryland was the first state to issue the proclamation following a nationwide request to all Governors by the Patent and Trademark Office.

The Fall River Chamber of Commerce and Industry in Massachusetts sponsored for the third year a three-day extravaganza called "Fall River Celebrates America," attended by 400,000 people and featuring a parade of seven tall ships sailing up Mount Hope Bay, military and naval reenactments of Colonial battles, a living pageant honoring the Stars and Stripes, a fireworks display on the waterfront, and a two-hour parade with Colonial emphasis. The DBC of Millbrae, California, had sponsored annual Bicentennial projects since 1986. Its 1990 September activity was an Admission Day Ball honoring California's 140th year of statehood. It also featured a BELLS ACROSS AMERICA activity during CONSTITUTION WEEK and several events by local organizations commemorating the Bicentennial of the Judiciary.

Harlee Little

Rhode Island citizens had prided themselves on their independence ever since 1663, when King Charles II granted them a charter providing a large measure of self-government. Rhode Island renounced allegiance to the King — without actually declaring independence — as early as 1775, and 12 years later refused to send delegates to the Constitutional Convention. It was the last of the original 13 states to ratify the Constitution and took two and one-half years to do so. On May 28-29, 1990, the state enthusiastically commemorated the 200th anniversary of its ratification of the Constitution with a gigantic fireworks display, the issuance at Pawtucket of the Statehood Commemorative Stamp, and numerous ceremonies throughout the state, including events at the Colony House, Newport; Roger Williams Park and North Providence Town Hall, Providence; and the Gilbert Stuart Homestead, North Kingstown.

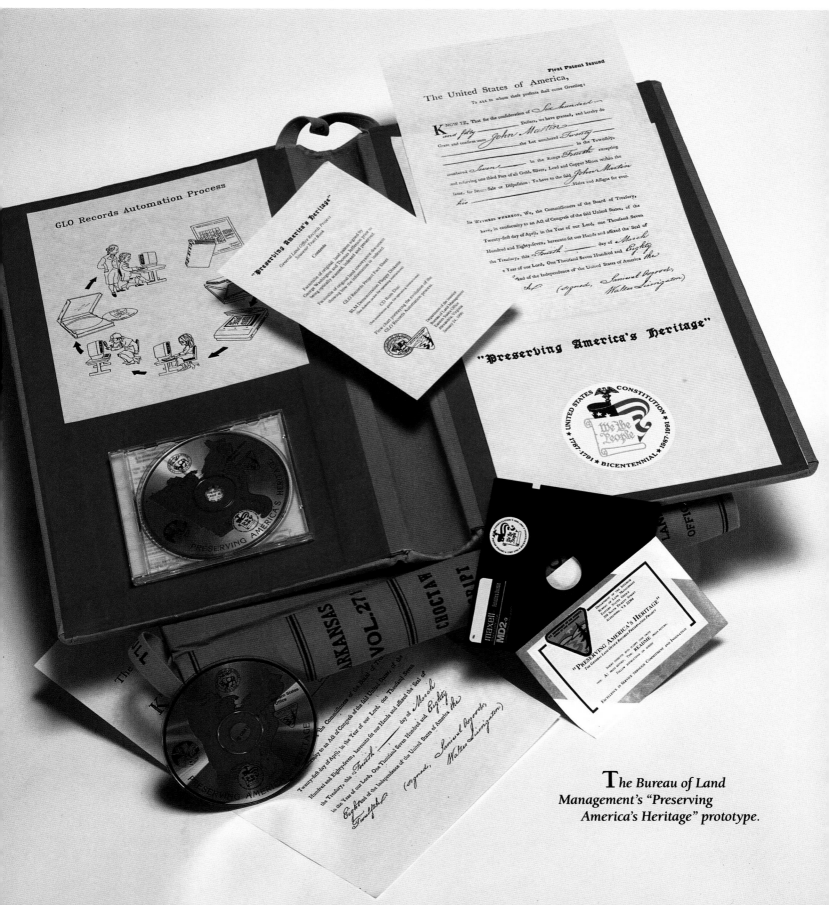

The Bureau of Land Management's "Preserving America's Heritage" prototype.

PRIVATE NONPROFIT GROUPS

During 1990, the Commission staff attended and distributed Bicentennial commemorative information and materials at selected annual conventions, including those of the Ruritan, the National Association for the Advancement of Colored People (NAACP), the U.S. Jaycees, the AFL-CIO, the American Association of Retired Persons (AARP), the League of Women Voters, the American Legion, the National Newspaper Association, and the Radio-Television News Directors Association. In addition, the Commission, through its representation at the national conventions of the National League of Cities, the National Association of Counties, and the U.S. Conference of Mayors, was able to reach over 10,000 city and county officials and Mayors.

In the 53rd Annual American Legion Oratorical Contest, four finalists, survivors of several rounds of local, state, and regional competition/delivered without microphone or notes their prepared eight-to-ten minute orations on selected aspects of the Constitution. They then gave five-minute extemporaneous talks on an "Article of Amendment" to the Constitution. Joshua E. Boyd of Fort Thomas, Kentucky, won the first-place plaque and an $18,000 scholarship. The other final contestants, Johnny Goff of Stantonsburg, North Carolina; Matthew Malone of Mashpee, Massachusetts; and Arthur Pai-Shih Chu of Albuquerque, New Mexico, received scholarships ranging from $12,000 to $16,000. Over 4,000 students from all 50 states participated.

In 1990, the Commission worked closely with the National Flag Day Foundation to promote public awareness of National Flag Day, June 14, and its theme, "We the People Pledge Our Allegiance." The Flag Day Foundation distributed through its network a large number of Commission materials and publications, and the Commission's Chairman was the speaker at the National Flag Day luncheon in Baltimore.

The U.S. Capitol Historical Society, working with the national Commission, issued its 1990 medal — the

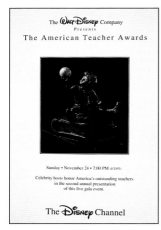

Winner of the American Legion's oratorical contest (below) on the Constitution.

Disney Channel's "American Teacher Award" for teaching achievement (above).

fourth in its Bicentennial series — on the Federal-state dual court system (see Chapter II). The obverse side featured the grand facade of the Supreme Court Building with the seated figure of Chief Justice John Marshall in the foreground. The reverse side saluted the judicial system of the states with a standing figure of Justice and the design inscription, "The Judicial Systems of the several states and the United States of America — Dual Guardians of the rights of all citizens under Law."

In October 1990 the Federal Judiciary Center hosted a Federal judicial history seminar, designed to help courts and court history programs in their efforts to preserve and make accessible the history of the United States Federal courts. Representatives of district and circuit courts across the country attended the seminar, one of whose sessions examined the role of Bicentennial celebrations.

PRIVATE CORPORATIONS

The Walt Disney Company, continuing its support of the educational goals of the Bicentennial, introduced the Disney Channel's "American Teacher Awards" program, which recognized outstanding achievements in the teaching profession. Some three dozen teachers, representing all disciplines, were chosen in each school year, 1988-1989 and 1989-1990, from many hundreds of candidates. A committee representing educational associations and other organizations, including the national Commission, made the selections in a process administered by the CCE. Promotion of the program began in September 1989 with a half-hour special, "The Disney Channel Salutes the American Teacher," hosted by First Lady Barbara Bush. Chief Justice Burger and Senator Edward Kennedy were among several prominent Americans who contributed testimonials to the influence of great teachers in their lives. Thereafter, brief profiles were periodically broadcast on the Disney Channel honoring each teacher selected. In October 1990, Disney broadcast its first "American Teacher Awards" show, and announced the nation's "outstanding teacher." Disney continued the program in subsequent years.

MEDIA

The Bicentennial Commission and the National Press Foundation once again cosponsored the Benjamin Franklin Awards, designed to recognize the best newspaper and magazine writing on various features of the Constitution. The 1990 winner of $1,000 in the category of general publications was the *Philadelphia Daily News* for a spread of 17 stories, published March 13, 1990, on operations in all 41 criminal courtrooms of the Common Pleas Court of Philadelphia during the previous day. The *National Law Journal* also won $1,000 in the category of specialized publications for a special project on the death penalty, published June 11, 1990. It involved staff interviews of more than 70 lawyers and examination of 100 trial transcripts in six states. The program's cosponsors presented the awards in a ceremony at the U.S. Supreme Court on June 25, 1991.

*B*ronze profile of John Marshall in L. Baker's **John Marshall: A Life in Law.**

Under an agreement with the national Commission, Harcourt Brace Jovanovich published as a high school text the series of 44 articles on the Constitution written by Chief Justice Burger and syndicated by the Associated Press in 1987 (*see Chapter III*). This book, *The Constitution: Foundation of Our Freedom*, contained appendices with annotated texts of the Constitution, the Articles of Confederation, and Northwest Ordinance as well as profiles of the delegates present at the signing of the Constitution. Harcourt Brace also issued a separate teacher's guide.

Of many outstanding titles in law-related education, Arlene F. Gallagher's *Living Together Under the Law: An Elementary Education Law Guide* provided a well-integrated curriculum on basic legal themes for use by younger students. Prepared by the Law, Youth, and Citizenship Program of the New York State Bar Association and the New York State Education Department, a new edition of the text was published in 1988 with support from Merrill Lynch and the New York State Bicentennial Commission. The New York State Bar Association, along with the American Judges Association, also issued *The Judge,* a pamphlet on law-related resources. Another title in law-related education, *The*

Federalist, a student edition of *The Federalist Papers* with an introduction and notes by editors George W. Carey and James McClellan, also appeared in 1990.

Among other books issued during the year was *Confronting the Constitution*, edited by Allan Bloom, a collection of essays on the intellectual foundations of American constitutionalism and the subsequent challenges to those foundations. Easton Press of Norwalk, Connecticut, reprinted Leonard Baker's 1974 biography, *John Marshall: A Life in Law.* Issued in two volumes with classic binding, the biography included a new foreword by Chief Justice Burger and a frontispiece illustration of his bronze bas-relief profile of John Marshall, which hangs in the U.S. Supreme Court.

INTERNATIONAL

The whirlwind of change in various parts of the world brought new meaning and renewed emphasis to the international activities of the Commission. A symbol of the movement toward freedom and democracy, Lech Walesa — the Polish shipyard electrician who launched the Solidarity union, which set Poland on the road to freedom and provided the example for the rest of

Foreign students from the Overbrook School for the Blind visit Independence Park (below); Lech Walesa is greeted by Chief Justice Burger (right).

Liberty Bell Foundation

Send-off ceremony at the White House for Peace Corps Volunteers (left).

Eastern Europe— made a week-long tour of the United States. On the final day, in a meeting of the Copernicus Society, the society's president, Edward M. Piszek, recognized Walesa as a true hero and said his "presence in our country . . . signifies the importance of liberty and freedom . . . [and his] steadfast determination and belief in the democratic system are inspirations for every human being in the world today." Piszek then presented to Walesa a copy of the bronze bust of Benjamin Franklin sculpted by Chief Justice Burger. When told of Franklin's discovery of electricity, Mr. Walesa pointed out that he too knew something of electricity.

Mr. Piszek also served as president of the Liberty Bell Foundation, which had lent its support to many Bicentennial activities (see Chapters III and IV). In 1990 the Foundation cosponsored Peace Corps Partners in Teaching English, a project that sent the first Peace Corps volunteers into Eastern Europe. In a special June 15 sendoff ceremony in the White House Rose Garden, President Bush spoke to the volunteers and the distinguished guests, including Commerce Secretary Robert A. Mosbacher, Deputy Secretary of State Lawrence S. Eagleburger, Deputy Secretary of the Treasury John E. Robson, and Chief Justice Burger. The President said that "today, we launch a new people-to-people effort through which the citizens of America, Poland and Hungary can work together in the exhilarating process of building new democratic societies." All of these volunteers left the White House with a supply of the special Eastern European edition of the POCKET CONSTITUTION, logo pins, and other Bicentennial materials.

The International Visitors Center in Philadelphia launched "Discover America: Behind the Headlines with Benjamin Franklin," a program that sponsored seminars and lectures on the Constitution, the Bill of Rights, and the statesmanship of Philadelphian Benjamin Franklin. Funded by the Pew Charitable Trusts, the program was part of a nationwide nonprofit network effort to acquaint foreign visitors with the Constitution's history and evolution. For example, the Center conducted a seminar at Independence Historical Park for 50 Fulbright and Humphrey scholars from 29 countries as part of a USIA cultural exchange. Federal District Judge Charles R. Weiner, one of the principal speakers, referred to the Declaration of Independence as "the birth certificate of our country" and to the Constitution as a model used by many nations. He added, however, that many of these other constitutions were several volumes long and in "mint" condition "because they are never used." "Discover America" continued through 1990, the Bicentennial of the Judiciary—also the anniversary year of the death of Franklin in 1790 — and 1991, the Bicentennial of the ratification of the Bill of Rights.

The Center also coordinated a program for international students from the Overbrook School for the Blind, who took part in a tour of Philadelphia, the site of the 1787 Constitutional Convention where the Constitution was debated, drafted, and signed. A tactile model of the Independence Hall area allowed the students, who were from 15 countries, to visualize the area by touch. The students also "read" the motto on the Liberty Bell by

Winners of international school debate sponsored by the Swiss chapter of the SAR.

tracing the characters with their fingers. The school has become internationally famous for its work with blind foreign students between the ages of 16 and 21, who are admitted based on their academic achievement in their native countries and their knowledge of English.

Negar Shapaeddin Bandaki of Iran and Ayita Hussain of India were winners of a constitutional school debate sponsored by the Swiss chapter of the Sons of the American Revolution. With their teacher-escorts, the two came to Washington, D.C., for a tour as guests of Trans World Airlines and the national Commission. They had lunch at the U.S. Capitol with three Commissioners — Representative Lindy Boggs, Senator Edward Kennedy, and Betty Southard Murphy — and visited Chief Justice Burger in his chambers at the Supreme Court. Both winners were students at the College du Leman, an international school in Switzerland.

In another international program, American students from the Kansas City People-to-People project had the opportunity to participate in a Young Pioneers Camp in Odessa, Ukraine, in the Soviet Union. The Commission supplied Constitutions and logo pins, which the students passed along to their Soviet counterparts. The Ukrainian students were eager to learn about the U.S. Government, economic system, and people. Coincidentally, the Ukraine declared itself independent of the Soviet Union a few months later.

CONCLUSION

Although the commemoration of the Judiciary and the dual court system lacked some of the media attention and emotional appeal present in other Bicentennial themes, activities in 1990 were in keeping with the Commission's goal of promoting a "history and civics lesson" for all Americans and did much to further programs in law-related education. Public awareness of the importance of the Judiciary, and educational programs focusing on that subject, received a substantial boost, in large part from the nation's legal profession, whose members took the initiative in planning and carrying out special ceremonies, and from educational activities in the schools. The year's focus on the rule of law and the role of an independent Judiciary in America's system of constitutional government also provided an appropriate prologue to the Bicentennial's concluding commemoration of the Bill of Rights. 🦅

CHAPTER VII

1991

The
Bill
of
Rights
and
Beyond

The Bicentennial programs concluded in 1991 with the commemoration of the Bill of Rights, probably the part of the Constitution Americans hold most dear. This commemoration also honored subsequent Amendments to the Constitution that abolished slavery, better secured the equal protection of the law, and broadened the base of American democracy with women's rights. The year's commemorative theme — "The Bill of Rights and Beyond" — therefore spanned from the Founding Era to the present day.

Few could have guessed at the outset of the Bicentennial what a dramatic backdrop world events would provide to America's celebration of its legacy of freedom. The anniversary year of the Bill of Rights also saw the virtual collapse of totalitarian regimes in Eastern Europe and the rush of newly liberated peoples to reach for those principles of constitutionalism and individual liberty — the ordered liberty Americans had enjoyed for two centuries. Perhaps no greater or more appropriate tribute was given to the Constitution's 200th anniversary than this witness of contemporary events. As the new President of Czechoslovakia, Vaclav Havel, said in his address to a Joint Session of Congress:

Wasn't it the best minds of your country . . . who wrote your famous Declaration of Independence, your Bill of Human Rights and your Constitution? . . . Those great documents . . . inspire us all; they inspire us despite the fact that they are over 200 years old. They inspire us to be citizens.

In a striking example of historical coincidence, the commemoration of the world's oldest written constitution had taken place in momentous times, with political changes unparalleled in human history.

Major Events

PLANNING FOR THE BILL OF RIGHTS COMMEMORATION

During 1991, the Bill of Rights theme appeared frequently and extensively in the media and in a wide range of events and activities over the breadth of the nation and around the world. The Commission sponsored a nationwide TEACH ABOUT reaching literally millions of students. Essay and other educational

Keith Jewel/US House of Representatives

President Vaclav Havel of Czechoslovakia addresses a Joint Session of Congress.
"These great documents inspire us all; they inspire us to be citizens."

(Mason) Virginia Museum of Fine Arts and Gunston Hall (left) (Madison) Thomas Gilcrease Institute of Art (right) Calligraphy by Julian Waters (above)

George Mason (inset, left) and James Madison (inset, right), two great champions of the Bill of Rights; the Liberty Bell (above).

contests adopted the Bill of Rights theme. BELLS ACROSS AMERICA rang in commemoration. *Life* magazine published a special Bill of Rights edition. *Parade* magazine sponsored a Bill of Rights photo contest. Numerous countries, particularly in Europe and Latin America, sponsored essay and oratory contests. Songs, plays, speeches, articles, parades, sports events, concerts, lectures, symposia, books, posters — and almost any other medium one could name — featured or publicized the year's commemorative theme. Betty Debnam's Sunday tabloid, *The Mini Page,* continued to tell the story, focusing on the Bill of Rights.

Background: The Bill of Rights was what Chief Justice Warren Burger has called the "Great Afterthought." Pressed for by George Mason of Virginia, it had been briefly considered and then rejected at the Constitutional Convention. Most of the Framers believed that such a provision was unnecessary in a Constitution of enumerated powers, which contained other safeguards of individual rights. Some feared that any general declaration of fundamental rights might suggest by implication that any other rights not mentioned did not exist. Others feared conflict with bills of rights already in place in most of the states.

Of the three delegates who would not sign the Constitution at the Philadelphia Convention, George Mason had refused because of the absence of such guarantees, and their omission proved to be the Anti-Federalists' most telling argument against ratification. The Anti-Federalists lost that struggle, but in so doing paved the way for the Bill of Rights. It soon became clear that the Constitution would not be approved without assurance being given to many states that a bill of rights would soon follow ratification. On May 4, 1789, Representative James Madison of Virginia — who had originally opposed the inclusion of a bill of rights in the Constitution — introduced the subject in the House. Finally, on September 25, 1789, the two Houses agreed on a list of 12 proposed amendments and referred them to the states for ratification.

The process of ratification began quickly. By the end of 1789, three states — New Jersey, North Carolina, and Maryland — had ratified the third through the twelfth of the proposed amendments. Then the pace slackened. Two more years would be required to secure ratification by the necessary three-fourths states — a number which had increased to 11 with the entry of Vermont into the Union as the 14th state in March 1791. On December 15, 1791, Virginia became the 11th state to ratify the Bill of Rights, and thereby made it part of the Constitution. Connecticut, Georgia, and Massachusetts did not ratify the Bill of Rights at all until the Constitution's Sesquicentennial in 1939.

Technically, the document now on display in the Rotunda of the National Archives (which was moved there from the State Department in 1938) is not the Bill of Rights. It is one of 11 surviving letters of transmittal of the 12 proposed amendments sent by the Congress to the states. The states never did ratify the first proposed amendment, which dealt with congressional representa-

tion. The second, prohibiting any variation in congressional pay from taking effect until "an election of Representatives shall have intervened," had been ratified by only six states by the end of 1791. Two centuries later, a sufficient number of states added their approval to the proposed amendment, thus providing the required concurrence of three-fourths of the states in the Union. On May 18, 1992, the Archivist of the United States, pursuant to his mandate, certified its adoption as the Twenty-seventh Amendment.*

The authors of the Bill of Rights intended it to be a restraint upon the power of the Federal Government, not upon state or local government. In its early career, the Bill of Rights had little impact on the courts or the course of American history. But this obscurity ended following the Civil War when the Thirteenth, Fourteenth, and Fifteenth Amendments abolished slavery and the disqualifications associated with it. Moreover, the Fourteenth Amendment gave new meaning to the Bill of Rights by making some of its provisions applicable to the states as well. By gradual incorporation in the years that followed, the Bill of Rights entered the mainstream of American life and acquired the central importance it enjoys today in the nation's constitutional system. Subsequent Amendments (the Nineteenth, Twenty-fourth, and Twenty-sixth) have expanded the nation's commitment to democracy by securing the franchise for women, 18-year-olds, citizens hitherto prevented from voting because of tax requirements, and (in Presidential elections) citizens of the District of Columbia.

The Coffin Committee: The national Commission's planning for the commemoration of the Bill of Rights began almost two years earlier with the appointment, in the spring of 1989, of an ad hoc advisory committee, which met formally June 9 and issued its report later that summer. Chaired by Judge Frank M. Coffin of the United States Court of Appeals for the First Circuit, with Rodney A. Smolla, Professor of Constitutional Law at the College of William and Mary and Director of the Institute of Bill of Rights Law, as Vice Chairman, the committee included jurists, scholars, historians, and journalists *(see Appendix)*. The report laid out a "Call to Action," including a "Statement of Principles Governing the Celebration of the Bicentennial Anniversary of the Bill of Rights." It set out what the key elements of a successful commemoration with education as its foundation should be. It also included a number of imaginative program suggestions, several of which found their way into a fall 1989 Commission Task Force Report. In preparing this report the Commission was assisted by the National Education Advisory Committee, which met at the U.S. Supreme Court in December 1989 to consider plans for the commemoration of both the Judiciary and the Bill of Rights.

The Commission, at its March 3, 1990, meeting, approved the recommendations of the Task Force Report, including the adoption of the commemoration theme for 1991, "The Bill of Rights and Beyond." It also

*At the time this book went to press, the final status of the proposed amendment had not been resolved.

Romanian journalist Alina Enista
speaks on liberty.

adopted the concept of a "Call to Action," setting forth the objectives of the 1991 Bill of Rights commemorations and encouraging participation from all segments of American society. The Commission approved a continuation of its education programs as well as other Bill of Rights programs — the printing of 2 million response brochures, the development of an advertising program of multimedia public service announcements (PSAs), a program of professional sports involvement, plans for regional, state, and local meetings to promote Bicentennial activities, and publication of a range of educational materials focusing on the Bill of Rights.

National Meeting: On September 21-22, 1990, over 150 state and national leaders gathered in Washington, D.C., for a national Bill of Rights planning conference. Dr. Herbert Atherton, the Commission Staff Director, outlined the threefold objective of the meeting: (1) to motivate participants to undertake the coming year's commemoration, (2) to indicate the Commission's leadership plans for 1991, and (3) to give participants an opportunity to share information and ideas. Attendees reviewed exhibits and participated in workshops and other activities, and the Commission introduced several new publications on the Bill of Rights. The meeting included a COLLEGE-COMMUNITY FORUM demonstration, which focused on the rights and responsibilities of citizenship and was moderated by Professor Isidore Starr, with Commissioners Thomas O'Connor, Harry McKinley Lightsey, Jr., and Betty Southard Murphy participating.

The gathering also featured three addresses. Dr. Walter Berns, John M. Olin Professor of Government at Georgetown University, examined the changing role of the Bill of Rights in the nation's history. Alina Enista, a former Romanian journalist who emigrated to the United States and became a naturalized citizen in 1982, spoke eloquently of the fear, the restrictions, and the oppressions associated with her journalistic career under Communism and of her dramatic experiences upon returning to Romania after the fall of the Ceausescu government in December 1989. In the United States, she noted, her children had taught her the national anthem and the Pledge of Allegiance, and she compared that experience with her childhood in Romania:

[I was compelled] to swallow other anthems, glorifying songs, political slogans and the contrivances of a communist education. . . . I chose to forget them all. . . . I pray to God that my children will never need to forget. The pride and touching dignity in their voices are the real guarantees that they will "secure the blessings of liberty to ourselves and our posterity" for which I, their mother, immigrated to the United States of America.

Syndicated columnist Carl T. Rowan, a former director of the United States Information Agency and United States Ambassador to Finland, discussed the Bill of Rights, the Civil War Amendments (Thirteenth, Fourteenth, and Fifteenth), and the arduous road African-Americans had to travel to become equal members in American society. He spoke of his interview during the 1950s with Gus Courts, an African-American who was shot when he tried to register to vote. "When I asked him why he persisted in risking his life, he said, 'Young man, maybe you won't understand, but I just wanted to be able to say that I voted once before I died.'"

Regional Meetings: As a follow-up to the national meeting, the Commission initiated a series of ten state and regional leadership conferences. The Commission staff organized and conducted three of these in the fall of 1990 — in San Diego, California; Topeka, Kansas; and Lansing, Michigan — with the remainder following in

State leadership conference in Kenner, Louisiana,
one of many Bicentennial meetings across the country in 1991.

President Bush signs the proclamation while National Security Advisor Scowcroft (left) and Chief Justice Burger look on.

1991 in Louisiana, Massachusetts, Ohio, and Nevada. The national Commission joined with Louisiana's state Commission in cosponsoring four separate meetings in Louisiana on the last four days in February 1991 — in Kenner, Lafayette, Shreveport, and Monroe — with educators, civic and service club representatives, and community leaders. Each meeting attracted from 150 to 200 attendees and carried the theme "The Bill of Rights and Beyond: La Liberté en Louisiane [Liberty in Louisiana]." Each meeting included a keynote speech by a scholar or jurist who outlined the history of the Bill of Rights and its significance in America. The meetings included workshops on potential civic and educational activities for the commemoration.

The meeting in Stoneham, Massachusetts, on April 27, 1991, included 200 representatives from six New England states plus a large number of other attendees. It was sponsored by the national Commission in cooperation with the state Commissions of Connecticut, Maine, Massachusetts, New Hampshire, Rhode Island, and Vermont, and the local Stoneham Commission. National Commissioner O'Connor urged the audience to use the information provided at the conference to commemorate the Bill of Rights not only in 1991 but in the years to follow. The conference featured two special events — a tree-planting ceremony with six trees representing each of the New England states and a plaque marking "The Bill of Rights Grove" in Stoneham, and a naturalization ceremony at the town hall where immigrants from 47 nations took the oath of citizenship.

A May 4th regional meeting in Columbus, Ohio, attracted 135 attendees and featured a welcome by Chief Justice Thomas J. Moyer of the Ohio Supreme Court and an appearance by "James Madison," portrayed by a college professor who examined the history of the Bill of

Rights and Madison's role in its development and ratification. Conducted at the Greek Orthodox Church in Columbus, the meeting included a discussion on whether the Bill of Rights had fulfilled or gone beyond its original purpose and a debate between two Columbus attorneys on "How does the Bill of Rights function in American life today?" The last leadership conference, at the University of Nevada in Reno on June 22, 1991, involved 150 representatives of professional, business, and labor groups, community organizations, local Bicentennial committees, and educational institutions in Nevada and California and a special workshop on suggested Bill of Rights programs. John C. Mowbray, Chief Justice of Nevada's Supreme Court and Chairman of the state Commission, addressed the gathering, as did national Commission member Judge Charles Wiggins. Among the subjects discussed were the citizen's role in keeping the Bill of Rights alive in American society and the constitutional implications of voting on special ballot initiatives in state elections.

During the five-year period of the Bicentennial (1987-1991), the national Commission sponsored 30 regional and state meetings in 23 states. These gatherings played an important role in mobilizing local, state, and national resources in this commemorative effort.

THE COMMEMORATION BEGINS

In a sense, the official commemoration of the Bill of Rights began with these words of President Bush: "As we enter the bicentennial year of our Bill of Rights, we celebrate more than the great freedom and security this document symbolizes for the American people — we also celebrate its seminal role in the advancement of respect for human dignity and individual liberty around the world." The President was reading from his proclamation marking Human Rights Day, Bill of Rights Day, and Human Rights Week, issued on the afternoon of December 10, 1990, at a special signing ceremony in the Old Executive Office Building. He thanked the Commission for creating a public awareness of the Bicentennial of the Constitution and the Bill of Rights and urged the Commission's Chairman to sign with him. This may have been the only occasion when a Presidential proclamation was attested by a Chief Justice of the United States. In the proclamation, the President reminded all Americans:

[The documents we celebrate —] the Bill of Rights, the Universal Declaration of Human Rights, and the more recent Helsinki accords — derive their value and promise from the timeless, immutable truths they contain and our solemn commitment to upholding them. As we reflect on the historic significance of these documents, let us vow to ensure that they remain meaningful guarantees of individual dignity and liberty.

Contemplating the year of events just ending — the collapse of Communism, the end of the Cold War, and the diminution of the East-West conflict — the President suggested that the revolution of 1989 had given way to the "renaissance of 1990" and the arduous related task of building democracy. He added that the Constitution was written not for one era or generation but for all ages — and that the nation's founding documents were "nothing less than the sum of human hope."

In a preliminary ceremony earlier that same day, the Department of State conducted a colloquium, cosponsored by the national Commission, commemorating the 42nd anniversary of the United Nations Declaration of Human Rights as well as the 199th anniversary of the ratification of the Bill of Rights. Speakers from Europe, Asia, South America, Central America, and Africa discussed the current state of the human rights movement. Quoting words of Soviet President Gorbachev, "The world is no longer what it was two years ago," Assistant Secretary of State for Human Rights and Humanitarian Affairs Richard Shifter referred to the signing of the United Nations Declaration of Human Rights 42 years earlier as the "bright side" of

STATE RATIFICATION COMMEMORATIONS

In another sense, the Bicentennial of the Bill of Rights began over a year earlier with the first of the state Ratification commemorations. New Jersey had been the first state to ratify, November 20, 1789, and it honored its historic role 200 years later with a four-day celebration in Perth Amboy, the 1789 state capital. Festivities included a naturalization ceremony for 125 new Americans, a Market Square Colonial fair, a reception at the Proprietary House (the Governor's mansion during the Founding Era), a ceremony in front of the original city hall where the Bill of Rights was ratified, parades, writing and art competition awards, and a mock "debate" in which an actor portrayed Benjamin Franklin (an early New Jersey landowner).

Maryland had ratified on December 19, 1789, less than a month after New Jersey. With the Bicentennial date so close to the Holiday Season, Maryland chose to

human rights progress. Other speakers included Dr. Pavel Bratinka, a member of the Czech federal parliament and former member of the opposition in communist Czechoslovakia; Gopal Siwakoti, an attorney from Nepal; Professor Martin Poblete of Chile and Rutgers University; Marta Patricia Baltodano of Nicaragua, a member of the opposition to the Sandinistas and the Somosa dictatorship; and Dr. George Ayittey of Ghana and American University in Washington, D.C. Chief Justice Burger concluded the program with a summary of the events leading to the adoption of the Bill of Rights and its subsequent history. He counseled patience on the part of emerging democracies, with the reminder that the American experiment in democratic government had been going on for 200 years and was still far from perfect. The Commission's Chairman then stated that we must "spread true freedom as far as possible and hope it will become universal."

Bill of Rights celebrations:
a rain-soaked parade in Virginia;
a re-created arch in
Perth Amboy, New Jersey.

recognize and honor the Bill of Rights two years later, on the anniversary of its adoption, with a proclamation issued by Governor William Donald Schaefer. North Carolina — because it had ratified the proposed amendments on December 22, 1789, only one month after ratifying the Constitution — celebrated both commemorations at the same time (see Chapter V). In Fayetteville, an encampment by the North Carolina Historical Reenactment Society featured citizens in period dress, while the Museum of Cape Fear staged a special exhibit entitled "1789 and Beyond: North Carolina and the United States Constitution," and various other activities highlighted the commemoration. South Carolina, to honor its ratification of the Bill of Rights on January 19, 1790, held a joint assembly of the legislature at the State House in Columbia on January 14, 1990, featuring speakers from the state Commission and the University of South Carolina. The Commission also set up a display of historic documents, including the South Carolina copy of the proposed amendments received from Congress 200 years before. New Hampshire had been the ratifying state that put adoption of the Constitution "over the top" and became the fifth state to ratify at least ten of the proposed amendments, on January 25, 1790. Two centuries later, on January 23 in Concord, Governor Judd Gregg welcomed members of the New Hampshire House and Senate in a Joint Commemorative Convention, noting that "people in Eastern Europe are now seeking those same rights."

Delaware, "The First State" to ratify the Constitution, had been the sixth, on January 28, 1790, to ratify the amendments that became the Bill of Rights. To commemorate the 200th anniversary, Governor Michael Castle issued a proclamation designating the week of January 28 through February 3, 1990, as "Bill of Rights Week in Delaware." A banner hung across Wilmington's Market Street Mall heralded the commemoration, which included a resolution by the General Assembly, the January 28th ringing of bells at noon in the houses of worship, and sermons on religious freedom under the Bill of Rights. New York's Commission, commemorating that state's ratification of the Bill of Rights on February 27, 1790, joined with the New York State Humanities Council to distribute 100 Bill of Rights mini-exhibits to schools throughout the state. The state Commission also published a new book, "A Trust . . . to Our Children": New York and the Adoption of the Bill of Rights, and distributed it to teachers statewide.

Pennsylvania had been the eighth state to ratify the Bill of Rights, March 10, 1790, and commemorated its Bicentennial at Harrisburg in a quiet ceremony at the state capitol. Governor Robert P. Casey issued a proclamation calling upon every man, woman, and child to remember the freedoms "denied to others, and strive to ensure that such rights and liberties will someday be denied to no one." Rhode Island had ratified the Bill of Rights on June 11, 1790, just two weeks after ratifying the Constitution, the last of the 13 original states to do so. Its Bicentennial commemoration on May 28 and 29 was a major two-day affair, combining not only both ratifications but Memorial Day as well (see Chapter VI). To honor the occasion, the Rhode Island Bicentennial Foundation also cosponsored a special noon ceremony at the State House on June 11, 1990, featuring a Bill of Rights exhibit and a proclamation by the Secretary of State, the keeper of Rhode Island's original copy of the document. Vermont's Bicentennial Commission issued a teacher's guide on the Bill of Rights and subsequent Amendments, and Carl Rowan spoke on the Bill of Rights via radio and television broadcast within the state *(see page 250)*.

These Ratification commemorations culminated in Virginia, which celebrated its part in the making of the Bill of Rights with a yearlong series of educational programs, publications, and special events. The commemoration reached its climax at the September 25th opening of the 1991 Virginia State Fair in Richmond, to which representatives of the 13 original states were invited to celebrate the anniversary of the Bill of Rights. During the days preceding, four caravans of Virginians in period costume had traveled from the far corners of the state — on foot, by boat, on horseback, and in a wagon train (transportation typical of the Founding Era). They converged on the Fair's arena before the Governor's reviewing stand, to be joined by similarly dressed representatives from the other original states, aboard horse- or mule-drawn wagons and buggies.

Governor L. Douglas Wilder was the keynote speaker at the opening ceremony, which also included the dedication of a Bill of Rights Commemorative Postal Card, the last in a series of 21 stamps and three postal issues commemorating the milestones of the Bicentennial Era. The national Commission's Staff Director, Dr. Atherton, represented the Commission on the occasion. The State Fair, visited by more than 500,000 people during the 12 days, included an eighteenth-century fair and several special exhibits on the Constitution and Bill of Rights. One, "Cultivating Freedom," was a reconstruction of the "Miracle at Philadelphia" exhibition on display at Independence Historical Park in Philadelphia four years earlier *(see Chapter II)*. The national Commission helped arrange for the transport and construction of the exhibit at its permanent home on the Virginia State Fair Grounds and provided copies of the POCKET CONSTITUTION for wide distribution at the Fair.

H.M.S. ROSE BILL OF RIGHTS TOUR

In a nautical reprise of the 1987 ROADS TO LIBERTY TOUR *(see Chapter III)*, the 24-gun frigate, H.M.S. Rose, took one of the original copies of the Bill of Rights on tour during the spring, summer, and autumn of 1991. Visiting 24 ports along the eastern seaboard from Portland, Maine, to Jacksonville, Florida, the world's largest operational wooden tall ship carried on its gun deck a special exhibit, which contained not only an original copy of the Bill of Rights, but a collection of other documents and reproductions as well, including an original of Roger Williams' *Bloody Tenent of Persecution* and replicas of the Magna Carta, the Petition of Right, the English Bill of Rights, and the Virginia Declaration of Rights. Crew in period costumes served as docents.

The tour was sponsored by the H.M.S. *Rose* Foundation of Bridgeport, Connecticut, which was also the owner of the ship, a replica of a Royal Navy frigate of the same name, whose effectiveness in suppressing Colonial trade during the War of Independence led to the establishment of the American Navy. The national Commission officially recognized and gave financial support to the tour, which was cosponsored by the NYNEX Corporation. Visitors' donations went to support the 1992 United States Olympic Team, Save the Children, the H.M.S. Rose Foundation, and the U.S. Constitution Council of the 13 Original States. The Commission assisted in the design of the exhibit and also provided copies of a special edition of the POCKET CONSTITUTION, as well as a supply of teaching materials on the Bill of Rights, for distribution to school groups. Students and teachers, in fact, were among the ship's most frequent visitors. Approximately 36,000 students saw the exhibit during its eight-month tour. Over 39,000 adults visited the ship, which was also used by several thousand more visitors attending special social functions on board. The tour was officially launched with ceremonies in Washington, D.C., on April 21 and concluded in Philadelphia, where the ship and its exhibit took part in the festivities during the weekend of December 13-15.

The H.M.S. Rose, the world's largest operational wooden tall ship, during its Bill of Rights Tour along the east coast.

Photos by Dan Beigel

Sailors aboard the H.M.S. Rose hoist the Stars and Stripes and put on sail during the frigate's Bill of Rights Tour; the Rose carried an original copy of the Bill of Rights and other historic documents.

© 1991 Dan Beigel (2)

Resembling a vision out of the
18th century, the H.M.S. Rose sails from
Annapolis, Maryland, headed for its next
port of call; the ship's 1991 tour of the east
coast began in Washington, D.C., and
ended 23 ports later in Philadelphia.

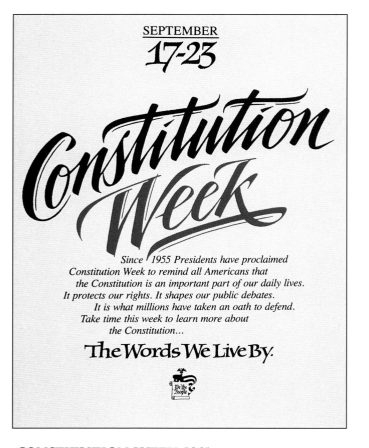

CONSTITUTION WEEK 1991

Another avenue for commemorating the Bill of Rights was the annual observance of Citizenship Day and Constitution Week. In his proclamation of this annual observance, President Bush took the opportunity to review the importance of the Constitution and the Bill of Rights. Quoting John Adams, who in 1787 had received word in London of the Constitution's approval by the Confederation Congress, President Bush said that the Constitution was, "if not the greatest exertion of human understanding, the greatest single effort of national deliberation that the world has ever seen." The President also extolled the provisions of the Bill of Rights as the guarantors of the nation's basic liberties—but only if citizens understand the principles enshrined in that document:

Accordingly, each of us has a responsibility to uphold the ideals of tolerance and justice; to teach our children the difference between liberty and license; and to share in the hard work of freedom — at the ballot box, in the workplace, on the farm, in the military, or through our homes, schools, and places of worship. This is the essence of good citizenship.

Chief Justice Burger took up this theme of citizenship in his "Chairman's Corner" of the Commission's summer 1991 *We the People* newsletter. He pointed out that the Constitution did not define the word *citizen* until the Fourteenth Amendment, passed following the Civil War. Nevertheless, the Chairman said, the Founders believed civic virtue meant more than just loyalty to the country. "To them, citizenship meant an understanding of, and active involvement with, the affairs of the nation. Could anything less be expected in a nation whose Constitution was chartered by 'We the People'?" Then the Commission's Chairman noted:

During the past five years, most of the Commission's energy and resources have gone to educational programs. By keeping Constitution Week alive as an annual observance, that educational commitment to an informed citizenry will continue — now and in the generations to come.

Many Americans were still unaware of these annual observances, which offered an opportunity for schools, organizations, and communities to focus on the importance of the Constitution in contemporary life and on the role of the citizen in a constitutional form of government. In this last observance of the Bicentennial era, the national Commission continued in its efforts to lay a broad foundation for the continued observance of Citizenship Day and Constitution Week. Accordingly, it prepared a Constitution Week packet for use not only in 1991 but in the years to follow. The Commission distributed 105,000 copies of the packet to civic groups, government agencies, schools, and other organizations. Each packet included a 48-page illustrated handbook of commemorative activities and resources, a promotion poster, a program brochure for BELLS ACROSS AMERICA, a series of reproducible ads, and a bumper sticker promoting "The Constitution: The Words We Live By."

Organizations and local governments across the nation responded with both traditional observances and new initiatives. The citizens of Mesa, Arizona, for example, honored Constitution Week beginning September 16 with a public discussion of the Bill of Rights in contemporary society. The program, "Let Freedom Ring," featured as discussants Chief Justice Stanley Feldman of the Arizona Supreme Court, an editor of the local newspaper, and a professor of law from Arizona State University. Following activities in schools and promotions in supermarkets, the week ended with an evening of patriotic music and with local government and civic officials reading the Bill of Rights.

In Hempstead, New York, Hofstra University President Dr. James M. Shuart and Judge Damon Keith, who represented the national Commission, dedicated a monument on the Hofstra campus featuring a statue of a Colonial patriot and a plaque engraved with a reproduction of the Bill of Rights. They were joined in the ceremony by Federal judges and other local and national dignitaries. Massachusetts celebrated Citizenship Day and Constitution Week alongside the U.S.S. *Constitution* ("Old Ironsides") at the Charlestown Navy Yard in Boston. The celebration featured students — including children with special needs — from various Boston school districts in a reading of the Bill of Rights. Governor William F. Weld proclaimed September 17 as Citizenship Day and spoke on the importance of the Constitution and the Bill of Rights. Commissioner Thomas H. O'Connor, who was master of ceremonies, and Commissioner Frederick K. Biebel represented the national Commission.

The Bill of Rights

Amendment I
Congress shall make no law respecting an establishment of religion, or prohibiting the free exercise thereof; or abridging the freedom of speech, or of the press; or the right of the people peaceably to assemble, and to petition the Government for a redress of grievances.

Amendment II
A well regulated Militia, being necessary to the security of a free State, the right of the people to keep and bear Arms, shall not be infringed.

Amendment III
No Soldier shall, in time of peace be quartered in any house, without the consent of the Owner, nor in time of war, but in a manner to be prescribed by law.

Amendment IV
The right of the people to be secure in their persons, houses, papers, and effects, against unreasonable searches and seizures, shall not be violated, and no Warrants shall issue, but upon probable cause, supported by Oath or affirmation, and particularly describing the place to be searched, and the persons or things to be seized.

Amendment V
No person shall be held to answer for a capital, or otherwise infamous crime, unless on a presentment or indictment of a Grand Jury, except in cases arising in the land or naval forces, or in the Militia, when in actual service in time of War or public danger; nor shall any person be subject for the same offence to be twice put in jeopardy of life or limb; nor shall be compelled in any criminal case to be a witness against himself, nor be deprived of life, liberty, or property, without due process of law; nor shall private property be taken for public use, without just compensation.

Amendment VI
In all criminal prosecutions, the accused shall enjoy the right to a speedy and public trial, by an impartial jury of the State and district wherein the crime shall have been committed, which district shall have been previously ascertained by law, and to be informed of the nature and cause of the accusation; to be confronted with the witnesses against him; to have compulsory process for obtaining witnesses in his favor, and to have the Assistance of Counsel for his defence.

Amendment VII
In Suits at common law, where the value in controversy shall exceed twenty dollars, the right of trial by jury shall be preserved, and no fact tried by a jury, shall be otherwise re-examined in any Court of the United States, than according to the rules of the common law.

Amendment VIII
Excessive bail shall not be required, nor excessive fines imposed, nor cruel and unusual punishments inflicted.

Amendment IX
The enumeration in the Constitution, of certain rights, shall not be construed to deny or disparage others retained by the people.

Amendment X
The powers not delegated to the United States by the Constitution, nor prohibited by it to the States, are reserved to the States respectively, or to the people.

JUDICIAL CONFERENCE OF THE UNITED STATES
COMMITTEE ON THE BICENTENNIAL OF THE CONSTITUTION

Judge Damon J. Keith
Chairman

December 15, 1991

Brian Ballweg

H*ofstra University dedicated this monument consisting of a Colonial patriot statue and a reproduction of the Bill of Rights.*

BELLS ACROSS AMERICA

On September 17, 1987, millions of Americans had participated simultaneously in a BELLS ACROSS AMERICA celebration of the anniversary of the signing of the Constitution (*see Chapter III*). Four years later, the national Commission contacted churches and other organizations to encourage a similar celebration of the ratification of the Bill of Rights on December 15. This nationwide bell-ringing eventually involved thousands of religious organizations, military installations, and other entities, as well as hundreds of thousands of Americans. One of the most active was B'nai B'rith International. Most of its districts in the country joined in, and the project's national chairman, Harry O. Hirsch, later reported: "I have never been privileged to chair a committee . . . that created such a great deal of enthusiasm and involvement. The cooperative spirit of all those people . . . around the country was most encouraging." B'nai B'rith's most notable participation in the project was a bell-ringing ceremony in front of Independence Hall in Philadelphia on December 15, involving religious leaders from many denominations. In addition to their bell-ringings, many religious organizations held special observances and sermons on the Bill of Rights for the weekend of December 13-15, 1991, in honor of the First

Amendment guarantee of religious freedom. BELLS ACROSS AMERICA would continue locally in many jurisdictions across the nation as an annual activity in honor of the Constitution and the Bill of Rights.

RADIO TRIBUTE TO THE BILL OF RIGHTS

Public radio station WETA in Washington, D.C., with support from the Pew Charitable Trusts, the National Education Association, and the national Commission, coordinated production of a one-hour, star-studded radio tribute to the Bill of Rights entitled "We Hold These Truths 1991." Broadcast via American Public Radio during the weekend of December 15, the program was created by distinguished author and scriptwriter Norman Corwin and was based on a similar radio tribute on December 15, 1941, which honored the Sesquicentennial of the ratification of the Bill of Rights. The earlier production, also written by Corwin, had been a landmark in the history of radio, with a live hookup that included Hollywood stars in a California studio, a symphony orchestra in New York City, and President Franklin D. Roosevelt speaking from the White House in Washington, D.C. The 1941 cast of participating film stars and other artists featured James Stewart, Lionel Barrymore, Marjorie Main, Walter

© John Mayer

James Earl Jones (left) and Norman Corwin recording.

Brennan, Edward G. Robinson, Orson Welles, and Leopold Stokowski. Broadcast just a week after the attack on Pearl Harbor, the program reached 60 million listeners and became not only a tribute to the Bill of Rights, but an eloquent and moving statement of what America was fighting for.

The 1991 anniversary program, which was brought up to date to reflect the changes in American society since 1941, engaged a similar cast of celebrities, including Richard Dysart, James Earl Jones, Lloyd Bridges, Brenda Vacarro, Rene Auberjonois, Fess Parker, Dan O'Herlihy, George American Horse, Rod McKuen, Anderson Wong, and Ben Vereen. Chief Justice Burger contributed a closing message to the program, which was carried by radio networks including NBC, CBS, ABC, Mutual, National Public Radio, American Public Radio, and the Unistar Radio Network. The National Association of Broadcasters and newspapers such as the *Wall Street Journal* promoted the program. Charles Kuralt featured it on his regular CBS television program, "Sunday Morning," in which portions of the original broadcast were read. Later, Mr. Kuralt wrote to Mr. Corwin: "Well, the Mercury Theater we are not, but your words seem to have rung a powerful bell in the country. I cannot remember when we've had such reaction to a piece on *Sunday Morning*. Thank you for letting us do it!" The positive reaction of stations and listeners around the country was such that Public Radio decided to rebroadcast the program on July 4, 1992.

THE "BICENTENNIAL CONSTITUTION" PROJECT

On December 15, Independence National Historical Park in Philadelphia staged its final event of the Bicentennial Era, with ceremonies concluding a nation-wide "Bicentennial Constitution" project. Nearly 5,000 visitors to the park that day added their signatures to a large copy of the Constitution, whose text had been inscribed by hand by each state's Governor and an outstanding teacher and student in that state. (Each of these 50 teams had been assigned a small segment of the Constitution to inscribe, and were sent a piece of handmade linen paper on which to enter it. When all the paper segments were assembled in Philadelphia, the result was a Constitutional mosaic.) ABC's "Good Morning America" covered the launching of the project. In one of the youngest states, Alaska, which entered the Union in 1959, Ketchikan High School math teacher Dick Sander and Juneau-Douglas High School student government president Tara Nolan joined Governor Walter J. Hickel in hand-copying their assigned portion of Article II, which describes the powers and duties of the President. "I'm glad I could be a part of this bicentennial celebration," the Governor said. "I hope all Alaskans will take a moment to reflect on how very important the Bill of Rights is to protecting our freedoms." Funded in part by the national Commission, the project was administered by Franklin S. Roberts Associates and the staff of Independence Park, with financial and in-kind support from many organizations, including USAir, Bell of Pennsylvania, Eastern National

*E*very state in the Union took part in the "Bicentennial Constitution" project.

*G*overnors, teachers, and students inscribed parts of the Constitution. The Alaskan contingent (top); closing ceremonies at Independence Hall (middle); the Maryland delegation (bottom).

Park and Monument Association, Friends of Historic Rittenhouse Town, the National Constitution Center, and the U.S. Postal Service.

To affix their signatures to the "Bicentennial Constitution" on December 15, thousands of people gathered in Philadelphia from dawn to midnight at Congress Hall, the home of the Congress (1790-1800) at the time the Bill of Rights was added to the Constitution. Activities began at 7:15 a.m. and included entertainment by various groups, readings of the Bill of Rights, and a public discussion involving participants in the project led by Lindy Boggs, Chair of the Commission on the Bicentenary of the House of Representatives and a member of the national Commission. The events of the day climaxed when Park Superintendent Martha P. Aikens presented the "Bicentennial Constitution" to Herbert Brownell, representing the national Commission.

PRESIDENTIAL ADDRESS AT MONTPELIER

Two hundred years after the Virginia ratification of the Bill of Rights, President Bush honored that occasion — and also brought the Bicentennial period to a symbolic conclusion — in a December 16, 1991, ceremony at James Madison's partially restored home, Montpelier, in Orange County, Virginia. At the event, sponsored by the National Trust for Historic Preservation, the President said:

The Framers . . . gave us not a declaration of rights but a bill of rights, not a piece of propaganda but a set of legally enforceable constraints on government. Most important, they drafted a bill of rights that reflected the higher nature, the aspirations of the American people, a bill that grew out of the American character, not one grafted onto it for the sake of some abstract theory.

Montpelier was an appropriate location for the last major event of the Bicentennial — home of the man who is often called the "Father of the Constitution" and who could with equal justice be called the "Father of the Bill of Rights." Here, President Bush said, "is where Madison developed and sustained his deep love of liberty, of religious freedom, economic freedom, intellectual freedom. Here at Montpelier Madison immersed himself in the historical and philosophical study that shaped our Constitution. And here he promised his constituents he would work to enact a Bill of Rights." Among many dignitaries attending the event were representatives of Estonia, Russia, Bulgaria, Poland, and Czechoslovakia. Local television covered the entire program, while the major networks highlighted it on national news broadcasts, and stories and briefs appeared in the press.

Commission Programs and Publications

"TEACH ABOUT" THE BILL OF RIGHTS

The Commission had begun the Bicentennial commemoration with one of its most successful educational projects: a national teach-in undertaken in connection with 1987's CELEBRATION OF CITIZENSHIP (*see Chapter III*). It concluded the Bicentennial with a similar project, a TEACH ABOUT THE BILL OF RIGHTS. Through this national program, the Commission distributed over half a million packets of curriculum materials, including a poster and study guide. These materials and their promotion encouraged schools to participate in a nationwide study and celebration of "The Bill of Rights and Beyond," beginning with Constitution Week in September and continuing through "Rights in History" week, December 9-15, 1991.

An ad hoc committee, including representatives of the National Education Advisory Committee (NEAC) and staff from the National Archives, helped put the program together. One member of the committee, Betty Debnam, designed the materials' centerpiece, a four-color poster in the style of *The Mini Page* depicting the 26 Amendments to the Constitution. The companion piece distributed with the poster, *A Study Guide for Elementary and Secondary Schools,* provided younger students with a simplified explanation of the first ten Amendments and eight additional Amendments that secured rights under the Constitution. Classroom activities stimulated by the TEACH ABOUT materials included citizenship bees, poster contests, special assemblies, studies of court cases, simulations of court hearings, research projects comparing life before and after the Bill of Rights, field trips, and Bill of Rights bookshelves. Younger students were encouraged to participate in class readings and discussions of the various Amendments.

Many educational posters were created
for the Bill of Rights, including those
for the Montpelier ceremony (left)
and the "Teach About" (opposite page).

The Bill of Rights

The original Constitution was signed in 1787. Many people agreed to support it only if basic rights were added.
This was done in 1791. The first 10 Amendments to the Constitution are called the Bill of Rights.

1st: Freedom of religion

Symbols of the five major religions
Christianity Judaism
Islam Hinduism Buddhism

 Freedom of speech

 Freedom of the press

 Freedom of assembly and petition

 2nd: Right to bear arms

 **3rd:** Limits the quartering of soldiers

 4th: Limits searches and seizures

 5th: The right to due process of law, including protection against self-incrimination

 6th: Rights of a person accused of a crime, including the right to be represented by a lawyer

 **7th:** Jury trial in civil cases

 8th: Unfair bail, fines, and punishment forbidden

 9th: Citizens entitled to rights not listed in the Constitution

10th: Powers reserved to the states or the people

and Beyond...

Since 1791, only 16 Amendments have been added to the Constitution.
Some of these Amendments have extended our rights as citizens.

 11th: Rules for lawsuits against states (1795)

 **12th:** New way of electing the President and Vice President (1804)

 13th: Abolishes slavery (1865)

14th: Guarantees citizenship, due process and equal protection under the law (1868)

 **15th:** Voting rights for former slaves (1870)

 16th: Power of the federal government to collect income taxes (1913)

 17th: Election of Senators by the people (1913)

 **18th:** Bans the sale of alcohol (1919)

 **19th:** Gives women the vote (1920)

 **20th:** Sets the date when President's and Congress's terms begin (1933)

 **21st:** Repeals 18th Amendment (1933)

22nd: Limits the President to two terms (1951)

 **23rd:** Gives people in the District of Columbia the right to vote for President (1961)

24th: Forbids having to pay a tax to vote. (1964)

 25th: Says who is next in line if something happens to the President (1967)

26th: Sets 18 as the voting age (1971)

Sponsored by The Commission on the Bicentennial of The United States Constitution. The Amendments in red are those concerned with rights. From **The Mini Page** by Betty Debnam © 1991 Universal Press Syndicate.

In addition to its own distribution of the TEACH ABOUT materials to every school in the country, the Commission contracted with nine major educational publications, including *Instructor, Creative Classroom, Leadership, Learning K-8 News, Principal, Scholastic, Social Education, Teacher,* and *Teaching K-8,* to insert copies of the poster as supplements to regular issues of their magazines. In all, approximately 2 million copies were distributed during the life of the program. Dr. William Carr, the former executive director of the National Education Association, whose career in education spanned 60 years, commented that he had rarely seen teachers respond more enthusiastically to any educational materials.

NATIONAL HISTORY DAY

Another of the Commission's most successful educational ventures was its cosponsorship of the National History Day competitions for 1990-1991, on "Rights in History." National History Day began in the late 1970s as a pilot project of the History Department of Case Western Reserve University, involving 100 secondary school students in the greater Cleveland, Ohio, area. Its aim was to promote better teaching and learning of history at the precollege level and to reward students for excellence in that study. With funding from the National Endowment for the Humanities, the pilot project grew into an ongoing national program, with about 500 state and district coordinators and 30,000 teachers in all 50 states as well as the District of Columbia. Both junior

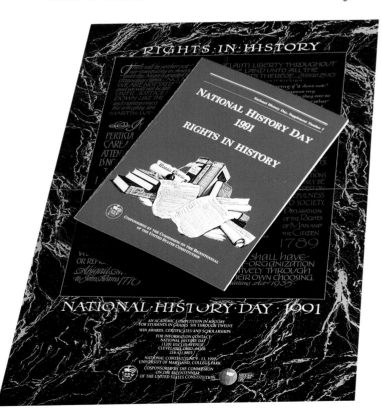

Instructional materials
for the National History Day
1991 competition.

and senior high school students participated in a variety of competitions, including essay writing, dramatic performances, art projects, and video and slide presentations. The theme for 1990-1991 was chosen to commemorate the 200th anniversary of the Bill of Rights.

In cosponsoring the 1990-1991 competitions, the Commission underwrote most of the administrative costs of the program and provided the national prizes. Early in 1990, it published a teachers' handbook, *National History Day 1991: Rights in History,* which included an introductory essay, suggested study approaches to the subject of rights in history, a collection of appropriate quotations, suggested topics, resource materials, and a bibliography. Together with a promotional poster produced by the staff of National History Day, copies of the handbook were distributed to teachers at preparatory workshops around the country in the spring, summer, and fall of 1990.

The 1990-1991 competitions proved to be one of the most successful in more than a decade of the National History Day program, with nearly 500,000 students and teachers participating. In June 1991, over 1,800 finalists gathered at the University of Maryland to compete for the national championship in the various categories at the junior and senior high school levels. Topics ranged from the Magna Carta and the Salem Witch Trials to the demolition of the Berlin Wall. The winning entries included such titles as "Impounded Americans: The Violation of Japanese Americans," "Deny Your Faith or Die," "The Reapportionment Revolution," "The Nazi/Skokie Conflict," "Cherokee Removal," "Clear & Present Danger," and "Frederick Douglass on Independence Day."

DEAF ORATORICAL CONTEST

Gallaudet University in Washington, D.C., joined with the national Commission to cosponsor the first nationwide "oratorical contest" for deaf and hard-of-hearing students. Contestants, age 13 through 19 in grades 7 through 12, competed first at the regional level in written essays and then at the national level through formal presentations, which could be delivered in American Sign Language or any other form of signed English, in spoken English, or in any combination of options. The contest topic was "What do the Bill of Rights and other constitutional amendments mean to me as a deaf or hard-of-hearing individual?" First-place regional winners competed at the U.S. Capitol in June 1991. Roberta Mather, 14, a student at Kendall Demonstration Elementary School in Washington, D.C., won the national first prize — a cash award and a trip as a guest to the National Convention of American Instructors of the Deaf, in New Orleans. Speaking from her own personal experience with Bill of Rights issues when she participated in a 1988 student protest at Gallaudet, she said: "I was so terrified it was illegal, but the Bill of Rights allowed us to do that." With the other five finalists, Mather visited with President Bush at the White House. Second- and third-place winners were Darby Jared of the Dalton School in New York City and Rita Ribera of

Competitor at the Deaf Oratorical Contest (above); Visitors at an IMPACT III exhibit (below).

the Oregon School for the Deaf. Honorable mentions went to Tiffany Logsdon of the Illinois School for the Deaf, Carolyn Kobek of Wando High School in Mount Pleasant, South Carolina, and Alicia Pena of Memorial High School in Mercedes, Texas.

BICENTENNIAL EDUCATIONAL GRANT PROGRAM

The Commission's BICENTENNIAL EDUCATIONAL GRANT PROGRAM (BEGP) sponsored one round of competition in its last year. The program received 216 applications, of which 33 were funded in a total amount of $1,889,620, a per-award average of $56,352. Next to the Constitution in general, the Bill of Rights (and subsequent Amendments) had been the most popular subject—comprising 28 percent of the funded projects—among all the grants awarded during the life of the program. Some of these projects have been described in earlier chapters. The 1991 grant awards included the following:

The Alabama Center for Law & Civic Education produced five videotapes, together with supplemental resource and teaching materials, focusing on contemporary Alabamians who played major roles in the development and interpretation of basic constitutional rights.

The Los Angeles Unified School District sponsored a series of 14 two-day workshops on the Constitution and Bill of Rights for 435 elementary school teachers in the District.

The National Institute for Citizen Education in the Law (NICEL), working with the Consortium of Universities of the Washington, D.C., metropolitan area, adapted existing lesson plans on the Bill of Rights for use by the deaf and hard-of-hearing.

ORBIS Associates developed curricular materials on citizenship and Bill of Rights issues for use by Native American students. The materials addressed the special, and generally not understood, constitutional status of Native Americans.

The Jefferson Parish Public Schools in Louisiana presented a two-week summer institute for 30 teachers, who taught grades 5 through 10, on the Constitution and Bill of Rights, with special emphasis on the Fifth Amendment.

Bates College in Lewiston, Maine, hosted a two-week summer institute for 20 secondary school teachers; the institute examined the philosophical and historical origins of the rights Amendments, their interpretation in the nineteenth and twentieth centuries, and the Bill of Rights in the light of current issues.

The New York City Public Schools' Social Studies Unit, in collaboration with the Constitution Works Project at Federal Hall, sponsored a three-week summer institute for 20 elementary and secondary teachers and their principals. Scholars led the institute's participants through a study of the antecedents of the Bill of Rights, the conflicts surrounding the adoption of that document, and its impact on their own lives and on the world community.

The Literacy Volunteers of America, Washington County, Rhode Island Chapter, with the Westerly Public Library in that county, developed 12 lesson plans on the Bill of Rights and related Amendments for the functionally illiterate and for adults whose native language was other than English.

Theatre IV, in cooperation with the Virginia Historical Society, the Virginia Department of Education, and the Virginia PTA, sponsored a 120-performance school tour throughout Virginia depicting the story of James Madison and the Bill of Rights. Teachers' and students' guides supplemented the performances.

During its five years the BEGP sponsored eight rounds of competition. It received 1,428 applications, of which 253 were funded in a total amount of $12,865,571 with an average grant award of $68,626. Although many of the projects included a combination of teacher training and curriculum development components, approximately 61 percent of the funded projects were devoted primarily to the former and 32 percent to the latter; the remainder (about 7 percent) contained a miscellany of special projects. About 47 percent of the grants encompassed all grade levels from kindergarten through grade 12. Nineteen percent focused on secondary education, 13 percent on middle and secondary, 6 percent on middle and elementary, and 6 percent on elementary education alone. A few, concentrating on the needs of the functionally illiterate, reached into the area of Adult Basic Education. Four percent responded to the needs of Special Education. Projects that were of special interest to ethnic and minority audiences (including English-as-a-second-language projects) constituted about 16 percent of the total.

The program immediately benefited an estimated 16,000 teachers through training projects, an additional 123,000 teachers through in-service training and curriculum development projects, and — in the projects' first year of implementation — 7.3 million students. Playing a key role in sustaining the momentum generated by this program was the Center for Research and Development in Law-related Education (CRADLE) at Wake Forest University in North Carolina. With support from the BEGP, CRADLE established a national repository and clearinghouse for all of the curricular materials generated by BEGP grants as well as many other materials created during the years of the Bicentennial. It would continue to provide teachers with easy access to useful educational materials on the Constitution.

The BEGP represented one of the Bicentennial's major investments in the future of American education, and its long-term impact will doubtless be much greater than can be measured in the short run. Quoting Henry Adams in his foreword to the program's *Final Report,* the Commission Chairman said: "A teacher affects eternity; he can never tell where his influence stops."

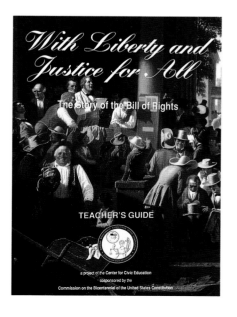

The Center for Civic Education's Bill of Rights textbook (right); a few of the thousands of entries for the National Historical/Pictorial Map Contest (opposite page).

NATIONAL BICENTENNIAL COMPETITION

Lincoln High School in Portland, Oregon, became the first repeat winner in the fourth NATIONAL BICENTENNIAL COMPETITION ON THE CONSTITUTION AND BILL OF RIGHTS (1990-1991). East High School of Denver, Colorado, took second place, and Maine South High School in Park Ridge, Illinois, took third. Over 1,000 students from 43 state championship teams participated in the three-day competition in Washington, D.C., with the top ten teams contending for the national title in U.S. Senate hearing rooms on Capitol Hill. Former Representative Lindy Boggs, a member of the Commission, and Charles E. Kolb, Deputy Assistant to the President for Domestic Affairs, participated in the awards ceremony. Optimist International president-elect Don Mills presented plaques to the winning teams, the top three of which also each received a 24-volume set of *The Annals of America* from Encyclopaedia Britannica.

The year also saw the appearance of a new textbook for the program, *With Liberty and Justice for All: The Story of the Bill of Rights,* to complement the three existing texts *(see Chapter II).* Made possible with a supplemental grant from the national Commission, the book offered 31 lessons on the origins, history, and meaning of the Bill of Rights. Like its predecessors, it included expository text, glossaries, and critical thinking exercises. The student text was accompanied by a teacher's guide. In honor of the Bicentennial of the Bill of Rights, *With Liberty and Justice for All* became the principal text in the NATIONAL BICENTENNIAL COMPETITION for the school year 1991-1992.

Administered by Center for Civic Education (CCE), the WE THE PEOPLE PROGRAMS reached about 4 million students and 56,000 teachers during the 1990-1991 school year. During their first five years, the programs, including the NATIONAL BICENTENNIAL COMPETITION, engaged over 12 million students and 170,000 teachers. Studies by the Educational Testing Service of Princeton, New Jersey, and other organizations confirmed the exceptional effectiveness of the curricula. Few programs could claim as great an impact on American education. Their continuation in subsequent years promised to be another important and enduring legacy of the Bicentennial.

NATIONAL HISTORICAL/PICTORIAL MAP CONTEST

In June 1991 the Commission hosted the national winners (and their teachers) of the third HISTORICAL/PICTORIAL MAP CONTEST for two days in Washington, D.C. During the awards ceremony, Chief Justice Burger presented the winners with plaques and checks for $5,000 toward the purchase of educational materials and supplies for their schools. Six thousand schools nationwide participated in the contest, once again sponsored by the Commission and administered by the CCE. Eleven fifth- and sixth-grade students from Wellsville Elementary School in Wellsville, Missouri, produced one winning entry, "Keep the Bell of Freedom

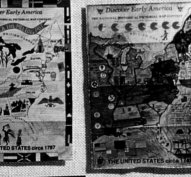

Official White House portraits of Presidents Richard Nixon, Gerald Ford, Jimmy Carter, and Ronald Reagan (left to right).

Ringing." At the middle school level, first place went to seventh- and eighth-grade students from Edward Hand Junior High School in Lancaster, Pennsylvania, who had researched the name origins of towns, rivers, and other geographical sites for their entry, "The Naming of a Nation." Finally, seniors Jeff Smithey and Tony Rainey, from Perkins-Tryon High School in Perkins, Oklahoma, won first prize at the high school level for their entry on Revolutionary War battle sites.

With the Bicentennial near its termination, funds were not available for a continuation of the program in the 1991-1992 school year. Many teachers expressed their disappointment in the lapse. One, an expert in geography teaching, wrote to the Commission's Chairman to say:

This contest has to go on. . . . "We" in geography are trying hard to promote a true sense of this subject, and for young people . . . this contest was one of the best to do that. . . . Kids like contests, but teachers like to be able to involve all the students. This wonderful project does just that and provides "naturally" for peer group interaction and activities across the curriculum. They [the students] worked together and the end project was not somebody succeeding, but rather a group succeeding with cooperative efforts. This is truly teaching a social studies ethic in a very kinesthetic way. . . . The contest showed the applied aspects of geography and how it is tied to history and human activity. That is what "we" in geography need!

Congress subsequently provided funding for the program to be reinstated in the 1992-1993 school year under the Department of Education and also gave it a new title, "The Warren E. Burger Historical/Pictorial Map Contest," in honor of its principal author.

WE THE PEOPLE: THE PRESIDENT AND THE CONSTITUTION

One of the Commission's last and most important projects premiered in late 1991 with the release of four one-hour television interviews with Presidents Nixon, Ford, Carter, and Reagan. This series, "We the People: the President and the Constitution," represented the culmination of an enterprise over two years in the making.

Early on, the Commission had considered the idea of creating "study groups" to examine each of the three branches of government. Each group would be located at an institution of higher learning and would enlist the

President Ford and Hugh Sidey before the taping session.

participation of scholars, public servants, and others in an examination of the state of a particular branch of government and its role in the nation's system of government. The requirements of time and expense ultimately persuaded the Commission not to pursue this ambitious idea, but in it was the essence of another project: an oral history of the American Presidency, drawing on the experience and reflections of the individuals still living who had once held that office. The rare historical coincidence of four surviving former Presidents argued strongly for such an enterprise. Not since Lincoln's first administration had there been so many surviving past occupants of the nation's highest office at one time. Capturing on film these men's views on the institution of the Presidency and its constitutional role was an opportunity too important to miss. The Commission recognized that, while such a film's contemporary interest was great, its historical value was beyond measure.

During 1989 the Commission explored the idea with several scholars and public servants, including the former Librarian of Congress, Dr. Daniel Boorstin; Professor Kenneth Thompson of the White Burkett Miller Center at the University of Virginia; Frank Shakespeare, the former Director of the United States Information Agency and Ambassador to the Vatican; and G. Gordon Hoxie of the Center for the Study of the Presidency. The project began in earnest in 1990 with the award of a grant to the Trust for the Bicentennial of the United States Constitution. After considering several possible candidates, the Trust awarded a contract to Anthony Potter Productions, Inc., of Greenwich, Connecticut, an organization with considerable experience in the production of historical television documentaries, to produce the four one-hour interviews with the former Presidents.

Meanwhile, the four Presidents had agreed to participate, and veteran Washington journalist Hugh Sidey was engaged as moderator. The John M. Olin Foundation and the Lynde and Harry Bradley Foundation awarded grants to help fund the project. The producer, working with the Commission and the Trust, refined the major "talking points" on which the interviews would focus, e.g., nomination and election of a President, selection of Cabinet members, and relations with Congress. The first interview to be taped was with President Ford in August 1990, followed by sessions with Presidents Carter and Reagan, and concluding with President Nixon in January 1991. Each interview was shot "on location" at the subject's office and ranged in length from two to four hours. Once completed, the interview material was edited and incorporated into four one-hour segments, which also included archival footage illustrating the points made in the interviews.

By the summer of 1991, the four interviews, each introduced by Chief Justice Burger, were ready. From the outset, the Commission saw three aspects to the educational value of this project. The first was widespread public exposure of the interviews on broadcast or cable television. The second was the dissemination of the interviews on videocassette, either in their original format or in a composite version, to colleges and schools. Third, the project provided for eventual distribution of the unedited tapes to archives and research libraries for the use of scholars in the future.

The first objective was realized in the fall of 1991 when the Trust entered into an arrangement with the Public Broadcasting System (PBS) to release the four interviews via satellite through its Education Services. PBS was chosen because of its well-established reputation for high-quality educational programs and its extensive national network, which included a large number of universities, colleges, and schools. PBS agreed to feed the interviews to its member stations on four weekend evenings in December 1991 and to release them again by satellite in 1992. Member stations were free to broadcast the interviews at the time of their satellite release or at later times. The network also publicized the series through a promotional campaign that included press releases and a special flyer sent to all public television stations and to the network's contacts at colleges and universities. Despite a short lead time, the initial response to the series was excellent, especially among educational institutions. PBS would release the interviews a third time by satellite in September 1992.

"We the People: the President and the Constitution" was not intended to be a comprehensive documentary history of its subjects' administrations. Although the interviews included references to various particulars in those administrations, the principal focus was on the broader, perennial issues that informed the Office of the Presidency and its place in the constitutional framework of American government. Among those issues were the President's relationship with Congress, the media, and foreign countries; the process of choosing a Chief Executive; the appointment of Supreme Court Justices; and the qualifications of members of the Cabinet. Among more specific issues addressed in the interviews were the War Powers Act, proposals for a line-item veto, and alterations in the Presidential term of office. Introduced in the closing days of the Bicentennial Era, the interview series promised to be one of the most enduring legacies of the commemoration, an extraordinary history of interest to present and future generations of Americans.

THE 1991 COMMISSION AD CAMPAIGN

A key element in the national Commission's plans for commemorating the Bill of Rights was a new advertising campaign, following on the print and electronic media ads it had sponsored with the assistance of the Advertising Council in previous years (*see Chapters III and V*). Working again with the Ad Council and the advertising firm of Scali, McCabe, Sloves, Inc., the Commission produced one 30-second television ad, two radio spots, and three print ads. The overall objective of the campaign was to demonstrate the importance of the Bill of Rights and subsequent Amendments in the lives of contemporary Americans.

The Commission's television ad, which premiered during the telecast of the 1991 Super Bowl, included four vignettes portraying religious freedom, due process under law, security in one's home, and the right to vote. One of the radio spots took up the same idea in a collage of voices, each representing the exercise of a particular right. The other radio message consisted of tributes to the Bill of Rights by Presidents Carter, Reagan, and Bush. The print campaign included a reformatted ad from

*P*rint ads from the 1991 advertising campaign.

1987 ("The Constitution . . . The Words We Live By"); an ad featuring a montage of sayings and expressions related to the exercise of freedoms under the Bill of Rights with the central message: "Each day Americans exercise freedoms guaranteed by the Constitution and the Bill of Rights . . . and they don't even know it"; and a series of ads offering reminders of the struggle for, and denial of, freedom in other parts of the world. The Ad Council disseminated these ads to 900 television stations, 450 cable systems, the four networks, 7,000 radio stations, 1,000 consumer magazines, and 9,000 newspapers. During the year the Ad Council provided support valued at $3.35 million, and the total estimated value of this ad exposure was over $78 million for the entire Bicentennial.

OTHER COMMISSION PROGRAMS

The Commission's COLLEGE-COMMUNITY FORUMS PROGRAM concluded in 1991 after a final round of competition in which the Commission awarded $303,454 for 30 projects designed to engage faculty, community leaders, and citizens in public discussion of constitutional issues. Most of the funded programs took place during the 1991-1992 academic year. The program also published the fourth educational booklet in its series, *The Bill of Rights and the Constitutional Order.* Among the final-round projects, Martin University in Indianapolis, Indiana, held a series of forums — several in local churches, one on campus, and one to a largely teenage audience at the Indiana Black Expo in July — on "The Afro-American and the Constitution." Some of the discussions were broadcast on local radio. The forums centered on a study book produced by the university for this project. The book and the forums were well received on the Martin campus and in the community and, as a result, *The Federalist Papers* received new emphasis in the university's curriculum.

The Virginia Foundation for the Humanities and Public Policy coordinated a statewide series of 50 forums in 1991 on "The Bill of Rights, the Courts, and the Law," held in ten Virginia communities with the cosponsorship of 27 other organizations. The series concentrated on landmark Supreme Court cases and the constitutional issues they raised. A 244-page casebook, containing abridged versions of the cases, served as a reading-and-discussion text for the program. Almost 7,000 people participated in the forums, which were led by distinguished scholars and jurists, including U.S. Solicitor General Kenneth Starr and Chief Justice Harry Carrico of the Virginia Supreme Court. During its existence, the Commission's COLLEGE-COMMUNITY FORUMS PROGRAM sponsored five rounds of competition, including the initial series of pilot programs begun in the summer of 1988 *(see Chapter IV)*. It funded or partially funded 108 projects, many including more than one event, in a total amount of $932,572.

In one of the Commission's other programs, Christopher J. Hand of Jacksonville, Florida, won first prize in the 1990-1991 CONSTITUTION WEEK ESSAY CONTEST, cosponsored by the Daughters of the Ameri-

can Revolution for high school students. The assigned essay topic was "How do we as Americans help preserve the Bill of Rights and other rights guaranteed in the Constitution of the United States?" The nine regional winners were each able to choose a teacher to accompany them to Washington. They were recognized in a ceremony at the Supreme Court in Washington, D.C., by the Commission Chairman.

The Commission's ADULT EDUCATION PROGRAM materials, *The Constitution . . . Let's Talk About It,* were completed and disseminated in 1991. They included an abridged edition for those with reading deficiencies in English, accompanied by a *Supplementary Guide* for teachers of intermediate and pre-college English-as-a-second language, adult secondary education, and programs leading to a General Equivalency Diploma (GED). The Commission completed evaluation of these materials using results from the final two of three pilot test groups. (The first test had been conducted in 1989, as described in Chapter IV.) The second test was conducted in the Federal Correction Center, Morgantown, West Virginia, where some of the 20 participating inmates had attended two or three years of college. Members of this group were able to relate their own experiences in dealing with the judicial system to the Constitution. The third test was held at Fort Myer, Virginia, in cooperation with the Military District of Washington and with the participation of 13 high school graduates serving in the 3rd Infantry (The Old Guard) and ranging in age from 18 to 22. The results of these tests assisted the final editing of the adult education materials, which the Commission then disseminated nationally.

*C*oordinators of a statewide lecture series.

To facilitate their dissemination and use, the Commission cosponsored 30 statewide orientation and in-service training workshops in 1991. The Federation of State Humanities Councils, the Center for Applied Linguistics, and the National Council on the Aging administered the training and worked with national, state, and local representatives of educational and community organizations, with the potential of reaching 220,000 participants. The American Association of Retired Persons (AARP) assisted in the dissemination of the materials. The Commission also made plans for use of the materials in the nation's correctional institutions. During 1991, the Commission received over 2,000 requests for sets of *The Constitution . . . Let's Talk About It.*

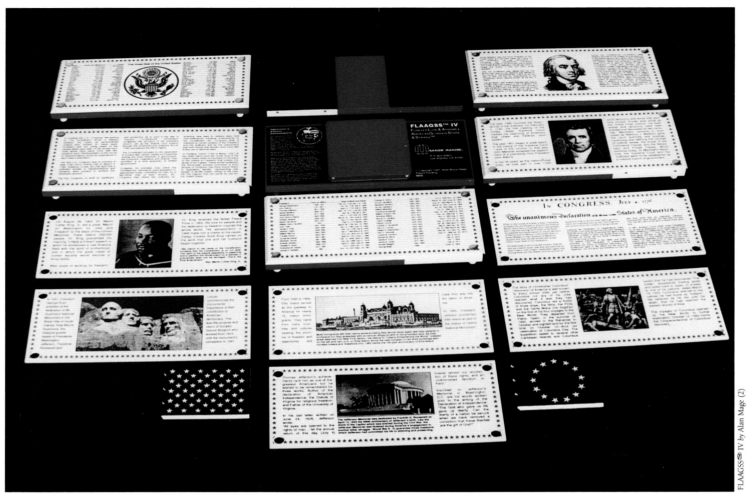

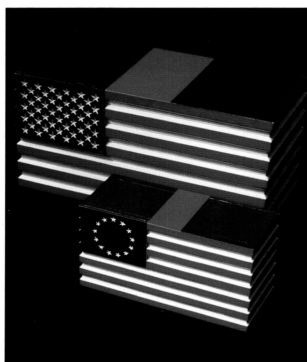

Among 1991's logo-licensed
products are two flag boxes (above);
the smaller is a music box,
the larger a puzzle,
shown disassembled (top).

The Commission's LIVING LEGACY program continued to provide a popular focus for commemorative ceremonies at the state and local levels. Since its inception in 1986, the program had stimulated thousands of plantings. During 1991 the Commission lent its support to a derivative program entitled ROOTS OF LIBERTY, in which the National Forest Service, the National Park Service, the American Forestry Association, and various state agencies also participated. This multifaceted program included the planting of "Trees of Liberty" in the nation's state and national forests, the planting of groves of trees in public parks in honor of the Constitution and Bill of Rights, and the creation of "Liberty Gardens" on public lands.

Under the PROJECT RECOGNITION PROGRAM, the Commission recognized 15 projects during 1991 to bring the grand total to 351 projects recognized out of 493 applications submitted over the life of the Bicentennial Commission. The projects recognized in 1991 ranged from an international seminar on the "Origin of Human Rights," sponsored by the Nicholaus Copernicus University of Torun (Poland), to a large patriotic exhibit featuring all 50 states and including signatures of every Governor. In addition, during the six years of commemoration, the Commission approved 103 licenses under the LOGO-LICENSING PROGRAM. Two 1991 examples were a Bill of Rights plaque entitled "The Four Freedoms," with four sterling proof medals patterned after works of Norman Rockwell, and "The Bill of Rights," the fifth in the Constitution Bicentennial Ornament Series in 24-karat gold (see Chapter III).

PUBLICATIONS

The national Commission's commemoration of the Bill of Rights included a wide range of publications, some of which have already been mentioned. The last COMMEMORATIVE CALENDAR of the six-year series, *The Bill of Rights and Beyond, 1791-1991,* was designed as a resource of educational information and reference material on the Bill of Rights. Richly illustrated, each month of the calendar provided historical background and modern applications of one part of the Bill of Rights and subsequent Amendments. In addition, each month listed pertinent events and dates and highlighted a biographical vignette of a prominent historical figure connected in some way to the right or rights covered during that month. The United Parcel Service distributed the calendar free of charge to 100,000 schools. Copies from the total printing of 225,000 also went to colleges and universities, courts, and public libraries as well as embassies and USIA posts abroad.

The enthusiastic response to the 1991 calendar from educators and others convinced the Commission to adapt the material as a book with the identical title. Published in November 1991, this book, *The Bill of Rights and Beyond, 1791-1991,* expanded both the list of key historical dates and the bibliography and added a list of suggested learning activities for teachers and an index. The Commission distributed the book to schools, colleges, public libraries, and other institutions in this country, and American embassies and USIA libraries overseas. The book would become an enduring resource for teachers and other students of the Bill of Rights.

The Commission also produced several new brochures in 1991. *The Bill of Rights and Beyond: Securing the Blessings of Liberty 1791-1991* became the fourth and final leaflet in a series begun in 1988 *(see Chapter IV).* This gatefold promotional brochure described the origins and history of the Bill of Rights and subsequent Amendments, their effect on American society, and a summary of Commission plans and programs for 1991. A companion brochure, *Each Day Americans Exercise Freedoms,* provided basic information about the Bill of Rights in a question-and-answer format. Included were such questions as "Why do we need a Bill of Rights" and "How does the Bill of Rights affect me?" The Commission printed and distributed 350,000 copies of the former pamphlet and 2 million of the latter to schools, libraries, civic organizations, and the general public.

Learning magazine promoted several Commission programs, including the NATIONAL HISTORICAL/PICTORIAL MAP CONTEST, Constitution Week, and other resources available through the Commission. Included as a special supplement to *Learning's* 1990 back-to-school issue, which went to 311,000 subscribing teachers, was a four-color poster insert, "Our American Rights." Sponsored by the Commission, the poster illustrated various rights enjoyed in everyday life and on its reverse side contained a list of 12 suggested learning activities for elementary and middle school students, together with a selected bibliography for both students and teachers. Approximately 80,000 copies of the poster

were distributed. Joining again with Scholastic, Inc., the Commission produced two Skills Handbooks on the Bill of Rights, one for elementary schools, the other for secondary schools. Each had a different cover design but the same title — *1791 to 1991, 200 Years of Our Bill of Rights: The Bill of Rights and Beyond.* The two Handbooks contained reading skills, explanations of the various Amendments, historical timelines, case studies, cartoon analyses, quizzes, and other learning activities. Scholastic distributed copies of the Handbooks to 144,000 subscribers as supplements to editions of its publications, and the Commission distributed an additional 50,000 copies.

The *Bill of Rights Resource Guide,* a softbound update and redesign of its 1987 predecessor, contained a history of the Bill of Rights, significant dates in the struggle for human rights, and other historical facts, plus suggested programs, contests, and competitions for commemorating the Bicentennial. The book listed hundreds of resources, including books, films, videotapes, posters, and prints.

In May 1990, the Commission's Chairman and staff had met with representatives of major religious organizations to enlist their participation in the Bill of Rights celebrations. Several program suggestions, including participation in BELLS ACROSS AMERICA, came out of these discussions. The following February, the Commission issued *A Resource Guide for Religious Communities,* an illustrated 36-page booklet containing suggestions for ceremonies to commemorate the Bill of Rights (particularly the First Amendment); a section of readings on religious liberty; an analysis of Supreme

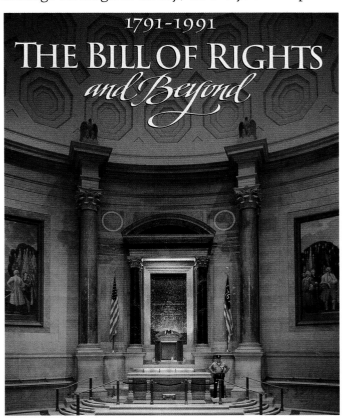

The **Bill of Rights and Beyond** *book, an expanded edition of the 1991 calendar.*

OUR AMERICAN RIGHTS

Court decisions regarding the religion clauses; and pages of significant dates and clip art for reproduction in religious publications. More than 20,000 copies of the four-color guide went to religious groups nationwide. The Commission also distributed to some 1,500 major religious denomination offices and headquarters a collection of thoughts on religious liberty and First Amendment provisions suitable for use in sermons and publications.

The Church of Jesus Christ of Latter-day Saints, for example, rounded out its Bicentennial activities by placing a four-page supplement on the Bill of Rights in the *Church News,* its nationwide weekly. Since 1987, the Church had provided several points of focus, including a yearlong exhibit on the Constitution at its world headquarters; a Bicentennial ball and banquet with entertainment from 1,200 dancers and choir singers, which was broadcast by satellite to 500 locations throughout the nation; the Mormon Tabernacle Choir's participation in the September 1987 gala Philadelphia celebration; BELLS ACROSS AMERICA and "Balloons Across America" celebrations throughout the Church; and the distribution to the homes of all Church members in the United States of a family home evening booklet designed to help parents teach their children about the importance of the Constitution.

During 1991, the Commission's Information Services Division — created in 1987 to provide an automated system to respond to the heavy request load — fulfilled 57,000 orders and distributed 2,833,385 Bill of Rights items. During its lifetime, the Commission disseminated an estimated 10.3 million information items on the Constitution, not including copies of the POCKET CONSTITUTION (*see Chapter II*).

COMMISSION ORGANIZATIONAL CHANGES

During 1991, the Commission began the orderly phaseout of its operations and the reduction in its staffing according to a plan approved by the Commissioners in December 1990. By autumn less than two dozen people were managing the remaining functions of the Commission, which had employed some 220 people during the years of the Bicentennial. They came from private industry, government (some detailed from other agencies), the military, and academe. The Chairman, after the approval of the full Commission at its final meeting in December 1991, signed an appropriate certificate of appreciation for each member of the staff and wrote his own general message of appreciation in the December 1991 *We the People* newsletter: "Since this may be the last Newsletter of the Commission, it is a good time to say thank you to all of the Staff, past and present, for their contribution to the success of the whole enterprise."

At the closing banquet on December 14, each Commissioner was presented with a framed set of Bicentennial ornaments, together with a note of appreciation from the Chairman. The Commissioners, in turn, presented Chief Justice and Mrs. Burger with the gift of a porcelain American eagle and a porcelain flag of the United States. In presenting this gift on behalf of the other Commissioners, Obert C. Tanner said:

Under your leadership we have helped our fellow citizens better understand the Constitution of the United States. The nation owes you a debt of gratitude. . . . Today our Constitution is better understood by millions of Americans, in our schools, our churches, our business life, indeed every segment of American life, including our homes . . . the greatest political document ever written in the history of mankind.

Mr. Tanner spoke of the new dimension that had come into the lives of the Commissioners over the previous six years and raised the toast: "God bless our citizens, and save the Constitution of the United States."

Outside Activities

EDUCATIONAL ORGANIZATIONS

Sponsored by the American Historical Association and the American Political Science Association, and supported by the Pew Charitable Trusts, the Bill of Rights Education Collaborative coordinated special initiatives for 1991-1992 to strengthen precollegiate education about constitutional rights. Competitions for funding ranged from mini-grants ($500 to $1,500) to teachers through state humanities council grants (up to $25,000); ten History Teaching Alliance collaboratives with yearlong seed grants (up to $10,000); "short course" grants for institutions; and in-service teacher workshops with grants between $5,000 and $20,000. Chief Justice Burger served as honorary chairman of the program,

Bill Fitzpatrick (2)

The Commission's closing banquet at the Court (above), where the Chairman receives an eagle statue from the Commissioners (left).

Logo of the James Madison Memorial Fellowship Foundation, which supports graduate study of the Constitution.

JAMES MADISON
MEMORIAL FELLOWSHIP
FOUNDATION

which complemented the Commission's BICENTENNIAL EDUCATIONAL GRANTS PROGRAM (BEGP), and would assist in carrying on its work.

Also supported by a grant from the Pew Charitable Trusts (and in addition to its other Bicentennial activities), CCE developed a seminal curricular document, *CIVITAS: A Framework for Civic Education,* as part of a collaborative project with the Council for the Advancement of Citizenship. *CIVITAS* provided detailed guidelines to public and private elementary and secondary schools for the promotion of civic competence, civic responsibility, and the widespread participation of youth in the political and civic life of their communities and the nation. A group of scholars and educators, with advice from public leaders, individual teachers, and educational and civic associations, helped to write the book, which was distributed nationally by the National Council for the Social Studies.

In the spring of 1992, the James Madison Memorial Fellowship Foundation began awarding fellowships worth up to $24,000. Chartered by Congress in 1986 with the assistance and encouragement of the national Commission, the Foundation administered an educational trust fund for the support of graduate study of the

Constitution by experienced social studies or American history teachers and by outstanding students who desired to become so qualified. In-service teachers (senior fellows) received support for part-time study over five years, while college seniors or recent graduates (junior fellows) were funded for up to two years of full-time study. The program also provided for summer institutes, bringing fellows and constitutional scholars together after a year of independent study.

The National Constitution Center of Philadelphia, which had undertaken a variety of educational projects during the Bicentennial, sponsored a traveling artwork exhibit, for which ten outstanding artists had been commissioned to produce visual representations of specific freedoms in the Bill of Rights. The premier showing took place at Independence National Historical Park in Philadelphia during March and April 1991, and the exhibit traveled through the remainder of the year to three national historic parks — Guadalupe, Texas; Cuyahoga Valley Park, Ohio; and Atlantic National Park, Georgia.

The American Bar Association (ABA) concluded its many contributions to the Bicentennial with a variety of conferences, publications, and other programs related to the Bill of Rights. One was a nationwide ad campaign — the "Bill of Rights in Transit" — to educate commuters via PSAs about the role of the Bill of Rights in American life. Tested in five cities early in 1990, the program was extended nationwide into 32 cities during 1991-1992, with transit advertising space donated by the Gannett Co., Inc. The award-winning campaign featured five posters on freedom of speech, freedom of religion, right to assembly, right to counsel in criminal cases, and equal protection. Two of the ads were printed in Spanish. The ABA also developed billboards, newspaper ads, radio PSAs, a television spot, and posters. The poster series and a companion instructor's guide were used in community centers and schools.

Other ABA activities included "The Bill of Rights 2000," featuring a national conference of teachers and students at Williamsburg, Virginia, on December 16, 1991. This project also included the development and dissemination of a student newsletter on Bicentennial programs and a variety of other educational materials. For example, a videotape and accompanying study guide, produced by the Young Lawyers Division of ABA and the Texas Young Lawyers Association, dramatized for students the Fourth and Fifth Amendments through case examples. For the fifth straight year, the American Lawyers Auxiliary Bicentennial Committee of the ABA sponsored a videotape competition in which students did research, prepared scripts, and produced videotapes on the theme "Balancing Rights and Responsibilities." First-place prizes in the two divisions went to a third-grade class from Flour Bluff School in Corpus Christi, Texas, and to 12th-grade students from Castle High School in Newburgh, Indiana.

On December 12, 1991, some 2,000 lawyers, judges, and other legal experts visited 2,000 ninth-grade social studies classrooms under a program sponsored by Friends of the Constitution of the U.S. (FOCUS) in

Artwork inspired by specific freedoms in the Bill of Rights and created for the
National Constitution Center (this page and following pages).

North Carolina. Mock Supreme Court arguments included experts and students arguing a hypothetical case on individual liberties and government authority. The program also produced a 28-minute television documentary on the evolution of the Bill of Rights. With the assistance of a 1989 BEGP award, KIDSNET — the computerized clearinghouse for audio, video, radio, and television resources—made available over 100 programs about, or related to, constitutional issues to schools, libraries, community groups, social service institutions, and civic and cultural organizations seeking educational materials for children from preschool through high school. Another project supported by the BEGP, "Impact II: Share the Spirit II," made it possible for the Boston Public Schools to disseminate exemplary teacher-developed programs on the Bill of Rights and subsequent Amendments. With support from the University of Massachusetts and the Boston National Historical Park, over 200 of the city's teachers showcased exemplary programs at a city-wide conference and adapted those programs for individual classrooms.

First Amendment/Press by Benny Andrews

Third Amendment by Janet Fish

During 1991, the national Commission's BICENTENNIAL SCHOOL RECOGNITION PROGRAM grew to 455 institutions, including one school in Nigeria. Many schools incorporated the Commission's TEACH ABOUT materials and its other programs into their activities, and some undertook altogether distinctive projects of their own. As in previous years, creativity and initiative characterized the activities of this network. San Marino High School in San Marino, California, for example, initiated a "Spotlight on a Right" project. An adaptation of the state's Mock Trial Competition, it involved a yearlong focus on a particular right, examined through simulated mock trial and appellate court hearings. Local attorneys provided expert advice, and a special school newspaper and wall display promoted the project. James Madison High School in Fairfax, Virginia, launched a "Bringing the Constitution to Life" program, in which students produced 30-second commercials using puppets to show the importance of the Constitution in contemporary society. At the Hillsdale High School in Hillsdale, New Jersey, students participated in "The Bill of Rights Experience," an interdisciplinary program designed to improve reading, writing, critical thinking, and planning skills. One activity was a hypothetical exercise in which students were asked to write letters from someone in the eighteenth century to a recipient in the twentieth century.

In Mentor, Ohio, the Ridge Junior High School concluded a comprehensive four-year program of commemorative activities with "Voice of Freedom" announcements on the school's PA system. Each announcement, prepared by a student, consisted of a brief biography of, and a quotation from, a historical figure. Other projects included the creation of a "Freedom Shrine" of replicas of historic documents, a "Book of Scholars" recognition program for outstanding students in the social studies, a "historic forest" on the school's property, and an annual "Profile of an American" composition competition at each grade level. The John L. Costley Senior School in East Orange, New Jersey, whose activities throughout the Bicentennial years had been featured in a regular school newsletter, concluded its celebrations with an all-day Constitution program on November 1.

Younger students also joined in the commemoration with a wide range of innovative educational activities. The Shaw Visual Performing Arts Center in St. Louis, Missouri, for example, produced and distributed to area public elementary and middle schools, copies of *The Bill of Rights Speaks,* a book containing stories and interdisciplinary lesson plans. The Pickney Elementary School in Lawrence, Kansas, focused on the writings of an African-American alumnus, Langston Hughes, whose lifelong protest against discrimination provided an appropriate focus for the study of the Bill of Rights and subsequent Amendments. The Menger Elementary School in Corpus Christi, Texas, participated in a yearlong social studies project on the Bill of Rights called "Up Close and Personal—Your Bill of Rights." Using the Civic Achievement Award Program of The Close Up Foundation and the U.S. House of Representatives, the program sponsored a series of outside speakers, field trips, pictorial essays, a photo contest, and poetry readings. The year's program culminated in an assembly for the whole school community, featuring a choral cantata, "Our Country 'Tis of Thee."

During its four years, the BICENTENNIAL CAMPUS PROGRAM recognized nearly 400 colleges and universities, many of which were junior colleges. One exemplary program, at Dyke College in Cleveland, Ohio, planned activities for each year of the Bicentennial: monthly films on the legislative process (1988), a constitutional quiz competition among clubs on campus (1989), a workshop on the Presidency (1989), a social studies course on the American judicial system (1990), and programs on the Bill of Rights (1990-1991).

What may have been the largest public event commemorating the Bill of Rights ratification took place on December 29, 1991, during the halftime show at the annual Liberty Bowl football game in Memphis, Tennessee. There, 1,500 high school and college musicians representing the 50 states joined author Alex Haley and Grammy-award-winning gospel artist Sandi Patti for a nine-minute salute to the Bill of Rights. The Commission officially recognized the game, which was broadcast live on the ESPN cable network. With the cooperation of the National Collegiate Athletic Association, the Commission provided public service announcements, large numbers of POCKET CONSTITUTIONS, uniform logo patches, and other materials to collegiate sports-information departments. Numerous colleges and universities promoted the Bill of Rights Bicentennial at football and basketball games throughout the fall of 1991. Austin Peay State University; Williams College; Massachusetts Maritime Academy; Bowling Green University; Cheyney University; California State University, Northridge; California State College, Stanislaus; Mount Union College; Texas A&I University; and Drake University all displayed the logo patches. On December 15, Bill of Rights Ratification Day, all 14,000 basketball fans in Mackey Arena at Purdue University received personal copies of the POCKET CONSTITUTION.

FEDERAL GOVERNMENT DEPARTMENTS AND AGENCIES

In December 1990, the U.S. Office of Personnel Management (OPM) initiated the Bill of Rights commemoration for Federal agencies at a special meeting of representatives from most Federal departments and agencies. OPM Director Constance Berry Newman conducted the meeting, which featured speakers from her agency addressing Bill of Rights topics. Designating "We the People" as the three most important words in the Constitution, Chief Justice Burger thanked the OPM representatives for their continued efforts. Director Newman discussed the Bill of Rights as it pertained to Federal workers and encouraged broad agency involvement in the commemoration.

On September 25, 1989, exactly 200 years after Congress approved its draft of the Bill of Rights and submitted it to the states for ratification, the U.S. Postal Service had dedicated a new 25-cent Bill of Rights stamp

Fifth Amendment by Fritz Scholder

Liberty
Bowl Games of

T*he Bill of Rights was the theme of the 1991 Liberty Bowl in Memphis, Tennessee, where 1,500 high school and college musicians joined celebrities in a halftime tribute.*

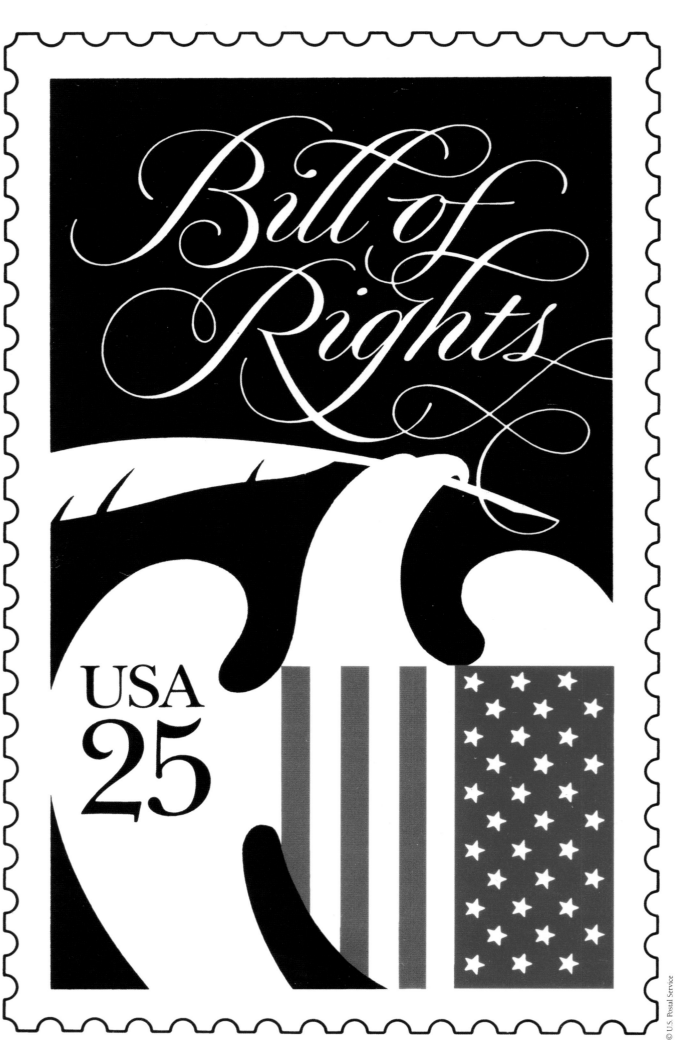

Bill of Rights

USA 25

Postage stamp issued to commemorate the drafting of the Bill of Rights by Congress.

at Independence Hall in Philadelphia. The stamp featured the words "Bill of Rights" in white script lettering on a black background, a white American eagle clutching a quill pen in its beak, and a representation in full color of an American flag in the lower-right corner. Two years later, the Postal Service issued a commemorative postal card at the opening of the Virginia State Fair in Richmond (see page 219). The card featured white quill pens against a red background, with wording that commemorated the December 15, 1791, ratification of the Bill of Rights by the states. The postal card completed a five-year philatelic program commemorating the Bicentennial of the United States Constitution, during which 23 stamps and postal cards were issued. The Postal Service also issued a special cancellation, "The Bill of Rights — 200 Years Old — And Still Working," that was used through December 31, 1991, in 20 of the largest post offices in the country.

In anticipation of the Bill of Rights anniversary, the National Archives in Washington, D.C., opened a major 80-item, two-part exhibition June 9, 1989, "This Fierce Spirit of Liberty: The Making of the Bill of Rights." Displayed in the Rotunda through 1991 in 26 cases flanking the U.S. Constitution and the Bill of Rights, the exhibition explored the ideological foundations and political struggles from which the Bill of Rights emerged. The first part traced the background and development of the Bill of Rights, while the second depicted the political struggle to adopt it. The Archives also sponsored a "One-Act Bill of Rights Playwright Competition." The winning play, *Scarecrow,* by Chuck Cummings of Decatur, Georgia, was based on records in the Georgia Regional Archives. It told the story of Essic Harris, a freed slave beaten and shot by the Ku Klux Klan during Reconstruction, who sought protection under the Bill of Rights. The scarecrow in the title, a sentinel in Harris's garden resembling Abraham Lincoln in top hat, kept the crows from the corn and, said the play's protagonist, "it might keep the Klan away, too."

During 1991, some 10,000 miners carried into the mines with them each day a "reflection" of the Bill of Rights Bicentennial. Safety regulations required that miners' helmets be marked with light-reflective materials. Working with Bureau of Mines officials in the Department of the Interior, the national Commission provided the miners with reflective decals of its "We the People" logo, which thereafter became a collector's item. The Department of Health and Human Services celebrated Constitution Week with a historical human rights drama presented by the Eastern High School Drama Department from the District of Columbia. During the same week, the U.S. Geological Survey presented a daily public showing of the video series, "Equal Justice Under Law," which deals with major court decisions of Chief Justice Marshall (see Chapter VI). At the showings, the Geological Survey also distributed the Commission's adult education package, *The Constitution . . . Let's Talk About It.*

The Department of Defense (DOD), continuing its outstanding leadership in the Bicentennial, developed in 1991 an information packet on the Bill of Rights,

which included a poster, a resource guide, a pamphlet, and a booklet discussing the Bill of Rights and the military. Eight more Designated Bicentennial Defense Communities (DBDCs) were recognized during the year, including Bad Aibling Station in Germany as well as units in the United States. During the Bicentennial period, the national Commission, in cooperation with DOD, recognized 198 DBDCs—installations throughout the world that developed constitutional programs for both military and civilian populations. Recognized installations represented the four major branches of the Armed Forces and comprised domestic and overseas bases as well as ships at sea.

On April 17, 1992, DOD concluded its commemoration of the Bicentennial with a ceremony at the Pentagon. There, a time capsule was dedicated containing a copy of the legislation authorizing the Bicentennial Commission, a POCKET CONSTITUTION, and other artifacts of the commemoration. Former Secretary of the Army John Marsh presented the Department of the Army's Decoration for Exceptional Service to Lt. Gen. Robert Arter for his role in coordinating the Defense Department's Bicentennial programs. Army Secretary Michael P. W. Stone presented to Chief Justice Burger DOD's medal for Distinguished Public Service in recognition of his leadership of the commemoration.

Among the other Federal Government programs honoring the anniversary of the Bill of Rights was a symposium in November 1991 sponsored by the Department of Justice, in which the speakers were former Attorney General Benjamin R. Civiletti, Solicitor General Kenneth W. Starr, and Dr. Ralph A. Rossum, the president of Hampden-Sydney College. On the evening of December 15, 1991, the National Archives hosted an address by Chief Justice of the United States William Rehnquist, "The Bill of Rights and an Independent Judiciary."

STATES AND COMMUNITIES

Throughout five commemorative years — encompassing the CELEBRATION OF CITIZENSHIP in 1987, the Constitution ratification ceremonies, the honoring of the establishment of the new nation's government, the reenactment of the George Washington inaugural journey, and more—the 53 state, district, and territorial commissions and the over 2,500 Designated Bicentennial Communities (DBCs) had been the most widespread network of Bicentennial activities. They were vital in assuring the collaborative efforts of a multitude of organizations across the nation. The outstanding performance of this state and local constellation continued through the Bill of Rights commemorations.

The River Oaks, Texas, DBC conducted a tree-planting ceremony on November 9, 1991, in honor of the Constitution and the Bill of Rights, in which 12-foot small-leaf oak trees were planted along River Oaks Boulevard and Highway 183 in that suburb of Fort Worth. In Hartford, Kentucky, monetary donations and the work of volunteers established Hartford House, a permanent Constitution and Bill of Rights resource center, in an unused building on Main Street. Bonneville County, Idaho, published a monthly newsletter containing historical accounts of the Founding Era and commentary on constitutional issues by local citizens and community leaders. In Boulder, Colorado, the Department of Community Services, under its Safeguard Law-Related Education Program and with partial funding by the national Commission, produced a set of 12 posters featuring Bill of Rights topics for classroom use along with a teachers' resource guide.

San Juan County, Washington, honored the Bill of Rights in its annual Fourth of July celebration with a parade depicting the variety of rights protected under the Constitution, a community picnic with fireworks, and a series of programs spotlighting the Bill of Rights. A 1991 Washington State Senate resolution recognized the county as a "shining example of local participation" in the commemoration. During Constitution Week in Wasilla, Alaska, the Wasilla Bicentennial Committee sponsored a "We the People" parade, a Bicentennial Park dedication, and a citizenship ceremony. The Committee then dedicated a six-ton boulder with a plaque marking Wasilla as a Designated Bicentennial Community and the boulder as the burial spot for a time capsule filled with letters, photos, and memorabilia from local leaders.

A *Bill of Rights plaque was dedicated at the Grand Rapids, Michigan, courthouse (below); present were Commissioner Keith (left) and Chief District Judge Douglas W. Hillman.*

As part of the "Florida Supreme Court Teach-In," Justices visited high school history classes across the state to talk with students about the Constitution and the Bill of Rights. The Florida Bicentennial Commission, in honor of Carol Bellamy, its Executive Director, endowed an annual $10,000 scholarship for social studies teachers pursuing an advanced degree in a field related to the Constitution at the University of South Florida. In Louisiana, the Centroplex Theater for the Performing Arts in Baton Rouge hosted a swearing-in ceremony for new citizens featuring the premiere of "The Rights of Freedom," a new musical composition by

Louisiana State University Music Department Professor Dinos Constantinides, who was an immigrant to the United States. The Mississippi Educational Television Network, with a grant from the national Commission and the Mississippi State Bar, produced a five-part instructional television series, "You've Got That Right," designed to instill into secondary students a basic understanding of how the Bill of Rights affects every American every day.

To conclude the Bicentennial, state Commissions undertook many outstanding programs. The Michigan Commission, for example, with partial funding from the national Commission, sponsored a series of "Blessings of Liberty Education Conferences" in the fall of 1990. The conferences took place at six locations around the state and were designed to assist educators and local leaders in promoting the observance of the Bicentennial in Michigan's schools. The Louisiana State Commission sponsored a resolution of the state legislature proclaiming December 15 "Bill of Rights Day" and December 16, "Bill of Responsibilities Day." With funding provided by the Connecticut State Commission, filmmaker Ken Simon produced "Crusaders and Criminals," an hourlong documentary for public television dramatizing seven landmark Supreme Court cases relating to privacy and the First Amendment.

In March of 1990, Vermont opened its 18-month statehood Bicentennial commemoration with a debate circuit on the topic "Should Vermont Secede From the Federal Union?" Local citizens wrestled with the question of belonging to the Union, as Vermonters had 200 years before. After a decade as a independent republic, Vermont joined the Union on March 4, 1791, becoming the first state to do so under the Constitution and increasing the number of states needed for ratification of the Bill of Rights to 11. Over 200 communities in Vermont sponsored statehood celebrations including town meetings, colonial craft fairs, chautauquas, concerts, plays, dances, parades, picnics, bell-ringings, exhibits, seminars, and school programs. The statewide commemoration concluded with a daylong "Bicentennial Birthday Bash" on the state house grounds in Montpelier on August 17, 1991.

PRIVATE NONPROFIT GROUPS

A number of private nonprofit groups honored the Bill of Rights anniversary in a wide range of programs and activities. Bicentennial involvement of the various American ethnic and minority communities had long been a priority of the Commission, which encouraged such participation in the commemoration — for example, in the BICENTENNIAL EDUCATIONAL GRANT PROGRAM and through its publications. The significance of the Bill of Rights and subsequent Amendments to the history of religious, cultural, and racial diversity in America made the concluding theme of the Bicentennial celebration especially important for such involvement.

To further the participation of ethnic communities in the commemoration of the Bill of Rights, the Chairman met with representatives from national

One of a series of editorial cartoon posters created by Brian Duffy of the Des Moines Register.

organizations concerned with the status of ethnic groups: the National Association for the Advancement of Colored People (NAACP), the Office of Personnel Management, the Organization of Chinese Americans, the Japanese American Citizens League, the National School Boards Association, the National Center for Urban Ethnic Affairs, the Association for the Study of Afro-American Life and History, and the League of United Latin American Citizens (LULAC). In addition, during the Bill of Rights anniversary year, Commission staff members attended national conventions of the NAACP and other groups to obtain ideas and suggestions and promote Commission programs.

At a seven-state regional NAACP meeting involving 1,200 delegates in Cleveland, Ohio, in March 1991, the national Commission presented a workshop on the history of the Bill of Rights and its influence in American life, conducted a demonstration of its ADULT EDUCATION PROGRAM, and handed out Bill of Rights materials. The NAACP distributed Commission publications among its regional offices. LULAC, the nation's largest Hispanic membership organization, commemorated the Bill of Rights Bicentennial by awarding several $5,000 scholarships for Hispanic students entering law school in 1991. Chief Justice Burger served as honorary chairman for the program. Students were judged on essays they submitted about the significance of the Bill of Rights as related to Hispanic civil rights, aptitude for law study, and community involvement.

The Constitutional Rights Foundation brought together 200 community leaders in law, education, the arts, and religion to promote 1991 as the "Year of the Bill of Rights in Los Angeles." Programs designed to involve the entire community, especially thousands of immigrants in the area, included conferences, mock trials, poster and essay contests, seminars for teachers and librarians, and the encouragement of a Bill of Rights semester in all Los Angeles city and county schools beginning in September. The Foundation's newsletter, *Bill of Rights in Action,* containing articles and other information on the history of rights, was made available to schools.

With a grant from the national Commission and the use of the Commission's adult education materials, the National Institute for Citizen Education in the Law and the Correctional Education Association developed a program designed to educate the U.S. prison population about the values, rights, and responsibilities of the Constitutional system. Through training provided for 36 teachers, 12 librarians, and 12 administrators, the 18-month program projected the involvement of 59,000 student-inmates. Meeting for the first time in July 1991, the program's advisory board, chaired by Chief Justice Burger, included officers of eight organizations involved with the correctional system nationwide.

State Humanities Councils continued to initiate outstanding educational programs for the general public. The Pennsylvania Humanities Council, for example, produced a 12-poster display, *To Preserve These Rights,* for schools, universities, and other public facilities. Each panel illustrated a particular set of rights along with the

Pennsylvania Humanities Council poster.

text of the relevant Amendments, captioned photographs, and quotations by key statesmen and jurists who had helped shape modern understanding of the Bill of Rights. An educational user's guide, which contained historical background and the development of the various rights, accompanied the posters, which were mounted on three free-standing kiosks.

The Virginia Foundation for the Humanities published a limited edition of George Mason's Virginia Declaration of Rights on vellum in a six-page folder, including a portrait of Mason and the Great Seal of the Commonwealth of Virginia, which had been adopted in 1776 on Mason's recommendation. Other such state humanities councils, with the assistance of the Federation of State Humanities Councils, used the Commission's adult education booklet series, *The Constitution . . . Let's Talk About It,* as discussion materials in workshops in Idaho, New Mexico, Ohio, Oregon, Pennsylvania, South Carolina, South Dakota, Texas, Utah, and Washington. Participants included representatives of civic organizations, ethnic groups, libraries, correctional education programs, junior and community colleges, religious organizations, women's organizations, and senior citizen centers.

Phi Beta Kappa Associates, under a Bill of Rights theme, presented its 1991 Career Achievement Award to Dr. John Hope Franklin, Duke University Professor of History, October 18, 1991, at the National Archives. A former president of Phi Beta Kappa and of the American Historical Association, Dr. Franklin discussed "The

Erratic Course of the Bill of Rights in the Early Days" and explained how its provisions may have been unevenly applied in the early history of the United States under the Constitution.

The U.S. Capitol Historical Society sponsored a two-day symposium, "The Bill of Rights: Government Proscribed," as part of its annual series on important issues in American history. Scholars such as Forrest McDonald and Kenneth Bowling provided analyses on the drafting and ratification of the Bill of Rights and its influence on American society during the previous two centuries. The Council for the Advancement of Citizenship concluded its Bicentennial programs in May 1991 with the tenth annual Jennings Randolph Forum, focusing on "The Bill of Rights — Our Common Compact: First Principles and Lasting Values," which was attended by representatives of educational and civic organizations.

In ceremonies at the U.S. Supreme Court in September 1990, Chief Justice Burger joined representatives of Kiwanis International in signing a proclamation launching that organization's commemoration of the Bill of Rights. The leaders encouraged individual chapters to undertake their own programs. The Kiwanis Club of Pittsburgh, for example, prepared a broadside on the Bill of Rights for distribution to immigrants from the Soviet Union. Rather than simply listing the Amendments, the document described the protections and rights that each amendment guarantees all citizens. Prepared for distribution to Pittsburgh schools and community organizations, the broadside was also picked up by other groups and used to help teach the U.S. system of government. Kiwanis arranged with the American Civil Liberties Union (ACLU) for a Russian translation, and the Legal Committee for Soviet Refugees in Pittsburgh distributed the document, which was also translated into Spanish. The ACLU, always involved in the many aspects of individual rights, commemorated the Bill of Rights Bicentennial through affiliates across the nation with a variety of speeches, programs, and posters.

Bar associations across the nation continued to make a significant impact. For example, in New Jersey, in addition to the commemorative events held in Perth Amboy (see page 217), the Committee on Public Education of the New Jersey Bar Foundation awarded U.S. Savings Bond prizes to elementary, middle, and high school students who submitted the winning original essay, short story, one-act play, poem, song, musical composition, or artwork promoting greater understanding of the Bill of Rights.

The American Legion produced a Bill of Rights coloring book for elementary schoolchildren, using pictures and simplified sentences to emphasize principles such as freedom of speech, the right to a speedy trial, and protection against cruel and unusual punishment. Many American Legion posts provided copies of the coloring book — a sequel to the 1987 version on the drafting and signing of the Constitution — to schools, while others used them in local coloring contests.

A needlepoint sampler, the creation of Mrs. Deborah Vanderwende of Greenwood, Delaware, was selected as a first-place winner in the annual National Grange "Loving Legacy" needlepoint competition. The Bicentennial Commission accepted the sampler at a September 11 ceremony at the headquarters building of the National Grange in Washington, D.C. The Grange conducted several educational programs and activities promoting the Bicentennial of the Constitution and distributed posters, a Bicentennial cookbook, and the Commission's adult education materials. The "Loving Legacy" contest, conducted by the Grange in partnership with the Coats and Clark thread company, generated over 1,000 needlepoint entries.

One of the winners of the National Grange's competition proudly displays her winning needlepoint entry.

National Grange

PRIVATE CORPORATIONS

The commemoration of the Bicentennial would not have been possible without the generous support of America's companies and corporations. The contributions of American Express, BellSouth, General Mills, IBM, International Paper, McDonald's, Merrill Lynch, Nabisco, United Parcel Service, USA Today, West Publishing, Xerox, and many others helped to bring about some of the Bicentennial's most successful events and programs. This outstanding support culminated with the commemoration of the Bill of Rights.

An original copy of the Bill of Rights sent to Virginia for ratification in 1789 was the featured attraction in a multimedia exhibit that traveled to all 50 states from October 1991 to February 1992. Sponsored by Philip Morris Companies, Inc., the display occupied a 5,000-square-foot pavilion complete with state-of-the-art sound, lighting, and audiovisual systems and protected 24 hours a day by security alarms and guards. Visitors learned the background and history of the Bill of Rights through a collection of video images and graphic displays — and could stand within arm's length of a special capsule that protected the original copy. They then entered a post-show area where they could reflect on the Amendments as they viewed a collection of displays. The exhibit was open to the public free of charge. Philip Morris also developed and distributed to schools a packet of materials on the Bill of Rights.

The Independent Insurance Agents of America (IIA), as part of their national citizenship program, released four public service radio spots featuring actor Raymond Burr promoting the Bicentennial of the Bill of Rights. The IIA, representing 35,000 agencies and 135,000 individual agents, underwrote production of a videotape about democratic principles and constitutional law and distributed it to its members in December 1991. The 14-minute video, which along with the "Equal Justice Under Law" tapes, was shown to local business and civic organizations, featured Chief Justice Burger with Raymond Burr and was shot in the Old Supreme Court Chamber at the U.S. Capitol.

Professional sports organizations, like college sports organizations before them, agreed to integrate the anniversary of the Bill of Rights into their activities. The National Football League gave the Commission's Bill of Rights print ad full-page treatment in the January 1991 Super Bowl XXV commemorative brochure and included the TV public service announcement on the Bill of Rights in its pregame show. With encouragement from the Commission, baseball's All-Star Game and World Series also featured the Bill of Rights, as did several U.S.-based clubs in the National Hockey League during games scheduled the weekend of December 15.

McDonald's, through its 8,764 restaurants — serving 18 million customers each day — produced and distributed in 1991 two commemorative trayliners entitled "Securing the Blessings of Liberty." The first, on "The Creation of the Bill of Rights," depicted the face of the Statue of Liberty, and the second, "The Guarantees of the Bill of Rights," quoted the first ten Amendments to the Constitution under a picture of the Supreme Court Building facade showing the words "Equal Justice Under Law." The BellSouth telephone company commissioned two Bill of Rights covers for its 1991 yellow page directories, more than 10 million copies of which were distributed in states covered by that company's service. IBM produced a poster, *What the Bill of Rights Means to Me,* on which it listed the first ten Amendments to the Constitution for an essay contest it sponsored in the Detroit Public Schools.

MEDIA

The Bill of Rights commemoration was especially important to the nation's media because of the First Amendment protections of freedom of the press and of speech. The 1991 commemoration generated many outstanding special editions, supplements, and documentaries by the print and electronic media.

To commemorate the Bicentennial of the Bill of Rights, the First Amendment Congress, which was organized in 1979 at the University of Colorado at

Denver's School of Public Affairs, opened its October 1991 conference, "A Time for Choices," at the state capitol in Richmond, Virginia, the site of that state's decisive Bill of Rights ratification. With 150 delegates and 40 speakers in attendance, the conference examined issues concerning freedom of speech, of the press, and of conscience. Chief Justice Burger, introduced by Rita Klimova, Czechoslovakia's Ambassador to the United States, was the keynote speaker at the final luncheon session of the three-day gathering. The conference compiled the final resolutions and published them in a report for distribution to key representatives of government, business, religion, education, and the media. The organization also published *A Time For Choices,* a book of 13 essays by leading scholars on topics related to the Bill of Rights.

Special Bill of Rights supplements appeared during 1991 in several prominent newspapers, including *The Philadelphia Inquirer,* which featured a score of articles dealing with the Bill of Rights in general and with specific rights as well. *The St. Louis Post-Dispatch* published 37 articles and a quiz on the Bill of Rights from October 8 through December 15, 1991. All of these features were later republished in a 28-page 12-part reprint special.

Parade magazine and Eastman Kodak cosponsored a yearlong photo contest to commemorate the Bicentennial of the Bill of Rights. The contest opening

LEARN ABOUT THE BILL OF RIGHTS

"IT'S THE SUPREME THING TO DO!"

Private corporations were deeply involved in the Bill of Rights celebration. McDonald's distributed commemorative trayliners throughout the country (opposite page); Knight-Ridder produced a poster (above) for the Newspapers in Education program; Parade magazine and Kodak cosponsored a Bill of Rights photo contest (left).

SHE'S BEEN ABLE TO VOTE FOR 71 YEARS.

OF COURSE, SHE WON'T BE GOING TO THE POLLS FOR QUITE A WHILE. NOT TOO LONG AGO, WOMEN COULDN'T VOTE JUST BECAUSE THEY WERE WOMEN. IN 1920, WITH THE PASSAGE OF THE NINETEENTH AMENDMENT TO THE U.S. CONSTITUTION, AMERICAN WOMEN'S SUFFRAGE BECAME A REALITY. THE TWENTY-SIX AMENDMENTS TO OUR CONSTITUTION ENSURE THAT THOSE FREEDOMS WE TREASURE REMAIN SAFE FOR FUTURE GENERATIONS. FIND OUT MORE ABOUT YOUR AMERICAN FREEDOMS, WRITE TO: THE COMMISSION ON THE BICENTENNIAL OF THE U.S. CONSTITUTION, 808 17TH STREET, N.W., WASHINGTON, D.C. 20006-3999. TELEPHONE (202)-USA-1787.

The opinions expressed herein do not necessarily reflect the views of the sponsoring organizations.

was announced in the January 27, 1991, issue, which also carried an accompanying introductory article on the Bill of Rights, "What It Means To Us," by Chief Justice Burger. Several subsequent 1991 issues carried several additional articles on various contemporary aspects of the Bill of Rights. *Life* magazine produced a Fall Special issue on the Bill of Rights, including a dozen articles on its history and meaning and on several of the most popular Amendments and their modern interpretation.

Through their Project '87, the American Historical Association and the American Political Science Association published in the fall of 1991 a special issue of *This Constitution* featuring the Bill of Rights. In addition to several scholarly articles on the subject, the journal contained a bibliography, list of resources, and chronology of historic dates and events. *Cobblestone,* the history magazine for young people, devoted its September 1991 issue to "Our Bill of Rights." With the collaboration of the national Commission, *Cobblestone* covered eight articles written at a middle school level on the history and application of the Bill of Rights to modern problems and issues. The magazine distributed 50,000 copies of this issue and provided an equal number to the Commission for further dissemination.

The American Newspaper Publishers Association (ANPA) Foundation and the International Reading Association cosponsored a Newspapers in Education (NIE) program, which used newspapers for educational purposes. During 1991, NIE encouraged students to study the daily news to learn more about the impact of the Bill of Rights on their lives. In connection with this program, the Knight-Ridder newspaper chain produced and distributed a poster—showing Chief Justice Burger standing with students from Washington area schools on the steps of the Supreme Court — with the caption "Learn about your Bill of Rights! It is the *supreme* thing to do!" ANPA provided its membership of 2,500 publishers and editors of 1,400 daily newspapers, as well as 2,000 NIE representatives, with Commission-produced materials that included an op-ed piece by Chief Justice Burger and a copy of the "Bill of Rights and Beyond Teach About" poster. ANPA also made copies of the Commission's pocket Constitution available to readers who requested them. The Commission's Chairman gave the keynote address on May 16, 1991, to the NIE conference in New Orleans, and the NIE Information Service developed and distributed a teaching guide on the history of the Bill of Rights and how the Amendments were used today.

As a sequel to its 1987 syndication of Chief Justice Burger's series of articles on the Constitution, the Associated Press made available to daily newspapers through its news service a 22-article series written by the Commission's Chairman on the Bill of Rights. The articles discussed not only those rights protected by the Bill of Rights, but also those safeguarded by subsequent Amendments to the Constitution. Sample titles included "Why Did We Need a Bill of Rights in 1787?" "First Amendment: Freedom of Religion," and "The

Framers' Failure to Outlaw Slavery." The Commission also sent the articles to some 2,000 weekly newspapers. As a sequel to its 1987 special supplement on the Constitution, the National Newspaper Association disseminated a six-page tabloid to its member newspapers for use as a supplement, including an introductory message by Chief Justice Burger, articles on the "Bill of Rights and Beyond," and camera-ready copies of the Commission's public service ads.

During the year, the National Press Foundation in cooperation with the National Press Club sponsored a series of lunches and forums on the Bill of Rights at the Club headquarters in Washington, D.C. Chief Justice Burger moderated one such forum on "The First Amendment: What's It Worth Today?" Topics ranged from the media's right to cover a war (in the Persian Gulf) without government censorship to the issue of whether or not journalists should be required to reveal their sources. Panel participants included former USIA Director Leonard Marks; Barbara Cohen, Vice President of CBS News; Clark Hoyt, Washington Bureau Chief for Knight-Ridder Newspapers; James Vicini, Reuters News Service; journalist Dan E. Moldea; and James E. Kirtley, Reporters Committee for Freedom of the Press.

In preparation for the Bill of Rights commemoration, the American Academy of Advertising and the International Newspaper Advertising and Marketing Executives joined with the national Commission in cosponsoring a nationwide competition for college students to develop a newspaper advertising campaign that would increase awareness of the Bill of Rights. Some 2,000 students responded and designed their own campaigns to answer the question: "What would life be like without the Bill of Rights?" The Commission provided research materials to help students gain insights into the subject. The national first- and second-place winners, Lynn Collins and James S. McMullen, were both from the University of Florida, while the third-place winner was Cheryl Warren from the University of Nebraska. The top regional and national ads were bound into a book that was made available for reproduction without cost to magazines, newspapers, newsletters, and brochures, and the Commission used some of the entries in its own ad campaign.

During 1991, Betty Debnam's *The Mini Page* featured a series of articles on the history of the Bill of Rights and its role in daily life, and on the men who inspired the amendments that became the Bill of Rights. Distributed in Sunday supplements around the nation, this series was followed by another on major Supreme Court cases that have defined and interpreted the Bill of Rights over the years. The series concluded Betty Debnam's many contributions to the Bicentennial.

The broadcasting industry also made a significant nationwide impact during the Bill of Rights commemoration. In addition to the special anniversary radio tribute already mentioned (*see page 226*), other activities are worthy of note. The National Association of Broadcasters, following its own 1987 example, produced and disseminated to all its member radio and television stations a 14-page booklet including 20 vignettes on the Bill of Rights; a mock news interview with Hamilton, Jefferson, and Madison; a Bill of Rights quiz; and suggested editorials urging Americans to learn more about the Constitution and Bill of Rights. CBS Radio produced in May 1991 a 30-minute interview with Chief Justice Burger on the evolution of courts and the legal system under the Constitution, how citizen awareness of the Constitution may have been heightened by the Bicentennial commemoration, and a discussion of each Amendment and its meaning. CBS disseminated the interview to its owned-and-operated stations.

New books appeared in 1991 on the Bill of Rights, including *In Our Defense: The Bill of Rights in Action,* by Ellen Alderman and Caroline Kennedy; *Images of a Free Press: The History of the Bill of Rights,* by Lee C. Bollinger; *A People's Charter: The Pursuit of Rights in America,* by James McGregor Burns and Stewart Burns; *Visions of Liberty: The Bill of Rights for All Americans,* by Ira Glasser; *A Culture of Rights: The Bill of Rights in Philosophy, Politics, and Law, 1791-1991,* edited by Michael J. Lacey and Knud Haakonssen; and *The Bill of Rights and the Politics of Interpretation,* by Robert S. Peck. The previous year, West Publishing had issued *The Bill of Rights and You,* edited by Steve Jenkins et al., a series of case histories and other material for use in secondary schools.

Among educational texts appearing in 1991 was John Patrick and Robert Leming's *Resources for Teachers on the Bill of Rights.* Published by the ERIC Clearinghouse for the Social Studies with financial support from the national Commission and the Bill of Rights Collaborative *(see page 241),* the book included a series of background papers on the Bill of Rights, a collection of primary documents, and selected lesson plans for elementary, middle, and high school use.

Patrick T. Conley and John P. Kaminsky edited *The Bill of Rights and the States: The Colonial and Revolutionary Origins of American Liberties,* a book sponsored by the U.S. Constitution Council of the Thirteen Original States and the Center for the Study of the American Constitution, with funding by the national Commission. With articles on each of the 13 states by leading scholars, the book was written for the general reader and as a standard reference for students at the high school and college level. Dr. Conley presented the bound page proofs of the new book to the Commission at the Philadelphia ceremony on December 15 *(see page 227).* Published in 1992, it followed a 1988 work by the same editors, *The Constitution and the States (see Chapter IV).* The Bill of Rights book brought to an end the work of the Constitution Council, which had been established in June 1970 and had thereafter done much to commemorate the nation's founding.

An important reference book on the Constitution in general also appeared in 1991 — *The Language of the Constitution: A Sourcebook and Guide to the Ideas, Terms, and Vocabulary Used by the Framers of the United States Constitution,* edited by Thurston Greene et al., with a foreword by Chief Justice Burger. A new biography of

Benjamin Franklin by William Carr, *The Oldest Delegate,* was published, focusing on Franklin's contribution to the Constitutional Convention. Project Innovation, of Chula Vista, California, used a Bill of Rights theme for the Fall 1991 issue of its scholarly journal, *Education,* which was officially recognized by the national Commission and contained several articles devoted to the subject. Many university law reviews published a wide range of articles on the Bill of Rights and other Constitutional rights during this commemorative year.

INTERNATIONAL

As the Bicentennial commemoration drew to a close, the influence of the enduring United States Constitution and Bill of Rights continued to gather momentum throughout the world. The national Commission provided assistance to *InterPulse* — a youth-oriented supplement in *Komsomolskaya Pravda* (then the former Soviet Union's largest newspaper, with 18 million readers) — for a special issue featuring Bill of Rights material, including an adaptation of Chief Justice Burger's Bill of Rights article from *Parade* magazine (*see page 255*). *InterPulse* published a Bill of Rights cover story with a guest editorial by President Bush and other articles that provided its Soviet readers with a distinctly American perspective.

Among other initiatives in commemorating the Bill of Rights, the Voice of America broadcast the story of the Bill of Rights to the Republic of Georgia on the Bicentennial of its ratification, December 15, 1991. The program incorporated portions of the text from the 1991 Commission Bill of Rights calendar. Following the broadcast, the Voice of America distributed throughout the republic the text of the program in booklet form. The Commission's Chairman participated in overseas broadcasts through the facilities of USIA's Worldnet system. One broadcast to Moscow, in July 1990 with the Russian broadcaster Vladimir Pozner, concerned the reform of Russian constitutional law. Another program, broadcast to Bulgaria in the fall of 1991, compared Bulgaria's new constitution with the U.S. Constitution. A third broadcast to Madrid, Spain, in April 1992, concerned the original copy of the Bill of Rights then on display at Seville Expo '92.

The Bill of Rights theme also prompted a number of international essay contests. In Latin America, the contests featured topics appropriate for each country, designed to encourage young students to consider the responsibilities of citizenship and freedom. First prize winners were Miss Tripti Lahiri from Peru and Mr. Francisco Jose Correa from Ecuador, who each won a trip to Washington D.C. American Airlines donated the air fare, and the Bicentennial Commission organized a two-day itinerary. In Poland, the law faculty at the University of Warsaw sponsored an essay contest for law school students on the topic "Constitutionalism in Poland and in the World." Mr. Krzysztof Golynski submitted the winning essay and was awarded a week-long trip to Washington as a guest of USIA. That year, Mr. Golynski received his Master of Law degree and

began to teach Constitutional Law at Warsaw University Law School. The Commission presented him with books and videotapes useful for his teaching.

The winner of another contest was Miss Eufrosinia G. Carlos, a 12-year-old sixth-grade student from Guagua, Pampanga, a remote village in the Philippines. In her winning essay she wrote, "All these written laws embodied in the Bill of Rights, I believe, are rooted in the Golden Rule: 'Do unto others what you would like them to do unto you,' or simply put, Do good to others." Miss Carlos received a $500 cash prize and a one-week all-expense-paid trip to Disneyland in Anaheim, California. In the United Kingdom, a contest for undergraduates at 30 British universities required an essay on "What lessons does the American experience have for the proposed Bill of Rights in Great Britain?" Barry Lee, a former police constable and a student at the University of Hull in northern England, won a Commission-sponsored trip to Washington, D.C., and subsequently enrolled at the University of South Carolina for his junior year abroad.

*E*ssay contest winners: Singapore (left), Latin America (above).

The USIA cooperated with the national Commission to provide 110 sets of reference books on the Constitution to colleges, universities, and high courts in Eastern Europe, Latin America, and Asia. This was in direct response to requests from USIA public affairs officers for more information on the Bill of Rights. An earlier effort placed "bookshelves" of reference books on constitutional law in the court libraries of 45 African countries. The Commission filled requests right to the end of its days for the "Bill of Rights Bookshelf" through USIA, and Peace Corps volunteers wrote frequently for extra copies of the POCKET CONSTITUTION and other materials to assist them in their service abroad.

CONCLUSION

Both the Bill of Rights commemoration and the Bicentennial itself drew to a close during the traditional season of hope and goodwill, in a year when peoples around the world looked forward to continued expansion of human freedom. America remained the great beacon for such aspirations. Her Constitution and Bill of Rights were — as President Bush said the year before — "nothing less than the sum of human hope."

EPILOGUE: 1992

Since it is unlikely that those who take part in one Constitutional anniversary will be available for a later one, we conclude this report to the President, the Congress, the Judiciary — and the American people — with the hope that apart from fulfilling the statutory mandate for a final report, it may also serve as a useful guide to our colleagues charged with the celebration in the year 2037.

The Spanish philosopher Ortega y Gasset said that nations are not defined by what they have been so much as what they are to become. Our country surely exemplifies this truism. People who came here in the seventeenth through the nineteenth centuries were looking ahead and sought to put the "old country" and all of its negative memories behind them. Swedish immigrants, for example, called America *framtidslandet* — land of the future. Fortunately those early arrivals were not burdened by the kind of past political, ethnic, and religious conflicts we see bearing bloody fruit in central Europe today.

Gorbachev's *perestroika* and *glasnost,* followed by Yeltsin's response to the dissolution of the Soviet Union and the collapse of Communism, came about just as the Bicentennial's celebration was evolving. These developments shed new light on the American experience of two centuries of "openness" and "change" and probably led the Eastern European states and the Russian republics — and indeed the rest of the world — to take a closer look at what happened in our own country beginning with Concord and Lexington, the Declaration of Independence, and the miracle at Philadelphia. Those who fought and died at Concord and Lexington were fighting for the values that were declared in the Bill of Rights — values that distinguish our system from most others. With these values as our guide, we made enormous progress from the signing of the Mayflower Compact to the birth of freedom around the world today. But in the long reach of history, America is still hardly more than an experiment in human government, albeit one that has remained on its original course under its original charter for longer than any other in history.

We must never forget Benjamin Franklin's warning at the close of the Constitutional Convention in 1787, when he said that the Framers had wrought "a Republic — if you can keep it." As we stand on the threshold of our third century, the challenges to our system of government should serve to remind us of the fragility of freedom and the impermanence of human institutions. Now it remains to be seen whether our leaders will have the wisdom and the courage to resist the accumulation of asserted "entitlements" and firmly declare that the only permanent "entitlements" are those defined in the Constitution and Bill of Rights. History tells us that more societies have disintegrated from internal weakness than from external attack.

We have every reason to hope that the young people of today, the leaders of tomorrow, will become better citizens because of the programs initiated during this Bicentennial. If so, our Commission will surely have made a difference.

Our priceless legacy of freedom now passes into the safekeeping of another generation of Americans. On the day of the great celebration in Philadelphia, at 4:00 p.m. on September 17, 1987 — the precise historic moment of the 200th anniversary of the signing of the Constitution — Chief Justice Burger, Chairman of the Bicentennial Commission, was asked to ring a replica of the Liberty Bell at Independence Hall. In a photograph of that event, which the Liberty Bell Foundation has preserved in an oil painting (see pages 62-63), the Commission Chairman handed the bell-rope to a cluster of children sitting nearby, saying, "It's yours, and it's up to you to keep it ringing."

Photography by Harlee Little

A SAMPLING OF COMMEMORATIVE ITEMS, TEACHING MATERIALS, SCHOLARSHIP, AND STUDENT SCHOOLWORK PRODUCED BY MANY ORGANIZATIONS AND INDIVIDUALS DURING THE YEARS OF THE BICENTENNIAL

An Act

To provide for the establishment of a Commission on the
Bicentennial of the Constitution.

*Be it enacted by the Senate and House of Representatives of the
United States of America in Congress assembled,* That there is
established a Commission on the Bicentennial of the United States
Constitution, hereinafter referred to as the "Commission". The
Commission shall have an official seal, which shall be judicially
noticed.

FINDINGS

SEC. 2. The Congress finds that —

(1) the bicentennial of the Constitutional Convention's adoption of the Constitution occurs on September 17, 1987;

(2) the Constitution enunciates the limitations on government, the inalienable rights, and the timeless principle of individual
liberty and responsibility, and equality before law, for the people of
the United States of America;

(3) this document has set an enduring example of representative democracy for the world; and

(4) the maintenance of the common principles that animate
our Republic depend upon a knowledge and understanding of their
roots and origins.

PURPOSE

SEC. 3. (a) It is the purpose of this Act to establish a Commission to
promote and coordinate activities to commemorate the bicentennial
of the Constitution.

(b) It is not the purpose of this Act to preempt any unit of State
or local government from celebrating the bicentennial of the
Constitution, and nothing in this Act shall prevent any such unit
from establishing its own logo, symbol, or mark in connection
therewith.

MEMBERSHIP

SEC. 4. (a) The Commission shall be composed of twenty-three
members as follows:

(1) twenty members appointed by the President, four of whom
shall be appointed from among the recommendations made by the
Speaker of the House of Representatives (in consultation with the
minority leader of the House of Representatives), four of whom shall
be appointed from among the recommendations made by the
President pro tempore of the Senate, in consultation with the
majority leader and minority leader of the Senate, and four of whom
shall be appointed from among the recommendations made by the
Chief Justice of the United States;

(2) the Chief Justice of the United States, or his designee;

(3) the President pro tempore of the Senate, or his designee;
and

(4) the Speaker of the House of Representatives, or his
designee.

(b) Each of the individuals making recommendations to the
President regarding appointments shall seek to achieve a balanced
membership representing, to the maximum extent practicable, the
Nation as a whole. The Commission members shall be chosen from
among individuals who have demonstrated scholarship, a strong
sense of public service, expertise in the learned professions, and
abilities likely to contribute to the fulfillment of the duties of the
Commission.

(c) Members of the Commission shall be appointed for the life
of the Commission.

(d) One of the members shall be designated as Chairman by,
and shall serve in the position of Chairman at the pleasure of, the
President.

(e) Twelve members of the Commission shall constitute a
quorum, but a lesser number may conduct meetings.

(f) A vacancy in the Commission resulting from the death or
resignation of a member shall not affect its powers, and shall be
filled in the same manner in which the original appointment was
made.

ADMINISTRATIVE PROVISIONS AND POWERS

SEC. 5 (a) The Commission shall appoint a staff director who shall
be paid at a rate not to exceed the rate of basic pay provided for level I
of the Executive Schedule pursuant to section 5312 of title 5, United
States Code.

(b) (1) The Commission is authorized to appoint and fix the
compensation of such additional publicly paid personnel as the
Chairman finds necessary to carry out the purposes of of this title.
Such personnel shall be compensated at a rate not to exceed a rate
equal to the maximum rate of pay for GS-18 of the General Schedule
under section 5332 of title 5, United States Code. The Chairman or
the staff director or both may, if so authorized by the Commission,
take any action which the Commission is authorized to take under
the preceding provisions of this paragraph.

(2) The Commission may appoint and fix the pay of such
additional personnel to be paid out of private donations. An
individual appointed to a position funded in such manner shall be
so designated at the time of such individual's appointment. The
Chairman or the staff director or both may, if so authorized by the
Commission, take any action which the Commission is authorized
to take under the preceding provisions of this paragraph.

(c) Appointments and compensation under subsection (b) (1)
or (2) of this section may be made without regard to the provisions
of title 5, United States Code, governing appointments in the
competitive service, and without regard to chapter 51 and
subchapter III of chapter 53 of such title relating to classification and
General Schedule pay rates.

(d) Each member of the Commission shall serve without being
compensated as a member of such Commission, except that each
member shall be reimbursed for travel, subsistence, and other
necessary expenses incurred by them in the performance of their
duties.

(e) Upon request of the Commission, the head of any Federal
agency may detail any of the personnel of such agency to the
Commission to assist the Commission in carrying out its duties
under this Act. Details under this subsection shall be without
reimbursement by the Commission to the agency from which the
employee concerned was detailed.

(f) The Commission is authorized to procure supplies, services,
and property, and make contracts, in any fiscal year, only to such
extent or in such amounts as are provided in appropriation Acts or
are donated pursuant to subsection (h) of this section.

(g) The Commission is authorized to enter into agreements
with the General Services Administration for procurement of
necessary financial and administrative services, for which payment

shall be made by reimbursement of funds of the Commission in such amounts as may be agreed upon by the Chairman and the Administrator of the General Services Administration.

(h) (1) The Commission is authorized to accept, use, solicit, and dispose of donations of money, property, or personal services.

(2) The Commission shall prescribe regulations under which the Commission may accept donations of money, property, or personal services, except that under such regulations, the Commission may not accept donations —

(A) the value of which exceeds $250,000 annually, in the case of donations from an individual; or

(B) the value of which exceeds $1,000,000 annually, in the case of donations from a corporation, partnership, or other business organization.

(3) The regulations prescribed under this subsection shall include procedures for determining the value of donations of property or personal services.

(4) The limitations set forth in this subsection shall not apply in the case of an organization if it is an organization described in section 501(c)(3) of the Internal Revenue Code of 1954 (26 U.S.C. 501 (c)(3)), and exempt from taxation under section 501(a) of such Code.

(i) The Commission may use the United States mails in the same manner and under the same conditions as other departments and agencies of the United States.

(j) (1) For the purpose of this Act, the term "Bicentennial logo" means the symbol or mark designated by the Commission for use in connection with the commemoration of the bicentennial of the Constitution.

(2) The Commission may, in accordance with rules and regulations which the Commission shall prescribe, authorize the manufacture, reproduction, use, sale, or distribution of the Bicentennial logo. Such rules and regulations shall provide, among other things, that all projects, goods, and services as to which use of the logo is authorized shall be educational or commemorative, and shall relate to the bicentennial of the United States Constitution, the establishment of the Federal Government, or the Bill of Rights, and none of such projects, goods or services shall exploit the United States Constitution or the Bill of Rights. The purpose of the Commission in authorizing use of the logo shall not be primarily or exclusively to raise funds.

(3) Rules and regulations referred to in paragraph (2) shall include provisions under which —

(A) fees may be charged for any authorization under this subsection (including circumstances under which any such fee may be waived);

(B) any authorization granted under this subsection shall not be subject to reassignment or transfer without approval by the Commission; and

(C) any authorization granted under this subsection may be revoked or otherwise terminated.

(4) (A) Whoever, except as authorized under this subsection, manufactures, reproduces, uses, sells, or distributes the Bicentennial logo —

(i) shall be fined not more than $250 or imprisoned not more than 6 months, or both; and

(ii) shall be subject to a civil penalty in an amount equal to the amount of the fee which would have been payable by that person under paragraph (3) (A).

(B) Section 701 of title 18, United States Code, shall not apply with respect to the Bicentennial logo.

(5) Amounts charged under paragraph (3) (A) shall be available to the Commission.

(6) Notice of designation under paragraph (1) shall be published in the Federal Register.

(k) The Commission may transfer funds received by it to another Federal department or agency if the Commission determines that the use of such funds by such department or agency would promote the commemoration of the bicentennial of the Constitution. This subsection is effective only to the extent and in such amounts as are provided in advance in appropriation Acts.

(l) The Commission may issue rules and regulations to carry out the purposes of this Act.

(m) Amounts received under subsection (h) and subsection (j) of this section shall be available to the Commission for official reception and representation expenses.

(n) An income account shall be available to the Commission without fiscal year limitations for printing, without regard to section 501 of title 44, and for distribution of Commission publications. The capital for the account shall consist of receipts from sales of Commission publications bearing the Bicentennial logo, including receipts received prior to the date of enactment of this subsection. Any obligated and unexpended balance in the account which the Commission determines to be in excess of amounts needed for printing and distribution of publications, and any unobligated balance remaining in the account on December 31, 1991, shall be deposited in the Treasury of the United States.

DUTIES OF THE COMMISSION

SEC. 6. (a) The Commission shall —

(1) plan and develop activities appropriate to commemorate the bicentennial of the Constitution, including a limited number of projects to be undertaken by the Federal Government seeking to harmonize and balance the important goals of ceremony and celebration with the equally important goals of scholarship and education;

(2) encourage private organizations, and State and local governments to organize and participate in bicentennial activities commemorating or examining the drafting, ratification, and history of the Constitution and the specific features of the document;

(3) coordinate, generally, activities throughout all of the States; and

(4) serve as a clearinghouse for the collection and dissemination of information about bicentennial events and plans.

(b) In planning and implementing appropriate activities to commemorate the bicentennial, the Commission shall give due consideration to —

(1) the historical setting in which the Constitution was developed and ratified, including such antecedents as the Federalist Papers, the Articles of Confederation, and the ratification debates in the States;

(2) the contribution of diverse ethnic and racial groups;

(3) the relationship and historical development of the three branches of the Government;

(4) the importance of activities concerning the Constitution and citizenship education throughout all of the States regardless of when such State achieved statehood;

(5) the unique achievements and contributions of the participants in the Constitutional Convention of 1787 and the State ratification proceedings;

(6) the diverse legal and philosophical views regarding the Constitution;

(7) the need for reflection upon both academic and scholarly views of the Constitution and the principle that the document must be understood by the general public;

(8) the substantive provisions of the Constitution itself;

(9) the impact of the Constitution on American life and government;

(10) the need to encourage appropriate educational curriculums designed to educate students at all levels of learning on the

CONTINUED NEXT PAGE

drafting, ratification, and history of the Constitution and the specific provisions of that document; and

(11) the significance of the principles and institutions of the Constitution to other nations and their citizens.

(c) The Commission shall seek the cooperation, advice, and assistance from both private and governmental agencies and organizations, including the National Endowment for the Arts, the National Endowment for the Humanities, the Library of Congress, the Smithsonian Institution, the National Archives, the Department of the Interior, State and local governments, learned societies, academic institutions, and historical, patriotic, philanthropic, civic, and professional groups, and bar associations. All such governmental agencies and organizations shall cooperate with the Commission, to the extent allowed by law, in providing advice and assistance requested by the Commission.

(d) The Commission may, in carrying out the purposes of this Act, delegate authority to State advisory commissions to assist in implementing this Act.

(e) Within two years after the date of enactment of this Act, the Commission shall submit to the President and each House of the Congress and the Judicial Conference of the United States a comprehensive report incorporating specific recommendations of the Commission for commemoration and coordination of the bicentennial and related activities. Such report shall include recommendations for publications, scholarly projects, conferences, programs, films, libraries, exhibits, ceremonies, and other projects, competitions and awards, and a calendar of major activities and events planned to commemorate specific historical dates. Each year after such comprehensive report, the Commission shall submit an annual report to the President, each House of the Congress, and the Judicial Conference until such Commission terminates.

TERMINATION

SEC. 7. The Commission shall terminate on June 30, 1992.

AUTHORIZATION OF APPROPRIATIONS

SEC. 8. There are authorized to be appropriated to carry out the purposes of this Act $300,000 for fiscal year 1984 and such sums as may be necessary for the subsequent fiscal years through fiscal year 1991.

EFFECTIVE DATE

SEC. 9. This Act shall become effective on the date of enactment.

LEGISLATIVE HISTORY

Pub. L. 98-101: S. 118; Senate Report 96-68 (Comm. on Judiciary)

Pub. L. 99-549: H.R. 3559; House Report 99-530 (Comm. on Post Office and Civil Service)

Pub. L. 100-459: H.R. 4782; House Report 100-979 (Comm. of Conference)

Pub. L. 102-181: H.R. 3728; S. 1969

DISCRETIONARY GRANT AUTHORITY

As a part of its FY 1989 appropriation, Congress authorized the Commission to make discretionary grants of federal assistance in accordance with the Federal Grant and Cooperative Agreement Act. (Title V of Public Law 101-62, 103 Stat. 1018, November 21, 1989)

". . . (I)n carrying out the purposes of this (Appropriation) Act, the Commission is authorized to enter into contracts, grants, or cooperative agreements as directed by the Federal Grant and Cooperative Agreement Act of 1977 (92 Stat. 3; 31 U.S.C. 6301) . . ."

COMMISSION BUDGET SUMMARY

FISCAL YEAR	85	86	87	88	89	90	91	92
BUDGET	$331,000	$12,226,000	$13,200,000	$21,000,000	$6,936,000	$15,005,000	$14,973,000	$1,882,000
EXPENDITURES	$11,400	$2,647,700	$11,200,672	$17,837,652	$16,822,871	$16,736,582	$15,038,000	$2,735,368
GRANTS	$0	$0	$3,700,000	$12,500,000	$7,500,000	$7,500,000	$7,500,000	$0
We the People 200			0	1,000,000	0	0	0	
Montpelier			0	1,000,000	0	0	0	
Law Centers (Loyola/Drake)			0	3,000,000	0	0	0	
Center for Civic Education			2,700,000	2,850,000	2,992,000	3,142,000	3,300,000	
Commission Education Grants			1,000,000	3,400,000	4,508,000	4,358,000	4,200,000	
Reprogram Authority			0	1,250,000	0	0	0	

INCOME ACCOUNT SUMMARY

Pocket Constitutions	$317,895.97
Calendars	107,871.38
Parchments	5,870.20
Videos	1,210.00
Other/Miscellaneous	75,223.07
Catalog Sales	29,040.29
TOTAL SALES INCOME	$537,110.91
Royalties	431,804.77
Interest	126,407.14
TOTAL INCOME RECEIVED	$1,095,322.82
EXPENDITURES	(623,923.07)
TOTAL AVAILABLE INCOME	$471,399.75

MEMBERS OF THE COMMISSION: SOURCE OF APPOINTMENT

Named by the Statute

Warren E. Burger, Chairman
Chief Justice, United States Supreme Court
Lindy Boggs
United States House of Representatives
(As Designated by the Speaker)
Strom Thurmond
United States Senate

Appointed by the President of the United States

Frederick K. Biebel
Chairman, Bicentennial Council of
the Thirteen Original States
Edward Victor Hill
Pastor, Missionary Hill Baptist Church
William Lucas
Chief Executive Officer,
Wayne County, Michigan
Betty Southard Murphy
Attorney, Baker & Hostetler
Phyllis Schlafly
President, Eagle Forum
Bernard H. Siegan
Professor, University of San Diego
Ronald H. Walker
Director, Korn Ferry International
Charles Alan Wright
Professor, University of Texas at Austin

Appointed by the Senate President Pro Tempore

Edward M. Kennedy
United States Senate
Harry McKinley Lightsey, Jr.
President, College of Charleston
Edward P. Morgan
Attorney, Welch & Morgan
Ted Stevens
United States Senate

Appointed by the Chief Justice of the United States

Herbert Brownell
Attorney, Lord, Day and Lord
Cornelia G. Kennedy
United States Circuit Court
Obert C. Tanner
Chairman, O. C. Tanner Corporation
Charles E. Wiggins
Unites States Court of Appeals

Appointed by the Speaker of the House of Representatives

Lynne V. Cheney
Chairman, National Endowment for
the Humanities
Philip M. Crane
United States Senate
William J. Green
Attorney, MacAndrews & Forbes
Thomas H. O'Connor
Professor, Boston College

Appointed to Replace Original Member

Dennis DeConcini
United States Senate
Mark O. Hatfield
United States Senate
Damon J. Keith
United States Circuit Court

ADVISORY COMMITTEES

Executive Committee

Warren E. Burger, *Chairman*
Herbert Brownell, *Vice Chairman*
Ronald H. Walker, *Vice Chairman*
Frederick K. Biebel
Lindy Boggs
Lynne V. Cheney
Cornelia G. Kennedy
Edward M. Kennedy
Betty Southard Murphy
Thomas H. O'Connor
Ted Stevens
Obert C. Tanner

Committee on Finance

Herbert Brownell, *Chairman*
Frederick K. Biebel
Lynne V. Cheney
William J. Green
Edward Victor Hill
Thomas H. O'Connor
Obert C. Tanner
Ronald H. Walker

Advisory Committee on Educational Projects

Philip M. Crane, *Co-Chairman*
Charles Alan Wright, *Co-Chairman*
Mark O. Hatfield
Cornelia G. Kennedy
Harry McKinley Lightsey, Jr.
Thomas H. O'Connor
Phyllis Schlafly
Obert C. Tanner

Advisory Committee on Federal Liaison

Frederick K. Biebel, *Co-Chairman*
Lindy Boggs, *Co-Chairman*
Herbert Brownell
Philip M. Crane
Strom Thurmond
Charles E. Wiggins

Advisory Committee on International Liaison

Betty Southard Murphy, *Chairman*
Frederick K. Biebel
Edward M. Kennedy
Thomas H. O'Connor
Bernard H. Siegan
Ted Stevens

Advisory Committee on Media

Lynne V. Cheney, *Co-Chairman*
Edward M. Kennedy, *Co-Chairman*
Lindy Boggs
Philip M. Crane
Edward Victor Hill
William Lucas
Bernard H. Siegan
Ronald H. Walker
Charles Alan Wright

Advisory Committee on Personnel and Administration

William Lucas, *Co-Chairman*
Phyllis Schlafly, *Co-Chairman*
William J. Green
Betty Southard Murphy
Ronald H. Walker
Charles E. Wiggins

Advisory Committee on Private Associations and Organizations

Edward Victor Hill, *Co-Chairman*
Obert C. Tanner, *Co-Chairman*
Dennis DeConcini
William Lucas
Phyllis Schlafly
Charles Alan Wright

Advisory Committee on Project Endorsements and Support

Cornelia G. Kennedy, *Chairman*
Frederick K. Biebel
Thomas H. O'Connor
Phyllis Schlafly
Charles E. Wiggins

Advisory Committee on State and Local Liaison

William J. Green, *Co-Chairman*
Phyllis Schlafly, *Co-Chairman*
Lynne V. Cheney
Dennis DeConcini
Harry McKinley Lightsey, Jr.
William Lucas

COMMISSION STAFF

Christine Abry, *Program Coordinator, Meeting Planning*
Vanessa Allen, *Assistant Systems Administrator*
Paul H. Anderson, *Grant Reviewer, Educational Programs*
Major Ronald Anderson, *Program Officer, Private Sector Programs*
Dr. Max N. Andrews, *Director, Special Events*
Patricia L. Andrews, *Publications Officer, Communications*
John Armor, *Program Officer, Private Sector Programs*
Carl Artman, *Federal & International*
Joya Ashe, *Receptionist, Office of Administration*
Dr. Herbert M. Atherton, *Staff Director and Director of Educational Programs*
Patricia Avery, *Senior Press Officer, Communications*
Walter Avis, *Research Assistant, Communications*
Gladys Baez, *Budget Assistant, Office of Administration*
Paul Balach, *Personnel Analyst, Personnel*
Barbara Bannon, *Secretary, Private Sector Programs*
Amy L. Barefoot, *Grant Fiscal Administrator, Educational Programs*
Latricia Barker, *Information Aide, Information Services*
Dr. J. Jackson Barlow, *Associate Director, Educational Programs*
John Barry, *Law Clerk, Office of the Chairman*
Brian Bauman, *Regional Director, Government Affairs*
Leslie Baumgartner, *Intern*
Julia Becker, *Program Manager, Marketing*
Mark Bedingfield, *Administrative Aide, Executive Secretariat*
Evelyn Beebe, *Paralegal, General Counsel*
Michele Bell, *Mail Clerk, Information Services*
Jeffrey Berger, *Intern*
Christopher P. Berns, *Manager of Grant Evaluation, Educational Programs*
Tracy Palmer Berns, *Research Assistant, Educational Programs*
Joanne Bielawski, *Librarian, Information Services*
Deanna Bird, *Project Manager, Marketing*
Charles Boesel, *Special Events Coordinator*
Mary Bohanan, *Program Officer, Marketing*
Specialist Franklin D. Bowen, *Supply Officer, Office of Administration*
Ashby Boyle, *Special Assistant/Law Clerk, Office of the Chairman*
Leo Brady, *Director of Support Services, Office of Adminstration*
Mary Braisted, *Intern*
Kent Brisley, *Coordinator, Special Events*
Steve Britt, *Research Associate, Office of the Staff Director*
Clifford Brown, *Information Assistant, Information Services*
Darrell Brown, *Intern*
Derreck Brown, *Administrative Assistant, Marketing*
Louise M. Brown, *Clerical Aide, Information Services*
Captain Terry Brown, *Program Manager, Private Sector Programs*
Yvonne M. Brown, *Executive Secretary, Office of Administration*
Jerry W. Browning, *Director of Private Sector Programs*
Louise Brunsdale, *Director of International Programs, Logo Licensing*
Renee Brutocao, *Information Assistant, Information Services*
Major William Buckingham, *Director of Project Recognition*
Yolanda Buran, *Secretary, Educational Programs*
Paul Burke, *Administrative Support*
Beth Burn, *Regional Director, Government Programs*
Beth Bush, *Special Event Coordinator*
Christine Butler, *Mail Clerk, Information Services*
York Butler, *Mail Clerk, Information Services*
Patricia Bye, *Executive Assistant, Office of the Staff Director*
Dr. Mark W. Cannon, *Staff Director*
Kathleene Card, *Program Officer, Private Sector Programs*
Susan E. Cardinale, *Grant Reviewer, Educational Programs*
Susan Carleson, *Project Cooordinator, Private Sector Programs*
Mary Carroll, *Executive Secretary, Office of the Staff Director*
A. Barbara Caselli, *Executive Secretary, Office of the Chairman*
Paulette Chapple, *Secretary, Federal and International Programs*
Cheryl Clagett, *Secretary, Office of the Staff Director*
Paul Clark, *Director of Government Affairs*
William Cohane, *Special Assistant, Office of the Chairman*
Katie Colton, *Office of the Staff Director*
William Cone, *Special Event Coordinator*
Doris Connel, *Information Assistant, Information Services*
John Craig, *Administrative Assistant, Office of Administration*
Matt Crook, *Intern*
Dustan Cross, *Intern*
Alice Cumberland, *Secretary, Information Services*

Mark Daniels, *Research Assistant, Educational Programs*
James Danos, *Mail Clerk, Information Services*
Dr. Richard L. Dargan, *Assistant Director, Educational Programs*
Joel Dawson, *Administrative Aide, Office of Administration*
Ann DeCain, *Intern*
M. Scott DeCain, *Intern*
Diane DeRoze, *Intern*
Virginia L. DeRoze, *Associate Director, Educational Programs*
Jennifer Demmon, *Intern*
Deborah L. Devault, *Comptroller, Office of Administration*
Patricia A. Devine, *Director, Meeting Planning*
Willie Diggs, *Mail Clerk, Executive Secretariat*
Edward Dingivan, *Development Committee*
Lois Douglas, *Secretary, Private Sector Programs*
Greg Dovel, *Law Clerk, Office of the Chairman*
Karen Dyson, *Research Assistant, Educational Programs*
Beverly Eakman, *Research Associate, Office of the Staff Director*
Mischa Eaton, *Intern*
Catherine Ecolovet, *Federal and International Programs*
Francene Engel, *Intern*
Darryl Fairley, *Intern*
Lisa Fechtel, *Intern*
Bob Feinman, *Development Committee*
Michael J. Feld, *Program Officer, International Programs*
Larry Ferezan, *Contracting Officer, Support Services*
Anne A. Fickling, *Associate Director, Educational Programs*
Seaman Cheryl Fischer, *Data Entry Clerk, Executive Secretariat*
Preston Ford, *Mail Clerk, Information Services*
Sherry Ford, *Secretary, Private Sector Programs*
Barbara Fraley, *Secretary, Private Sector Programs*
Inga D. Freivalds, *Program Officer, Educational Programs*
Gertrude Fry, *Acting Director, Private Sector Programs*
Maria Galindo, *Program Officer, Private Sector Programs*
Sandra Garcia, *Computer Programmer, Office of Administration*
Pamela Gartrell, *Information Assistant, Information Services*
John Gemma, *Administrative Specialist, Support Services*
Major Charles Gittins, *Contracts Manager, Office of Administration*
Catherine R. Giuffrida, *Clerk Typist, Support Services*
Steve Gold, *Editor and Public Affairs Associate, Communications*
Barbara Green, *Information Assistant, Information Services*
Roy Greenhill, *Administrative Aide, Office of the Chairman*
Steve Greenwood, *Intern*
Diedre Griffin, *Secretary, Office of Administration*
Maria Grindhart, *Intern*
Marilin Gruber, *Office Manager, International Programs*
Elizabeth Gudgell, *Government Affairs*
Donna Hafley, *Data Entry Clerk, Executive Secretariat*
LuVerne Hall, *Executive Secretary, Office of the Staff Director*
Sergeant William Hallem, *Administrative Aide, Office of the Staff Director*
Dr. Elizabeth Hallwell, *Administrative Assustant, Office of the Staff Director*
William G. Hamilton, Jr., *Historian/Writer*
Joan Hanover, *Executive Secretary, Office of the Staff Director*
Barbara A. Hanrahan, *Manager, Marketing and Advertising*
Kemp R. Harshman, *Attorney*
Malcolm Harshman, *Administrative Assistant, Information Services*
Melissa Hatch, *Receptionist, Support Services*
Deborah Hattes, *Federal and International Programs*
LaVerne Hicks, *Administrative Aide, Support Services*
Harriet Hightower, *Office of the Comptroller*
Glenda Hildreth, *Secretary, Office of Administration*
Valerie Hirsch, *Program Coordinator, Private Sector Programs*
Chuck Hobbs, *Intern*
Sandy Hoffman, *Program Analyst, Office of Administration*
Wendy Hoffman, *Intern*
Deborah Holland, *Secretary, Office of the Staff Director*
Catherine Horvath, *Special Events Coordinator*
Jeffrey Hovenier, *Intern*
Harriet Howath, *Private Programs*
Criss Hyde, *Systems Administrator, Office of Administration*

Kim Y. Jackson, *Administrative Assistant, Archives*
Dale Jerome, *Program Coordinator, Private Sector Programs*
Peter Johnson, *Administrative Aide, Support Services*
Everlener M. Jones, *Executive Secretary, Educational Programs*
Yvette Jones, *Intern*
Dr. Arthur P. Kaufmann, *Acting Director, Educational Programs*
Von Keetch, *Law Clerk, Office of the Chairman*
Sergeant Robert N. Kelley, Jr., *Computer Specialist, Information Services*
John Kelly, *Acting Associate Director, Office of Administration*
Julie Kessler, *Intern*
Jae Khu, *Intern*
Janell Khu, *Intern*
Patrick Killoran, *Research Aide, Communications*
Deborah H. Kirk, *Management Consultant, Office of the Chairman*
Nola L. Kotter, *Assistant Coordinator, Educational Programs*
Helen LaBelle, *Secretary, Office of the Staff Director*
Jennifer LaPointe, *Mail Clerk, Information Services*
Camille Landow, *Administrative Aide, Office of Administration*
Kent S. Larsen, *Archivist, and Director of Publications*
Sydney Arlene Lee, *Director of Information Services*
Barbara Lindsey, *Information Assistant, Information Services*
David Louthan, *Administrative Aide, Educational Programs*
Marti Luce, *Systems Analyst, Office of Administration*
Shaun Lund, *Mail Clerk*
John Lusk, *Administrative Assistant, Speakers Bureau*
Frank Maisano, *Intern*
Ronald M. Mann, *Deputy Staff Director*
April Martin, *Data Entry Clerk, Executive Secretariat*
Doreen Martinez, *Mail Clerk, Information Services*
Ronald Martinson, *Congressional Liaison Officer, Government Affairs*
Rhonda Mason, *Secretary, Private Sector Programs*
Gene Mater, *Director of Communications*
Timothy Matheney, *Intern*
Helen P. Mazzello, *Comptroller, Office of Administration*
Sheila McCauley, *Associate Director, Educational Programs*
Ted McConnell, *Associate Director, Marketing*
Mickey McCully, *Budget Analyst, Office of Administration*
John H. McDade, *Acting Director of Administration/Comptroller*
Joseph McGrath, *General Counsel*
Barbara McMahon, *Regional Director, Government Affairs*
Steve McManus, *Regional Director, Government Affairs*
Lt. Colonel Bobbie McMeans, *Program Director, Government Affairs*
Daniel Meador, Jr., *Intern*
Dana Merrill, *Secretary, Office of the Staff Director*
Bonnie Mersinger, *Regional Director, Government Affairs*
Joseph Miller, *Administrative Aide, Government Affairs*
William Moncrief, *Systems Administrator, Office of Administration*
Elizabeth Montalvo, *Budget Assistant, Office of Administration*
Anne Morrison, *Program Officer, Private Programs*
Ronald Morrison, *Assistant Regional Director, Government Affairs*
Nancy Moucha, *Research Associate, Communications*
Anne Murphy, *Intern, Private Sector Programs*
Neil Murphy, *Intern, Communications*
Norman Murphy, *Administrative Aide, Office of the Chairman*
Petty Officer Sophia L. Myles, *Information Assistant/Mail Clerk, Information Services*
W. Todd Nein, *Grant Reviewer, Educational Programs*
Robert Nelson, *Program Officer, Private Programs*
Matthew Neumeier, *Special Assistant, Office of the Chairman*
Major Kelly Nielsen, *Manager of Mail Services, Information Services*
Fred Nielson, *Coordinator, Private Sector Programs*
Patrice Nielson, *Executive Secretary, Office of the Staff Director*
Vadis Nipper, *Budget Analyst, Office of Administration*
Michael Noble, *Special Event Coordinator*
Terry Notari, *Deputy Staff Director, Director of Operations*
Janet O'Meara, *Special Events*
Colonel Patrick O'Meara, *Director of Administration*
Michael Orrick, *Administrative Aide, Support Services*
Sylvia Otten, *Intern, Educational Programs*
Jeanne Ozols, *Associate Director, Government Affairs*
Robert Patterson, *Editor, Communications*
Robert Patton, *Program Officer, Educational Programs*
Cynthia Paul, *Executive Secretary, Office of the Staff Director*
Betty Pendarvis, *Secretary, Personnel*
John Peschong, *Special Events Coordinator*
Joseph R. Phelan, *Associate Director, Educational Programs*
Howard Pickett, *Administrative Aide, Speakers Bureau*
Cora Preston, *Secretary, Federal and International Programs*
Jay N. Price, *Director of Private Sector Programs*

Sheila Probst, *Executive Secretary, Office of the Deputy Director*
Earl Proctor, *Deputy Director, Marketing*
William Pruitt, *Research Aide, Speakers Bureau*
Sheila Quinlin, *Special Events Coordinator*
Denise Rachal, *Intern*
Peter Radvanyi, *Intern*
Elizabeth Grahl Ray, *Administrative Assistant, Support Services*
Jeannie H. Reed, *Personnel Officer*
Bridgid Reidy, *Research Aide, Federal and International Programs*
Donald E. Reilly, *Director of Communications and International Programs*
Brooke Reuther, *Research Aide, Communications*
Steve Richards, *Computer Specialist, Information Services*
Kerry Riley, *Computer Specialist, Information Services*
Henry Ritchie, *Project Recognition Coordinator*
Seaman Rosa Rivera, *Mail Clerk, Information Services*
Denise Robinson, *Receptionist, Office of Administration*
Tom Rodriguez, *Word Processor, Office of Administration*
Elizabeth Rohn, *Assistant Director, Private Sector Programs*
Michael Ryan, *Intern*
Scott Sanders, *Project Coordinator, Private Sector Programs*
Rocio Santiago, *Information Assistant, Information Service*
Gloria L. Sandtner, *Secretary, Office of the Staff Director*
Gene Schaerr, *Law Clark, Office of the Chairman*
Charity Schofield, *Intern, Personnel*
Keith Schofield, *Private Sector Programs*
Fred Shields, *Mail Clerk, Information Services*
Valdenia V. Simmons, *Administrative Assistant, Educational Programs*
Thomas J. Simon, *Deputy Staff Director and Director of Administration*
Elizabeth Smith, *Intern*
Randy Smith, *Intern*
Stephen B. Sorensen, *Program Officer, Educational Programs*
Jocelyn A. Stevenson, *Receptionist, Office of the Staff Director*
Jocelyn Stevenson, *Secretary, Office of the Staff Director*
Mattie Stroman, *Grant Assistant, Educational Programs*
Jacklyn MacInnis Sunderland, *Director of Speakers Bureau*
Dr. Lane Sunderland, *Director of Educational Programs*
Norma Swanson, *Program Officer, Educational Programs*
Jane Symmes, *Office Manager, Marketing / Private Sector Programs*
Karen E. Symonds, *Grants Administrative Manager, Educational Programs*
Colleen Taggart, *Intern*
George Taylor, *Deputy Director, Marketing*
Therese Taylor, *Secretary, Project Recognition*
Sharon K. Thomas, *Computer Specialist, Information Services*
Petty Officer Roccio Thornton, *Information Assistant, Information Services*
Charles L. Timanus, *Director of Communications*
Eddie Timanus, *Intern, Private Sector Programs*
Daphne Torney, *Data Entry Clerk, Executive Secretariat*
Dr. Ronald L. Trowbridge, *Staff Director*
Charles Tait Trussell, *Director of Communications*
Carl Udler, *Intern*
Suzanne Valenzuela, *Assistant Director, Support Services*
Christine Vann, *Secretary, Educational Programs*
Ruth K. Vass, *Secretary, Government Affairs*
Elliott S. Waddell, *Grant Coordinator, Educational Programs*
Helen Wall, *Research Assistant, Communications*
David W. Warne, *Director of Support Services, Office of Administration*
Betsy Warren, *Assistant Director, Communications*
Della Watson, *Intern*
Penny Weaver, *Executive Director, Office of the Chairman*
Owen Werthmann, *Administrative Aide, Private Sector Programs*
Denise Whelton, *Intern*
Jill White, *Secretary, Office of the Chairman*
Julia White, *Marketing*
George Wilcox, *Assistant Director, Marketing*
Laura Wilharm, *Intern*
Winston Wilkinson, *Special Assistant to the Staff Director*
Lt. Colonel Chuck Williams, *Special Assistant to the Deputy Staff Director*
Rebecca Williams, *Confidential Assistant, General Counsel*
Judy Wilson, *Secretary, Office of the Chairman*
Angela Withers, *Regional Director, Government Affairs*
Seaman Johanna Witzen, *Data Entry Clerk, Information Services*
Roger Woodworth, *Editor and Assistant Director, Communications*
Peggy Wright, *Computer Specialist*
Vanessa Yarnell, *Office of the Chairman*

ADVISORY COMMITTEES

Article III Advisory Committee

Hon. Howard T. Markey, *Committee Chairman, United States Circuit Court of Appeals for the Federal District*
Chief Justice Harry Carrico, *Supreme Court of Virginia*
Judge Edward J. Devitt, *United States District Court*
Fred Fielding, *Wiley, Rein & Fielding*
Justice Edward F. Hennessey, *Martin, Magnuson, McCarthy & Kenney*
Judge Damon J. Keith, *United States Circuit Court*
Judge James Lawrence King, *United States District Court*
Edward McConnell, *National Center for State Courts*
Professor Rodney A. Smolla, *College of William and Mary*
Judge Kenneth Starr, *United States Court of Appeals for the District of Columbia*

Bill of Rights Advisory Committee

Judge Frank M. Coffin, *Committee Chairman, United States Circuit Court*
Professor Rodney A. Smolla, *Committee Vice Chairman, College of William and Mary*
Professor Stephen Burbank, *University of Pennsylvania Law School*
Professor Jack Greene, *The Johns Hopkins University*
Ewrin Griswold, *Jones, Day, Reavis & Pogue*
Judge Frank M. Johnson, Jr., *United States Court of Appeals*
Professor Marvin Kalb, *J.F.K. School of Government*
Chief Justice Vincent McKusick, *Supreme Judicial Court*
Eugene Methvin, *Reader's Digest Association*
Judge Constance Baker Motley, *United States District Court*
Professor Thomas H. O'Connor, *Boston College*
Judge Edward D. Re, *United States Court of International Trade*
Judge Kenneth F. Ripple, *United States Court of Appeals*
Judge Aubrey Robinson, Jr., *United States District Court for the District of Columbia*
Professor Lois Schwoerer, *George Washington University*
Professor Kenneth W. Thompson, *University of Virginia*
James Russell Wiggins, *The Ellsworth American*

Communications Advisory Committee

Edward O. Fritts, *Committee Chairman, National Association of Broadcasters*
Jerry Friedheim, *Committee Vice-Chairman, American Newspaper Publishers Association*
David Bartlett, *Radio-Television News Directors Association*
Rory Benson, *National Association of Broadcasters*
Doug Bennet, *National Public Radio*
Ben Cason, *United Press International*
Bruce Christensen, *Public Broadcasting Service*
Charles Dale, *The Newspaper Guild*
Brian Dickinson, *National Conference of Editorial Writers*
Dr. John Doolittle, *Association for Education in Journalism and Mass Communication*
William Gorog, *Magazine Publishers Association*
Ray Jenkins, *American Society of Newspaper Editors*
Donald D. Kummerfeld, *Magazine Publishers Association*
Brian Lamb, *C-SPAN*
Bob Lewis, *Society of Professional Journalists (Sigma Delta Chi)*
James Mooney, *National Cable Television Association*
Charles A. Perlik, Jr., *The Newspaper Guild*
Al Rossiter, *United Press International*
Ernie Schultz, *Radio-Television News Directors Association*
David Simonson, *National Newspaper Association*

International African Planning Committee

Brian Atwood, *National Democratic Institute for International Affairs*
Richard Bissell, *Department of State*
Herman Cohen, *Department of State*
Vivien Derryck, *African American Institute*
Frank Ferrari, *African American Institute*
Wayne Fredericks, *Ford Motor Company*
Norman Gross, *American Bar Association*
Robert Halligan, *National Rural Electric Cooperative*
Marshall Phelps, *IBM Corporation*
Ronald Roskens, *Department of State*
Keith Schuette, *National Republican Institute for International Affairs*

International Asian Planning Committee

Richard Allen, *Richard V. Allen Company*
Deswaix Anderson, *Department of State*
Brian Atwood, *National Democratic Institute for International Affairs*
Bob Bergland, *National Rural Electric Cooperative Association*
Peter Braestrup, *Library of Congress*
A. Lewis Burridge, *Chamber of Commerce of the Philippines*
William Clark, *Department of State*
Ray Cline, *United States Global Strategy Council*
James Cudney, *American Technology & Commerce*
Cinnamon Dornsife, *The Asia Foundation*
Chuck Gray, *Asian American Free Labor Institute*
Norman Gross, *American Bar Association*
James Holger, *United Nations Information Center*
Mark Joelson, *Morgan, Lewis and Bockius*
Jan Kalicki, *Shearson Lehman Hutton*
Omie Kerr, *United States Information Agency*
Paul Locigno, *Hill & Knowlton*
Leon Lynch, *United Steel Workers of America*
Dr. Ronald Morse, *Economy Strategy Institute*
Dr. Frederick Quinn, *United States Information Agency*
Charles Rhyne, *World Peace Through Law Center*
Eric Sanson, *U.S. Agency for International Development*
Keith Schuette, *National Republican Institute for International Affairs*
Jay Tolson, *Wilson Quarterly*
Mark Van Fleet, *U.S. Chamber of Commerce*

International European Planning Committee

William Archey, *U.S. Chamber of Commerce*
Brian Atwood, *National Democratic Institute for International Affairs*
Richard Berendzen, *American University*
Luigi Einaudi, *Department of State*
William Falsgraf, *Baker and Hostetler*
Robert Hunter, *Center for Strategic and International Studies*
Phyllis Kaminsky, *United Nations Information Center*
Abraham Katz, *Council for International Business*
Charles McC. Mathias, Jr., *United States Senate*
David Peterson, *Department of Commerce*
Dr. Frederick Quinn, *United States Information Agency*
Rozanne Ridgway, *Department of State*
Keith Schuette, *National Republican Institute for International Affairs*
Ambassador Richard Shifter, *Department of State*
Steven Slezak, *Department of International Affairs*
Joseph Sweeney, *Hastings University*

International Latin American Planning Committee

Dean Frederick Anderson, *American University*
William Archey, *U.S. Chamber of Commerce*
Brian Atwood, *National Democratic Institute for International Affairs*
Svend Brandt-Erichsen, *Office of the Honorable Ted Stevens*
Karen Cardran, *Department of Commerce*
John Dahlgren, *Inter-American Bar Association*
Luigi Einaudi, *Department of State*
William Falsgraf, *Baker and Hostetler*
Phyllis Kaminsky, *United Nations Information Center*
Langhorne Motley, *L.A. Motley and Company*
Carolyn Osolinik, *Office of the Honorable Edward Kennedy*
Dr. Frederick Quinn, *United States Information Agency*
Mark Schneider, *Pan American Health Organization*
Keith Schuette, *National Republican Institute for International Affairs*
Steven Slezak, *Department of International Affairs*
Holly Stewart-McMahon, *American Bar Association*

National Education Advisory Committee

Elliot L. Richardson, *Committee Chairman*
Dr. Sidney P. Marland, Jr., *Committee Vice Chairman*
Lamar Alexander, *U.S. Department of Education*
Dr. Greg Anrig, *Educational Testing Service*
Ed Argenbright, *State Superintendent, Office of Public Instruction, Montana*
Gen. Robert Arter (ret.), *Department of Defense*
Dr. Donald Bragaw, *New York State Department of Education*
Frederick Brigham, *National Catholic Education Association*
Lloyd Bromberg, *New York City Board of Education*
Kathy Brown, *Association for Supervision and Curriculum Development*
Marilyn Tyler Brown, *Washington, D.C., Schools*
Dr. Robert A. Burnham, *SEHNAP, New York University*
Betty Debnam, *Editor, The Mini Page*
Rosa Chapman DuCree
Donald Eklund, *Association of American Publishers*
Margaret Evans, *National Association of Elementary School Principals*
Jeremiah Floyd, *National School Boards Association*
Charlotte Frank, *McGraw-Hill Book Company*
Jean Fritz, *Author of Children's Books*
Dr. Thomas J. Galvin, *American Association of School Librarians*
Shirley Garner, *Andres Castillero Middle School, San Jose, California*
Kay Garvey, *Department of Defense Dependents Schools*
Warlene Gary, *National Education Association*
Charlene Gaynor, *Springhouse Corporation*
Dr. Richard Green, *New York City Board of Education*
Col. Ron Green, *Department of Defense*
Frances Haley, *National Council for the Social Studies*
Dr. J. Jerome Harris, *Superintendent, Atlanta City Schools*
Dr. James S. Haskins, *Professor of English*
Judith D. Hines, *American Newspaper Publishers Association Foundation*
Maureen Hunter-Bones, *Electric Company Magazine, Children's Television Workshop*
Sam Husk, *The Council of the Great City Schools, Washington, D.C.*
Dr. David G. Imig, *American Association of Colleges for Teacher Education*
Dr. Andrew Jenkins, III, *Superintendent of Schools, Washington, D.C.*
Lynell Johnson, *Field Publications*
Brother James Kearney, *FMS, Superintendent of Schools, Archdiocese of New York*
Roger Kennedy, *National Museum of American History, the Smithsonian Institution*
Judy Koloski, *American Association for Adult and Continuing Education*
Jean Krier, *Scholastic, Inc.*
Jack W. Kukuk, *John F. Kennedy Center*
Dr. Marvin Kurtz, *Department of Defense Dependents Schools*
Leanna Landsman
Mary Anne Lecos, *Fairfax County Schools, Virginia*
Lt. Col. Lewis Levy, *Department of Defense*
Marjorie W. Longley
Ann Lynch, *National Parents Teachers Association*
Gary Marx, *American Association of School Administrators*
Peter Massardo, *Alpine School, Sparta, New Jersey*
Joyce McCray, *Council for American Private Education*
Dr. Duncan McDonald, *Council of Chief State School Officers*
Dr. Floretta McKenzie, *The McKenzie Group*
Dr. Mabel McKinney-Browning, *American Bar Association, Special Committee on Youth Education for Citizenship*
Catherine T. McNamee, *CSJ, National Catholic Education Association*
Edward Meade, *Ford Foundation*
Marjorie Montgomery, *CRADLE*
Paula O'Connor, *American Federation of Teachers*
Dale Parnell, *American Association of Community and Junior Colleges*
J. W. Peltason, *Chancellor, University of California-Irvine*
Dr. David R. Pierce, *American Association of Community and Jr. Colleges*

Dr. Jon Quam, *Council of Chief State School Officers*
Billy R. Reagan, *Harcourt Brace Jovanovich, Inc.*
Harry Robinson, *National Conference of Christians and Jews*
Richard Robinson, *Scholastic, Inc.*
Paul Rowley, *Instructor Magazine*
Diane Ruffner, *United States Department of Education*
Charles B. Saunders, Jr., *American Council on Education*
Dr. Samuel G. Sava, *National Association of Elementary School Principals*
Charles M. Schulz, *Creator of the Peanuts Gang*
Bruce H. Seide, *Field Publications*
Eleanor Shannahan, *World Magazine, National Geographic Society*
Thomas Shannon, *National School Boards Association*
Sandra Siegel
Robert L. Smith, *Council for American Private Education*
Frances M. Sonnenschein, *Anti-Defamation League*
Dr. Robert R. Spillane, *Division Superintendent, Fairfax County Schools*
Rosalind Stark, *American Newspaper Publishers Association Foundation*
Dr. Isidore Starr
Dr. Donald R. Stoll, *Educational Press Association of America*
Lenora Talley-Burger
Dr. Scott Thomson, *National Association of Secondary School Principals*
Manya S. Ungar, *National Parents Teachers Association*
Jacqueline Wexler, *National Conference of Christians and Jews*
Dr. John Wherry, *National School Public Relations Association*
Gene Wilhoit, *National Association of State Boards of Education*
Ron Wolk, *Education Week*

Religious Advisory Committee

Dr. Ben Armstrong, *National Religious Broadcasters*
Dr. Robert Biscoe, *National Council of Churches*
Rev. Donald L. Brown, *Joint Educational Development Committee of the National Council of Churches*
Dr. Donald Campbell, *Local Ministerial Alliance*
Seymour S. Cohen, *B'nai B'rith International*
Dr. Robert P. Dugan, Jr., *National Association of Evangelicals*
Dr. James Dunn, *Baptist Joint Committee*
Maj. Gen. Norris L. Einertson, *Chief of Chaplains, Department of the Army*
Rev. James D. Ford, D.D., *Chaplain of the U.S. House of Representatives*
Brandt Gustavson, *National Religious Broadcasters*
Rev. Dr. Richard C. Halverson, *Chaplain of the U.S. Senate*
Dr. James Hamilton, *The National Council of Churches of Christ*
Donald F. Hetzler, *The Associated Church Press*
Most Reverend James A. Hickey, *Archbishop of Washington, D.C.*
Most Reverend Archbishop Iakovos, *The Greek Orthodox Archdiocese of North and South America*
Father Alexander Karloutsos, *The Greek Orthodox Archdiocese of North and South America*
Rev. Robert Kline, *Evangelical Church Alliance*
Rear Adm.l Alvin B. Koeneman, *Chief of Chaplains, United States Navy*
Msgr. William Lori, *Secretary to the Archbishop of Washington*
Msgr. Robert Lynch, *National Conference of Bishops*
Brig. Gen. Charles J. McDonnel, *Assistant to the Chief of Chaplains, United States Army*
Maj. Gen. John McDonough, *Chief of Chaplains, United States Air Force*
Louis Moore, *Religious Newswriters Association*
Rabbi James Rudin, *The American Jewish Committee*
Rev. Glen E. Seaborg, *Evangelical Church Alliance*
Rev. Alan J. Sorem, *Religion in American Life, Inc.*
Rev. Ivan E. Speight, *Associated Gospel Churches*
Gary Warner, *Evangelical Press Association*
Maj. Gen. Matthew A. Zimmerman, *Chief of Chaplains, United States Army*

STATE BICENTENNIAL COMMISSIONS

Alabama
Alabama Bicentennial Task Force, *Montgomery*
C.C. "Bo" Torbert, Jr., *Chairman*
Dr. Anita Buckley, *Executive Director*
Dr. Ed Bridges, Charles Carr & Bob Neel, *Office of the Governor*

Alaska
Alaska Commission to Celebrate the United States Constitution, *Juneau*
John E. Havelock, *Chairman*
Harry Gamble, *Executive Director*
Allison Elgee, *Office of the Governor*
Randall P. Burns, *Bicentennial Contact*

Arizona
Arizona Commission on the Bicentennial of the United States Constitution, *Phoenix*
William A. Holohan & Frank X. Gordon, Jr., *Chairmen*
Ellie Sbragia & Dick Wright, *Executive Directors*
Teena Olszewski & Lynda Rando, *Arizona Bar Association*
Trish Beck, *The Supreme Court of Arizona*

Arkansas
Arkansas Constitution Bicentennial Commission, *Little Rock*
Lt. Gov. Winston Bryant & Lt. Gov. Jim Guy Tucker, *Chairmen*
Mike Ross, *Bicentennial Coordinator*
Charles Miller & Howard Harper, *Office of the Lieutenant Governor*

California
State of California Commission on the Bicentennial of the United States Constitution, *Glendale/South Pasadena*
Jane A. Crosby, *Chairman*
Jeffrey D. Allen, *Executive Director*

Colorado
Colorado Commission on the Bicentennial of the United States Constitution, *Englewood/Denver*
Roger Alan Walton & William J. Hybl, *Chairmen*
Esther Marie Capps, *Executive Director*
Rebecca Smith, *Colorado Justice Department*
George Pramenko, *Coordinator, Office of the Lieutenant Governor*

Connecticut
United States Constitution Bicentennial Commission for the State of Connecticut, *Hartford*
Ralph G. Elliott, *Chairman*
Janet Crook & Wilson (Bill) Faude, *Executive Directors*

Delaware
Delaware Heritage Commission, *Wilmington*
Robert P. Barnett & Dr. James R. Soles, *Chairmen*
Dr. Claudia L. Bushman & Dr. Deborah P. Haskell, *Executive Directors*

District of Columbia
District of Columbia Bicentennial Commission
Jeannine Clark & Teri Y. Dokes, *Chairmen*
Peter Share, *Executive Director*

Florida
United States Constitutional Bicentennial Commission of Florida, *Tallahassee*
Ben F. Overton, *Chairman*
Carol Bellamy & Jeffrey Jonasen, *Executive Directors*

Georgia
Georgia Commission on the Bicentennial of the United States Constitution, *Atlanta*
Thomas O. Marshall, *Chairman*
Helen P. Dougherty, *Executive Director*

Hawaii
Hawaii Bicentennial Commission, *Honolulu*
Vernon F. L. Char, *Chairman*
Concetta Riccio, *Bicentennial Contact*

Idaho
Constitution Bicentennial Commission of Idaho, *Boise*
Dennis Harwick, *Chairman*
Constance M. Arana, *Executive Director*

Illinois
Committee to Commemorate United States Constitution in Illinois, *Chicago*
Richard E. Friedman & Cheryl I. Niro, *Chairmen*
Donna Schechter, *Illinois State Bar Association*

Indiana
Indiana Commission on the Bicentennial of the United States Constitution, *Indianapolis*
Randall T. Shepard, *Chairman*
Pamela Bennett, *Executive Director*
Ray Ewick, *State Librarian*

Iowa
Iowa State Commission on the Bicentennial of the United States Constitution, *Iowa City*
Dr. Joseph Walt, *Chairman*
Loren N. Horton, *Coordinator of Bicentennial Projects*

Kansas
Kansas Commission on the Bicentennial of the United States Constitution, *Topeka*
Frank Theis, *Chairman*
Marjorie Schnacke, *Executive Director*
Nancy Ingle, *State Coordinator*

Kentucky
United States Constitution Celebration Project, *Frankfort*
Alice McDonald, *Chairman*
Betty H. Seay, *Project Director*

United States Constitution Bicentennial Commission of Kentucky, *Louisville*
Penny P. Gold, *Chairman*
Glenda Donoho, *Project Director*

Louisiana
Louisiana Commission on the Bicentennial of the United States Constitution, *New Orleans/Baton Rouge*
James L. Dennis, *Chairman*
Michael M. Davis, *Vice-Chairman*
Terry Allbritton & Paul Baier, *Executive Directors*

Maine
Maine Commission to Commemorate the Bicentennial of the United States Constitution, *Portland*
Arthur M. Johnson & Hugh Calkins, *Chairmen*
Kay Evans, *Executive Director*
Rosalyne S. Bernstein, *Project Director*

Maryland
Maryland Office for the Bicentennial of the Constitution of the United States, *Annapolis*
Dr. Edward C. Papenfuse, *Chairman*
Dr. Gregory A. Stiverson, *Executive Director*

Massachusetts
Massachusetts Advisory Commission to Commemorate the Bicentennial of the United States Constitution, *Boston*
Edward F. Hennessey, *Chairman*
Margaret Cavanaugh, *Executive Director*

Massachusetts Advisory Commission on the Commemoration of the Bill of Rights, *Boston*
Joseph A. Milano, *Chairman*
Paul E. McDonald, *Executive Director*

Michigan
Michigan Commission on the Bicentennial of the United States Constitution, *Lansing*
Dr. David W. Adamany, Morley Winograd, & Jerry Roe, *Chairmen*
Ronald Russell & Dr. James McConnell, *Executive Directors*

Minnesota

Minnesota Commission on the Bicentennial of the United States
Constitution, *St. Paul*
Hubert H. Humphrey, III, Connie Levi, & Dorothy Molstad, *Chairmen*
Todd Lefko, *Executive Director*
Scott D. Fride & Tony Harris, *Project Coordinators*

Mississippi

United States Constitution Bicentennial Commission of Mississippi,
Jackson/Tupelo
William C. Keady & Harry Grey Walker, *Co-Chairmen*
James Dixon & Margaret DeMoville, *Executive Directors*
Fred Slabach, *Bicentennial Coordinator*

Missouri

United States Constitution Bicentennial Commission of Missouri,
Jefferson City
Albert L. Rendlen, *Chairman*
Joanne M. Hibdon, *Executive Director*

Montana

Montana Constitutional Connections Committee, Statehood Centennial
Office, *Helena*
Frank Haswell, *Chairman*
Richard Roeder, *Executive Director*
Carolyn Linden & Richard Roeder, *Bicentennial Contacts*

Nebraska

United States Constitution Bicentennial Commission of Nebraska,
Lincoln
Jack Schuetz, *Chairman*
Julie Garay & Lois Noble, *Executive Directors*
Allen Beerman, *Office of the Secretary of State*

Nevada

Nevada Commission on the Bicentennial of the United States
Constitution, *Las Vegas/Carson City*
John C. Mowbray, *Chairman*
Leslie B. Gray, Robert J. Miller & Larry Struve, *Executive Directors*
Frankie Sue Del Pappa, *Bicentennial Contact*

New Hampshire

State of New Hampshire Bicentennial Commission on the United States
Constitution, *Wolfeboro/Hampton*
Russell C. Chase & Ednapearl F. Parr, *Chairmen*
Natalie Flanagan, *Vice-Chairman*

New Jersey

Constitutional Bicentennial Commission of New Jersey, *Mahway/Trenton*
Jane Burgio, *Chairman*
Noreen Bodman & Lynne Edwards, *Executive Directors*
Mary Alice Quigley, *New Jersey Historical Commission Director*
Robert J. Flood, *Smith Administration Center Supervisor for Social Studies/
Media*

New Mexico

New Mexico Diamond Jubilee/United States Constitution Bicentennial
Commission, *Santa Fe*
Michael L. Keleher, *Chairman*
Virginia Hendley, *Executive Director*

New York

New York State Commission on the Bicentennial of the United States
Constitution, *Albany/Troy*
Sol Wachtler, *Chairman*
Dr. Stephen L. Schechter, *Executive Director*
Paul Schudiere, *State Historians*

North Carolina

North Carolina Commission on the Bicentennial of the United States
Constitution, *Raleigh*
Robert B. Jordan, III, *Chairman*
Gerry Hancock, *Director*

Friends of the Constitution of the United States, *Raleigh*
Marrianne Wason, *Executive Director*
Bob Geary & Steve Channing, *Assistants*

North Dakota

North Dakota Constitution Celebration Commission, *Bismarck*
Herbert L. Meschke, *Chairman*
Lawrence D. Spears & Jim Gange, *Executive Directors*

Ohio

Northwest Ordinance and United States Constitution Bicentennial
Commission, *Columbus*
Dr. Phillip R. Shriver, *Chairman*
James C. Miller, *Executive Director*

Ohio Historical Society
Gary Ness, *Director*
Steve George, *Assistant Director*

Oklahoma

Constitution 200, *Tulsa & Norman*
Dr. Joseph A. Blackman & Dr. Richard S. Wells, *Co-Chairmen*

Oregon

Oregon Governor's Commission on the Bicentennial of the United
States Constitution, *Portland*
Charles S. Crookham, *Chairman*

Pennsylvania

Commonwealth of Pennsylvania Commission on the Bicentennial of the
United States Constitution, *Harrisburg*
Samuel J. Roberts, *Chairman*
Mitch Akers, *Staff Director*
Dr. James J. Wetzler, *Pennsylvania Department of Education*

Puerto Rico

Puerto Rico Commission on the Bicentennial of the United States
Constitution, *Hato Rey*
Victor M. Pons, Jr., *Chairman*
Carmen I. Navas, *Executive Director*

Rhode Island

Rhode Island Bicentennial Foundation, *Providence*
Dr. Patrick T. Conley, *Chairman*
Thomas Shola, *Bicentennial Contact*

South Carolina

United States Constitution Bicentennial Commission of South Carolina,
Columbia
Alexia J. Helsley & P. Bradley Morrah, Jr., *Chairmen*
Ben F. Hornsby, Jr., *Executive Director*
Tray Stephenson, *Projects Director*

South Dakota

South Dakota Centennial Commission, *Pierre*
Kay Jorgensen & Shelly Stingley, *Chairmen*
David Martin & James Larson, *Executive Directors*

Tennessee

United States Constitution Bicentennial Commission of Tennessee,
Nashville
Douglas Henry & Harry W. Welford, *Co-Chairmen*
Mary Sewell, *Executive Director*
Dr. Milton M. Klein, *University of Tennessee Historian*

Texas

Texas Commission on the Bicentennial of the United States
Constitution, *Brownsville*
Ricardo H. Hinojosa, *Chairman*
Hope Lockridge, *Texas State Bar Association*

Utah

Governor's Commission on Law and Citizenship, *Salt Lake City*
Brinton R. Burbidge, *Chairman*
Donald C. Cobb, *Executive Director*

Council on the United States Constitution and the Bill of Rights,
Salt Lake City
Lt. Gov. Val Oveson & Keith A. Kelly, *Co-Chairmen*

CONTINUED NEXT PAGE

Vermont

Vermont Statehood Bicentennial Commission, *Burlington/Rutland*
Bill Schubart & William B. Gray, *Chairmen*
Carolyn Meub, *Executive Director*
Garry Schaedel, *Office of the Governor*

Virgin Islands

United States Constitution Bicentennial Commission of the Virgin
    Islands, *St. Thomas*
Dr. Roderick E. Moorehead, *Chairman*
Sherry Simmons, *Vice-Chairman*

Virginia

Virginia Commission on the Bicentennial of the United States
    Constitution, *Charlottesville*
Dr. A.E. Dick Howard, *Chairman*
Dr. Timothy G. O'Rourke, *Executive Director*

Washington

Constitutions Committee, Washington Centennial Commission,
    Olympia
Robert E. Mack, *Chairman*
Caryl Zenker, *Program Coordinator*
John Dziedzic, *Office of the Secretary of State*

West Virginia

United States Constitution Bicentennial Commission of West Virginia,
    Charleston
Charles H. Haden, II, *Chairman*
Ken Sullivan, *Executive Director*

Wisconsin

Wisconsin Bicentennial Committee on the Constitution, *Madison*
Roland B. Day, *Chairman*
George Brown & Karen McNett, *Executive Directors*
Philip S. Habermann, *Program Coordinator*

Wyoming

Wyoming Commission on the Bicentennial of the United States
    Constitution, *Cheyenne*
Bill McIlvain, *Chairman*
Becky Evans, *Executive Director*
Tony Lewis, *Wyoming Bar Association*

DESIGNATED BICENTENNIAL COMMUNITIES

Alabama

Alabaster
Anniston
Ashville
Athens-Limestone County
Bay Minette
Brookwood
Collinsville
Cullman
Demopolis
Dothan
Eufaula
Foley
Gadsden-Etowah County
Gardendale
Greensboro
Grove Hill
Gulf Shores
Hueytown
Huntsville-Madison County
Jacksonville
Jasper
Lipscomb
Mobile-Baldwin Counties
Montgomery
Northport
Opelika
Pine Hill
Rainbow City
Rutledge
Sylacauga
Talladega
Vestavia Hills
Waverly
Wetumpka

Alaska

Anchorage
Fairbanks
Haines
Houston
Juneau
Kenai
Kodiak
Saint Paul
Sitka
Valdez
Wasilla

Arizona

Avondale
Benson
Bisbee
Buckeye
Duncan
Eagar
Eloy
Fountain Hills
Gilbert
Glendale
Holbrook
Huachuca City
Kingman
Mesa

Parker
Payson
Phoenix
Pinetop-Lakeside
Prescott
Saint Johns
Scottsdale
Show Low
Sierra Vista
Snowflake
Tempe
Tombstone
Tucson
Willcox
Winslow
Youngstown
Yuma

Arkansas

Arkadelphia-Clark County
Arkansas County
Ash Flat-Sharp County
Ashley County
Baxter County
Benton
Benton County
Blytheville
Boone County
Bradley County
Calhoun County
Carroll County
Cave City
Chicot County
Clay County
Cleburne County
Cleveland County
Columbia County
Conway County-Morrilton
Corning
Craighead County
Crawford County
Cross County
Desha County
Drew County
Faulkner County
Fordyce-Dallas County
Fort Smith
Franklin County
Fulton County
Garland County
Grant County
Greene County-Paragould
Hazen County
Helena-Phillips County
Hempsted County
Howard County
Independence County
Jackson County
Jacksonville
Jefferson County
Johnson County
Lafayette County
Lee County-Marianna
Little River County
Logan County
Lonoke County
Madison County-Huntsville
Marion County
Miller County
Mississippi County
Monroe County
Montgomery County
Mountain View-Stone County

Nevada County
Newton County
Ouachita County
Parkin
Perry County
Pike County
Poinsett County
Polk County-Mena
Pope County
Prairie County
Pulaski County
Randolph County-Pocahontas
Scott County-Waldron
Sebastian County
Sevier County
Sherwood
Shirley
Star City
Stuttgart
Texarkana
Union County
Van Buren County-Clinton
Washington County
White County
Woodruff County
Wynne
Yell County

California
Agoura Hills
Alameda
Alhambra
Anaheim
Anderson
Antioch
Arcadia
Atascadero
Atwater
Avalon
Azusa
Banning
Beaumont
Bell
Bellflower
Belvedere
Beverly Hills
Big Bear Lake
Blythe
Brea
Buena Park
Burbank
Burlingame
Camarillo
Carpinteria
Carson
Ceres
Cerritos
Colusa
Commerce
Coronado
Costa Mesa
Culver City
Cupertino
Del Mar
Desert Hot Springs
Duarte
Dunsmuir

El Cajon
El Dorado
El Monte
El Segundo
Encinitas
Escalon
Escondido
Eureka
Fairfield
Ferndale
Fillmore
Fortuna
Foster City
Fresno
Fullerton
Gardena
Garden Grove
Glendale
Glenn County
Hawthorne
Hemet
Hidden Hills
High Desert
Hollister
Huntington Beach
Imperial County
Indio
Irvine
Kern County
Kingsburg
Lafayette
Laguna Beach
Laguna Niguel
La Habra
La Mesa
La Mirada
Lancaster
La Puente
Lawndale
Livermore
Livingston
Loma Linda
Lomita
Los Altos
Los Angeles
Los Angeles County
Manhattan Beach
Manteca
Mariposa County
Medera
Menlo Park
Millbrae
Milpitas
Monrovia
Montclair
Montebello
Monterey
Monterey County
Monterey Park
Moorpark
Moreno Valley
Morro Bay
Napa County
National City
Nevada City
Newark
Newport Beach
Norwalk
Novato

Oakdale
Ojai
Ontario
Orange
Orange County
Orange Cove
Oxnard
Pacific Grove
Palm Springs
Palo Alto
Palos Verdes Estates
Paradise
Paramount
Parlier
Pasadena
Petaluma
Pico Rivera
Piedmont
Pittsburg
Placerville
Pleasanton
Plymouth
Porterville
Portola
Rancho Cucamonga
Rancho Palos Verdes
Redlands
Redondo Beach
Rialto
Ripon
Riverbank
Riverside-Riverside County
Sacramento-
        Sacramento County
Salinas
San Bernardino
San Bruno
San Buenaventura
San Clemente
San Diego County
San Gabriel
San Juan Capistrano
San Marcos
San Mateo
San Mateo County
Santa Ana
Santa Barbara
Santa Fe Springs
Santa Monica
Santa Paula
Saratoga
Seal Beach
Seaside
Shafter
Simi Valley
Solana Beach
Sonoma County
South Lake Tahoe
South Pasadena
Suisun City
Thousand Oaks
Torrance
Tracy
Tulare
Tulare County

Ventura County
Victorville
Visalia
Vista
Walnut
West Covia
Westminster
West Sacramento
Whittier
Yountville
Yuba City
Yucaipa-Calimesa

Colorado
Alamosa County
Boulder County
Clear Creek County
Colorado Springs
Cortez
Douglas-Elbert County
Fountain
La Junta
Larimer County
Littleton
Mesa County
Northglenn
Rio Grande County
Weld County
Westminster

Connecticut
Barkhamsted
Beacon Falls
Bethlehem
Bloomfield
Bridgewater
Canaan (Falls Village)
Cheshire
Clinton
Colebrook
Coventry
Cromwell
Darien
Derby
East Hampton
East Hartford
East Windsor
Ellington
Greenwich
Higganum
Kent
Lebanon
Litchfield
Lyme
Madison
Mansfield
Meriden
Middletown
Milford
Monroe
Morris
Naugatuck
New Canaan
New Haven
Newington
Old Saybrook
Prospect
Putnam

CONTINUED NEXT PAGE

Roxbury
Salisbury
Seymour
Sherman
Simsbury
Southbury
Stamford
Stratford
Union
Voluntown
Wallingford
Waterbury
Waterford
Watertown
West Hartford
West Haven
Westbrook
Weston
Wethersfield
Windsor

Delaware
Camden
Dagsboro
Delaware City
Georgetown
Laurel
Leipsic
Milford
Millville
Milton
New Castle
Newark
Ocean View
Odessa
Seaford
Smyrna
South Bethany
Townsend
Wilmington
Woodside
Wyoming

Florida
Alachua County
Atlantic Beach
Avon Park
Baldwin (Town of)
Bay County
Belleair Beach
Branford
Brevard County
Broward County
Cape Coral
Cedar Key
Citrus County
Clay County
Cocoa
Cocoa Beach
Coral Springs
Cottondale
Dania
Davie
Deerfield Beach
De Funiak Springs
Deltona
Dunedin
Eustis
Fort Lauderdale
Fort Myers
Fort Pierce

Gadsden County
Hallandale
Hardee County
Hernando County
Hillsborough County
Holly Hill
Hollywood
Homestead
Hypoluxo
Jackson County
Jacksonville
Jacksonville Beach
Juno Beach
Keystone Heights
Key West-Monroe County
Lake County
Lake Mary
Lake Wales
Lake Worth
Lakeland
Lauderhill
Longboat Key
Longwood
Manatee County
Melbourne
Miami
Miami Shores
Mulberry
Naples
Niceville
North Bay Village
North Miami
North Palm Beach
North Port
Oakland Park
Ocala
Ocoee
Orlando-Orange County
Oviedo
Palm Bay
Palm Beach County
Palm Coast
Pasco County
Pembroke Park
Pembroke Pines
Pensacola
Pinellas County
Pinellas Park
Port St. Joe
Port St. Lucie
Putnam County
Redington Shores
Rockledge
Safety Harbor
Saint Augustine
Sanford
Sarasota-Sarasota County
Satellite Beach
Starke-Bradford County
Sweetwater
Tallahassee-Leon County
Tampa
Tequesta
Venice
Wakulla County
Waldo
Wauchula
West Melbourne
Winter Haven

Georgia
Alma-Bacon County
Americus-Sumter County
Appling County
Athens-Clarke County
Atkinson County
Augusta-Richmond County
Baker County
Banks County
Barrow County
Bartow County
Ben Hill County
Berrien County
Brantley
Brooks County
Burke County
Calhoun-Gordon County
Calhoun County
Camden County
Camilla
Candler County
Carroll County
Catoosa County
Charlton County
Chatman County
Chattahoochee County
Chattooga County
Cherokee County
Clay County
Clayton County
Clinch County
Cobb County-Kennesa College
Cochran-Bleckley County
Coffee County
Colquitt-Miller County
Colquitt County
Columbia County
Cook County
Coweta County
Crawford County
Crisp County
Dade County
Darien-McIntosh County
Dawson County
Decatur County
DeKalb County
Dodge County
Dooly County
Dougherty County
Douglas County
Early County
Echols County
Effingham County
Elbert County
Ellaville-Schley County
Emanuel County
Evans County
Fannin County
Fayette County
Forsyth County
Franklin County
Fulton County
Gainesville-Hall County
Gilmer County
Glascock County
Glynn County
Grady County
Greene County
Griffin-Spalding County
Gwinnett County

Habersham County
Hancock County
Haralson County
Harris County
Hartwell-Hart County
Heard County
Henry County
Houston County
Irwin County
Jackson-Butts County
Jackson County
Jasper County
Jeff Davis County
Jefferson County
Jenkins County
Johnson County
Jones County
Lamar County
Lanier County
Lauren County
Lee County
Liberty County
Lincoln County
Long County
Lowndes County
Lumpkin County
Macon-Bibb County
Macon County
Madison County
Marion County
McDuffie County
Meriwether County
Milledgeville-Baldwin County
Mitchell County
Monroe County
Montgomery County
Morgan County
Murray County
Muscogee County
Newton County
Oconee County
Oglethorpe County
Paulding County
Peach County
Pembroke-Bryan County
Pickens County
Pierce County
Pike County
Polk County
Pulaski County
Putnam County
Quitman County
Rabun County
Randolph County
Rockdale County
Rome-Floyd County
Savannah
Screven County
Seminole County
Statesboro-Bulloch County
Stewart County
Sylvester-Worth County

Talbot County
Taliaferro County
Tattnall County
Taylor County
Telfair County
Terrell County
Thomas County
Tift County
Toccoa-Stephens County
Toombs County
Towns County
Treutlen County
Troup County
Turner County
Twigg County
Union County
Upson County
Walker County
Walton County
Ware County
Warren County
Washington County
Wayne County
Webster County
Wheeler County
White County
Whitfield County
Wilcox County
Wilkes County
Wilkinson County
Worth County

Hawaii
Maui County
Weimea Valley

Idaho
American Falls
Ashton
Bonneville County
Coeur D'Alene
McCall
Nampa
Nez Perce County-Lewiston
Pocatello
Salmon Valley
Weston
Wood River Valley-Blaine County

Illinois
Addison
Aledo
Arlington Heights
Ashton
Auburn
Aurora
Barrington Village
Bloomington-Normal
Bolingbrook
Bradford
Brookfield
Bureau County

Calumet City
Calumet (Township of)
Canton
Carbon Cliff
Carol Stream
Champaign
Chatham
Chebanse
Chester
Clarendon Hills
Columbia
Country Club Hills
Crestwood
Crete
Danville-Vermillion County
Decatur
Deland
Dixon
Downers Grove
Dwight
East Alton
Ela Township
Fairbury
Flora
Forest Park
Fox Lake
Fulton County
Galesburg
Glencoe
Glenwood
Grayslake
Harwood Heights
Highland Park
Hillside (Village of)
Hinsdale
Homewood
Indian Head Park (Village of)
Itasca
Kendall County
Knoxville
LaGrange Park (Village of)
Lansing (Village of)
Lee (Village of)
LeRoy
Lincolnwood
Lisle
Livingston (Village of)
Maine Township
Mason County
Matteson
McHenry County
Merrionette Park (Village of)
Morton Grove
Mount Prospect
Murphysboro
Norridge
Northbrook
Ogle County
Orion
Orland Park
Peoria
Peotone (Village of)
Quincy
Rantoul (Village of)
River Forest
Riverside
Robbins
Rockford-Winnebago County
Round Lake Beach

Sandwich
Schaumburg
Schiller Park
Skokie
South Pekin
South Roxana
Stephenson County-Freeport
Sterling
Stickney
Streamwood (Village of)
Swansea (Village of)
Thomson
Thornton
Tinley Park (Village of)
Vernon Hills (Village of)
Warrenville
Waterloo
Wenona
Westchester
West Chicago
Wheeling
Wilmington
Woodlawn

Indiana
Attica
Bicknell
Bloomington
Brownburg
Carroll County
Cedar Lake
Chandler
Covington
Crawfordsville-
      Montgomery County
Crown Point
East Chicago
Elkhart
Evansville
Fort Wayne
Greenfield
Griffith
Hagerstown
Hammond
Hendricks County
Huntingburg
Huntington
Indianapolis
Jackson County
Jennings County
Lawrence County
Kokomo
Lebanon-Boone County
Lincoln City
Lowell
Martinsville
Michigan City
Mishawaka
Monticello
Montpelier
Mt. Vernon
Muncie
Newburgh
Noblesville
Parke County
Peru
Pulaski County
Richmond
Salem
Shelby County
6th Congressional District
South Bend

Syracuse
Tell City
Vincennes
Wakarusa
Washington-Daviess County

Iowa
Algona
Avoca
Bernard
Carson
Cascade
Charles City
Clarion
Decorah
Des Moines
Dubuque
Dubuque County
Dyersville
Emmetsburg
Everly
Forest City
Hampton-Franklin County
Hopkinton
Lee County
Marion
Murray
New Vienna
North Liberty
Norwalk
Rodney
Sherrill
Villisca
Webster City

Kansas
Concordia
Dodge City
Gypsum
Hillsboro
Hutchinson
Johnson County
Leawood
Lenexa
McPherson
Newton
Norton
Plainville
Rawlins County
Rice County
Salina
Southwest Dickinson County
Sumner County
Topeka
Winfield

Kentucky
Ashland
Bardstown-Nelson County
Boone County-Campbell County-
      Kenton County
Bowling Green-Warren County
Campbellsville-Taylor County
Carrollton
Crestview Hills
Danville
Elkton
Elsmere
Eminence

CONTINUED NEXT PAGE

Frankfort-Franklin County
Franklin-Simpson County
Glasgow-Barren County
Grayson County
Harrodsburg-Mercer County
Hartford
Henderson-Henderson County
Lawrenceburg-Anderson County
Lebanon-Marion County
Lexington
Livingston County
Louisville-Jefferson County
Madisonville-Hopkins County
Marion-Crittenden County
Mayfield-Graves County
Meade County
Monticello-Wayne County
Mt. Sterling-Montgomery County
Mt. Washington
Nicholas County
Owensboro
Paducah
Radcliff
Scott County
Shelbyville
Stanford-Lincoln County
Trigg County
Williamstown

Louisiana
Baton Rouge
Bogalusa
Claiborne
Delhi
De Quincy
Denham Springs
Eunice
Franklin
Gilbert
Gonzales
Jamestown
Kenner
Lafayette
Lake Charles
Lutcher
Mangham
Monroe
New Orleans
Opelousas
Ouachita Parish
Pineville
Port Barre
Ringgold
Ruston
Saint Francisville
Saint Helena
Shreveport
Sicily Island
Slidell
Springfield
Ville Platte
Welsh
West Carroll Parish
West Monroe
Winnsboro

Maine
Alna
Auburn-Lewiston
Bangor
Bar Harbor
Bath
Belfast
Berwick
Biddeford
Camden-Rockport
Cumberland
Dresden
East Millinocket
Hebron
Hermon
Houlton
Jay
Kennebunk
Lewiston
Livermore Falls
Norridgewock
Ocean Park
Orono
Paris
Portland
Saco
Sanford
Seboeis
Skowhegan
Southwest Harbor
Topsham
Van Buren
Westbrook
Wilton

Maryland
Annapolis
Baltimore
Calvert County
Caroline County
Charles County
College Park
Crisfield
Frederick County
Friendship Heights
Friendsville
Gaithersburg
Montgomery County
Prince George's County
Somerset County
Talbot County
Westernport
Williamsport

Massachusetts
Abington
Arlington
Ashburnham
Attleboro
Avon
Ayer
Barnstable
Becket
Bedford
Belmont
Beverly
Blackstone
Boston
Boxford
Bridgewater
Brockton
Brookfield

Chelsea
Chicopee
Cohasset
Dennis
Dighton
Douglas
Dover
Dracut
Dudley
East Bridgewater
Easton
Fall River
Fitchburg
Foxborough
Gardner
Grafton
Greenfield
Harvard
Haverhill
Hingham
Holbrook
Hull
Lancaster
Lanesboro
Lawrence
Leominster
Lexington
Lincoln
Lunenburg
Lynnfield
Malden
Manchester
Marblehead
Marion
Marlborough
Mattapoisett
Medfield
Medford
Merrimac
Methuen
Middlefield
Middleton
Milford
Milton
Monroe
Needham
Newton
North Adams
North Andover
North Reading
Northampton
Northbridge
Norwood
Orleans
Palmer
Plainville
Provincetown
Reading
Rehoboth
Rochester
Rowe
Salem
Salisbury
Sharon
Sherborn
Shrewsbury
Spencer
Stoneham
Sturbridge
Taunton
Topsfield

Upton
Wakefield
Waltham
Wareham
Warren
Webster
Wellfleet
Westborough
Westfield
Winthrop
Worcester
Wrentham

Michigan
Bark River
Bedford Township
Berkley
Beverly Hills
Brooklyn
Clinton County
Clinton Township
Crawford County
Crystal Falls
Eaton County
Farmington Hills
Flint-Genesee County
4th Congressional District
Grand Blanc
Grand Rapids-Kent County
Ironwood
Manchester
Marshall
Mecosta County
Michigan Reformatory
Midland
Milford
Mount Pleasant
Novi
Oakland County
Orion
Plymouth
Pontiac
Saginaw County
Saline
Southfield
Swartz Creek
Troy
Windsor Charter Township
Wixom
Wyandotte

Minnesota
Bertha
Bloomington
Brainerd
Brooklyn Center
Brooklyn Park
Clarissa
Columbia Heights
Dilworth
Dodge County
Eagle Bend
Eden Prairie
Goodridge
Hopkins
Houston
Long Prairie
Madison
Mankato-North Mankato
Moorhead-Clay County
Osakis

Pine Island
Red Wing
Rochester-Olmsted County
Roseville
Rush City
Rushford
St. James
Winona

Mississippi
Biloxi
Brandon
Calhoun
Crystal Springs
Jackson County
Long Beach
Lucedale-George County
Natchez-Adams County
Richland
Shelby
Tupelo

Missouri
Albany
Atchison County
Aurora
Belton
Blue Springs
Boone County
Branson
Bridgeton
Canton
Cape Girardeau
Chillicothe-Livingston County
Clarksdale
Clayton
Creve Coeur
De Soto
East Prairie
Edina-Knox County
El Dorado Springs
Ferguson
Festus
Florissant
Fredericktown
Garden City
Graham
Hamilton
Hannibal
Hazelwood
Hermann
Higbee
Houston
Howell County
Huntsville
Independence
Jackson
Jamesport
Jefferson City
Kahoka
Kansas City
Kimberling City
Kirksville-Adair County
Lamar
Lathrop
Lee's Summit
Liberal
Lockwood
Maryville
Moberly
Monett
Mount Vernon
Mountain Grove

New Madrid
North Kansas City
Olivette
Osage County
Osceola
Paris
Perryville
Poplar Bluff
Saint Ann
Saint Charles
Saint Joseph
Saint Louis
Saint Louis County
Saint Peters
Sedalia
Ste. Genevieve
Sullivan
Sumner
Tarkio
Trenton
Warrensburg
Warrenton-Warren County
Waverly

Montana
Bozeman
Butte-Silver Bow County
Cut Bank
Great Falls
Helena
Missoula
Missoula County

Nebraska
Aurora
Bruning
Gage County
Grand Island-Hall County
Hartington
Lexington
Lincoln
Logan County
Milford
Minden
North Platte
Omaha
O'Neill
Plattsmouth
Ralston
Scottsbluff-Gering
Seward
Sutton
York

Nevada
Carlin
Carson City
Elko
Eureka
Hawthorne-Mineral County
Henderson
Humboldt County-
    Winnemucca
Lander County
Las Vegas
Lincoln County
Lovelock-Pershing County
Pioche
Reno
Reno-Sparks-Indian Colony
Sparks
White Pine County
Yerington

New Hampshire
Alstead
Alton
Amherst
Antrim
Ashland
Belmont
Berlin
Bethlehem
Bradford
Brentwood
Bridgewater
Bristol
Campton
Canaan
Candia
Claremont
Derry
Dorchester
Durham
Ellsworth
Farmington
Franklin
Gilford
Goffstown
Goshen
Groton
Hampton
Hebron
Hillsborough
Holderness
Hollis
Jefferson
Kingston
Lancaster
Landaff
Londonderry
Lyme
Manchester
Meredith
Milford
Mont Vernon
Nashua
New Castle
Newton
Orange
Orford
Ossipee
Plaistow
Plymouth
Raymond
Rindge
Rumney
Salem
Somersworth
Sullivan
Tamworth
Thornton
Unity
Wakefield
Warren
Washington
Waterville Valley
Wentworth
Whitefield
Winchester
Wolfeboro

New Jersey
Allendale
Atlantic City
Avalon
Beach Haven
Bedminster Township
Belleville Township
Bergen County
Bergenfield
Berkeley
Berlin
Bloomfield
Boonton
Bradley Beach
Brielle
Burlington
Califon
Camden County
Cape May Court House
Carteret
Chatham
Cherry Hill
Chester
Clementon
Cliffside Park
Closter
Cranbury
Cranford
Cresskill
Cumberland County
Delran
Demarest
Denville
Dover
Eagleswood (Township of)
East Hanover
East Orange
Edison
Elizabeth
Englewood
Essex
Estell Manor
Ewing
Fanwood
Flemington
Franklin Lakes
Freehold
Garwood
Gibbstown (Greenwich Township)
Glen Ridge
Glen Rock
Gloucester County
Green Township
Haddonfield
Hampton (Township of)
Hanover (Township of)
Haworth
Hazlet
Highlands Borough
Hightstown
Hillsdale
Holmdel
Hopatcong
Hopewell
Hudson County
Hunterdon County
Irvington
Jefferson (Township of)
Jersey City
Keyport
Kinnelon

CONTINUED NEXT PAGE

Lavallette
Lawrence Township
Linden
Lindenwold (Borough of)
Little Silver
Livingston
Lower Alloways Creek
    (Township of)
Lumberton
Magnolia
Mahwah
Manasquan
Mantua Township
Maple Shade
Maplewood
Medford
Mendham
Middletown
Millburn
Monmouth County
Monroe Township
    (Gloucester Co.)
Monroe Township
    (Middlesex Co.)
Montclair
Montville Township
Morris County
Morris Township
Mount Olive
Mountainside
Neptune
New Providence
Newark
North Arlington
    (Borough of)
North Haledon
North Plainfield
Oakland
Oaklyn
Ocean City
Ocean Gate
Old Bridge
Oradell
Park Ridge
Perth Amboy
Plainsboro
Prospect Park
Ramsey
Randolph
Ridgefield Park
Ridgewood
Ringwood Borough
Roseland
Roselle Park
Runnemede
Saddle River
Sandyston
Sea Isle City
Seaside Heights
Shrewsbury
Somers Point
South River
Sparta
Springfield
Spring Lake
Spring Lake Heights
    Borough
Stratford
Teaneck
Union Beach
Wall

Wayne
West Caldwell
Wildwood Crest
Woodbridge
Woodcliff Lake
Wyckoff

New Mexico
Alamogordo
Albuquerque
Aztec
Bosque Farms
Carlsbad
Espanola
Gallup-McKinney County
Grants
Hatch
Hobbs
Las Cruces
Lincoln County
Los Alamos County
Mesilla
Roswell
Santa Fe
Tucumcari

New York
Albany
Albany County
Altamont
Aurora-East Aurora
Ausable Forks
Babylon
Ballston
Bayville
Bedford
Bellmont
Binghamton
Blooming Grove
Briarcliff Manor
Brighton
Broadalbin
Bronx County
Brookhaven
Brooklyn-Kings County
Broome County
Brunswick
Buffalo
Cambria
Cambridge
Canajoharie
Canandaigua
Cape Vincent
Cape Vincent Village
Carmel
Castile
Caton
Cattaraugus County
Cayuga County
Cedarhurst
Champion
Cheektowaga
Chemung County
Chester
Clifton Park
Clinton
Clinton County
Clinton-Dutchess County
Cobleskill
Colonie
Concord

Cortland County
Cortlandville
Coxsackie
Dansville
Darien Center
Deferiet
Delaware County
Deposit
Dobbs Ferry
Dutchess County
East Fishkill
East Syracuse (Village of)
Eastchester
Elmira
Ephratah
Essex County
Floyd County
Forestburgh
Frankfort
Franklinville
Friendship
Fulton County
Galway
Gates
Genesee County
Gerry
Gilbertsville
Glen Cove
Gloversville
Gouverneur
Grand Island
Greenburgh
Greenwood Lake
Hague
Harford
Harrison (Town)-
    Harrison (Village)
Hartwick
Hempstead
Hermon
Holland Patent
Hopkinton
Hornell
Hudson
Huntington
Hurley
Ilion
Ithaca
Jamestown
Java
Jay
Johnson City
Johnstown (City of)
Johnstown (Town of)
Jordan (Village of)
Kinderhook
Kingston
Kirkland (Town of)
Lake Carmel-Kent
Lake George
Lake Luzerne
Larchmont
Lewis County
Lisle
Livingston County
Lockport
Lynbrook

Madison County
Malta
Malverne
Mamaroneck
Manhattan (Borough of)
Marion
Marlborough (Town of)
Mayfield
Milton
Mineola
Monroe County
Montgomery County
Montour Falls (Village of)
Morristown
Mount Pleasant
Mount Vernon
Nelsonville
Newburgh
New Castle
New Hempstead
New Rochelle
New York City
Niagara County
Niskayuna
North Collins (Town of)
North Collins (Village of)
North Greenbush
North Haven
North Hempstead
North Salem
North Tonawanda
Northport
Norwich
Ogdensburg
Old Brookville
Olean
Oneida County
Onondaga
Onondaga County
Orange County
Orangetown
Oswego County
Oyster Bay
Palermo
Patterson
Pawling
Pelham
Perth
Plattsburgh
Poestenkill
Pomona
Port Chester (Village of)
Port Jervis
Port Leyden
Potsdam
Poughkeepsie (City of)
Poughkeepsie (Town of)
Prattsburg
Putnam County
Rensselaer County
Rensselaerville (City of)
Richmond County
Richville
Rochester
Rockland County
Round Lake
Roxbury
Rye
Rye Brook

Saint Johnsville
Salamanca
Salem
Saratoga
Saratoga County
Saratoga Springs
Scarsdale
Schenectady
Schenectady County
Schoharie
Schoharie County
Schuyler County
Seneca
Seneca Falls
Skaneateles
Smithtown
Somers
Somerset
South Glens Falls
Southampton
Southeast
Southold
Spafford
Stillwater
Stockholm
Stratford
Suffern
Suffolk County
Sullivan County
Syracuse (City of)
Tonawanda
Tuckahoe
Ulster County
Union
Utica
Vernon
Vestal
Virgil
Waddington (Town of)
Waddington (Village of)
Walworth
Wappinger
Warsaw
Warwick
Watervliet
Waverly
Wawarsing
Weedsport
Wellsville
West Seneca
Westchester County
Western
Whitestown
Whitney Point
Williamson
Wilson
Wilton
Wyoming County
York County
Youngstown

North Carolina
Alamance County
Alexander County
Alleghany County
Anson County
Ashe County
Avery County

Beaufort County
Bertie County
Bladen County
Brunswick County
Buncombe County
Burke County
Cabarrus County
Caldwell County
Camden County
Carteret County
Caswell County
Catawba County
Charlotte-Mecklenburg County
Chatham County
Cherokee County
Chowan County
Clay County
Cleveland County
Columbus County
Cramerton County
Craven County
Currituck County
Dare County
Davidson County
Davie County
Duplin County
Durham County
Edgecombe County
Elizabeth City-Pasquotank County
Fayetteville
Forsyth County
Franklin County
Gaston County
Gates County
Graham County
Granville County
Greene County
Guilford County
Halifax County
Harnett County
Haywood County
Henderson County
Hertford County
Hoke County
Hyde County
Iredell County
Jackson County
Johnston County
Lee County
Lenoir County
Lincoln County
Macon County
Madison County
Martin County
McDowell County
Mitchell County
Montgomery County
Moore County
Nash County
Northampton County
Onslow County
Orange County
Pamlico County
Pender County
Perquimans County
Pitt County
Polk County

Randolph County
Richmond County
Robeson County
Rockingham County
Rowan County
Roxboro-Person County
Rutherford College (Town of)
Rutherford County
Sampson County
Scotland County
Stanly County
Stokes County
Surry County
Swain County
Transylvania County
Tyrrell County
Union County
Vance County
Wake County
Warren County
Washington County
Watauga County
Wayne County
Wilkes County
Wilmington-
    New Hanover County
Wilson County
Yadkin County
Yancey County

North Dakota
Bismarck
Dickinson
Dunn Center
Rugby
Wahpeton

Ohio
Adams County
Adamsville
Arlington Heights
Ashland County
Ashville (Village of)
Athens
Aurora
Belpre-Little Hocking
Berea
Beverly-Waterford
Brook Park
Canfield
Canton
Chardon
Chillicothe-Ross County
Clermont County
Cleves
Clyde
Columbus
Crawford County
Dalton (Village of)
Darke County
Dayton-Montgomery County
Defiance
Delphos
Dublin
East Liverpool
Eastlake
Edgerton
Elyria
Euclid
Evendale
Fairborn
Fairfield County
Fairport Harbor

Gallia County
Geauga County
Groveport
Hillsboro
Hubbard
Huber Heights
Jefferson County
Kent
Kettering
Killbuck
Knox County
Lakewood
Lawrence County
Liberty
Licking County
Lorain County
Louisville
Mahoning County
Mansfield-Richland County
Marietta
Marion County
Mason
Medina County
Meigs County
Mentor
Mentor-on-the-Lake
Mercer County
Middleburg Heights
Middletown
Milford
Mingo Junction
Monroe County
Montgomery
Moraine
Mount Gilead
Mount Holly
New Lexington
North Olmstead
Norton
Oberlin
Orrville
Parma Heights
Perrysburg
Phillipsburg
Poland
Port Clinton
Putnam County
Russells Point
Saint Bernard
Seven Hills
Sheffield Lake
Solon
Spring Valley
Tiffin-Seneca County
Trotwood
Twinsburg
University Heights
Upper Arlington
Warren-Trumbell County
Westfield Center
Wickliffe
Willoughby
Wintersville
Wood County
Woodlawn
Worthington
Xenia

CONTINUED NEXT PAGE

Oklahoma
Ada
Agra
Alva
Boise City
Broken Arrow
Chelsea
Chickasha
Claremore
Collinsville
Del City
Duncan
Edmond
Elk City
Guthrie
Le Flore
Lincoln County
Mangum
Marietta-Love County
McAlester
Midwest City
Nash
Nichols Hills
Noble
Norman
Oklahoma City
Pauls Valley
Pawnee
Ponca City
Sac and Fox Tribe of Indians
Sapulpa
Shattuck
Shawnee
Skiatook
Stillwater-Payne County
Tatums
The Village
Tulsa
Warr Acres
Yukon

Oregon
Ashland
Astoria
Baker County
Beaverton
Brookings
Canby
Clatskanie
Estacada
Hermiston
Hillsboro
Hood River County
Independence-Monmouth
Jackson County
Klamath Falls
Molalla
Portland-Multnomah County
Reedsport
Roseburg
Salem
Stayton
Tillamook
Wasco County
West Linn
Wilsonville
Yamhill

Pennsylvania
Allegheny County
Aspinwall (Borough of)

Beaver County
Bell
Berks County
Big Run
Blair County
Boyertown
Brookville
California
Chambersburg (Borough of)
Chester County
Clinton County
Coplay
Cumru
Curwensville
Dallastown
Delaware County
Dubois
Fulton County
Hanover
Indiana County
Jefferson County
Jessup
Lackawanna
Lebanon County
Limerick
Mercer County
Moon (Township of)
Muncy
Nanty Glo
New Hope
New Wilmington
Newtown (Borough of)
Newtown (Township of)
Northampton County
Philadelphia
Pike County
Pine Creek Township
Portage
Pottsville
Punxsutawney
Slatington
Slippery Rock Borough
Upper Merion Township
Upper Southampton
Walnutport
Washington
West Chester Borough
West Reading
Whitehall
Whitpain

Puerto Rico
San Juan

Rhode Island
Barrington
Bristol
Burrillville
Central Falls
Charlestown
Coventry
Cranston
Cumberland
East Greenwich
East Providence
Exeter
Foster
Glocester
Hopkinton
Jamestown
Johnston
Lincoln
Little Compton
Middletown

Newport
New Shoreham
North Kingstown
North Providence
North Smithfield
Pawtucket
Portsmouth
Providence
Richmond
Scituate
Smithfield
Tiverton
Warren
Warwick
West Greenwich
West Warwick
Westerly
Woonsocket

South Carolina
Aiken
Anderson-Anderson County
Beaufort County
Belton
Brunson
Cayce
Charleston
Columbia
Florence
Gaffney
Georgetown
Greenville
Greenwood County
Greer
Hilton Head
Lake City
Landrum
Laurens County
McCormick County
Moncks Corner
North Charleston
Perry
Prosperity
Rock Hill
Saluda-Saluda County
Smoaks
Winnsboro

South Dakota
Aberdeen-Brown County
Elk Point
Madison
Pollock
Sturgis
Wessington Springs

Tennessee
Athens
Atwood
Chattanooga
Church Hill
Clarksville
Cleveland-Bradley County
Clinton
Cross Plains
Dayton
Decatur
East Ridge
Farragut
Fayette County
Gallaway
Gatlinburg
Germantown

Hawkins County
Hohenwald-Lewis County
Jackson
Jasper
Johnson City
Knoxville-Knox County
Lakeland
Lavergne
Lawrenceburg
Lenoir City
Madisonville
Manchester
Memphis-Shelby County
Newport-Cocke County
Norris
Obion
Polk County
Powell's Crossroads
Red Bank
Robertson County
Rutherford County
Sumner County-18th Judicial District
Tipton County
Tullahoma
Union City
Warren County
Woodland Mills

Texas
Arlington
Austin
Bay City
Blanco
Blanket
Boerne
Breckenridge
Brownsville
Caldwell
Canyon
Cedar Hill
Collin County
Corpus Christi-Nueces County
Crowley
Dalhart
Dallas County
Denton
Devine
Dumas
Eagle Pass-Maverick County
El Paso
Fairfield
Forest Hill
Grand Prairie
Garyson County
Haltom City
Hedwig Village
Henderson County
Hereford
Humble
Huntsville-Walker County
Irving
Jacksonville
Katy
Kirby
La Grulla
La Marque
Lexington
Llano
Lubbock
Martin County
McLendon-Chisholm
Memphis
Mesquite

Nacogodoches County
Nocona
North Richland Hills
Odessa-Extor County
Pampa
Palo Pinto County
Panola County
Plainview
Port Aransas
River Oaks
Robinson
Rowlett
San Antonio-Bexar County
San Augustine
Shoreacres
Springtown
Stafford
Stinnett
Terrell Hills
Texarkana
Tyler
Tyler County
Victoria
Waco-McLennan County
Wellington-Collingsworth County
Woodway

Utah
American Fork
Big Water
Blanding
Brigham City
Cache County
Cedar City
Circleville
Clearfield
Davis County
Duchesne County
Edinburgh
Fairview
Green River
Heber City
Honeyville
Junction
Kanab
Kaysville-Fruit Heights City
Kingston
La Verkin
Layton
Manila
Marysvale
Midvale
Murray
North Salt Lake
Ogden
Orem
Payson City
Piute County
Pleasant Grove
Price
Providence
Park City
Provo
River Heights
Roy City
Saint George
Salt Lake City
Salt Lake County
Sandy City
Sanpete County
Santa Clara
South Ogden

Spanish Fork City
Springville
Syracuse
Uintah County
Utah County
Wasatch County
Washington Terrace
West Jordan
West Valley City

Vermont
Arlington
Athens
Burlington
Castleton
Hinesburg
Middlebury
Plainfield
Rutland
Shelburne
Windsor
Winhall

Virginia
Alexandria
Alleghany County
Arlington County
Augusta County
Bedford
Blacksburg
Bluefield
Botecourt
Bridgewater
Brunswick County
Buckingham
Campbell County
Caroline County
Carroll County
Charles City County
Charlotte County
Charlottesville-Albemarle County
Chesapeake
Chesterfield County
Chincoteague
Clarke County-Frederick County-
    Winchester
Clifton Forge
Colonial Heights
Covington
Danville
Essex County
Fairfax County
Falls Church
Fauquier County
Fluvanna County
Franklin
Front Royal
Galax
Gloucester County
Halifax County
Hampton
Hanover County
Harrisonburg-Rockingham County
Highland County
Hopewell
Loudoun County
Lynchburg
Manassas Park
Mathews County
Mecklenburg County
New Kent County
Newport News
Nottoway County

Orange County
Petersburg
Pittsylvania County
Portsmouth
Powhatan County
Prince Edward County
Prince George County
Prince William County
Reston
Richmond
Roanoke-Roanoke County
Salem
Scott County
Smyth County
South Boston
Staunton
Suffolk
Tazwell County
Virginia Beach
Washington County
Waynesboro
Westmoreland County
Williamsburg-
    James City County
York County

Washington
Adams County
Asotin County
Auburn
Bellevue
Benton County-Franklin County
Clallam County
Clark County
Dayton-Columbia County
Grant County
Grays Harbor County
Island County
Kelso
King County
Kittitas County
Lincoln County
Mason County
Palouse
Pierce County
San Juan County
Snohomish County
Spokane County
Stevens County
Tacoma
Thurston County
Wahkiakum County
Yakima
Yakima County
Walla Walla

West Virginia
Aurora
Bluefield
Ceredo
Fairmont
Moundsville
New Martinsville
Nitro
Parkersburg
Point Pleasant
Princeton
Richwood
Shepherdstown
Shinnston

Sistersville
Vienna
Wellsburg
Wheeling

Wisconsin
Albany
Alma
Altoona
Ashland
Beloit
Brookfield
Cottage Grove
Dane County
Delavan
Elm Grove
Evansville
Green Bay-Brown County
Hartford
Janesville
Kenosha County
Kewaskum
Marinette County
Menomonie
Neenah
New London
Oak Creek
Oconto County
Oshkosh
Outagamie County
Pewaukee
Port Washington
Richland County
Sheboygan County
Stevens Point-Portage County
Stratford
Superior-Douglas County
Tigerton
Tomah
Two Rivers
Viroqua
West Allis
Whitewater
Winnebago
Wisconsin Dells
Woodville

Wyoming
Basin
Casper
Cheyenne
Cody
Dubois
East Thermopolis
Evanston
Gillette
Green River
Jackson-Teton County
Kemmerer
Lander
Laramie
Lovell
Luck-Niobrara County
Manderson
Newcastle-Weston County
Platte County
Rawlins
Saratoga
Sheridan
Shoshoni
Thermopolis
Torrington-Goshen County
Washakie County

DESIGNATED BICENTENNIAL DEFENSE COMMUNITIES

Department of Defense Joint Organizations

Americans on Okinawa, *Japan*
Defense Courier Service Station, *Guam*
Defense Depot, *Memphis, Tennessee*
Defense Logistics Agency Defense Depot, *Mechanicsburg, Pennsylvania*
Defense Logistics Agency Defense Electronics Supply Center,
    Dayton, Ohio
Defense Reutilization and Marketing Office, *Cannon, New Mexico*
Saudi Arabia Training Mission, *Dhahran, Saudi Arabia*
Spokane Military Entrance Processing Station, *Washington*

Department of the Air Force

9th Missile Warning Squadron, Robins Air Force Base, *Georgia*
22nd Air Refueling Wing, March Air Force Base, *California*
857 Combat Support Group, Minot Air Force Base, *North Dakota*
927th Tactical Airlift Group, Selfridge Air National Guard Base, *Michigan*
2002nd Communications Squadron, Altus, *Oklahoma*
Air Force Accounting & Finance Center, Lowry Air Force Base,
    Denver, Colorado
Bolling Air Force Base, *Washington, D.C.*
Bradley Air National Guard, *East Granby, Connecticut*
Chanute Air Force Base, *Illinois*
Davis-Monthan Air Force Base, *Tucson, Arizona*
District of Columbia Air National Guard, *Washington, D.C.*
Dover Air Force Base, *Delaware*
Luke Air Force Base, *Arizona*
Michigan Employer Support of Guard and Reserve State Executive
    Committee, *Selfridge Air National Guard Base, Michigan*
Norton Air Force Base, *California*
Tinker Air Force Base, *Oklahoma City, Oklahoma*
Vandenberg Air Force Base, *California*
Wilford Hall Air Force Medical Center, *San Antonio, Texas*
William Air Force Base, *Arizona*

Department of the Army

6th Infantry Division (Light) and U.S. Army Garrison, Headquarters,
    Alaska
8th Infantry Division, *Germany*
80th Division (TNG), 2nd Battalion, 319th Regiment, 2nd Brigade,
    Blacksburg, Virginia
81st United States Army Reserve Command, Headquarters, *East Point,*
    Georgia
125th United States Army Reserve Command, *Nashville, Tennessee*
132nd Support Battalion, *Madison, Wisconsin*
157th Separate Infantry Brigade, *Horsham, Pennsylvania*
Anniston Army Depot, *Alabama*
Ansbach Military Community, *Germany*
Arlington Hall Station, *Virginia*
Aschaffenberg Military Community, *Germany*
Augsburg Military Community, *Germany*

Bad Aibling Station, *Germany*
Bad Kreuznach Military Community, *Germany*
Bamberg Military Community, *Germany*
Baumholder Military Community, *Germany*
Berlin United States Command, *Germany*
Camp Beauregard, *Pineville, Louisiana*
Camp Carroll, *Korea*
Camp Dodge, *Johnston, Iowa*
Camp Mabry, *Austin, Texas*
Camp Lincoln, *Springfield, Illinois*
Camp Zama Kanagawa Prefecture, *Japan*
Cameron Station, *Alexandria, Virginia*
Carlisle Barracks, *Pennsylvania*
Caserma Ederle, *Vincenza, Italy*
Cold Regions Research and Engineering Laboratory, *Hanover,*
    New Hampshire
Colorado National Guard, *Denver, Colorado*
Corpus Christi Army Depot, *Texas*
Darmstadt Military Community, *Germany*
Defense Logistics Agency, *Alexandria, Virginia*
Defense Mapping Agency, *Washington, D.C.*
Dugway Proving Ground, *Utah*
Fort Belvoir — 310th Theater Area Command, *Virginia*
Fort Belvoir — Davison Aviation Command, *Virginia*
Fort Belvoir — Engineer Center, *Virginia*
Fort Benjamin Harrison, *Indiana*
Fort Benning, *Georgia*
Fort Bliss, *Texas*
Fort Bragg, *North Carolina*
Fort Campbell, *Kentucky*
Fort Carson, *Colorado*
Fort Devens, *Massachusetts*
Fort Dix, *New Jersey*
Fort Drum, *New York*
Fort Eustis, *Virginia*
Fort Gillem, *Georgia*
Fort Gordon, *Georgia*
Fort Hood — III Corps, *Texas*
Fort Hood — West Fort Hood (TCATA), *Texas*
Fort Huachuca, *Arizona*
Fort Jackson, *South Carolina*
Fort Leavenworth, *Kansas*
Fort Leonard Wood, *Missouri*
Fort Lee, *Virginia*
Fort Lewis, *Washington*
Fort McClellan, *Alabama*
Fort Meade — 97th Reserve Command, *Maryland*
Fort Meade — Headquarters, *Maryland*
Fort Monmouth, *New Jersey*
Fort Monroe, *Virginia*
Fort Myer, Virginia
Fort Ord, *California*
Fort Polk, *Louisiana*
Fort Sam Houston, *Texas*
Fort Shafter, *Hawaii*
Fort Sheridan, *Illinois*
Fort Sill, *Oklahoma*
Fort Stewart, *Georgia*
Fort Riley, *Kansas*
Fort Ritchie, *Maryland*
Fort Rucker, *Alabama*
Garmisch Military Community, *Germany*
Greater Stuttgart Military Community, *Germany*
Hanau Military Community, *Germany*
Heidelberg Military Community, *Germany*
Holston Ammunition Plant, *Kingsport, Tennessee*
Judge Advocates General's School, *Charlottesville, Virginia*
Karlsruhe Military Community, *Germany*
Kilbourne Kaserne Military Community, *Schwetzingen, Germany*
Livorno Military Community, *Tuscany, Italy*
Longhorn Ammunition Plant, *Marshall, Texas*
Louisiana National Guard — Headquarters, *Jackson Barracks, Louisiana*

Mannheim Military Community, *Germany*
Military District of Washington, *Washington, D.C.*
Military Ocean Terminal, *Bayonne, New Jersey*
Military Traffic Management Command, *Falls Church, Virginia*
Missouri National Guard, *Jefferson City, Missouri*
Munich Military Community, *Germany*
North Little Rock Bicentennial Committee, *Arkansas*
Papago Military Reservation, *Phoenix, Arizona*
Pennsylvania National Guard, *Annville, Pennsylvania*
Phoenix Military Entrance Processing Station, *Arizona*
Picatinny Arsenal, *New Jersey*
Piramasens Military Community, *Germany*
Red River Army Depot, *Texarkana, Texas*
Redstone Arsenal Support, *Huntsville, Alabama*
Rock Island Arsenal, *Illinois*
Roosevelt County, *Portales, New Mexico*
Schwaebisch GMUEND Sub-Community, *Germany*
Schwaebisch Hall Military Sub-Community, *Germany*
Schweinfurt Military Community, *Germany*
Seneca Army Depot, *Romulus, New York*
Storck Barracks, *Illeshrim, Germany*
Tank Automotive Command, *Warren, Michigan*
Tobyhanna Army Depot, *Monroe County, Pennsylvania*
Torii Station, *Okinawa, Japan*
United States Army Aviation Systems Command, *St. Louis, Missouri*
United States Army Concepts Analysis Agency, *Bethesda, Maryland*
United States Army Laboratory Command, *Adelphi, Maryland*
United States Army Test 7 Evaluation Command & Aberdeen Proving Ground, *Maryland*
Vicenza Military Community, *Italy*
Vint Hill Farms Station, *Warrenton, Virginia*
Waterways Experiment Station, *Vicksburg, Mississippi*
West Point Military Academy, *New York*
Wuerzburg Military Community, *Germany*
Yongsan and Area III, *Korea*

Department of the Navy
Assault Craft Unit Two, *Norfolk, Virginia*
Assault Craft Unit Five, *Camp Pendleton, California*
Bangor Naval Submarine Base, *Silverdale, Washington*
Guam Naval Facility, *San Francisco, California*
Mayport Naval Station, *Florida*
Naval & Marine Corps Reserve Center, *Encino, California*
Naval & Marine Corps Reserve Center, *New Haven, Connecticut*
Naval Air Engineering Center, *Lakehurst, New Jersey*
Naval Air Station, *Jacksonville, Florida*
Naval Air Station, *Pensacola, Florida*
Naval Aviation Supply Office, *Philadelphia, Pennsylvania*
Naval Base Norfolk, *Virginia*
Naval Communications Station, *Keflavik, Iceland*
Naval Communications Station, *United Kingdom*
Naval Construction Battalion Center, *Gulfport, Mississippi*
Naval District Washington, *Washington, D.C.*
Naval Facility Brawdy, *Wales, United Kingdom*
Naval Ocean Processing Facility, *Dam Neck, Virginia*
Naval Plant Representative Office, *St. Louis, Missouri*
Naval Reserve Center, *Corpus Christi, Texas*
Naval Security Group Activity, *Terceira Island, Azores*
Naval Surface Station, *Long Beach, California*
Naval Training Station, *Great Lakes, Illinois*
Naval Training Station, *Orlando, Florida*
Naval Training Station, *San Diego, California*
Naval Technical Training Center, *Corry Station, Pensacola, Florida*
Submarine Squadron Twenty-two, *La Maddalena, Sardinia, Italy*
United States Navy Fleet Activities, *Chinae, South Korea*
United States Navy Support Office, *La Maddalena, Sardinia, Italy*
USS Affray, *Newport, Rhode Island*
USS Aries, *Key West, Florida*
USS Constitution, *Charlestown, Massachusetts*
USS Dwight Eisenhower, *Norfolk, Virginia*
USS Edson (DD 946), *West Haven, Connecticut*
USS Estocin, *Philadelphia, Pennsylvania*
USS Exploit (MSO-440), *Newport, Rhode Island*
USS Gunston Hall, *Little Creek, Virginia*
USS John Hancock, *Miami, Florida*
USS Mahan, *Charleston, South Carolina*
USS Missouri, *Long Beach, California*
USS Orion (AS 18), *La Maddalena, Sardinia, Italy*
USS Oliver Hazard Perry, *Philadelphia, Pennsylvania*
USS Philippine Sea (CG-58), *Miami, Florida*
USS Prairie, *Long Beach Caliornia*
USS Robert E. Peary, *Pearl Harbor, Hawaii*
USS Samuel Eliot Morison, *Charleston, South Carolina*
USS Santa Barbara, *Miami, Florida*
USS Stark, *Mayport, Florida*
USS Taurus, *Mayport, Florida*
USS Thomas S. Gates, *Norfolk, Virginia*
USS Trippe, *New York, New York*
USS Valley Forge, *San Diego, California*
USS Wabash, *San Francisco, California*

Marine Corps
Marine Corps Air Stations, El Toro & Tustin, *Santa Ana, California*

BICENTENNIAL CAMPUSES

Alabama

University of Alabama, *Birmingham*
Livingston University, *Livingston*
Huntingdon College, *Montgomery*
Northwest Alabama State Junior College, *Phil Campbell*
Northeast Alabama State Junior College, *Rainsville*
Stillman College, *Tuscaloosa*
Southern Union State Junior College, *Wadley*

Arkansas

Henderson State University, *Arkadelphia*
Ouachita Baptist University, *Arkadelphia*
Mississippi County Community College, *Blytheville*
University of Central Arkansas, *Conway*
University of Arkansas, *Monticello*
Crowley's Ridge College, *Paragould*
John Brown University, *Siloam Springs*

California

Cabrillo College, *Aptos*
California State University, *Carson*
De Anza College, *Cupertino*
Christian Heritage College, *El Cajon*
Cuyamaca College, *El Cajon*
College of the Redwoods, *Eureka*
California State University, *Fresno*
University of California/San Diego, *La Jolla*
Biola University, *La Mirada*
Los Angeles Southwest College, *Los Angeles*
Northrop University, *Los Angeles*
Holy Names College, *Oakland*
Chapman College, *Orange*
Diablo Valley College, *Pleasant Hill*
Feather River College, *Quincy*
San Diego State University, *San Diego*
Mount San Jacinto College, *San Jacinto*
San Jose State University, *San Jose*
Santa Clara University School of Law, *Santa Clara*
West Valley College, *Saratoga*
Humphreys College, *Stockton*
El Camino College, *Torrance*
California State University/Stanislaus, *Turlock*
Rio Hondo College, *Whittier*

Colorado

United States Air Force Academy, *Colorado Springs*
Red Rocks Community College, *Golden*
Front Range Community College, *Westminster*

Connecticut

Fairfield University, *Fairfield*
Albertus Magnus College, *New Haven*
United States Coast Guard Academy, *New London*
Norwalk Community College, *Norwalk*
Briarwood College, *Southington*
University of Connecticut, *Storrs*
Saint Alphonsus College, *Suffield*
Saint Joseph College, *West Hartford*
University of Hartford, *West Hartford*
Northwestern Connecticut Community College, *Winsted*

District of Columbia

American University
Southeastern University

Florida

South Florida Community College, *Avon Park*
Brevard Community College, *Cocoa*
Santa Fe Community College, *Gainesville*
Florida Community College, *Jacksonville*
Jacksonville University, *Jacksonville*
Florida Southern College, *Lakeland*
Lake-Sumter Community College, *Leesburg*
Miami-Dale Community College, *Miami*
Barry University, *Miami Shores*
Central Florida Community College, *Ocala*
Valencia Community College, *Orlando*
Gulf Coast Community College, *Panama City*
University of West Florida, *Pensacola*
Flagler College, *St. Augustine*
Saint Petersburg Junior College, *St. Petersburg*
Florida A & M University, *Tallahassee*
Florida State University, *Tallahassee*
Tallahassee Community College, *Tallahassee*
University of South Florida, *Tampa*

Georgia

Georgia Southwestern College, *Americus*
Morehouse College, *Atlanta*
Bainbridge Junior College, *Bainbridge*
Gordon Junior College, *Barnesville*
Brunswick College, *Brunswick*
Columbus College, *Columbus*
Andrew College, *Cuthbert*
Agnes Scott College, *Decatur*
Brenau College, *Gainesville*
LaGrange College, *LaGrange*
Berry College, *Mount Berry*
Armstrong State College, *Savannah*
Thomas College, *Thomasville*

Iowa

Luther College, *Decorah*
Drake University, *Des Moines*
University of Dubuque, *Dubuque*
Vennard College, *University Park*

Idaho

Northwest Nazarene College, *Nampa*

Illinois

Kaskaskia College, *Centralia*
City Colleges of Chicago, *Chicago*
Northeastern Illinois University, *Chicago*
Robert Morris College, *Chicago*
Danville Area Community College, *Danville*
Northern Illinois University, *Dekalb*
Oakton Community College, *Des Plaines*
Southern Illinois University, *Edwardsville*
Elgin Community College, *Elgin*
MacMurray College, *Jacksonville*
Kankakee Community College, *Kankakee*
Olivet Nazarene University, *Kankakee*
DeVry Institute of Technology, *Lombard*
Western Illinois University, *Macomb*
Kishwaukee Community College, *Malta*
Monmouth College, *Monmouth*
Illinois Eastern Community College, *Mount Carmel*
Moraine Valley Community College, *Palos Hills*
Triton College, *River Grove*
Sangamon State University, *Springfield*

Indiana

University of Southern Indiana, *Evansville*
Indiana University Northwest, *Gary*
Butler University, *Indianapolis*
University of Indianapolis, *Indianapolis*
Ball State University, *Muncie*
Indiana University, *South Bend*
Saint Mary-of-the-Woods College, *St. Mary-of-the-Woods*
Indiana State University, *Terre Haute*
Rose-Hulman Institute of Technology, *Terre Haute*
Vincennes University, *Vincennes*
Purdue University, *West Lafayette*
Purdue University North Central Campus, *Westville*

Kansas

Benedictine College, *Atchison*
Fort Hays State University, *Hays*
Washburn University of Topeka, *Topeka*
Southwestern College, *Winfield*

Kentucky

Elizabethtown Community College, *Elizabethtown*
Madisonville Community College, *Madisonville*
Morehead State University, *Morehead*
Prestonburg Community College, *Prestonburg*

Louisiana

University of Southwest Louisiana, *Lafayette*
McNeese State University, *Lake Charles*
Tulane University, *New Orleans*
Pioneer Heritage Center, *Shreveport*

Massachusetts

Massasoit Community College, *Brockton*
Fitchburg State College, *Fitchburg*
Greenfield Community College, *Greenfield*
Holyoke Community College, *Holyoke*
Quincy Junior College, *Quincy*
Springfield Technical College, *Springfield*

Maryland

Catonsville Community College, *Catonsville*
Washington College, *Chestertown*
Prince George's Community College, *Largo*
Towson State University, *Towson*
Chesapeake College, *Wye Mills*

Maine

University of Maine, *Orono*

Michigan

Oakland Community College, *Auburn Hills*
Ferris State College, *Big Rapids*
Charles Stewart Mott Community College, *Flint*
Western Michigan University, *Kalamazoo*
Great Lakes Bible College, *Lansing*

Minnesota

Brainerd Community College, *Brainerd*
Bethany Lutheran College, *Mankato*
Dr. Martin Luther College, *New Ulm*
Hamline University, *St. Paul*
Winona State University, *Winona*

Missouri

Southwest Baptist University, *Bolivar*
Culver-Stockton College, *Canton*
Southeast Missouri State University, *Cape Girardeau*
Mineral Area College, *Flat River*
Missouri Southern State College, *Joplin*
Avila College, *Kansas City*
Penn Valley Community College, *Kansas City*
University of Missouri, *Kansas City*
Park College, *Parkville*
Drury College, *Springfield*
Evangel College of Arts & Sciences of the
     Assembly, *Springfield*
Southwest Missouri State University, *Springfield*
Missouri Western State College, *St. Joseph*
East Central College, *Union*
Central Missouri State University, *Warrensburg*

Mississippi

Delta State University, *Cleveland*
East Central Junior College, *Decatur*
Mississippi Gulf Coast Junior College, *Gautier*
Mississippi Delta Community College, *Moorhead*
Pearl River Community College, *Poplarville*

North Carolina

Anson Technical College, *Ansonville*
Lees-Mcrae College, *Banner Elk*
Campbell University, *Buies Creek*
Elizabeth City State University, *Elizabeth City*
Elon College, *Elon College*
Methodist College, *Fayetteville*
Bennett College, *Greensboro*
ECU School of Medicine, *Greenville*
Caldwell Community Technical Institute, *Hudson*
Coastal Carolina Community College, *Jacksonville*
Lenoir Community College, *Kinston*
Carteret Community College, *Morehead City*
Chowan College, *Murfreesboro*
Pembroke State University, *Pembroke*
Meredith College, *Raleigh*
Shaw University, *Raleigh*
NASH Community College, *Rocky Mount*
Mayland Community College, *Spruce Pine*
Mayland Technical College, *Spruce Pine*
Wingate College, *Wingate*

North Dakota

North Dakota State College of Science, *Wahpeton*

Nebraska

Chadron State College, *Chadron*
Kearney State College, *Kearney*

New Hampshire

New Hampshire College, *Manchester*

New Jersey

Salem Community College, *Carneys Point*
Stevens Institute, *Hoboken*
Jersey City State College, *Jersey City*
Brookdale Community College, *Lincroft*
Felician College, *Lodi*
Rutgers University, *New Brunswick*
New Jersey Institute of Technology, *Newark*
Bergen Community College, *Paramus*
Passaic County Community College, *Paterson*
Burlington County College, *Pemberton*
Raritan Valley Community College, *Somerville*
Cumberland County College, *Vineland*

New Mexico

Saint John's College, *Santa Fe*

Nevada

Clark County Community College, *Henderson*
University of Nevada, *Las Vegas*

New York

Albany Law School, *Albany*
College of Saint Rose, *Albany*
University of New York, *Bronx*
Long Island University, *Brookville*
Corning Community College, *Corning*
State Univesity of New York College, *Cortland*
Elmira College, *Elmira*
Hofstra University, *Hempstead*
Jamestown Community College, *Jamestown*
Sullivan County Community College,
     Loch Sheldrake
Iona College, *New Rochelle*
City University of New York, *New York*
Mount St. Mary College, *Newburgh*
Mater Dei College, *Ogdensburg*
Saint Joseph's College, *Patchogue*
College of Mount St. Vincent, *Riverdale*
Molloy College, *Rockville Centre*
State University of New York, *Saratoga Springs*
Utica School of Commerce, *Utica*
Westchester Community College, *Valhalla*

Ohio

Baldwin-Wallace College, *Berea*
Dyke College, *Cleveland*
Notre Dame College of Ohio, *Cleveland*
Sinclair Community College, *Dayton*
Wayne College, *Orrville*
Miami University, *Oxford*
Ursuline College, *Pepper Pike*
Clark State Community College, *Springfield*
Belmont Technical College, *St. Clairsville*
Jefferson Technical College, *Steubenville*
Otterbein College, *Westerville*
Youngstown State University, *Youngstown*

Oklahoma

Bartlesville Wesleyan College, *Bartlesville*
University of Science & Arts of Oklahoma,
     Chickasha
Rogers State College, *Claremore*
Southeastern Oklahoma State University, *Durant*
Phillips University, *Enid*
Oklahoma State University, *Stillwater*
Tulsa Junior College, *Tulsa*
University of Tulsa, *Tulsa*
Connors State College, *Warner*

Oregon

Oregon State University, *Corvallis*
University of Oregon School of Law, *Eugene*
Eastern Oregon State College, *La Grande*

Pennsylvania

Montgomery County Community College, *Blue Bell*
Butler County Community College, *Butler*
California University of Pennsylvania, *California*
Edinboro University, *Edinboro*
Gannon University, *Erie*
Seton Hill College, *Greensburg*
Thiel College, *Greenville*
Gwynedd-Mercy College, *Gwynedd Valley*
Immaculata College, *Immaculata*
Saint Vincent College, *Latrobe*
Lock Haven University, *Lock Haven*
Mansfield University, *Mansfield*
Chestnut Hill College, *Philadelphia*
Pierce Junior College, *Philadelphia*
Saint Joseph's University, *Philadelphia*
Duquesne University, *Pittsburgh*
Point Park College, *Pittsburgh*
Pennsylvania State University, *Sharon*
Shenango Campus, *Sharon*
Shippensburg University, *Shippenburg*
Villanova University, *Villanova*
Washington and Jefferson College, *Washington*
King's College, *Wilkes-Barre*
Williamsport Area Community College,
     Williamsport
Penn State, *York*

Rhode Island

Community College of Rhode Island/Flanagan
     Campus, *Lincoln*

South Carolina

Beaufort Technical College, *Beaufort*
Chesterfield-Marlboro Technical College, *Cheraw*
Clemson University, *Clemson*
University South Carolina Coastal Carolina
     College, *Columbia*
Horry-Georgetown Technical College, *Conway*
University of South Carolina, *Conway*
Francis Marion College, *Florence*
Limestone College, *Gaffney*
Greenville Technical College, *Greenville*

South Dakota

South Dakota State University, *Brookings*
Dakota State College, *Madison*
Black Hills State College, *Spearfish*
University of South Dakota, *Vermillion*

CONTINUED NEXT PAGE

Tennessee

Bristol College, *Bristol*
Columbia State Community College, *Columbia*
Lincoln Memorial University, *Harrogate*
Freed-Hardeman College, *Henderson*
Pellissippi State Community College, *Knoxville*
University of Tennessee, *Knoxville*
University of Tennessee, *Martin*
LeMoyne-Owen College, *Memphis*

Texas

Abilene Christian University, *Abilene*
Alvin Community College, *Alvin*
Lee College, *Baytown*
East Texas State University, *Commerce*
Del Mar College, *Corpus Christi*
Dallas Baptist University, *Dallas*
El Centro College, *Dallas*
Mountain View College, *Dallas*
Richland College, *Dallas*
University of North Texas, *Denton*
Texas Wesleyan College, *Fort Worth*
Cook County College, *Gainesville*
Houston Community College, *Houston*
Sam Houston State University, *Huntsville*
Tarrant County Junior College, *Hurst*
Texas A & I, *Kingsville*
North Harris County College East, *Kingwood*
East Texas Baptist University, *Marshall*
Wiley College, *Marshall*
Wayland Baptist University, *Plainview*
Southwest Texas State University, *San Marcos*
Southwestern Assemblies of God College,
    Waxahachie
Wharton County Junior College, *Wharton*
Midwestern State University, *Wichita Falls*

Utah

Utah State University, *Logan*

Virginia

Virginia Highlands Community College, *Abingdon*
Virginia Poyltechnic Institute & University,
    Blacksburg
John Tyler Community College, *Chester*
Paul D. Camp Community College, *Franklin*
Liberty University, *Lynchburg*
Christopher Newport College, *Newport News*
Tidewater Community College, *Portsmouth*
Radford University, *Radford*
Southwest Virginia Community College, *Richlands*
Virginia Commonwealth University, *Richmond*
Mary Baldwin College, *Staunton*
Tidewater Community College, *Virginia Beach*
Shenandoah College and Conservatory, *Winchester*

Washington

University of Washington, *Seattle*
Pierce College, *Tacoma*

Wisconsin

Northland College, *Ashland*
University of Wisconsin/Parkside, *Kenosha*
Edgewood College, *Madison*
University of Wisconsin/Fox Valley, *Menasha*
Marquestte University, *Milwaukee*
University of Wisconsin, *Oshkosh*
University of Wisconsin, *Platteville*
Ripon College, *Ripon*
University of Wisconsin, *Superior*
University of Wisconsin, *Waukesha*
University of Wisconsin, *Whitewater*

West Virginia

Fairmont State College, *Fairmont*
West Virginia State College, *Institute*
Potomac State College of WV University, *Keyser*
Fort New Salem College, *Salem*
Wheeling Jesuit College, *Wheeling*

Wyoming

University of Wyoming, *Laramie*
Eastern Wyoming College, *Torrington*

BICENTENNIAL SCHOOLS

Alabama
Aliceville High School, *Aliceville*
Brookwood Elementary School, *Brookwood*
Julian Harris Elementary School, *Decatur*
Bradshaw High School, *Florence*
Frisco City High School, *Frisco City*
Hokes Bluff Middle School, *Gadsden*
Riverton School, *Huntsville*
Louisville Elementary School, *Louisville*
St. John's Deliverance Christian Academy, *Mobile*
Trinity Presbyterian School, *Montgomery*
Pinecrest Elementary School, *Sylacauga*

Arkansas
Many Farms Elementary Public School, *Chinle*
Florence Elementary School, *Florence*

California
Cerritos School, *Anaheim*
Precious Blood School, *Banning*
LeConte Primary School, *Berkeley*
Pine Street School, *Bishop*
Ceres High School, *Ceres*
Dunbar Elementary School, *Glen Ellen*
St. Martin Academy, *La Mesa*
Los Coyotes School, *La Palma*
Mar Vista Elementary School, *Los Angeles*
Sierra Vista School, *Los Angeles*
Grace Lutheran School, *Los Angeles*
Peninsula School, *Menlo Park*
Victory Boulevard Elementary School, *North Hollywood*
Cole Elementary School, *Oakland*
Patterson Junior High School, *Patterson*
St. Francis de Sales School, *Riverside*
Cavitt School, *Roseville*
Barton Elementary School, *San Bernardino*
Blessed Sacrament Catholic School, *San Diego*
Union's History Committee-UMS, *San Jose*
Christ Church School, *San Rafael*
Saddleback High School, *Santa Ana*
Margaret S. Grant Elementary School, *Santa Ana*
Twenty-nine Palms Elementary School, *Twenty-nine Palms*

Colorado
Thunder Mountain Elementary School, *Grand Junction*

Connecticut
Calf Pen Meadow School, *Milford*
Fawn Hollow Elementary School, *Monroe*
North Haven Junior High, *North Haven*

Delaware
Sussex Technical High School, *Georgetown*

District of Columbia
W.B. Patterson Elementary School
John Q. Adams Elementary School
D.C. Public Schools/Instructional Service Center
Van Ness Elementary School
Garrison Elementary School

Florida
Bay Harbor Elementary School, *Bay Harbor Islands*
St. Jude Academy, *Boca Raton*
Branford School, *Branford*
Our Saviour's School, *Cocoa Beach*
Winston Park Elementary School, *Coconut Creek*
Country Hills Elementary, *Coral Springs*
James S. Hunt Elementary School, *Coral Springs*
Forest Hill Elementary School, *Coral Springs*
Coral Park Elementary School, *Coral Springs*
Unity Elementary School, *Delray Beach*
Alimacani Elementary School, *Jacksonville*
Mildred Helms Elementary School, *Largo*
Madison County High School, *Madison*
North Beach Elementary School, *Miami Beach*
Shores Academy, *Miami Shores*
Springview Elementary School, *Miami Springs*
Avalon Elementary School, *Naples*
Oneco Elementary School, *Oneco*
Westridge Middle School, *Orlando*
Tedder Elementary School, *Pompano Beach*
Sebring High School, *Sebring*
Tamarac Elementary School, *Tamarac*
Villa Madonna School, *Tampa*
Tildenville Elementary School, *Winter Garden*

Georgia
Pace Academy, *Atlanta*
Venetian Hills Elementary School, *Atlanta*
Heards Ferry Elementary School, *Atlanta*
West Bainbridge Elementary School, *Bainbridge*
Marie Archer Teasley Middle School, *Canton*
Eddy Junior High School, *Columbus*
Kelsey Avenue Middle School, *Griffin*
Ila Elementary School, *Ila*
Toombs County High School, *Lyons*
Pennsylvania Avenue Elementary School, *Savannah*
Valdosta High School, *Valdosta*

Idaho
Salmon Junior High School, *Salmon*

Illinois
Our Lady of the Wayside School, *Arlington Heights*
Bolingbrook High School, *Bolingbrook*
Brookport Elementary School, *Brookport*
St. Mary's School, *Buffalo Grove*
St. Paul — Our Lady of Vilna, *Chicago*
Lindblom Technical High School, *Chicago*
Von Steuben Upper Cycle School, *Chicago*
William B. Ogden School, *Chicago*
High School for Agricultural Sciences, *Chicago*
Fenger High School, *Chicago*
F.W. Reilly Elementary School, *Chicago*
Indian Trail Elementary Committee, *Frankfort*
Caroline Bentley School, *New Lenox*
Warren P. Shepherd Junior High School, *Ottawa*
Pana Junior High School, *Pana*
MacArthur Junior High School, *Prospect Heights*
Queen of Apostles School, *Riverdale*
Jordan Catholic Schools, *Rock Island*

Indiana
North Knox Central Elementary School, *Bicknell*
North Knox High School, *Bicknell*
Dyer Elementary School, *Bloomington*
Harris Elementary School, *Brownsburg*
White Lick School, *Brownsburg*
Lincoln Elementary School, *Brownsburg*
North Knox West Elementary School, *Bruceville*
Cascade High School, *Clayton*
Fayette Central Elementary School, *Connersville*
North Knox East Elementary & Jr. High, *Edwardsport*
Concord Junior High School, *Elkhart*
Concordia Lutheran High School, *Fort Wayne*
Griffith High School, *Griffith*
Orange Elementary School, *Glenwood*
Mary Frank Elementary School, *Granger*
Deer Creek School — Indiana State Farm, *Greencastle*
Kenwood Elementary School, *Hammond*
Columbia Elementary School, *Hammond*
Washington Irving School, *Hammond*
Abraham Lincoln Elementary School, *Hammond*
Holton Elementary School, *Holton*
Hebrew Academy of Indianapolis, *Indianapolis*
The Gage Institute, *Indianapolis*
Kokomo-Center Township School Corp., *Kokomo*
Liberty Middle School, *Liberty*
Twin Lakes School Corporation, *Monticello*
Lowell Elementary School, *Princeton*
Le Mans Academy, *Rolling Prairie*
Bradie Shrum Elementary School, *Salem*
Grimmer Middle School, *Schererville*
Silver Creek Junior High School, *Sellersburg*
Shelbyville Junior High School, *Shelbyville*
Shoals Elementary School, *Shoals*
St. Patrick's School, *Walkerton*
Westfield Middle School, *Westfield*
Yorktown Middle School, *Yorktown*

Iowa
English Valleys Community School, *North English*

Kansas
Southeast High School, *Cherokee*
Indian Trail Junior High School, *Olathe*
Pioneer Trail School, *Olathe*
Wichita High School West, *Wichita*

Kentucky
Berea Community Elementary School, *Berea*
Woodlawn Elementary School, *Danville*
Green County Middle School, *Greensburg*
Harrodsburg High School, *Harrodsburg*
Auburndale Elementary, *Louisville*
Phelps High School, *Phelps*
South Williamson School, *South Williamson*

Louisiana
St. Francis Xavier School, *Baton Rouge*
Crestworth Elementary School, *Baton Rouge*
Bossier High School, *Bossier City*
Central Park Elementary School, *Bossier City*
Upper Pointe Coupee Elementary School, *Innis*
Northwood High School, *Lena*
St. Mary's Academy, *New Orleans*
Crescent Elementary & Jr. High School, *Plaquemine*
John Curtis Christian School, *River Ridge*
Sunset Acres Elementary School, *Shreveport*
Starks High School, *Starks*

CONTINUED NEXT PAGE

Maine

St. Mary's School, *Houlton*
Wales Central School, *Sabattus*

Maryland

Annapolis Senior High School, *Annapolis*
Mater Amoris Montessori School, *Ashton*
Hammond High School, *Columbia*
Upper County Elementary School, *Cordova*
Immaculate Conception School, *Elkton*
Frederick Academy of the Visitation, *Frederick*
Nicholas Orem Middle School, *Hyattsville*
Kenmoor Middle School, *Landover*
Wayside Elementary School, *Potomac*
Stonegate Elementary School, *Silver Spring*

Massachusetts

Brackett School, *Arlington*
Berkley Middle School, *Berkley*
Dr. O.S. Marshall Middle School, *Billerica*
Bondsville Elementary School, *Bondsville*
Mather Elementary School, *Dorchester*
Webster School, *Everett*
Crocker Elementary School, *Fitchburg*
St. Margaret School, *Lowell*
Charles H. Taylor School, *Mattapan*
North Andover High School, *North Andover*
The New Testament Christian School, *Plymouth*
Kiley Junior High School, *Springfield*
Lincoln Street School, *Worchester*

Michigan

Lindemann Elementary School, *Allen Park*
Post Elementary School, *Battle Creek*
Oakley W. Best Middle School, *Dearborn Heights*
Cass Tech High School, *Detroit*
St. Henry School, *Rosebush*
Eisenhower Elementary School, *Southfield*
Rancho Elementary School, *Taylor*
White Pigeon School, *White Pigeon*

Minnesota

Dilworth School, *Dilworth*
St. Francis de Sales School, *Moorhead*
Trinity Lutheran School, *Sauk Rapids*

Mississippi

Whitten Junior High School, *Jackson*
St. Martin East Elementary School, *Ocean Springs*
Ripley Middle School, *Ripley*

Missouri

Carver Christian Day School, *Kansas City*
Oak Park High School, *Kansas City*
Hatton McCredie Elementary School,
    Kingdom City
West County R-IV High School, *Leadwood*
Holman Middle School, *St. Ann*
Neely School, *St. Joseph*
Washington Junior High School, *St. Louis*
Parkway East Junior High School, *St. Louis*
Shaw Visual and Performing Arts Center, *St. Louis*
Our Lady of Loretto, *St. Louis*

Montana

Deer Creek School, *Glendive*
Scobey Elementary School, *Scobey*

Nebraska

Rabbit Hill School, *Auburn*

Nevada

Ruth School, *East Ely*

New Jersey

Belleville School Number Ten, *Belleville*
Marion T. Bedwell Elementary School,
    Bernardsville
Bernardsville Middle School, *Bernardsville*
St. Joseph's School, *Beverly*
Walter T. Bergen School, *Bloomingdale*
Brick Township High School, *Brick*
Saint Anthony of Padua School, *Butler*
Clifton Public Schools, *Clifton*
Applegarth School, *Cranbury*
Lincoln School, *Dumont*
Benjamin Franklin Elementary School, *Edison*
Delsea Regional High School, *Franklinville*
Abraham Lincoln School No. 6, *Garfield*
Glen Ridge Middle School, *Glen Ridge*
Indiana Avenue School, *Iselin*
Keansburg High School, *Keansburg*
Long Valley Middle School, *Long Valley*
Sacred Heart School, *Lyndhurst*
Washington School, *Lyndhurst*
Highland Elementary School, *Midland Park*
Morris Plains Borough School, *Morris Plains*
Mountview Road School, *Morris Plains*
Warren Street School, *Newark*
McKinley School, *Newark*
Dogwood Hill School, *Oakland*
Ogdensburg Public School, *Ogdensburg*
Public School No. 4, *Paterson*
Fairview School, *Red Bank*
Orchard Elementary School, *Ridgewood*
J. Ackerman Coles Elementary School,
    Scotch Plains
Our Lady of Sorrows School, *South Orange*
Corpus Christi School, *South River*
St. Catharines School, *Spring Lake*
Kennedy Elementary School, *Succasunna*
Jefferson School, *Summit*
Toms River Intermediate School West,
    Toms River
St. Cassian School, *Upper Montclair*
St. Mary School, *Williamstown*
Mary S. Shoemaker Elementary School,
    Woodstown

New Mexico

House Municipal School, *House*
University High School, *Roswell*
La Plata Junior High, *Silver City*

New York

Northwest Elementary School, *Amityville*
Lake Shore Central Senior High School, *Angola*
Bayville Primary & Intermediate School, *Bayville*
Saint Anne School, *Brentwood*
The Bronxwood School, *Bronx*
Beth Jacob/Beth Miriam School, *Bronx*
I.S. 180 at Truman High School, *Bronx*
P.S. 205 Bronx, *Bronx*
Beth Rivka School, *Brooklyn*
P.S. 221 Empire School, *Brooklyn*
P.S. 236, *Brooklyn*
Oceanhill-Brownsville I.S. 55, *Brooklyn*
Unlocking the Constitution School Committee,
    Brooklyn
Saint Ann's School, *Brooklyn*
North Park Academy, *Buffalo*
Canajoharie High School, *Canajoharie*
Canisteo Central School, *Canisteo*
Dover Elementary School, *Dover Plains*
East Meadow High School, *East Meadow*
Woodland Junior High School, *East Meadow*
Fenner Elementary School, *Falconer*
Northside School, *Farmingdale*
Adrien Block I.S. 25Q, *Flushing*
West Frankfort School, *Frankfort*
Glenmont Elementary School, *Glenmont*
August Martin High School, *Jamaica*
North Park Junior High School, *Lockport*
Ann MacArthur Primary School, *Locust Valley*
Locust Valley Intermediate School, *Locust Valley*
Queens Vocational & Technical High School,
    Long Island City
McGraw Elementary School, *McGraw*
Millbrook Jr./Sr. High School, *Millbrook*
Charminade High School, *Mineola*
Mt. Sinai Elementary School, *Mt. Sinai*
Regional Alternative-High School, *N. White Plains*
Laurel Plains Elementary School, *New City*
School of Graphic Communication Arts, *New York*
Amalia Castro School P.S. 142, *New York*
George Washington High School, *New York*
Niskayuna Middle School, *Niskayuna*
Dr. Grant C. Madill Elementary School, *Ogdensburg*
Ossining High School, *Ossining*
Owego Apalachin Middle School, *Owego*
Carrie Palmer Weber Jr. High School,
    Port Washington
Overlook School, *Poughkeepsie*

St. Peter Claver School, *Queens*
P.S. 34Q, *Queens Village*
Rochester Area Council: Social Studies, *Rochester*
Carthage School No. 8, *Rochester*
Hillel School, *Rochester*
Hoosic Valley Central School, *Schaghticoke*
Amherst Middle School, *Snyder*
Spring Valley Senior High School, *Spring Valley*
Springfield Gardens High School, *Springfield Gardens*
Holland Patent Central School, *Stittville*
William Sidney Mount Elementary School, *Stony Brook*
Stony Point Elementary School, *Stony Point*
Edison Elementary School, *Tonawanda*
T.R. Proctor Junior High School, *Utica*
Notre Dame South, *Utica*
Notre Dame North, *Utica*
John F. Kennedy Junior High School, *Utica*
Wheeler Avenue School, *Valley Stream*
Elm Street School, *Waverly*
Clarkstown South High School, *West Nyack*
Junior High School 194 Queens, *Whitestone*
Whitesville Central School, *Whitesville*
Wyoming Central School, *Wyoming*
Gorton High School, *Yonkers*

North Carolina
Valley Springs Middle School, *Arden*
Phillips Junior High School, *Chapel Hill*
Quail Hollow Junior High, *Charlotte*
Charlotte Christian School, *Charlotte*
Goldsboro Junior High School, *Goldsboro*
Alamance Christian School, *Graham*
F.D. Bluford School, *Greensboro*
Hollister Elementary School, *Hollister*
Moss Hill Elementary, *Kinston*
Madison High School, *Marshall*
Western Union Elementary School, *Waxhaw*

North Dakota
Bismarck High School, *Bismarck*

Ohio
David Hill Elementary School, *Akron*
Margaret Park Elementary School, *Akron*
Crestview Elementary School, *Brunswick*
Linwood Fundamental Academy, *Cincinnati*
Bishop Watterson High School, *Columbus*
Pleasant Valley School, *Coshocton*
Radcliff Heights Upper Elementary School, *Dayton*
Spaulding Middle School, *Goshen*
Grand Rapids Junior High School, *Grand Rapids*
Graysville Elementary School, *Graysville*
Lewisville Elementary School, *Lewisville*
Maple Heights Middle School, *Maple Heights*
South Junior High School, *Martins Ferry*
Mason Middle School, *Mason*
St. Mary School, *Massillon*
Fort Miami School, *Maumee*
Newton Falls Middle School, *Newton Falls*
St. Boniface Elementary School, *Oak Harbor*
St. Pius X School, *Reynoldsburg*
Shreve Elementary School, *Shreve*
Lincoln Elementary School, *Steubenville*
Allen Elementary School, *Strongsville*
Bethel Elementary School, *Sycamore Valley*
Troy Junior High School, *Troy*
Warrensville Heights Junior High, *Warrensville Heights*
St. Anthony School, *Youngstown*

Oklahoma
Byng School, *Ada*
Anadarko Junior High School, *Anadarko*
Beavers Memorial S.D.A. Jr. Academy, *Ardmore*
Boise City Public Schools, *Boise City*
Longfellow School, *Chelsea*
Lincoln Elementary School, *El Reno*
Emmanuel Christian School, *Enid*
Lexington Public Schools, *Lexington*
Mangum High School, *Mangum*
Roland Senior High School, *Roland*
Limestone Elementary School, *Sand Springs*
Sharon-Mutual Elementary, *Sharon*
Weatherford High School, *Weatherford*

Oregon
John Ball School, *Portland*

Pennsylvania
Economy Elementary School, *Baden*
St. Mary's School, *Beaver Falls*
St. Luke Lutheran School, *Cabot*
Cecil Elementary School, *Cecil*
Shawnee Intermediate School, *Easton*
St. James School, *Erie*
Muhlenberg Middle School, *Laureldale*
Lehighton Area High School, *Lehighton*
Highlands Senior High School, *Natrona Heights*
Bilingual Middle Magnet, *Philadelphia*
E.T. Richardson Middle School, *Springfield*
Wallingford Elementary School, *Wallingford*
Cheltenham High School, *Wyncote*

Rhode Island
Western Coventry School, *Coventry*
Bernon Heights Elementary School, *Woonsocket*

South Carolina
St. Helena Elementary School, *St. Helena Island*
Ebenezer Elementary School, *Travelers Rest*

South Dakota
Newell Elementary School, *Newell*

Tennessee
Northeast High School, *Clarksville*
Elizabethton High School, *Elizabethton*
East Chester Elementary School, *Henderson*
Parrottsville Elementary, *Parrottsville*
Tellico Plains Elementary School, *Tellico Plains*

Texas
Crockett High School, *Austin*
Caldwood Elementary School, *Beaumont*
Faulk Intermediate School, *Brownsville*
East Elementary School, *Brownwood*
Bethel Temple Christian Academy, *Bryan*
Incarnate Word Junior High School, *Corpus Christi*
William L. Cabell Elementary School, *Dallas*
Daniel Intermediate School, *Duncanville*
Westcreek Elementary School, *Fort Worth*
Giddings State Home and School, *Giddings*
St. Rose of Lima School, *Houston*
Almeda Elementary School, *Houston*
Beth Yeshurun Day School, *Houston*
Pines Montessori School, *Kingwood*
Leggett Independent School District, *Leggett*
Lubbock-Cooper High School, *Lubbock*
Lytle Elementary School, *Lytle*
Quail Valley Elementary School, *Missouri City*
Pearland Intermediate School, *Pearland*
W.W. Jackson Middle School, *San Antonio*
Sullivan Elementary School, *San Benito*
Jefferson Elementary School, *Temple*
Wills Point Primary School, *Wills Point*

Utah
North Ogden Junior High School, *Ogden*
Valley View Elementary School, *Pleasant Grove*
Oquirrh Hills Middle School, *Riverton*
Wasatch Junior High School, *Salt Lake City*
Bingham High School, *South Jordan*

Vermont
The Dover School, *East Dover*
Whitingham School, *Jacksonville*

Virginia
Powhatan School, *Boyce*
Western Branch Elementary, *Chesapeake*
Collinsville Primary School, *Collinsville*
Bayview Christian School, *Norfolk*
The Williams School, *Norfolk*
Robert E. Lee Elementary School, *Richmond*
Sully School, *Sterling*

Washington
Adventist Christian School, *Hadlock*
Meadows Elementary School, *Olympia*
Redmond Christian School, *Redmond*

West Virginia
Piedmont Elementary School, *Charleston*
Sacred Heart School, *Charleston*
Mallory Grade School, *Mallory*
North Elementary School, *Ravenswood*
Liberty Elementary School, *Weirton*
Bicentennial Committee, *Winfield*

Wisconsin
Franklin Elementary School, *Appleton*
Saint Isidore School, *Newton*
Greenland School, *Oconomowoc*

Department of Defense Overseas Schools
Chaffee High School
Mannheim Middle School
Schweinfurt American School

RECOGNIZED PROJECTS

Agency for Instructional Technology (AIT)
"The U.S. Constitution" Video Program

Alliance Francaise
National Essay Contest

American Association of Retired Persons
Lifetime Learning Video Mini-course, "The Constitution: That Delicate Balance"

American Association of School Administrators
"Citizenship: Goal of Education" Book

American Bar Association
National Bicentennial Mock Trial Program and Student Seminar on the Judiciary, the Constitution, and Dispute Resolution

American Cancer Society
"Constitutionalist Salute Concert Commemorative Book"

American Chamber of Commerce of El Salvador
Essay Contest "The Significance of the Principles of the U.S. Constitution for Other Nations and Their Citizens"

American Club of Zurich
"A Constitutional Evening," September 17, 1987

The American-European Community Association Trust
"The Role of the European Court of Justice and the U.S. Supreme Court in Creating Policy" Conference

American Forestry Association
"American Bicentennial Forest"

The American Franklin Friends Committee
September 17th Commemoration of the Franklin House

American Hellenic Alliance
"The American Constitution and the Influence of Ancient Greece on Its Writing" Classroom Video

American Hotel and Motel Association
"Summer of Great American Hospitality" Public Awareness Adversiting Campiagn

American Indian Artists / American Indian Institute
"The Iroquois Confederacy and the U.S. Constitution" Public Service Announcements

American Institute of Fellows in Free Enterprise
"You Can Do It Baseball!" Quiz Competititon on the Constitution

American Jewish Committee
"The U.S. Constitution: Where We Are; Where We Are Going" Materials and Activities on Religious Liberty

American Lawyers Auxiliary
"Law and The Bicentennial" National Videotape Competition
"Law and the Bicentennial" A Third-Grade Teaching Unit

American Legion
Bicentennial Program
National High School Oratorical Contest

The American Legion Auxiliary
Bicentennial of the U.S. Constitution Program

*American Newspaper Publishers Association Foundation
"A Celebration of Citizenship" National Teach-In on the Constitution

The American Radio Relay League, Inc.
"People to People" Amateur Radio for the Bicentennial of the U.S. Constitution

The American Whig — Cliosophic Society
Constitution Bicentennial Forum Series

Anima International, Inc.
"Misa Pacis" (Mass of Peace) Orchestral-Choral Concert

Appalachian Regional Commission
Appalachian Quilt Project

Army War College, Corresponding Studies Course
Class of 1987 Gift to the Army War College, Commemorative Stained Glass Window

Association of Catholic Colleges and Universities
"Celebrating the Constitution" Clearinghouse

Association of Jesuit Colleges and Universities
A National Dialogue on the United States Constitution

*The Big Ten Universities Alumni Associations
Northwest Ordinance Regional Project

B'nai B'rith International, Committee on Community Volunteer Services
"Bicentennial Constitutional Sabbath" Project

Bowl Games of America
1991 Liberty Bowl Halftime Salute to the Bill of Rights

Brigham Young University Motion Picture Studio
"A More Perfect Union: America Becomes a Nation" Film

California State University, Northridge, Pre Law Society
Bicentennial Celebration of the United States Constitution Conference/ Lecture Series

Cameo Productions, Ltd.
"LIBERTY!" (The Archers)

Camp Fire, Inc.
"We the People" Project

Carleton College
"Mr. Adams and Mr. Jefferson: A Dramatization for the Radio"

The Carter Center of Emory University, Georgia State University, and The Jimmy Carter Library
"Women and the Constitution: A Bicentennial Perspective" Symposium

The Catholic University of America
"Comparative Constitutional Developments in the Republic of Ireland (1937-1987) and the U.S. (1787-1987)" Conference

CBN University
"Reviving the American Republic" Conference Series

Center for Civic Education / Law in a Free Society
International Conference on "Constitutional Government and the Development of an Enlightened Citizenry"
National Bicentennial Competition

Center for Strategic and International Studies
Conference on the Constitution and Legislative-Executive Relations in International Affairs

Center for the Study of the Constitution
"Our Peculiar Security: The Constitution and Limited Government" Lecture

Chromosohm Media, Inc.
The New World Experience Multi-Media Production

Citicorp/Citibank
Pocket Constitution Distribution Program

City Club of Cleveland
Celebration of the 200th Anniversary of the Bill of Rights

Claremont Institute for the Study of Statesmanship and Political Philosophy
"Novus Ordo Seclorum: A New Order of the Ages" Project of Lectures, Conferences, and Speakers' Bureau

Close Up Foundation
Bicentennial Program Initiative on Citizenship Education
Civic Achievement Award Program, Student Citizenship Education

College of William and Mary, Institute of Bill of Rights Law
Charter Day Bill of Rights Ceremony

Columbia University School of Law
Conference to Commemorate the Bicentennial of the U.S. Constitution

Convention II, Inc.
Convention II National Education Program

Council for the Advancement of Citizenship
"Bicentennial Leadership Project: A Collaborative Approach" Conference Series

Creighton University
"A More Perfect Union" Live and Video Tape Performance

Dana-Farber Cancer Institute
40th Anniversary Gala Concert — Salute to the Constitution

D.E.A.F Media, Inc.
Rainbow's End Television Show #301, "Rules, Laws and the U.S. Constitution"

Denver Public Schools
"We the People — The Dream Lives On" Slide-Tape Presentation

Department of Defense
Bicentennial Coloring Book, "We the People"
Bicentennial Defense Communities Program
Bicentennial Foot Race Packet
Bicentennial Logo Awareness
Bicentennial Program Cover
"Celebrate Youth '87: Leaders For Tomorrow" Armed Forces Youth Activities
Commemorative Medallion
Constitution Grove Cherry Tree Planting
"Defenders of the Constitution: Past, Present, Future" Dedication of Constitution Bicentennial Tank
"Department of Defense Commemoration of the Bicentennial of the United States Constitution — The Year in Review" Videotape
Fall 1987 Issue of Military Chaplain's Review, on "The Constitution"
Foreign Language Translations of the United States Constitution
Fort Bragg Naturalization Ceremony
Oath Reaffirmation Certificates
Pentagon Library, "Quotations on the Constitution" Booklet
"Proud to Serve Freedom's Family" Program
"Provide for the Common Defense" Bicentennial Poster
Ratification Bicentennial 1788/1988 Souvenir Card
Ratification Oak Tree Planting to Commemorate New Hampshire's Ratification
"Reaffirmation Day" Oath Ceremony at Fort Monmouth
Renaming and Dedication of "Constitution Square"
Soldier-Statesmen of the Constitution Souvenir Card
389th Army Band Constitutional Bicentennial Concert
"Your Oath" Brochure

Armed Forces Inaugural Committee, *Advertorial Promoting Inaugural and Constitution Bicentennials*
Defense Logistics Agency — Personal Support Center, Philadelphia, *"We the People Flags"*
Headquarter Forces Command, *Bicentennial Band Concert Tour*

"We the People" Record
Air Force Military Airlift Band (MAC), *"We the People: Birth of a Dream" Patriotic Music Recording*

The Army Constitution Grove at Valley Forge National Park
"Bicentennial of the Establishment of the Department of War" August 7, 1989 Ceremony
"Bicentennial of the Establishment of the United States Army Under the Constitution" September 29, 1989 Ceremony
Bicentennial of the French Revolution and the Declaration of the Rights of Man and of the Citizen
A Bicentennial Resource Guide
Bicentennial Resource Guide: Supplement I
Bicentennial Resource Guide: Supplement II
Bicentennial Resource Guide: Supplement III
Bicentennial Resource Guide: Supplement IV
"Bill of Rights 1791-1991" Poster
"Bill of Rights 1791-1991" Souvenir Card
"The Bill of Rights" Pamphlet, Soldier-Statesmen Series
Captain Michael Doudel Oak Dedication
Commemorative Wreath Ceremonies to Honor Constitution Signers
Constitution/History Lecture Series
Constitution Lecture Series
Constitution Week 1988, Federal Oak Dedication at Mount Vernon
Department of Defense Certificate of Recognition
Establishment of the Judiciary 1790/1990 Poster
"Establishment of the Judiciary 1790-1990 Medallion"
General William Darke Oak Dedication Commemorative Ceremony
George Washington Oak Dedication
James Monroe Oak Dedication
Leave and Earnings Statement Bicentennial of the Constitution Message
Living Legacy Tree Planting Program
Morgan-Stephanson Oak Dedication
Museum Exhibit Honoring Signers of the Constitution
Oath Reaffirmation Ceremony, Letter of Instruction
Outreach to Department of Defense Attache Worldwide
Ratification Bicentennial 1788/1988 Poster
The Runnymede Oak Dedication
Soldier-Statesmen Presidents 1789/1989 Souvenir Card
Soldier Statesmen Presidents 1789/1989 Poster
"Soldier-Statesmen Justices 1790-1990" Souvenir Brochure
Tercentennial of the English Bill of Rights Ceremony
"This We Will Support and Defend" Constitution Exhibit at the National Infantry Museum
Washington, D.C., to Philadelphia Constitution Relay-Run

Headquarters, Office of Public Affairs
Annapolis Convention
"Bicentennial Bullets" Public Service Announcements
Constitution Touring Exhibit
Pentagon Exhibits
"Signers of the Constitution" Videotapes
"Soldier Statesmen of the Constitution" Pamphlets
"To Provide for the Common Defense" exhibit
"We the People" Commemorative Album
"We The People" Traveling Exhibit

Military District of Washington
"Spirit of America" Military Pageant 1987
"Spirit of America" Military Pageant 1988
Twilight Tattoo 1988
"Spirit of America" Military Pageant 1989
Twilight Tattoo 1989
American Presidential Pageant 1989
"Spirit of America" Military Pageant 1990
Twilight Tattoo 1990

CONTINUED NEXT PAGE

U.S. Army Center of Military History
Hard-bound volume, Soldier-Statesmen of the Constitution
"The Ratification of the Constitution" Pamphlet
"Soldier Statesmen of the Constitution: The Presidents' Pamphlet"

89th U.S. Army Reserve Command, *Bicentennial Army Reserve Band Concert Tour*
101st Airborne Division *"Week of the Eagles 1988"*
927th Tactical Airlift Group, *The American Flag and the 927th Tactical Airlift Group*
Army Material Command, *Constitutional Bicentennial Exhibits*
Anniston Army Depot, *Constitution Bicentennial Outreach, Educational Collaborations with Local Schools*
Combined Arms Center, *War Department Bicentennial Symposium*
Corps of Engineers, *Constitution Bicentennial Poster*
Corps of Engineers, Missouri River Division, *Dedication of Freedom Grove*
Headquarters, Second United States Army, Office of Public Affairs, *Constitution Bicentennial Coloring Book*
HHC 104th Division, Vancouver Barrack, Washington, *Commemorative Constitution Issue of "The Wolf Print"*
Office of the Chief, Army Reserve, *History Teachers' Posters*
Picatinny Arsenal, *Bicentennial of the Constitution Float*
ROTC Cadet Command, *Dedication of Cadet Park*
Training and Doctrine Command, *Constitutional Relay*
U.S. Army Field Band, *Bicentennial Concert at the Kennedy Center*
U.S. Army Intelligence Center and School, *Constitution Wall*
U.S. Army Logistics Management College, *Bicentennial Celebration*
U.S. Army Reserve, *National Essay Contest*

NATIONAL GUARD

Missouri National Guard, *Bicentennial of the Constitution Program*
National Guard Bureau, *Bicentennial Program*

DEPARTMENT OF THE NAVY

"America on the March" Record
Constitution Weekend in Boston
USS Constitution Turnaround Cruise

Assistant Secretary of Navy, Financial Management, *Reaffirmation of Oath*
Department of the Navy and Smithsonian Institution, National Portrait Gallery, *"Constitution Quest: Why a Navy?" Program for Students*
Naval District of Washington, *"Your Constitution" Weekly Page in Command Newspaper*

Disabled American Veterans (DAV)
Educational Materials and Activities Supporting the Bicentennial of the U.S. Constitution

The Documentary Heritage Trust of the United States

Eagle Forum Education and Legal Defense Fund
Constitution Radio Jingle "Standing Proud for the Constitution"
"We The People" Slide Program
"How American Inventors Changed the Way We Live" Multi-Media Production

Fairfax County (Virginia) Bicentennial Commission
Bill of Rights Day Celebration

Farmington Committee on the Constitution
Liberty Gazette, "The People and the Constitution"

Federal Bar Association, Young Lawyers Division
"These Inalienable Rights" Bill of Rights Program for Students

The Federalist Society for Law and Public Policy Studies
Symposium and Speakers Bureau on Federalism, Constitutional Checks and Balances, and Protections

Festival Williamsburg, Ltd.
"To Preserve and Protect the Constitution" Festival

Foundation for a Creative America
Bicentennial of U.S. Patent and Copyright Acts 1790-1990 Programs

Franklin and Marshall College
The John Marshall Lectures on the Constitution, the Supreme Court and the Justices

Freedoms Foundation at Valley Forge Pennsylvania
"Freedoms Foundation Bill of Responsibilities"

Friends of Libraries U.S.A.
Sir Zelman Cowen Address on "Constitution or No — Which Works Better?"

Future Business Leaders of America — Phi Beta Lambda, Inc.
"Linking Leaders" Mentor Program

Gannon University and the Chatauqua/The Center for the Study of the Presidency Institute
National Conference, "The American Presidency: Origins, Development, and Future"

General Federation of Women's Clubs
GFWC Patriotism Through Constitutional Studies Program

General Services Administration, Public Buildings Service
Bicentennial of First Federal Building

Gloria LeVaggi, Illustrator
"America the Beautiful, America the Bountiful" Series of Paintings in Exhibition

Grand Lodge of District of Columbia
Cherry Blossom Parade, "To Form A More Perfect Union" Float
July 4th Parade Float
Apple Blossom Parade Float

Hamilton Heights Homeowners Association, Inc.
Hamilton Grange Restoration

Hellenic Law Society
"The Hellenic Idea of Justice and The Hellenic Roots of the U.S. Constitution" Symposium and Retreat

H.M. S. Rose Foundation, Inc.
H.M.S. Rose Bill of Rights Tour

Hokkaido University and Japan / U.S. Friendship Commission
Sapporo Seminar in American Studies "The United States Constitution — Its Myth and Reality"

Hugh O'Brian Youth Foundation
"200 Years of Progress — Moving Toward the Future" Leadership Seminars

Indian Rights Association
"In Search of a More Perfect Union" National Symposium

The Intercollegiate Studies Institute and Villanova University
ISI Bicentennial Celebration

International Foundation for Human Sciences, Inc.
"The Constitution of the United States: American and European Perspectives" Conference at the University of Virginia

*International Newspaper Advertising and Marketing Executives Foundation
Student Newspaper Advertising Competition on the Bill of Rights

International Platform Association
First Amendment Awareness Program

James Madison University
Bicentennial Program

Jewish War Veterans
92nd Annual National Convention Salute to the U.S. Constitution

John M. Ashbrook Center for Public Affairs and United Telephone of Ohio
"Salute to the Constitution" Conference

K.A.R.E. TV/Gannett Broadcasting Corp.
"We The People: Revolution to Constitution" News Broadcast Series on the Constitution

Kenneth Walsh
"The Trail of the Eagle" Advertising Campaign

League of Women Voters Education Fund/Project '87
Bicentennial Project

Liberty Bell Foundation
Liberty Bell Replica, Tour of Original 13 Colonies

*Library of Congress
Acquisition of Jean de Crevecoeur Manuscripts

Los Angeles Arts Council
"Spirit of America" Monument

Lou Reda Productions
"Constitution Minutes" Television and Radio Vignettes

Macalester College
Wallace Conference on the Liberal Arts, "The Constitution, Freedom of Expression, and the Liberal Arts"

Magna Carta in America
Magna Carta Touring Exhibit

The Malaysian Association for American Studies
"The United States and Malaysia: The Socio-Cultural Experience"National Seminar"

Malmark, Inc.
"We The People" Handbell Composition

Maryland Public Television
"This Constitution" Public Television Series / College Course

McPhail-Pridgen & Associations, Inc.
"Two Hundred Years of the U.S. Presidency" 60-Minute Documentary

Meredith Slobod Crist Memorial Fund
"The Great Tree of Peace: Iroquois Contributions to the United States Constitution" Educational Materials

Merrill Lynch and Company, Inc.
Series of State "Ratification Celebrations"

Modern Woodmen of America / Putnam Museum (Iowa)
"We The People: The United States Constitution Celebrates 200 Years" Exhibit and Lecture Series Project

Mortar Board, Inc.
"Constitution Trees: 200"

Music Educators National Conference
September 17, 1986, Bicentennial Concert
March 19, 1987, Concert

National Archives and Records Administration
Constitution Exhibits
Supplemental Teaching Kit "The Constitution: Evolution of a Government"
87-hour Vigil at the Archives Building: National Tribute to the U.S. Constitution
"This Fierce Spirit of Liberty: The Making of the Bill of Rights" Exhibition
"The Bill of Rights: Evolution of Personal Liberties" Teaching Package

National Association for Court Management
"Charting Our Course" Bicentennial Program

National Association of Area Agencies on Aging
"Aging America: Building on Our Heritage" Annual Training

National Association of Parliamentarians Committee
Bicentennial Celebration

National Association of Retired Federal Employees
Bicentennial Program

National Catholic Educational Association
Bicentennial Communications and Clearinghouse Project

National Conference of Christians and Jews, Inc.
"Sign on to the Constitution at the Polls"

*National Council for the Social Studies
Constitution Day Broadcasts and Workshops

National Defense University
"The President, Congress, and National Security: A View from the Bicentennial of the Constitution" Symposium

National Exchange Club
"An American Masterpiece" brochure

National Fraternal Congress of America
U.S. Constitution Bicentennial Celebration

National Grange
National Grange Bicentennial Cookbook

National Independence Day Parade, Inc.
National Independence Day Festival and Parade (7th Annual)

National Inventors Hall of Fame and National Invention Center
"Induction 1990" Program

*National Newspaper Association
"We the People at 200: The Constitution Bicentennial" Newspaper Supplement

National Radio Theatre of Chicago
"Dateline 1787" Radio Project

National Society of Hebrew Day Schools
Constitutional Bicentennial Projects

The National Society of the Colonial Dames of America
The Washington Workshops Congressional Seminar "Why Has The U.S. Constitution Endured?" Essay Contest
XVII Century — Commemorative Church Service for 200th Anniversary of the Ratification of the Constitution

National Society of the Daughters of the American Revolution
Three-Year Celebration of the Bicentennial with over 50 Projects

The National Society of the Sons of the American Revolution
"Celebrate Your Heritage" Bicentennial Program

The National Society of the Sons of the American Revolution, Switzerland Society
Interscholastic Debate

National Sojourners, Inc.
"Freedom and Responsibilities of Citizenship under the United States Constitution" Project for Students

National Trust for Historic Preservation
Formal Opening of Montpelier, James Madison's home
Montpelier Crafts Celebration

National Trust for Historic Preservation and the Society for Photographic Education
"America's Uncommon Places: The Blessings of Liberty" Photographic Exhibit

CONTINUED NEXT PAGE

National Year of Thanksgiving Foundation
"1787 The Year of Thanksgiving" Promotion

The Navy League
83rd Annual Dinner — Salute to the Constitution

Nevis Philatelic Bureau
Developing and Issuing of Commemorative Stamps

New York Alliance for Public Schools and the Federal Bar Council
MENTOR Education Project

New York Public Library, Schomburg Center for Research in Black Culture
"Blacks and the United States Constitution" Exhibit

Nichiren Shoshu Soka Gakkai of America
"New Freedom Bell" Tour
"New Freedom Bell" World Freedom Trail International Tour

Nicholaus Copernicus University of Torun (Poland)
International Seminar on the Origin of Human Rights

Old Christ Church Preservation Trust
Forum Exploring the Religious Roots of the Writers of the U.S. Constitution

Outdoor Advertising Association of America
Outdoor Advertising Celebrates the Bill of Rights

Parade Publications, Inc.
"We The People" Bicentennial Photo Contest

The Pennsylvania Humanities Council
"To Preserve These Rights" Bill of Rights Exhibit

Phi Alpha Delta Public Service Center
Bicentennial Law-related Seminars

Phi Kappa Phi, The Honor Society
"Toward the Bicentennial of the Constitution" National Forum (Fall 1984)

Phi Theta Kappa Fraternity, Inc.
"The U.S. Constitution: Assuring Continuity through Controversy," Topic of Annual Honors Institute

The Philadelphia School
"The Great Experiment, 1787" Musical Dramatization

Phillips Petroleum Company
Reprint and Distribution of U.S. Constitution and Declaration of Independence Booklet

Pirandello Lyceum, Inc.
Bicentennial Celebration of the U.S. Constitution

Prism Magazine
Special Issue on the U.S. Constitution

Project '87
"The Blessings of Liberty" Poster Exhibit Project

Public Broadcasting Service, Adult Learning Service
"Constitution: That Delicate Balance" Telecourse

Puerto Rico Commission on the Bicentennial of the Constitution of the United States of America
"Human Rights: 200 Years of Constitutional Experience in the U.S. and its Influence on Latin America" Forum

Quadrus and Friends, Inc
"Quadrus and His Friends Celebrate the Bicentennial of the U.S. Constitution" Educational Comic Workbook

Romanian-American Chamber of Commerce, Inc.
Romanian-American Chamber of Commerce Essay Contest

Rosenstiel Foundation
Constitutionalism and Human Rights in Poland, France, and America

Satellite Education Services, Inc.
"Securing Liberty: The Genius of the U.S. Constitution" Television Series

Second Baptist Church of Houston, Texas
"We The People: Freedom Under God" Televised Bicentennial Program

Second Circuit Court Committee on the Bicentennial of the Constitution
"Egbert Benson: First Chief Judge of the Second Circuit" Exhibit
Plaque honoring authors of The Federalist Papers
The Bicentennial of the U.S. Patent System

Sister Cities International
U.S.-Australia Sister Cities Teacher Exchange Constitution Project

The Smithsonian Institution, National Portrait Gallery, Office of Education
"The Constitution and the Presidency" Student Program
"Before the Constitution: The Roots of Self Government" Student Program

The Smithsonian Institution, Office of Interdisciplinary Studies
"Constitutional Roots, Rights and Responsibilities" Symposium

Social Science Assocation of Thailand
The Federalist Papers Translation Project

The Society of English and American Lawyers
Commemorative Brochure for Annual Dinner

Society for Preservation and Encouragement of Barber Shop Quartet Singing in America, Inc., Dallas Metropolitan Chapter
"We the People" Concert

Southern California Rapid Transit District
RTD's Transit Rider Bill of Rights

State and Local Government Labor-Management Committee
"To Promote the General Welfare" Public Service Project

The Supreme Council, 330, Ancient and Accepted Scottish Rite of Freemasonry
"Keystone of Liberty" Public Awareness Program

Supreme Forest, Tall Cedars of Lebanon of North America
Annual Convention Parade

Temple University, Center for the Study of Federalism
"State Constitutional Law in the Third Century of American Federalism"
Conference

Texas A&M University, Memorial Student Center
Wiley Lecture Series, "Constitution and Foreign Policy: A Question of Control"

Theatreworks/USA
"We The People" Touring Musical Dramatization

Thomas Schwenke, Inc., and Georgetown University
The Bicentennial Exhibition of American Federal Furniture

Toastmasters International
Speak Up For Freedom!

The Tocqueville Forum, Wake Forest University
"We The People: Citizenship and Political Life Under the United States Constitution"

Tuskegee Airmen Incorporated
Tuskegee Airmen National Conference: Salute to the Bicentennial of the U.S. Constitution

*The United States Constitution Council of the Thirteen Original States, Inc.
1987 Magna Carta Tour — Freedom Documents Project

United States Constitutional Council, U.S. Coast Guard, and New York State Commission
Law Day on America's Tall Ship, the "Eagle"

United States Department of Agriculture: Forest Service
"Constitution Trees"

United States Department of Commerce
Commerce People *Bicentennial Articles, January 1986 — August 1986*
Commerce People *Bicentennial Articles, January 1987 — December 1987*
"Counting for Representation: The Census and the Constitution" Brochure
Minority Enterprise Development Week 1987 "We the People — A Legacy of Minority Business 1787-1987"

United States Department of Education
National Elementary School Essay Contest, "What the Constitution Means to Me and to Our Country"

United States Department of the Interior
Bureau of Land Management
"Public Lands, USA" Brochure
"Preserving America's Heritage" Preservation of Lands Office Documents

National Park Service
Bicentennial Theme Slides
"Four Little Pages" One-Act Musical
Second Bank of the U.S.
The "Miracle at Philadelphia" Exhibit
U.S. Geological Survey
"An Emerging Nation — Maps of the United States of America 1787-1987"

United States Department of Justice
United States Marshals Service
Smithsonian Exhibit — "America's Star: The United States Marshals, 1789-1989" Traveling Exhibit

United States Department of Labor (Office of Federal Contract Compliance Programs, San Antonio)
Planting a "Constitution Tree"

United State Global Strategy Council
Constitutionalism in Modern Chinese Societies Conference

United States Information Agency
Exhibit of American Experience in Constitutionalism
The American Participant Program for the Bicentennial of the U.S. Constitution Symposium, Conferences, and Panel Discussions Abroad
Colloquium, "Multi-Ethicity and Constitutionalism: The American Model and Africa"
"We the People" Poster Display

INSTITUTO CULTURAL ARGENTINO — NORTE AMERICANO
Seminar on the U.S. and Argentine Constitutions

VOICE OF AMERICA
Series of Documentaries on the Constitution
"American Profiles on the Framers of the U.S. Constitution" Five-minute Broadcasts
Radio feature programs on the U.S. Constitution
"We the People" Broadcast Series of 26 Documentaries on the Creation of the Constitution
"Constitutional Law: U.S. vs. U.S.S.R." Radio Broadcast Series

United States Office of Consumer Affairs
National Consumer Week Theme, "Consumers Celebrate the Constitution"

The United States Office of Personnel Management
"The Constitution: Let's Talk About It"
"Constitutional Issues" Module

University of Bologna
International Conference, "The U.S. Constitution and What It Means Today"

University of Dallas
"Constitutionalism in America" Symposiums, Meetings, and Speakers' Bureau

University of San Diego School of Law / Tel Aviv University Faculty of Law
Constitutional Law Conference

University of South Carolina
"Federal Courts — The Next 100 Years" Symposium

Veterans of Foreign Wars of the United States
Bicentennial Projects

Volunteer — The National Center
National Volunteer Week 1987, "Our Constitutional Heritage"

VP Fair Foundation
"We the People" VP Fair

Wake Forest University/Center for Research and Development In Law-Related Education (CRADLE)
SPICE II, Seven-day Institute for Elementary and Secondary School Teachers

Washington Antiques Show
"Crafting a Nation: A Celebration of the 200th Anniversary of the United States Constitution" Loan Exhibition

West Point Society of New York
"To Preserve and Defend: 200 Years" Bicentennial Celebration

*West Publishing Company
Reproduction and Distribution to High Schools of Alton S. Tobey "Signing of the Constitution" Prints

WETA-TV
"This Honorable Court" Television Documentary

The Williamsburg Charter Foundation
The Williamsburg Charter, First Amendment Statement

World News Institute, Inc.
"American Forum" Pilot Program for Television

Yale Center for Parliamentary History
Program of Publications of English Parliamentary Records of the Stuart Period

Ben Yarmolinsky
"The Bill of Rights: A Secular Oratorio"

Young Astronaut Council
"Space Bill of Rights" National Writing Competition

BICENTENNIAL EDUCATIONAL GRANT PROGRAM*

FISCAL YEAR 1987 AWARDS

California

Auxiliary Services Enterprises, Inc., of California State University at Los Angeles
$34,843 ($43,554)
A set of 38 lessons for grade 8 on the Constitution with an accompanying teacher's guide.

California State Department of Education
$42,500 ($99,820)
A two-week institute for 45 primary and secondary school teachers, focusing on the deliberations that produced the Constitution, its philosophical and historical antecedents, and the context of the Founding Era.

Long Beach Unified School District
$13,677 ($112,742)
A "Constitutional Forum" for 140 teachers focusing on the substantive background of the Constitution and its classroom applications.

Colorado

Colorado State Department of Education
$49,060 ($61,961)
A curriculum guide distributed to all elementary and middle schools in the state.

Social Science Education Consortium, Inc.
$24,064 ($34,114)
A one-week institute for 25 elementary and middle school teachers, with in-service follow-up, on an integrated humanities approach to the study of the Founding Era and development of lesson plans on the Constitution related to students' lives.

Connecticut

Connecticut Humanities Council
$29,199 ($42,355)
A four-week training course on the Constitution for 20 teachers, with in-service follow-up.

District of Columbia

American Studies Center
$50,000 ($140,240)
Development of a 44-minute videotape on the Constitutional Convention.

Catholic University of America
$49,429 ($61,787)
A two-week institute for 30 elementary school teachers, focusing on the use of existing curriculum materials on the Constitution.

History Teaching Alliance
$100,000 ($316,570)
Fourteen two-week institutes followed by a year of monthly seminars on the Constitution in 12 states, each institute/seminar involving 15 to 20 elementary and secondary teachers and four to five university faculty.

Georgia

Vinson Institute of Government at the University of Georgia
$20,887 ($85,705)
A three-day conference on The Federalist Papers and related documents, for 45 teachers and curriculum coordinators.

Kansas

Dr. James B. Schick of Pittsburg State University
$10,000 ($14,431)
A computer-based simulation of the Constitutional Convention and the Ratification process.

Kentucky

Jefferson County Public Schools
$55,000 ($95,960)
A ten-day institute on the Constitution with in-service follow-up, for 44 elementary and secondary teachers.

Louisiana

Professor John S. Baker of Louisiana State University Law Center
$20,162 ($28,832)
A seminar on The Federalist Papers for 28 secondary school teachers.

Maine

Maine Humanities Council
$50,000 ($128,038)
A conference for 35 elementary and secondary teachers, with in-service follow-up, to develop and apply curricular units on Constitution history.

Maryland

Anne Arundel County Public Schools
$19,224 ($30,175)
A two-week institute in national and state constitutional history for 30 participants, using local historical resources to develop lesson plans and a resource guide.

Massachusetts

Massachusetts Council for Social Studies
$50,000 ($169,390)
A series of research activities on the Massachusetts Ratification Convention for 355 secondary school teachers and their students.

Mississippi

Mississippi Committee for the Humanities
$14,227 ($72,900)
A two-day training conference on the Constitution for 100 teachers, four scholars, and other consultants.

Rust College
$47,652 ($56,218)
A three-week institute for 30 high school teachers on the Founding Era, the structure of the Constitution, and its historical development, together with the development and field-testing of teaching units.

New York

Hofstra University
$55,000 ($95,960)
A three-day workshop for 30 elementary and secondary teachers on the nation's constitutional heritage.

New York Historical Society
$50,000 ($67,950)
A ten-part radio series, videotape, and accompanying teacher and student guides on the Constitution, together with workshops on their use.

North Carolina

Center for Research and Development in Law-related Education (CRADLE) at Wake Forest University
$85,000 ($108,443)
A three-week institute and curriculum development program, with in-service follow-up, for 25 elementary teachers.

Center for Research and Development in Law-related Education (CRADLE) at Wake Forest University
$9,692 ($9,692)
Development of a national resource depository for teaching materials on the Constitution.

North Dakota

Bureau of Governmental Affairs of the University of North Dakota
$3,865 ($7,144)
Lessons on the Constitution for upper elementary school students.

*First funding figure in each program indicates the amount of the grant award; the second figure, in parentheses, indicates the total cost of the project.

306   We the People

Pennsylvania

Pennsylvania Humanities Council
$49,961 ($74,081)
A five-day institute for 45 teachers on "The Constitution and the Franchise."

Vermont

Vermont Department of Education
$12,317 ($23,467)
A five-day institute on major constitutional themes for 21 teachers, with in-service follow-up.

Virginia

Dr. George Blume of Virginia Polytechnic Institute
$5,900 ($25,185)
The writing of "The Constitution: Little Short of Miracle" for use in elementary schools.

Virginia Department of Education
$7,000 ($7,650)
A booklet of essays, resource materials, lesson plans, and teaching strategies on the drafting and ratification of the Constitution.

Washington

YMCA of Greater Seattle
$25,463 ($37,456)
A three-day conference for 40 middle school teachers on the use of lesson plans and resource materials prepared by the Washington Commission for the Humanities.

Wisconsin

Nicolet High School
$25,000 ($30,000)
A two-day conference/workshop for 40 secondary school teachers, with follow-up discussion and evaluation session.

University of Wisconsin System-Parkside
$23,176 ($30,214)
Three-day conference, a one-day meeting, and four dissemination seminars for 44 elementary and junior high school teachers on the Constitution and its historical background.

FISCAL YEAR 1988 AWARDS

Alabama

Auburn University
$73,137 ($77,583)
A four-week institute for 30 middle school teachers on the Constitution, with emphasis on Ratification and the development of the legislative branch.

Stillman College
$7,325 ($8,325)
Development of instructional materials on the Constitution for use in four inner-city elementary schools.

University of Montevallo
$6,787 ($6,787)
A one-day conference for 30 secondary school teachers on constitutional government, federalism, republicanism, and separation of powers.

Arizona

Tucson Unified School District
$9,229 ($24,169)
Three in-service workshops and follow-up sessions for 42 elementary school teachers on the creation and use of constitutional resource materials.

California

AMICUS
$106,700 ($106,700)
Production of a videotape with accompanying teachers' and students' guides, on the meaning of the Constitution, open-captioned for use with hearing-impaired students.

California State University, Chico
$66,770 ($77,402)
A two-week training seminar for 25 teachers in grades 5-12 on the use of effective teaching strategies for the Constitution.

Citizenship and Law-Related Education Center for the Sacramento Region
$61,787 ($473,866)
A year-long Constitution Mentor Teacher Institute for primary and secondary school teachers on the philosophical foundations of the Constitution and Bill of Rights.

Chaffey Joint Union High School
$44,816 ($120,337)
A program to train teachers in the use of teaching strategies and lesson plans on the Constitution, and to hold a model U.S. Congress involving 525 students.

Foundation for California State University, San Bernadino
$27,635 ($34,735)
A three-day conference on Congress and separation of powers for 35 secondary school teachers.

Foundation for California State University, San Bernadino
$22,503 ($32,427)
A six-day institute and follow-up conference for 60 primary and secondary teachers on the development and demonstration of classroom materials on the Constitution.

Santa Clara County Office of Education
$21,701 ($77,675)
Development and field-testing of an 8th-grade training model with accompanying videotape on the Constitution.

William B. Allen of Harvey Mudd College
$71,457 ($71,457)
Development of a 14-part radio program/audiocassette, with accompanying teacher guides and student workbooks, on the Constitutional Convention.

Connecticut

Area Cooperative Educational Services
$10,252 ($117,212)
Three two-hour in-service training sessions within a framework provided by the National Bicentennial Competition on the Constitution and Bill of Rights.

Connecticut Consortium for Law-Related Education
$6,000 ($29,367)
An institute for thirty-two 5th, 8th, and 11th grade teachers who were trained by constitutional scholars on the concepts and history of federalism.

Connecticut Consortium for Law-Related Education
$4,500 ($19,740)
A one-day in-service training workshop for 120 elementary and junior high school teachers on the National Bicentennial Competition on the Constitution and Bill of Rights.

University of Hartford, College of Engineering
$32,735 ($36,468)
A five-day institute for 50 science and history teachers in middle and high schools on the copyright and patent provisions of the Constitution.

Delaware

Delaware Heritage Commission
$20,822 ($35,713)
Development of a packet of primary resources, bibliography, and other materials for use in the 5th, 9th, and 12th grades.

CONTINUED NEXT PAGE

District of Columbia

American Political Science Association
$68,260 ($68,260)
A three-week institute for 25 master teachers on the Constitution, with in-service follow-up.

American Political Science Association's Project '87
$74,797 ($74,797)
Development of 10,000 copies of a guide and lesson plan to accompany selected essays on the Constitution.

Council for the Advancement of Citizenship
$64,826 ($64,826)
Four training sessions for elementary and secondary school teachers and administrators, together with other activities including a clearinghouse of Bicentennial resource materials.

National Trust for Historic Preservation
$50,000 ($76,123)
Development of an educational program at James Madison's home, Montpelier, for elementary and secondary school students.

Florida

Florida State University
$62,648 ($69,098)
A three-week institute for 25 secondary school social studies teachers on constitutional history, Congress, and separation of powers.

Georgia

Bainbridge College
$2,872 ($4,491)
A program of workshops for 50 elementary and secondary school teachers on the principles of, and controversies over, the Constitution.

Vinson Institute of Government at the University of Georgia
$20,816 ($26,649)
A three-day conference for 45 secondary school teachers to develop lesson plans focusing on Ratification and the legislative branch.

Idaho

Idaho Centennial Foundation
$84,500 ($101,935)
Development and distribution of 50,000 facsimile kits, containing curricular materials and reproductions of key documents in the history and statehood of the territories of the Great Northwest.

Illinois

American Bar Association
$71,393 ($137,423)
A one-week institute with in-service follow-up for 120 educators and community leaders, with lectures, discussion seminars, workshops, and an exhibit of exemplary materials.

Constitutional Rights Foundation
$30,490 ($41,562)
A five-day institute for 30 secondary school teachers on the history and principles of the Constitution.

Constitutional Rights Foundation
$32,968 ($43,646)
A five-day institute for 30 junior and senior high school teachers, focusing on the theoretical background of the legislative branch.

Southern Illinois University
$38,954 ($63,840)
A one-week institute and follow-up conference for 30 elementary and secondary school teachers on issues related to the ratification of the Constitution.

Indiana

Indiana Law-Related Education Bicentennial Project
$105,108 ($339,977)
A training program on the use of two sets of curricular materials for grades K-12 on the ideas, principles, issues, and continuing intellectual dialogue of American constitutionalism.

Joe Dunbar of the Kokomo-Center Township Consolidated Corporation
$35,050 ($35,050)
A school program which included visits by a constitutional scholar who portrayed Benjamin Franklin and taught constitutional lessons, and two-week seminars for 8th, 11th, and 12th grade students; videotapes of the Franklin character were distributed nationally at cost.

Iowa

Center for Educational Experimentation, Development, and Evaluation, of the University of Iowa
$46,944 ($50,319)
Materials, including Apple computer programs, focusing on the Legislative and executive branches for use by secondary school students with limited proficiency in English.

Loess Hills Area Education Agency
$9,996 ($12,971)
A series of in-service programs for 45 teachers of grades 5-12, focusing on the Ratification debates and the creation of the legislative branch.

Professor Clair Keller of Iowa State University
$20,000 ($31,797)
An elementary and secondary school program, which included historical "press conferences" related to the creation of the First Congress.

Louisiana

Louisiana School for Math, Science, and the Arts
$55,450 ($66,000)
A two-week institute and six follow-up sessions for 50 junior and senior high school teachers, focusing on the origins of the legislative branch and the Constitutional period.

Louisiana State University
$80,745 ($80,745)
A two-week institute, with in-service follow-up, for 30 secondary school teachers on the Ratification debates and The Federalist Papers.

Maine

Maine Humanities Council
$30,328 ($58,013)
Curricular materials focusing on the lives of the 56 Maine delegates to the Massachusetts Ratification Convention.

Maryland

Board of Education of Prince George's County
$74,058 ($108,550)
A three-week institute for 36 teachers of grades 5, 8, and 11 on the creation and development of the legislative and executive branches and the evolution of the electoral process.

Maryland Office for the Bicentennial
$38,457 ($45,457)
Creation of two audiovisual learning activity kits on the ideas and concepts that shaped the Constitution.

Patricia M. Cuff of the Montgomery County School District
$3,834 ($3,884)
Development of a drama on the executive branch and two workshops for teachers on the use of this material in grades 5-8.

Somerset Professional Development Center
$2,700 ($6,500)
In-service training of 50 elementary and secondary school teachers on the history, development, and structure of the Constitution.

Massachusetts

Massachusetts Global Education Program
$7,600 ($7,600)
A two-day conference for 30 junior and senior high school teachers, administrators, and curriculum specialists on the origins of the Constitution and its global impact.

Salem State College
$74,134 ($79,889)
A four-week institute for 20 middle and secondary school teachers on the role of Massachusetts in the drafting and ratification of the Constitution and in the creation of Congress.

Minnesota

Mankato State University
$48,754 ($74,879)
A two-week institute and follow-up sessions for 30 secondary social studies teachers on the history and principles of the Constitution, with a focus on the legislative branch and the doctrine of separation of powers.

Minnesota Center for Community Legal Education
$93,350 ($97,992)
A training institute for 5,000 teachers on the integration of constitutional studies into school curricula, and a Youth Constitutional Convention involving 50,000 students.

Mississippi

Mississippi State University
$48,917 ($48,917)
A statewide program involving development and dissemination of exemplary lesson plans on the Constitution.

Petal School District
$9,967 ($14,659)
A three-day conference for 45 elementary school teachers focusing on the use of writing exercises in constitutional studies.

Missouri

Central Missouri State University
$57,870 ($88,601)
A three-week institute and in-service follow-up for 30 secondary school teachers focusing on the philosophical roots of the Constitution.

U.S. Constitution Bicentennial Commission of Missouri
$46,250 ($75,000)
A statewide conference training a cadre of 45 teachers, who then served as co-conveners at six regional workshops to train teachers in the use of the We the People . . . texts of the Center for Civic Education.

New York

Buffalo City School District
$42,673 ($42,673)
Development of curricula for all grade levels on topics that included ratification, separation of powers, checks and balances, the functions of the three branches, and the impact of the Constitution on New York State.

Central New York Bicentennial Consortium and North Syracuse CSD
$58,651 ($71,133)
A two-week institute for 30 elementary and secondary school teachers on the first presidential administration and the development of the executive branch.

Iona College
$23,820 ($30,193)
An interdisciplinary three-week institute and in-service training of 40 junior and senior high school social studies teachers on the background of the Constitution.

Mamaroneck Union Free School District
$6,450 ($13,000)
Production of an elementary and middle school course on the executive branch.

New York Historical Society
$80,000 ($145,280)
Development of a mobile exhibit for the boroughs of New York City, based on the Society's 1987 exhibit on the Founding Era, "Government by Choice: Inventing the Constitution," with dissemination of exemplary instructional materials and teacher workshops, and establishment of a resource room and network.

New York Historical Society
$140,250 ($287,230)
Development of a mobile exhibit tour of five cities across the nation, based on the Society's 1987 exhibit on the Founding Era, with the development of resource guides for each site.

Project PATCH (Participatory Awareness Through Community Help)
$82,011 ($191,011)
Statewide dissemination of scholarly works, exemplary instructional programs, media projects and other learning activities on the Constitution through ten regional training centers.

Richard Skolnik of City University of New York
$18,195 ($18,195)
An original historical newspaper series, American Observer, with teacher's manual, featuring contemporary accounts of episodes in early American history, with an emphasis on Congress.

Syracuse University
$55,175 ($124,263)
A two-week institute for 30 elementary and secondary school teachers on the Constitution and ratification debates.

North Carolina

Center for Research and Development in Law-related Education (CRADLE), Wake Forest University
$59,610 ($81,610)
Implementation of a project to collect, evaluate, catalogue, establish a national repository for, and disseminate nationally, lesson plans on the Constitution.

Ohio

Hamilton County Office of Education
$30,200 ($40,795)
A ten-day institute for 40 secondary school teachers on the issues and debates of the Constitutional Convention and Ratification.

New Richmond Exempted Village School District
$10,191 ($29,762)
A staff development conference to train 80 teachers, a parents' newsletter, speakers bureau on the Constitution, and the expansion of a documents and artifacts museum.

Oklahoma

Harmony School
$6,803 ($20,556)
Continuation of the "Kids in Harmony with the Constitution" program, including teacher in-service training, development of a curriculum guide, and Constitution-related activities for school and community.

CONTINUED NEXT PAGE

Oregon

Columbia Education Center
$93,345 ($169,830)
Training of 36 master teachers from 12 Western states, with follow-up instruction of 100 teachers, on the philosophical and historical background of the Constitution.

Oregon Law-Related Education Program
$39,815 ($82,896)
A three-day seminar for 30 elementary and secondary school teachers, with in-service follow-up, on the nature of republican government and the views of the Federalists and Anti-Federalists on the three branches of government

Pennsylvania

National Constitution Center
$55,000 ($67,500)
Twenty-five yearlong reading and discussion groups comprising a total of 500 teachers on the Constitution, with an emphasis on the application of primary source materials in the classroom.

Rhode Island

Rhode Island Bicentennial Foundation
$9,230 ($20,330)
A daylong, in-service program, with additional in-service follow-up, for middle and secondary school teachers on "Congress and the People."

Rhode Island Legal/Educational Partnership Program
$64,970 ($79,945)
A three-week institute and follow-up sessions for 50 elementary school educators on the Constitution's antecedents, provisions, and modern applications.

South Carolina

South Carolina Bar Foundation
$27,200 ($29,800)
Production of four one-hour television sessions on the Constitution, each with teacher training and demonstration lessons; two sessions for secondary school, and one each for middle and elementary school.

Tennessee

Tennessee Technological University
$20,617 ($20,617)
A two-week interdisciplinary institute for 30 social studies teachers, grades 5-9, in the Upper Cumberland region of Tennessee, with special emphasis on teaching constitutional studies in small, rural school systems.

Texas

Association for Retarded Citizens of the United States
$46,154 ($58,920)
Development of a workbook and audiotape on the Constitution appropriate for students with mental retardation.

Northside Independent School District
$12,700 ($18,645)
A two-week institute, with in-service follow-up, for 15 secondary school teachers on the writing and ratification of the Constitution.

Southwest Texas State University
$64,302 ($87,693)
A three-week institute for 30 secondary school teachers on the Constitution and its principles.

Utah

Utah State Department of Education
$38,200 ($111,400)
Training of elementary school teachers in the integration of constitutional studies with children's literature and reading programs, together with statewide distribution of a guide to children's books on the Constitution.

Wisconsin

University of Wisconsin-Eau Claire
$50,708 ($59,329)
A four-week institute for 20 elementary and secondary school teachers on government under the Articles of Confederation and the philosophical background to the Constitution's drafting and ratification.

FISCAL YEAR 1989 AWARDS

Alabama

Auburn University
$60,444 ($74,067)
A two-week institute for 30 high school social studies teachers on the historical development and functioning of the executive and judicial branches.

Alaska

Anchorage School District
$37,110 ($58,520)
A one-week institute for 30 master teachers, focusing on both the U.S. and Alaska Constitutions; state legislators and original framers of the state constitution addressed the conference.

Arizona

Phoenix Union High School
$51,904 ($62,504)
Training activities involving 50 teachers and the development of curriculum materials, all focusing on the Constitution as the foundation of judicial decision-making.

California

Azusa Pacific University
$48,125 ($76,740)
A two-week teacher-training project, "Institute on the Principles of American Democracy," for thirty 12th-grade teachers, on the teaching of a state-required course on the Constitution.

California State University, Chico
$70,633 ($81,153)
A two-week institute, with in-service follow-up, for 25 social studies teachers and the development of a resource book on the Constitution and the Presidency.

Ninth Judicial Circuit Historical Society
$6,500 ($31,000)
Development and nine-state dissemination of essays and a teacher's guide on the history of the Bill of Rights in the American West and Pacific.

Sacramento LRE
$59,960 ($269,080)
A week-long institute, with in-service follow-up, for 40 teachers of grades 5, 8, 11, and 12 on the historical and philosophical foundations of the Constitution and Bill of Rights.

Colorado

Boulder County Safeguard LRE Program
$44,664 ($75,814)
A one-week institute for 40 teachers of grades 5-9 on the origins, history, and enduring principles of the Bill of Rights and subsequent Amendments.

Social Science Education Consortium, Inc.
$39,351 ($50,006)
A seven-day institute and post-institute activities for 23 elementary and middle school teachers on Congress, the Presidency, and separation of powers.

Connecticut

Connecticut Consortium for Law-Related Education
$21,516 ($22,905)
A week-long teacher training and curriculum development seminar for 21 middle and high school teachers on the deliberations, debates, and decisions of the First Congress.

District of Columbia

Council for Basic Education
$45,630 ($49,930)
A two-week institute for 28 secondary school teachers on teaching the Constitution using Socratic methods.

KIDSNET, Inc.
$29,740 ($35,665)
Creation and national distribution of a compendium of Constitution-related educational resources for grades K-12, including both print and computer materials.

National Council for the Social Studies
$91,600 ($191,662)
Development and field-testing of a poster series on the Judiciary for use at all grade levels.

National Institute for Citizen Education in the Law (NICEL)
$75,625 ($88,871)
Development of lessons for a 9th-grade course in D.C. history and for a two-week institute for more than 40 teachers, with in-service follow-up.

National Park Foundation
$100,000 ($142,750)
Development of curricular materials, including a videotape, student books, and lesson plans, for use in the "Constitution Works" program at Federal Hall in New York City.

Shepherd Elementary School
$7,638 ($47,838)
Expansion of the school system's Paideia project with additional teacher training in the use of U.S. history and government texts and other activities.

Georgia

Kennesaw State College
$33,018 ($46,983)
Development and distribution of a supplemental teaching unit on the Federal courts, together with a workshop for teachers.

Idaho

University of Idaho
$41,226 ($49,342)
A two-week teacher training and curriculum development institute for 15 secondary school social studies teachers on the evolution of the Presidency, with in-service follow-up.

Illinois

American Bar Association
$104,501 ($158,090)
A five-day institute on the Presidency, for six-member teams of educators from school districts nationwide with follow-up activities in each district.

Chicago Public Schools
$7,704 ($70,004)
A two-day training seminar for instructional coordinators, with in-service follow-up, on basic constitutional principles, with an emphasis on the legislative branch and The Federalist Papers.

Chicago Public Schools
$9,946 ($9,946)
Production of audiovisual learning materials for 8th and 11th grade students on the judicial system.

Constitutional Rights Foundation
$46,415 ($62,415)
An institute for 30 junior and senior high school teachers, with follow-up seminars and conference, on the role of the Federal Judiciary.

Constitutional Rights Foundation
$152,720 ($164,468)
Development and field-testing of an eight-week curriculum on the Bill of Rights for use by junior and senior high school English- as-a-second-language students.

University of Illinois at Chicago
$77,863 ($97,707)
A four-project activity, including production and distribution of 21 lessons on the Constitution, an institute for 15 area teachers, and follow-up workshops.

Indiana

Organization of American Historians
$52,193 ($72,821)
Production and dissemination of a series of secondary-school booklets on issues raised by the Bill of Rights.

Iowa

Loess Hills Area Education Agency
$9,993 ($14,048)
Second in a planned series of in-service programs and institute for 25 teachers of grades K-8 on the Constitution.

Maine

University of Southern Maine
$93,836 ($111,465)
Extension and integration of earlier programs on constitutional studies, including a curriculum-writing project on Maine's role in ratification and the development of adult education materials.

Maryland

INTEC Division of the Maryland State Department of Education
$61,380 ($225,108)
Development of a 20-minute video and teacher's guide on the Bill of Rights for use in upper elementary and middle schools.

Maryland LRE Program Center for Development
$60,027 ($105,114)
A two-week institute for 25 middle and high school teachers on the history of the Bill of Rights and related constitutional issues.

Prince George's County Public Schools
$74,793 ($116,793)
A two-week institute on the Constitution for 40 social studies teachers and library media specialists, with in-service follow-up.

Massachusetts

New England Foundation for the Humanities
$18,881 ($131,557)
Production and videotape distribution of a play, The Other Boston Tea Party, with follow-up workshops and PBS broadcast.

Minnesota

Mankato State University
$52,537 ($79,852)
An institute and two in-service follow-up sessions for 30 secondary school teachers on the executive and legislative branches.

Mankato State University
$55,248 ($80,868)
An institute for 30 teachers on the history and principles of the Constitution, with an emphasis on the Bill of Rights and subsequent Amendments.

Missouri

St. Louis Public Schools
$66,650 ($66,650)
A three-week institute and ancillary activities for 12 interdisciplinary teams of three teachers each on the Bill of Rights.

New Jersey

Rutgers University
$72,248 ($129,126)
A three-week institute for 25 middle and secondary school teachers on the philosophical and historical origins of the Constitution, the Bill of Rights, the Fourteenth Amendment, and the evolution of the Presidential selection process.

CONTINUED NEXT PAGE

New York

City School District of New Rochelle
$9,696 ($9,696)
Development by teams of teachers of study units on ten major constitutional issues, with in-service follow-up.

Forest Hills High School
$10,759 ($17,410)
Development and dissemination of four "Jigsaw Cooperative Learning Strategies" on the Bill of Rights.

New York State Bar Association
$85,000 ($135,600)
An institute for 27 master teachers with in-service follow-up on the creation and development of the legislative and executive branches.

Northport-East Northport Union Free School District
$109,547 ($109,547)
Support of ten regional centers training 1,000 teachers in the use of exemplary instruction programs on the First Inaugural, the Judiciary Act of 1789, and the first session of the U.S. Supreme Court.

Port Washington Union Free School District
$9,578 ($10,785)
Dissemination to classrooms of The Triumph of the Constitution, *an original play about the Ratification struggle in New York State, with a study guide.*

Project LEGAL
$48,917 ($109,626)
Development and dissemination of educational materials on the Constitution for learning-disabled and remedial reading students.

North Carolina

Center for Research and Development in Law-related Education (CRADLE)
$103,680 ($155,630)
Development of an interactive video program with teacher's guide on the Supreme Court and Bill of Rights.

Center for Research and Development in Law-related Education (CRADLE)
$157,140 ($347,243)
Continued development of CRADLE's project to collect, evaluation, catalogue and disseminate lesson plans on the Constitution.

North Carolina Bicentennial Commission
$59,777 ($94,317)
A week-long institute for 32 secondary school teachers on the "Courts and the Constitution," with subsequent dissemination of institute materials to teachers in the state.

Oklahoma

Oklahoma State University College of Arts and Sciences
$63,520 ($64,320)
Creation of a computer bulletin board of educational materials on The Federalist Papers for use in 7th grade through college, for both teachers and students.

Oregon

Oregon Law-Related Education Program
$46,698 ($67,198)
An institute for 30 teachers with in-service follow-up on the "Supreme Court's Review of Presidential Power."

Oregon Law-Related Education Program
$39,506 ($120,012)
A three-day seminar for 30 elementary and secondary school master teachers on the role of the Judiciary in American history, with subsequent publication of lesson plans.

Pennsylvania

Pennsylvania State University
$105,090 ($200,076)
Development of an interactive, multi-discipline television course on citizenship for dissemination through the Public Broadcasting System, including ten scripts, a teacher's guide, and a textbook.

School District of Philadelphia
$64,125 ($117,918)
Development, through two teacher training sessions, and distribution of materials in law-related education to educators in the school district.

Rhode Island

University of Rhode Island
$29,211 ($29,211)
A two-week institute for participants from all 40 of the state's school districts on the judicial branch.

South Carolina

South Carolina Bar Foundation
$36,900 ($62,000)
Production of four one-hour television sessions on the Constitution, each with teacher training and demonstration lessons.

University of South Carolina
$13,635 ($12,486)
A two-day conference for 50 secondary school teachers on Congress and the executive branch.

Tennessee

Vanderbilt University
$164,000 ($309,766)
Development of an interactive video on the Bill of Rights, with 14 lessons and a reference database of background materials using a hypertext reference system, for use at the junior high school level.

Texas

Association for Retarded Citizens of the U.S. (ARC)
$65,782 ($73,586)
Development and dissemination of instructional materials on the Bill of Rights for use in special education classes at all levels.

Intercultural Development Research Association (IRDA)
$91,827 ($107,305)
Development of a set of instructional materials on citizenship teaching applicants for amnesty under the Immigration Reform Act of 1986 and their children.

Southwest Texas State University
$66,640 ($87,570)
A three-week institute with in-service follow-up for 30 teachers of grades 7-12 on Congress and the executive branch.

Southwest Texas State University
$70,500 ($98,096)
An institute for 30 secondary school teachers on "The Constitution and the Federal Judiciary."

Utah

Ogden Area History Teaching Alliance
$13,650 ($30,900)
Replication and use in two Utah counties for elementary school teachers, of an exemplary secondary school program produced by the History Teaching Alliance, on the historical origins and development of the nation's constitutional system.

Utah State Office of Education
$79,600 ($114,900)
Additional development of the "Teaching About the Constitution Through Literature" project, including creation of a collection of constitutional stories, plays, and mock trials, and two training seminars out-of-state to implement it nationally.

Virginia

John Marshall Foundation
$55,589 ($69,209)
A four-day institute for 48 middle and high school teachers on the role of the Judiciary in resolving issues arising from the separation of powers.

Wisconsin

University of Wisconsin at Whitewater
$36,377 ($36,377)
A six-week institute with follow-up meetings for 30 middle and high school teachers on the Judiciary.

FISCAL YEAR 1990 AWARDS

California

Azusa Pacific University
$49,960 ($68,115)
A two-week institute for 30 history/social studies teachers on the primary documents of the founding of the United States.

Colorado

Boulder County Board of County Commissioners Safeguard Law-Related Education Program
$54,419 ($92,869)
Development and distribution of a resource guide of writing and lessons on individual liberties protected in the Constitution, together with a series of workshops on the Bill of Rights for teachers, and later, 100 secondary school students.

Social Science Education Consortium
$102,305 ($121,205)
Development and distribution of seven curriculum units with materials offering a case-study, comparative approach to the study of the Bill of Rights and its global significance, together with an institute and follow-up workshops.

Connecticut

Connecticut Consortium for Law-Related Education, Inc.
$18,912 ($23,362)
A follow-up training institute for participants in the National Bicentennial Competition on the Constitution and Bill of Rights.

District of Columbia

Constitutional Education Foundation
$88,997 ($118,526)
Development of a curriculum on the executive branch for simulated executive decision-making exercises by students in the "Constitution Works" project.

Constitutional Education Foundation
$101,726 ($148,382)
Development of a supplemental videotape for the "Constitution Works" project.

Council for Basic Education
$49,887 ($58,695)
A two-week institute on the Judiciary for 30 secondary school history teachers in the Washington, D.C. public school system.

National Institute for Citizen Education in the Law (NICEL)
$97,495 ($111,176)
Continuation of a broad-based program of curriculum development, teacher training, and innovative student projects, focusing on leadership training of 40 teachers and constitutional studies related to a required course in local history.

Florida

Florida State University
$85,414 ($100,063)
A three-week institute for middle and high school teachers on the Bill of Rights, with follow-up workshops.

Idaho

Idaho Humanities Council
$85,832 ($140,917)
A two-week institute for 40 secondary school teachers and students on the Bill of Rights.

Illinois

American Bar Association
$144,074 ($222,681)
A three-part project on the Bill of Rights, including a five-day institute for six-member teams from 20 schools districts, a series of follow-up programs in the school districts, and dissemination of the program's publications and resource materials.

Rich East High School
$22,400 ($22,400)
A four-day institute for 30 secondary school teachers from five states on teaching the history of the Founding Era through the use of a mock Constitutional Convention.

Sangamon State University
$31,900 ($47,475)
Production and dissemination of a series of three videotapes on the history and function of the judicial branch.

Indiana

Social Studies Development Center of the University of Indiana
$50,298 ($62,529)
Development and dissemination of a handbook of teaching and learning resources on the Bill of Rights.

Iowa

Clair Keller of Iowa State University
$18,000 ($27,284)
An adaptation of his elementary and secondary school program of "Historical Press Conferences" to the teaching of the Bill of Rights.

Maryland

College of Notre Dame
$51,441 ($97,680)
A two-week institute for 35 middle and high school teachers on the Bill of Rights, together with statewide dissemination of a workbook.

Phi Alpha Delta Public Service Center
$35,175 ($35,175)
Development of a resource guide and nationwide training program on the Bill of Rights, for use in elementary and middle schools.

Professional Development and Training Center, Inc.
$62,424 ($99,084)
A two-week institute with follow-up in-service workshops for 20 teacher-trainers on the Bill of Rights, for application in grades 5-12.

Professional Development and Training Center, Inc.
$61,921 ($75,301)
A two-week institute with follow-up workshops for 20 teacher-trainers on the historical background and functioning of the Judiciary, for application in grades 5-12.

William Donald Schaefer Center for Public Policy at the University of Baltimore
$35,197 ($47,579)
Two three-day workshops for 60 secondary school social studies and civics teachers on the origin of the Federal Judiciary.

Massachusetts

Boston Public Schools
$83,000 ($424,400)
"IMPACT II: Share the Spirit" program of dissemination through an estimated 220 teachers of exemplary teaching programs on the Bill of Rights and subsequent Amendments.

Arlene F. Gallagher, Ph.D.
$62,670 ($84,040)
Development and dissemination of a book of interactive plays demonstrating constitutional principles and their application, for use in elementary schools.

CONTINUED NEXT PAGE

Michigan

Michigan Commission on the Bicentennial of the U.S. Constitution
$47,581 ($183,254)
Development and distribution of a curriculum resource guide on the Bill of Rights, creation of a student Bicentennial internship program, and sponsorship of five regional workshops in the state.

Wayne County Intermediate School District
$72,407 ($121,522)
Development of guidelines for a multicultural education program on the Constitution, the Bill of Rights, and the U.S. Government for use in grades K-9.

Minnesota

Minnesota Center for Community Legal Education
$38,556 ($69,156)
Development of ten curriculum units and two regional teacher training conferences on the Bill of Rights and subsequent Amendments, for grades 5-12.

Mississippi

Mississippi Authority for Educational Television
$97,923 ($212,393)
Production of an instructional project, including a video, teaching materials, and teacher workshops, on the Bill of Rights for use by 9th grade social studies teachers, their students, and "at-risk" secondary school students.

New Mexico

New Mexico Bar Foundation
$81,215 ($217,220)
A four-part secondary school project on the Bill of Rights, including a ten-day institute for 25 teachers, compilation of a teacher resource manual, dissemination of training and materials to schools, and follow-up evaluation.

New York

Amity Public Schools
$29,237 ($30,000)
Development of a district-wide learning styles curricula on the Constitution and Bill of Rights for use in grades 4-12.

Community School District 11
$40,877 ($104,613)
Production of an exhibition on the First Amendment in the "Museum of Migrating People," for use by secondary schools.

Community School District 11
$22,305 ($68,535)
Production and distribution of a videotape and accompanying materials on the First Amendment, for use in the "Museum of Migrating People."

New York City Board of Education/Community School District #30
$65,988 ($88,559)
Adaptation of Federal Hall's "Constitution Works" programs on the Constitution for use with Limited English Proficiency (LEP) junior high school students.

New York State Bar Association — Law, Youth, and Citizenship Program
$85,600 ($135,600)
A teacher training program, including institute and regional workshops, on the creation and development of the Bill of Rights.

Northport-East Northport Union Free School District, Project PATCH
$124,959 ($124,959)
Ten regional training centers for 1,000 teachers on the use of exemplary programs, together with dissemination of exemplary programs and materials on the Constitution, the Bill of Rights, and subsequent Amendments.

Project Reach Youth
$48,958 ($48,958)
Development and dissemination of a mock First Congress program to teach high school students about the drafting of the Bill of Rights.

Society for the Preservation of Long Island Antiquities
$14,292 ($18,625)
Production of a set of instructional materials on local African-American history to be made available to approximately 180 Long Island middle and high schools.

North Carolina

Center for Research and Development in Law-related Education (CRADLE)
$93,873 ($145,200)
Expansion of the operation of the national repository and cataloging of teacher-developed lesson plans on the Constitution.

Friends of the Constitution of the U.S. (FOCUS)
$47,875 ($165,200)
A statewide program of 9th grade classroom role-playing exercises on constitutional rights, led by visiting jurists and other experts.

Ohio

Ashbrook Center of Ashland University
$55,056 ($77,995)
A two-week institute in 1990 for 30 high school history/social studies teachers on the founding principles of the United States Government.

Ashbrook Center of Ashland University
$59,600 ($92,423)
A two week institute in 1991 for 30 high school/social studies teachers on the founding principles of the United States Government.

Hamilton County Office of Education
$32,965 ($41,715)
A five-day institute with in-service follow-up for 40 middle and high school teachers on the judicial branch, with emphasis upon state history.

Western Reserve Historical Society
$104,417 ($128,992)
Production and dissemination of a multi-disciplinary film documentary and teacher's guide, focusing on Connecticut's Western Reserve lands in Ohio, with specific reference to constitutional issues in the context of this frontier settlement.

Oregon

Oregon LRE Program
$73,309 ($93,809)
A one-week institute, with in-service follow-up, for 30 teachers on the "Impact of the Bill of Rights on Federalism."

Pennsylvania

Chester County Intermediate Unit
$8,386 ($13,879)
Five-day in-service training for 25 secondary school history and government teachers on the structure and history of the modern judicial system.

National Constitution Center
$22,100 ($25,300)
Development and dissemination of a teacher's guide to educational materials on the Constitution and Bill of Rights, together with establishment of a telephone hotline.

PATHS/PRISM
$127,405 ($170,508)
A four-week institute for 25 teachers, grades 1-8, on the Bill of Rights, together with curriculum development and dissemination and with an in-service follow-up weekend retreat on teaching strategies.

Pennsylvania Humanities Council
$49,603 ($62,747)
Development and field-testing of an in-service course for 240 social studies teachers on the Bill of Rights.

South Carolina

South Carolina Bar Foundation
$35,900 ($35,900)
Production of four one-hour television sessions on the Constitution, including its impact around the world, with each session offering teacher training and demonstration lessons, two sessions for high school use, one for middle school, and one for elementary school.

South Dakota

University of South Dakota
$59,562 ($96,585)
A three-week institute, with a follow-up workshop, for 30 upper elementary and secondary school social studies teachers from three states on the Bill of Rights and the Fourteenth Amendment.

Tennessee

Memphis State University
$121,180 ($289,180)
A six-week course for 20 secondary school social studies teachers on the Bill of Rights, together with the development of an in-service training manual and dissemination of the project's materials.

University of Tennessee
$52,033 ($68,868)
A three-week institute for middle and high school teachers on the concept of separation of powers and right of due process.

Texas

San Elizario Independent School District
$24,510 ($35,250)
In-service teacher seminars for teachers of all grade levels that focused on connecting local history with the Constitution.

Southwest Texas State University
$72,751 ($93,406)
A three-week institute, with in-service follow-up, for 30 secondary school teachers on the Bill of Rights.

Virginia

Dr. George Blume of Virginia Polytechnic Institute and State University
$15,397 ($15,397)
Development and dissemination of a one-act play on various aspects of the Bill of Rights, for use in elementary schools.

Virginia Commonwealth University
$44,070 ($75,514)
A seven-day institute for 40 secondary school social studies teachers on the Bill of Rights.

Western Branch Elementary School
$6,000 ($8,600)
Continuation of a student project in oral history on the meaning and impact of the Constitution as revealed through the testimony of individual citizens in the community.

Wisconsin

Milwaukee SER-Jobs for Progress
$9,239 ($13,439)
Two three-hour study/training sessions for 36 teachers in 18 alternative high school programs on the teaching of the Constitution and Bill of Rights to at-risk, economically disadvantaged, and high school students with limited English proficiency.

FISCAL YEAR 1991 AWARDS

Alabama

Alabama Center for Law & Civic Education
$82,588 ($112,879)
Production of five videotapes and accompanying printed materials on contemporary Alabamians with major roles in the development and interpretation of constitutional rights.

Shelby County Board of Education
$6,450 ($7,450)
A one-day seminar and workshop for approximately 50 teachers on the Bill of Rights.

California

Calexio Unified School District
$21,095 ($21,095)
In-service training of 28 teachers, grades 5, 8, 11, and 12, on the basic principles of democracy and the development of lessons on the Constitution and the Bill of Rights.

Citizenship and Law-Related Education Center for the Sacramento Region (CLRE)
$59,970 ($241,690)
A training program for 40 mentor teacher/curriculum leaders, with in-service follow-up, on the historical and philosophical foundations of the Constitution and Bill of Rights.

Los Angeles Unified School District (LAUSD)
$112,893 ($219,532)
A series of 14 two-day workshops for 435 elementary school teachers on the Constitution and Bill of Rights.

Thomas Jefferson Center
$18,350 ($18,350)
A three-day institute with in-service follow-up for ten teacher-trainers on the use of the Center's teacher guides.

District of Columbia

Catholic University of America
$64,604 ($193,124)
A three-week institute, with in-service follow-up, for 30 elementary and secondary teachers and librarians throughout the nation on various topics in U.S. history, including the origins of the Bill of Rights, the Civil War Amendments, and modern Civil Rights Acts.

District of Columbia Public Library
$1,696 ($4,884)
Three weekly sessions for teachers of Adult Basic Education classes and English-as-a-Second-Language classes on the Bill of Rights.

National Institute for Citizen Education in the Law (NICEL)
$86,829 ($99,705)
Development and adaptation of lesson plans on the Bill of Rights for use with deaf and hard-of-hearing students.

ORBIS Associates
$54,383 ($68,391)
Development of curricular materials on citizenship and Bill of Rights issues relating to Native Americans, for use in secondary schools.

Illinois

Constitutional Rights Foundation — Chicago
$129,500 ($145,336)
Continued development, testing, and dissemination of curricular materials on the Bill of Rights, for use with English-as-a-Second-Language classes.

Rich East High School
$34,655 ($35,655)
A four-day institute for 30 master teachers of U.S. history on the use of mock Constitutional Conventions and other methods of teaching the Founding Era.

Kentucky

Jefferson County Public Schools
$32,989 ($101,810)
A series of six-hour in-service workshops for 30 middle and high school teachers, with in-service follow-up, on cultural pluralism and the role of women in the historical development of rights in the United States.

Louisiana

Jefferson Parish Public Schools
$74,500 ($98,778)
A two-week institute, with in-service follow-up, for 30 teachers of grades 5-10 on the Constitution and Bill of Rights, with emphasis on the Fifth Amendment.

CONTINUED NEXT PAGE

Maine

Bates College
$23,453 ($36,540)
A two-week institute, with follow-up workshops, for 20 secondary school teachers on the historical development and current impact of the Bill of Rights.

University of Southern Maine
$62,970 ($88,060)
Development of an adult education project on the Bill of Rights for use in Adult Basic Education and high school equivalency programs.

Minnesota

Minnesota Center for Community Legal Education
$49,954 ($66,412)
A one-week institute for 30 elementary and secondary school teachers on the development of educational materials on the Fourth, Fifth, Sixth, Eighth, and Fourteenth Amendments, with subsequent dissemination of the materials throughout the state.

Missouri

Webster University
$58,875 ($58,875)
A three-week institute for 20 elementary and secondary school teachers and their principals, on contemporary implications of the Constitution and Bill of Rights.

New York

New York City Public Schools' Social Studies Unit
$39,936 ($79,457)
A one-week institute for 32 social studies teachers and supervisors, grades 7-12, on the Bill of Rights, with emphasis upon its impact on ethnic and cultural groups.

New York State Bar Association
$125,000 ($221,220)
A five-day teacher training institute for 45 teachers on the creation and development of the Bill of Rights and on topics concerning freedom and responsibility in a contemporary society.

Project LEGAL
$36,267 ($40,267)
On-site training and technical assistance for 50 Special Education teachers on constitutional studies and related teaching methods.

North Carolina

Center for Research and Development in Law-related Education (CRADLE)
$124,906 ($170,984)
Continued expansion of the national repository of lesson plans on the Constitution.

Oregon

The Constitution Project
$88,920 ($88,920)
Production of a film and accompanying curricular materials on the internment of Japanese Americans in World War II.

Ninth Judicial Circuit Historical Society
$30,999 ($63,593)
Production of a videotape about the history of the nation's courts in the West and their role in the application of the Bill of Rights, designed as a supplement to the grantee's publications on Western legal history.

Oregon Law Related Education Program
$62,843 ($83,093)
A week-long institute, with follow-up school activities, for 30 teachers on the application of the Bill of Rights to ethnic minorities, students, and criminal defendants.

Pennsylvania

Temple Law Education and Participation (LEAP) Program
$53,967 ($132,095)
A four-day teacher training and materials development institute on the Bill of Rights.

Rhode Island

Literacy Volunteers of America, Washington County Chapter
$15,904 ($17,829)
Development of a set of 12 lesson plans on the Bill of Rights and related Amendments for use by the functionally illiterate and English-as-a-second-language adults.

Tennessee

Memphis State University
$90,591 ($889,145)
A six-week institute, with development of learning modules and in-service follow-up, for 20 elementary school teachers on the Bill of Rights and the Fourteenth Amendment.

Texas

Association for Retarded Citizens of the U.S.
$61,531 ($66,973)
An in-service training program on the Constitution for teachers in high school students with mental retardation.

Virginia

Jamestown-Yorktown Foundation
$40,640 ($57,080)
A six-day institute for 30 secondary school teachers, with in-service and other follow-up, on Virginia's contribution to the origins and adoption of the Bill of Rights.

Theatre IV
$61,000 ($123,426)
Sponsorship of a 120-performance tour of the play James Madison and the Bill of Rights, *together with teacher's guide, suggested classroom activities, and other materials for use in elementary and middle schools.*

Virginia Commonwealth University
$48,793 ($88,638)
A seven-day institute, with in-service follow-up, for 40 social studies teachers on the Bill of Rights and the concept of American constitutionalism from an international perspective.

Washington

University of Puget Sound School of Law Institute for Citizen Education in the Law (UPSICEL)
$75,000 ($126,499)
Development of eight lessons on the Bill of Rights for use in upper elementary and middle schools, together with a one-week institute to instruct 40 teachers in their use.

COLLEGE-COMMUNITY FORUMS

Alaska

Alaska Pacific University

The Impact of the Bill of Rights and Civil War Amendments: Four three-hour forums examined the competing perspectives of the various Rights Amendments involving speakers, panelists, and a question and answer period. Cosponsors included the state bar association and the Alaska Bicentennial group.

California

California State University, Los Angeles

Whither Civil Rights? Congress, the Presidency, the Courts and Civil Rights in the 1990s: Two forums were held on contemporary civil rights questions, featuring panelists from academic, legal, governmental, and community backgrounds.

California State University

Land-Use Control and the Bill of Rights: Three forums in April and May 1991 focused on the conflict between community rights and individual property-owner rights, placing current issues in the broader context of the First, Fifth, and Fourteenth Amendments.

College of the Redwoods

Legislative and Executive Powers: The College conducted a series of three forums on two government branches, one of which used a high school student essay contest to promote interest and encourage debate.

Fresno City College

Congress vs. the President: Contemporary Challenges Over the Separation of Powers Doctrine: Cosponsored by the League of Women Voters and promoted among local minority organizations, this forum on the separation of powers included the showing of a Public Broadcasting Service film on the Constitution.

Fresno City College

Judicial Restraint vs. Judicial Activism: The forum on the Judiciary was held in March 1991 and was cosponsored by the local League of Women Voters, the American Association of University Women, and the Fresno Bar Association. It also involved groups from the NAACP, the Mexican American Political Association, and the ACLU.

Colorado

Colorado Supreme Court Commission on Public Education

The Judiciary and the Bill of Rights: Past, Present, and Future: Five forums cosponsored with the Colorado Judicial Institute and selected Colorado colleges featured panels consisting of state and Federal jurists, academics, and members of local bar associations and special interest groups.

Regis College

U.S. Courts — The Least Dangerous Branch of Government?: A three-day forum was held on the Judiciary, with each day consisting of two sessions — an afternoon panel and an evening address.

Regis College

Bill of Rights: Protector of Individual Freedoms: A three-day program on the Amendments included five sessions — three afternoon panel discussions and two evening public forums.

Connecticut

Middlesex County Chamber of Commerce

Three April 1991 forums concentrated on the ratification of the Bill of Rights in Connecticut, and considered both the issues of the time and the same issues today. Wesleyan University and local historians cooperated in the effort.

District of Columbia

American University

Managing Presidential Transitions; Political Honeymoon or Impending Divorce? President Bush Meets the 101st Congress; Congressional Oversight and the Constitution in the Reagan-Bush Era; Congress, the President, and War Powers: Perspectives for a Third Century: A series of four forums included men and women working in, or closely associated with, the institutions of the Federal Government, including members of Congress, the executive branch, and the press.

American University, Center for Congressional and Presidential Studies

Understanding Congress, the Presidency, the Courts and the Constitution: A series of four forums was presented by a consortium of universities in the metropolitan area, featuring roundtable discussions with congressional representatives, scholars and experts on the executive branch.

Florida

Brevard Community College

The Judiciary: A series of six forums featured discussion panels made up of local judges, state attorneys, and local members of the bar, the press, and minority organizations.

Broward Community College

Securing Voting Rights for African-Americans and the Role of the Federal Judiciary: A February 1991 forum on legal and philosophical views of voting rights, was cosponsored by two local universities, two African-American community organizations, the county school board, and the county library.

Central Florida Community College

The Supreme Court — Continuity and Change: A day-long forum featured panel and small group discussions, and was produced in consortium with the local library and chamber of commerce.

Florida State University

The Federal Judiciary and Freedom of Political Expression and The Bill of Rights for the 21st Century: Two forums were produced with assistance from the state bar association, the state law-related education program, and the state Constitution Bicentennial Commission.

Florida State University

The Constitution in Times of Crisis: Congress, the President, and the Power to Make War: The two-session event consisted of an afternoon colloquium and an evening mock trial.

Gulf Coast Community College

Rethinking the Separation of Powers — The "Delicate Balance" of Presidential and Congressional Power: The forum was presented by the college, the North Florida Regional Libraries, and the Florida Institute for Policy Studies, and featured a debate between two main speakers, followed by discussion from two respondents.

Manatee Community College Foundation, Inc.

We the People: A Forum on the Bill of Rights: Eight public forums were held during 1991, conducted by members of the Institute for Retired Executives and Professionals (REAP).

Okaloosa-Walton Community College

Town Meeting on the Bill of Rights: Four town meetings were held on selected Bill of Rights Amendments and subsequent Amendments, with presentations by local experts followed by audience participation.

Polk Community College

Impact: The Constitution Today: The forum consisted of four events, conducted in February and March 1991; each consisted of a skit depicting an Amendment's historical background followed by a debate on the Amendment between experts and audience discussion.

St. Petersburg Junior College

The Judiciary and Civil Rights: A series of three forums was held at a local church, a community facility, and the college itself, with representatives of local groups serving as panelists.

Valencia Community College

The United States Constitution: Responding to the Nation's Diversity: A series of forums was presented in fall, spring, and summer of 1990-1991 on the courts and the Constitution, before audiences that included African-American, American-Asian, women's, and senior citizens' groups and communities.

CONTINUED NEXT PAGE

Georgia

Albany State College

The Federal Judiciary — Nonelected Defenders of Democracy: A series of five forums focused on all aspects of the Judiciary and featured background lectures by judicial scholars, followed by panel and audience discussions.

Albany State College

The Freedom of Expression — Assessing the First Amendment: A series of five forums covered the history, meaning, and impact of free expression, with an address by a judicial scholar and a panel discussion. Videotapes of the proceedings were made available to other communities.

Clark Atlanta University

African-Americans and the Bill of Rights: Continuity or Change?: With the cosponsorship of the Southern Center for Studies in Public Policy, a series of three forums was presented, each concentrating on a specific historical era.

Macon College

The Constitution and Our Judges: The Human Face of the Judiciary: An evening forum was held featuring speakers who included local civic, business and academic leaders, and three members of the Federal Judiciary. The local League of Women Voters assisted with the project.

Morehouse College

First, Fourth, and Fifth Amendment Rights and The Relationship Between the Bill of Rights and the 14th Amendment: A series of forums was held in four different cities (including Atlanta) near the college, with speakers who were scholars in history, religion, philosophy, sociology, and other disciplines.

Illinois

Eastern Illinois University

The Bill of Rights and Our Community: In cooperation with seven community organizations, a series of forums was held discussing the role of the Bill of Rights in everyday life. A keynote address was given by an Illinois State Supreme Court Justice.

Native American Educational Services — NAES College

Appropriate Judicial Power: Federal Models and American Indian Tribal Courts: The forum, held at the Field Museum of Natural History in Chicago, compared tribal court systems with the U.S. Federal court system.

Oakton Community College

Judicial Restraint vs. Judicial Activism; the First Amendment: Two forums were cosponsored by the college and the Skokie Public Library, where the gatherings took place, and featured scholars, jurists, local elected officials, and members of the press as guest speakers and panelists.

Richland Community College

The Impact of Controversial Issues on the [Supreme] Court's Decision-Making Processes: The forum, cosponsored by the Decatur Bar Association, featured three addresses, followed by a panel discussion led by a moderator.

Sangamon State University

Spring 1991 Intersession — The Bill of Rights After 200 Years: A week-long program was held in March 1991 covering Bill of Rights issues, as well as the history of the Fourteenth Amendment, including discussions with attorneys or litigants, and concluding with a two-day town meeting.

South Suburban College of Cook County

The Presidency: The forum featured a keynote address by John Rohr, author of To Run a Constitution: The Legitimacy of the Administrative State. *Among the groups assisting were the state League of Women Voters and the state political science association.*

Western Illinois University

Fighting All the Way to the Supreme Court: The Genesis of a Constitutional Right: Two forums cosponsored with the Macomb League of Women Voters were held in April 1991, focusing on four landmark Supreme Court cases, West Virginia v. Barnette, Wisconsin v. Yoder, Gideon v. Wainwright, and Bradwell v. Illinois.

Indiana

Calumet College of St. Joseph

The Bill of Rights and 20th-Century Immigrants in Northwest Indiana: Two community forums on the Bill of Rights were held, in which the forum presenters were both sitting judges — one from the Federal District Court, the other from Superior Court.

Indiana State University, Terre Haute

The Bill of Rights and the Limits of Individual Liberty: A series of three forums was cosponsored by a local technical college and a local community college.

Martin University

The Afro-American and the Constitution: The four-forum series was held in 1991 featuring pre-forum discussion sessions that then governed the structure of the forums.

Iowa

Coe College

The Bill of Rights: A Living Document: Four forums were held in May 1991, one per week, on the history of the Bill of Rights, freedom of speech, freedom of religion, and human rights in the 20th century.

Drake University Law School

The Judiciary and Freedom of the Press: A symposium was presented to mark the 25th anniversary of the New York Times v. Sullivan ruling and the freedom of the press guaranteed by the First Amendment.

Kentucky

University of Kentucky

The Courts, the Community and the Bill of Rights: Each in a series of four forums on the Bill of the Rights featured a keynote address followed by two panel discussions, with publicity and resources assistance from a local library.

Western Kentucky University

The Judiciary and the Living Constitution: Each in a series of three forums featured an introductory lecture followed a week later by a roundtable forum, with assistance from the local bar association.

Louisiana

Louisiana Technical University

Substance Abuse — A Challenge to Constitutional Law Enforcement: The forum was produced with assistance from the local bar association, mayor's office, public library, and local Bicentennial Commission.

Maine

Bates College/Muskie Archives

The Expansion of the Bill of Rights: Two forums were held in the spring of 1991 on the Thirteenth, Fourteenth, and Fifteenth Amendments, focusing on race and gender issues, with keynote addresses by recognized scholars. Videotapes of the programs were subsequently used by the University of Maine Law School's Law Related Education Project.

Edmund S. Muskie Archives at Bates College

The Judiciary: The series of four forums on the Judiciary featured two principal speakers offering opposing viewpoints, followed by questions from a panel and audience discussion. Videotapes of the programs were subsequently used by the University of Maine Law School's Law Related Education Project.

Maryland

St. John's College

Our Constitution: The Executive and Judicial Powers: A series of 15 seminars was presented for students and community members, utilizing as texts such primary sources as The Federalist Papers.

Massachusetts

Fitchburg State College

Judging the Judiciary: Vision and Reality: A one-day, three-part forum was held, and included participation by high school and college debate teams, as well as scholars and legal professionals.

Mount Ida College

Rights and Duties in the American Constitutional System; the Founders' Perspective and the 21st Century: Two forums were held covering the Constitutional System and featuring opening presentations, small discussion groups, and a final plenary session.

Springfield Technical Community College

A Sociological and Historical Overview of the First Amendment — An African-American Perspective: A two-day program was held at the Springfield Armory National Historic Site, comprising three panel meetings followed by workshops, film presentations and small-group discussions.

Stonehill College

An On-Air Open Town Meeting on the Bill of Rights: A town meeting was held concerning local Bill of Rights issues, such as opposition to an adult bookstore, and police searches directed at minorities. Cosponsored with the county bar association, the City of Brockton Bicentennial Commission, and other organizations, this forum was broadcast live over WBZ radio in Boston.

Michigan

Charles Stewart Mott Community College

The Judiciary in the Third Century: Each in a series of four forums featured an introductory speech by a local-area judge or constitutional authority, followed by a panel response and discussion.

Hope College

The Supreme Court And the People: The forum, which covered such principles as original intent and constitutional rights, consisted of three addresses followed by a panel response and audience discussion.

Minnesota

Minnesota Commission for the Humanities

The Bill of Rights: The state agency purchased and distributed the Bill of Rights poster series created by the Pennsylvania Humanities Council to organizations throughout Minnesota, encouraging their use to promote constitutional discussions.

Mississippi

Mississippi Delta Community College

Literacy and Its Impact on the Judicial System: The forum was developed to increase the public's understanding of the basics of civics, the legal processes, and the administration of justice, and was sponsored by a consortium of local universities.

Mississippi State University

The Judiciary: Two events made up this forum program — a forum on the selection of Federal and state Judges, and a mock trial on the First Amendment. The Stennis Institute of Government assisted with the project.

Mississippi University for Women

Bill of Rights Forum: The forum was held in February 1991, cosponsored by the local branch of the American Association of University Women and the county public library and covering issues related to the First, Fourth, and Sixth Amendments.

Pearl River Community College

Leadership in the Legislative Branch: A series of four forums was held in various locations, and featured a video presentation on Thomas Jefferson that was used to introduce the panel discussions.

Missouri

Crowder College

Legislative and Judicial Branches: Two forums on the Legislature and Judiciary were held at local high schools and were cosponsored by local political parties and the local bar association and historical society.

Mineral Area College

Congressional Powers: A series of six forums was held on the legislative branch.

Montana

Rocky Mountain College

The Bill of Rights in Montana History: Pathways to the Present: Cosponsored with the Yellowstone Bar Association, this forum consisted of a keynote address on the history of the Bill of Rights, followed by four workshops the following day on the document's applications and effect on Montana.

Rocky Mountain College

Constitutional Law and Native American Issues: A two-day workshop focused on the influence of Supreme Court rulings on the development of Federal Indian law, utilizing discussion groups led by jurists, attorneys, and other participants.

New Hampshire

Colby-Sawyer College

The Executive Branch and the Judicial Branch — A Delicate Balance: The forum, focusing on the Executive and the Judiciary, consisted of Friday evening and Saturday morning sessions and followed the format of traditional town meetings, with a keynote speaker and panel and audience discussions, followed by six small-group workshops.

New Jersey

Kean College of New Jersey

The Redress of Grievances: The New Jersey Tax Revolt and the First Amendment: The forum held in April 1991 focused on the right to petition the government for redress, an issue relevant to the tax revolt then under way in New Jersey.

New Mexico

Eastern New Mexico University

The Politics of Public Discourse: Two evening programs, which also served as components of university courses, covered the First Amendment; the first concerned the arts and censorship, the second, the media's freedoms and responsibilities.

CONTINUED NEXT PAGE

New York

Canisius College

The Federal Courts and Social Problems and Policies: The forum covered the subject of judicial activism and featured a panel presentation and discussion, followed by audience discussion.

Empire State College

President v. Congress: Accountability in War and Peace: An evening session featured presentations by Dr. Louis Fisher and Professor Jeremy Rabkin and a discussion with a panel of community leaders. Groups involved in the event were the League of Women Voters, the local bar association, the county legislature, the local chamber of commerce, and others.

Hofstra University

The Importance of a Judicial Nominee's Political Views and Ideology During Consideration for Confirmation: The forum featured a discussion by panelists who were lawyers, scholars, members of the press, and representatives of community organizations.

Russell Sage College

Constitutional Rights in Comparative Perspective: American and East Asian Views: A series of three forums was conducted in cooperation with the Chinese-American Alliance of the Capital District.

State University of New York, Oswego

Changing in Interpretation: The Courts and the Constitution: The forum focused on the role of the courts in defining the Constitution and featured panel and audience discussions.

Syracuse University

Articles I and II of the Constitution: A series of three forums was presented, one each in Syracuse, Binghamton, and New York City, including a dramatized debate between Alexander Hamilton and New York Governor George Clinton, who had been on opposites sides of the constitutional ratification debates.

Syracuse University

Federalism and the Judiciary Throughout American History: Eight forums were presented from September 18 through November 20, 1990, in which a moderator portraying Chief Justice John Marshall examined the creation of the Judicial System and the impact of Supreme Court decisions on federalism.

Syracuse University

The Creation of the Bill of Rights and Our First Amendment Freedoms: Then and Now: The series of four forums was held during the spring of 1991 in conjunction with the Central New York Bicentennial Commission, and covered the history of the Bill of Rights and First Amendment issues.

North Carolina

Methodist College

A series of three forums was cosponsored by the county bar association, county school system, the state Department of Public Instruction, and the North Carolina Museum of Cape Fear.

University of North Carolina at Charlotte

Congress, the Presidency and Democracy: Past and Present: Two evening forums featuring panel discussions covered "looking back" and "looking forward" at popular control of the government.

Wake Forest University

The Judicial Enforcement of Civil Rights in the Work Place: The forum featured a keynote speaker and two panel discussions and was cosponsored by the Wake Forest University School of Law, and the Department of Political Science and School of Management at the university.

Ohio

Cuyahoga Community College

The Fourth Amendment: A Man's Home Is His Castle — Or Is It?: The forum, consisting of speakers and a panel, was held in May 1991 and concentrated on the protections of the Fourth Amendment in an age of electronic surveillance, random drug testing, and other challenges.

Defiance College

Judicial Review: Check, Balance, or Legislation? The forum was produced with the assistance of the county bar association and the local chamber of commerce and library.

University of Cincinnati

Defiance or Compliance? Cincinnati's Response to the Supreme Court: Consisting of three forums on court cases that included racist speech and separation of church and state, this series featured panelists who were attorneys or plaintiffs involved in Supreme Court cases that originated in Ohio.

Pennsylvania

Community College of Allegheny County

The Bill of Rights vs. the Bill of Wrongs: Individual Rights vs. Common Good: The forum was held in April 1991; its panelists included a Federal Judge, a newspaper editor, a member of a county bar association, and a vice president of Duquesne University.

Pennsylvania Humanities Council

The Bill of Rights in Everyday Life: Two forums were held in the fall of 1991, the first addressing the Bill of Rights and criminal procedure, the second weighing the Bill of Rights as a model for the new emerging democracies of Eastern Europe.

Perkiomen Valley Public Library

Dialogues on the Bill of Rights: Three meetings focused on the constitutional protections enjoyed by controversial individuals and groups, the philosophy behind the Bill of Rights, and how the Supreme Court has protected it.

St. Vincent College

The Bill of Rights: Its Past, Its Present, and Its Future: A March 1991 forum on civil liberties protections in the Bill of Rights — specifically the First, Second, Fourth, and Fifth Amendments, and the rights of refugees — opened with a skit on the political atmosphere of the 1790s and was followed by plenary and small-group discussion sessions.

St. Vincent College

The Constitutional Tug-of-War Between Congress and the Presidency: Who Controls the Outcomes?: The forum concentrated on the legislative and judicial branches, featuring small-group discussion sessions and a final plenary session.

St. Vincent College

The Federal Judiciary — Its Role as Arbiter and Policymaker in American Society: The evening forum focused on the Judiciary and featured small discussion groups made up of local community and civic group leaders, followed by a final plenary session.

Wilson College

The First Amendment in a Small Community Context: Two panel discussions were held in April 1991 in cooperation with the Chambersburg (Pa.) Mayor's office — the first on First Amendment issues affecting the press in a small community (such as libel suits), and the second on reaction to the Supreme Court's decision on obscenity, Miller v. California.

South Carolina

University of South Carolina

Congress into the 21st Century: Would the Framers Approve?: Chief Justice Warren Burger gave the opening address at the forum, which continued with a panel discussion on foreign policy, domestic policy, and the representativeness of Congress. Veteran TV correspondent Edwin Newman was the panel moderator.

University of South Carolina — Spartanburg

200 Years of the Bill of Rights: Individual Freedoms in 1991: Five panel discussions were held on topics that included freedom of religion, freedom of expression, search and seizure, cruel and unusual punishment, and right to privacy.

South Dakota
Sioux Falls College
We the People: Our Bill of Rights: The forum, held in the afternoon and evening, included lectures, small-group discussion, and a panel discussion and was conducted in cooperation with Augustana College and the Sioux Falls League of Women Voters.

Tennessee
Lincoln Memorial University
Constitutional Anachronism? The Place of the Electoral College: The forum, which focused on the governmental mechanism that selects the President, consisted of presenters' remarks followed by audience discussion, and was broadcast by the campus radio station.

The University of Tennessee-Knoxville
Federalism: Original Intent and Current Reality: The forum covered the debates over the Constitution's ratification and the original understanding of the role of the States in the Federal system.

Walters State Community College/Lincoln Memorial University
They Are the Tyrant's Pleas — Abraham Lincoln and the Constitution: The forum focused on Lincoln's and other Presidents' interpretations of certain constitutional provisions, and was broadcast live over Lincoln Memorial University's radio station.

Texas
Hispanic Chamber of Commerce of Austin
The Constitution and the Bill of Rights: Empowerment for Minorities?: Three three-hour town meetings were conducted during the fall of 1991, focusing on Constitutional provisions that directly affect minorities in America. Panels included an ethnic mix of state and local lawyers, judges, educators, and others.

Sam Houston State University
The Bill of Rights — into the 21st Century: Four forums were held during 1991 on due process, the right to privacy, minority issues, and freedom of expression, and received commitments of support from the city of Huntsville, the local DAR, the Colonial Dames, and other organizations.

Southwest Texas State University
The Bill of Rights and the Community: Three town meetings were held, each comprised of two segments, and each including a keynote address and panel response followed by questions from the audience.

Texas A & M University
The Flexible Constitution: Four forums from January through April 1991 covered the First, Second, Fourth, Fifth, and Twenty- second Amendments, with assistance from the Galveston Historical Foundation, the World Affairs Council, and the Rosenburg Library.

Utah
Brigham Young University
The Judiciary and the Bill of Rights: As part of a continuing series on the Constitution, five forums were held, including lectures by constitutional scholars followed by audience discussion.

Virginia
Averett College
The Separation of Powers — Invitation to Conflict, but Safeguard of Our Liberties: Ten mini-forums and two public forums were presented on the Separation of Powers; the mini-forums were held in conjunction with local civic and community organization meetings.

Averett College
A Question of Justice: Ten mini-forums and two public ones focused on judicial philosophy; again, the mini-forums were held in conjunction with local civic organizations' meetings.

New River Community College
Equality and the Due Process Clause of the Fourteenth Amendment: The forum, held in November 1991, covered the history of the Fourteenth Amendment and its impact on women and minorities, particularly in Virginia, and was cosponsored by the New River Historical Society.

Old Dominion University
Safeguarding Civil Liberties — The Bill of Rights as a Living Document: Activities in this 1991 forum included the production of 26 public service announcements, a speakers' bureau on Bill of Rights topics, a town meeting on First Amendment issues, and a Mini Bill of Rights Convention Workshop.

Shenandoah College and Conservatory
The Constitution and the Rights of Property: The Individual and Community in Modern America: The series of three forums focused on land use planning and constitutional rights to property and was cosponsored by local preservation groups, the local board of realtors, the local bar association, and others.

Tidewater Community College
Individual Rights — Civic Responsibilities: The six-part symposium, conducted during February and March 1991 and cosponsored by the Virginia Beach Bicentennial Commission and the Virginia Beach Public Library, included the topics of search and seizure, the right to bear arms, and the right to peaceful assembly.

Virginia Foundation for the Humanities
The Bill of Rights, the Courts, and the Law: A series of 50 forums was organized across Virginia in 1991 under the cosponsorship of the Virginia Foundation for the Humanities and 27 other organizations. The series concentrated on landmark Supreme Court cases and the constitutional issues they raised.

Washington
Fort Vancouver Regional Library
Freedom of Speech and Community Standards: An Historical Context and Current Dialogue: The October 1991 forum cosponsored by The Forum at Clark College, concentrated on the First Amendment, and resulted in publication of a special book list on the subject as well as a videotape for local public television and for programs at branch libraries.

Wisconsin
Blackhawk Technical College
The First Amendment and the Media: The discussion panel, cosponsored with the Janesville Chamber of Commerce, consisted of speakers from the Judiciary, the bar, the media, and local government, and was videotaped for use by local schools and residents.

University of Wisconsin — Little Falls
Freedom of Expression and the First Amendment: Three panel discussion were held during spring of 1991 on the history of, and present issues regarding, freedom of expression, as protected by the First Amendment. Cosponsors were the League of Women Voters of Pierce and St. Croix Counties and the St. Croix Valley Bar Association.

University of Wisconsin-Parkside, and the Kenosha-Racine Bicentennial Committee
Political Action Committees and the Constitution — Are They Compatible?: The forum centered on the constitutional role of the legislative branch as the representatives of the people; panelists, two in favor of PACs and two against, included U.S. Senator William Proxmire of Wisconsin and three leaders from the community.

SPECIAL GRANTS*

Akron University Law School
$800,000 (1988)
A congressionally directed grant.

African-American Institute
$27,172 (1991)
The grant supported a series of essay contests on the Bill of Rights in several African countries.

Bicentennial Council of the Original Thirteen States
$58,000 (1989)
The grant supported production of a book of essays, The Bill of Rights and the States.

Big Ten Alumni Association Northwest Ordinance Bicentennial Project
$100,000 (1987)
The grant supported the touring exhibit "Liberty's Legacy: Our Celebration of the Northwest Ordinance and the Constitution."

Center for Civic Education
$11,988,904 (1987-1992)
Five directed grants assisted the administration of the National Bicentennial Competition on the Constitution and the Bill of Rights.

Center for Civic Education
$1,945,899 (1988-1990)
Three grants assisted the administration of the National Historical/Pictorial Map Contest.

Center for Civic Education
$364,034 (1990-1991)
Two grants supported the creation and dissemination of a textbook on the Bill of Rights, With Liberty and Justice for All.

Contact Center
$510,000 (1988-1989)
Two grants supported the distribution of copies of the Commission's Pocket Constitution through a literacy "hotline."

Drake University
$1,500,000 (1988)
A congressionally directed grant to establish a law center.

Drake University
$800,000 (1988)
A congressionally directed grant.

First Federal Congress Project
$120,000 (1989)
The grant supported production of five volumes of the Documentary History of the First Federal Congress.

Gallaudet University
$45,036 (1991)
The grant supported the administration of an oratorical contest for the deaf and hard-of-hearing.

HMS Rose Foundation
$300,000 (1991)
Two grants supported the operation of the HMS Rose/Bill of Rights Tour.

Howard University School of Law
$800,000 (1988)
A congressionally directed grant.

Loyola University
$1,500,000 (1988)
A congressionally directed grant to establish a law center.

National History Day
$357,000 (1990)
The grant supported administration of the 1990-1991 program "Rights in History."

National Institute for Citizen Education/Correctional Education Association
$45,000 (1991)
The grant supported training for teams of teachers in citizenship education in state and Federal penal institutions.

National Portrait Gallery
$110,000 (1989)
The grant supported an exhibit on the First Federal Congress.

National Trust for Historic Preservation
$1,000,000 (1988)
The grant supported the restoration of James Madison's home, Montpelier, in Virginia.

Public Broadcasting Service Station WETA
$25,000 (1990)
Three grants supported the radio tribute to the Bill of Rights, "We Hold These Truths," and its dissemination to schools on audiocassette.

Trust for the Bicentennial of the United States Constitution
$1,315,963 (1990)
The grant supported production of the oral history "We the People: the President and the Constitution."

University of South Carolina Law School
$800,000 (1988)
A congressionally directed grant.

University of Texas and the LBJ Foundation
$790,000 (1989)
The grant supported the Encyclopedia of Congress.

We the People 200 Inc.
$1,000,000 (1988)
The grant supported commemorative activities in Philadelphia.

---

*List does not include projects the Commission supported through contracts.

LOGO LICENSEES

Abelexpress, *Carnegie, Pennsylvania*
Adirondack Park Agency, *Raybrook, New York*
Allen Company, *Blanchester, Ohio*
Allen Mage FLAAGSS IV, *Los Angeles, California*
American Bicentennial Study Group, *Washington, D.C.*
Andersen Lamb, Inc., *East Moriches, New York*
Annin Flag Company, *Roseland, New Jersey*
Aristoplay, Ltd., *Ann Arbor, Michigan*
Black Star and Frost, Ltd., *Vienna, Virginia*
Boehm, Inc., Edward Marshall, *Trenton, New Jersey*
Brunner Music Publishing Co., *Los Angeles, California*
Bureau of Engraving and Printing, *Washington, D.C.*
Button Works, Inc., *Nevada City, California*
Byron Preiss Visual Publications, Inc., *New York, New York*
C & P Telephone Company, *Washington, D.C.*
Catania Et Al, *Chicago, Illinois*
Chalk and Vermillion Fine Arts, *Greenwich, Connecticut*
Charles Goldberg, Ltd., *Glenshaw, Pennsylvania*
Charleston Mint, *Charleston, South Carolina*
Collegeville Flag Company, *Collegeville, Pennsylvania*
Constitutional Society, *Midlothian, Virginia*
Countryside Studio, Inc., *Gallatin, Tennessee*
Creative Imprints, Inc., *New Bedford, Massachusetts*
Custom Pin and Design, *Lake Placid, New York*
Daughters of the American Revolution, *Washington, D.C.*
Design Masters Associates, Inc., *Williamsburg, Virginia*
Dettra Flag Company, Inc., *Oaks, Pennsylvania*
Document House, *Solvang, California*
Eder Manufacturing Corporation, *Milwaukee, Wisconsin*
Family Heir-Loom Weavers, *Red Lion, Pennsylvania*
Fisher Pen Company, *Forest Park, Illinois*
Folk Era Production, Inc., *Nashua, New Hampshire*
Forward Company, *Van Nuys, California*
Frankoma Pottery, Inc., *Sapulpa, New Hampshire*
Gallery of the Republic, *Austin, Texas*
General Mills, *Minneapolis, Minnesota*
Hampton Hall, *New York, New York*
Hansen Classics, Ltd., *West Sandy, Utah*
Heritage Collections, Ltd., *Alexandria, Virginia*
Heroes Are Forever, *Houston, Texas*
Historic Cards and Prints, *Alexandria, Virginia*
Historical Documents, Inc., *Philadelphia, Pennsylvania*
Instant Buttons Machine, *Hamden, Connecticut*
International Paper Company, *Memphis, Texas*
J. H. B. Designs, *San Clemente, California*
Knowledge Products, *Nashville, Tennessee*
Lenox China and Crystal, *Lawrenceville, New Jersey*
Lenox Collections, *Langhorne, Pennsylvania*
Lewis Glaser, Inc., *Charlottesville, Virginia*
Liberty Mint, *Provo, Utah*
Lion Brothers Company, *Owings Mills, Maryland*
Louisville Stoneware Company, *Louisville, Kentucky*
Macrobit, Miami, *Florida*
Madonna Educational Systems, Inc., *Clearwater, Florida*
Magna Carter in America, *Portland, Oregon*
Marathon Marketing Corporation, *Norwalk, Connecticut*
Massillon Plaque Company, *North Canton, Ohio*
McDonald's Corporation, *Oak Brook, Illinois*
Metro Flag, Inc., *Dover, New Jersey*
Minnesota Educational Computing Corp., *St. Paul, Minnesota*
Mottahedeh, *New York, New York*
Mount Vernon Ladies Association, *Mt. Vernon, Virginia*

Nabisco Brands, Inc., *Parsippany, New Jersey*
National Association of Realtors, *Washington, D.C.*
National Foundation to Protect the American Eagle, *Nashville, Tennessee*
Neal H. Korpi, Inc., *Minneapolis, Minnesota*
New Continental Congress Research Education Foundation,
    Washington, D.C.
O.T. Dime, Inc., *Washington, D.C.*
Orion Marketing, *Manassas, Virginia*
Panda Cachets, *Clifton, Virginia*
Philip K. Smith Woodcarving, Inc., *Cincinnati, Ohio*
Pitney Bowes, *Stanford, Connecticut*
Polaroid Corporation, *Cambridge, Massachusetts*
Printing Industry of the Carolinas, *Charlotte, North Carolina*
Reynolds Metals Co., *Richmond, Virginia*
Savoy Music, *Schenectady, New York*
Seven Star, *Wyandotte, Michigan*
Silvertip Studio, *Twin Falls, Idaho*
Society for Visual Education, *Chicago, Illinois*
Specialty House Candies, *Elmer, New Jersey*
Spouting Whale, *Fall River, Massachusetts*
Steuben Class/Corning Glass, *New York, New York*
Stickley, Inc., *Manlius, New York*
Stonyfield Display, Inc., *White Plains, New York*
Supreme Court Historical Society, *Washington, D.C.*
T. Foley Designs, Ltd., *New York, New York*
TBW Industries, Inc., *Los Gatos, California*
Texoma Leather and Brass, *Denison, Texas*
Theme Merchandise, Inc., *Attleboro, Massachusetts*
Thomas Schwenke, Inc., *Wilton, Connecticut*
Tracey-Knifewing, Inc., *Gallup, New Mexico*
Unicover, *Cheyenne, Wyoming*
United States Capitol Historical Society, *Washington, D.C.*
Valley Forge Flag Company, *Great Neck, New York*
Washington Pops, *Washington, D.C.*
Watercrest China, Inc., *Nanuet, New York*
Weekly Reader, *Middletown, Connecticut*
Weiner Jennings and Vane, Inc., *Washington, D.C.*
Windsor Crystal (Touch of Glass), *Moundsville, West Virginia*
WO-DI Manufacturing, Inc., *Knoxville, Tennessee*
Xerox Corporation, *Stamford, Connecticut*

Every effort has been made in this appendix to include all the organizations and individuals who participated in the Bicentennial of the U.S. Constitution. We take this opportunity to thank any groups or individuals not listed; any omission is inadvertent and regretted, and the groups' and individuals' contributions are deeply appreciated.

"…a Republic, if you can keep it."

Benjamin Franklin, September 17, 1787

ACKNOWLEDGMENTS

The Commission, acknowledging the many organizations and individuals who contributed accounts of their Bicentennial activities to the Commission's archives, could include only a representative sampling of that record of accomplishment in this Final Report. The following individuals were especially helpful in the preparation of the Report: Max Andrews, Richard Baker, Frederick Biebel, Yvonne Brown, Louise Brunsdale, William Buckingham, Mark Cannon, Paul Clark, Virginia DeRoze, Larry Ferezan, Trudy Fry, Ronald Green, Kemp Harshman, Kim Jackson, Nola Kotter, Sydney Lee, Ronald Mann, Sheila McCauley, Joseph McGrath, Barbara McMahon, Bobby McMeans, Thomas O'Connor, Patrick B. O'Meara, Jeannie Reed, Thomas J. Simon, Raymond Smock, Greg Stiverson, Obert Tanner, and the staffs of the Friends of Independence National Historic Park, the General Services Administration, the Government Printing Office, the National Archives and Records Administration, and the Office of Justice Programs.

Editors:
Herbert M. Atherton
William G. Hamilton
Kent S. Larsen

Designer Director:
David Moore

Photo Editor:
Elisabeth M. Hartjens,
Imagefinders

Production Coordinator:
Patricia Andrews

Copy Editor:
Arthur Haupt

Design Assistant:
John Campbell

Production Assistant:
Jon Davies

Mechanical Art:
Ann Bacon
Martha Jo Chaconas
Sherry Haymen

Typesetting:
General Typographers
Jennifer H. Gray
Marge Wilson

Special Photography:
Harlee Little, Jr.